Essentials of
Financial Accounting
For Business Managers

SIXTH EDITION

ASISH K. BHATTACHARYYA
Distinguished Professor, Shiv Nadar University, Noida
Formerly, Professor, Finance and Control
Indian Institute of Management Calcutta

PHI Learning Private Limited
Delhi-11009
2026

In fond memory of ***Shri Asoke K. Ghosh*** *(October 1942 – February 2024), Founder Chairman and Managing Director of PHI Learning, whose vision endlessly inspires.*

The Legacy Continues....

Published by Pushpita Ghosh, PHI Learning Private Limited, Rimjhim House, 111, Patparganj Industrial Estate, Delhi-110092 and Printed by Syndicate Binders, A-20, Hosiery Complex, Noida, Phase-II Extension, Noida-201305 (N.C.R. Delhi).

₹895.00

ESSENTIALS OF FINANCIAL ACCOUNTING—For Business Managers, Sixth Edition
Asish K. Bhattacharyya

ISBN-978-93-91818-52-4 (Print Book)
ISBN-978-93-91818-53-1 (e-Book)

The export rights of the book are vested solely with the publisher.

Contents

Preface

I have revised and updated this popular book based on the feedback received from the students and instructors. However, the core structure of the book has not been changed, as they find the sequence of the topics appropriate. I have simplified the presentation without sacrificing rigour and tried to support every accounting principle with maximum possible examples to illustrate the subject matter more comprehensively and understandable. Some new examples and assignments have also been included to enhance clarity and acceptability of the subject.

The changes have enhanced the suitability of the book for teaching financial accounting to students who join undergraduate and graduate management programmes like MBA, MBA (Executive). PGDM, BMS and BBA programmes without any formal education in accounting. The material remains highly suitable for self-learning.

I hope that the students as well as instructors will continue to enjoy learning the fundamentals of financial accounting using this textbook.

Asish K. Bhattacharyya

CHAPTER 1

Conceptual Framework

CHAPTER OBJECTIVES

The objective of this chapter is to introduce to readers important accounting principles that cut across all the topics covered in this book. In particular, the objective is developing and understanding of:

- Business firms—purpose, activities, and structure;
- Nature of accounting—financial accounting, and management accounting;
- Financial capital—equity, borrowings, and preference shares;
- Accounting conventions, and qualitative characteristics of financial statements;
- Accounting standards, accounting policy, accounting estimates, materiality, true and fair view, and concept of fair value;
- Internal control, internal audit, and external audit.

1.1 BUSINESS FIRMS

1.1.1 Business Purpose

Business firms are for-profit organisations. Their purpose is to make money—earn a reasonable return on the amount invested in the firm. They innovate products and services by applying scientific innovations to perform current tasks being performed by the members of the society better and more efficiently or to fulfil the latent needs of a particular segment of the society. For example, metro rail, household electronic appliances, and robots are examples of products that have helped us to do existing tasks better and more efficiently. Smart phones and OTT (over the top) platforms are examples of products that have fulfilled our latent needs. Business firms create customers for those products and sell them at a price which is higher than the cost of producing those items to generate surplus for a reasonable return on investment. In the process of making money they improve the standard of living of the members of the segments of the society they serve. Even when they spend money on so called corporate social responsibility (CSR) activities, they aim to internalise the benefits.

Business firms are expected to comply with the applicable laws and deal ethically with stakeholders, such as employees, communities around which they operate, customers, vendors and investors, who do not participate in the governance and management of the firm (for example, lenders and non-controlling shareholders of a company). They are duty bound to preserve the natural resources and align their policies with the global sustainability goals.

1.1.2 Business Activities

Table 1.1 presents classification of activities performed by a firm.

TABLE 1.1 Classification of Activities Performed by a Firm

S. No.	Classification	Description
1.	Operating	Operating activities are core business activities. They include all the activities performed for producing and selling goods, such as creating customers (marketing), procurement of inputs, converting inputs into finished goods, selling those to customers, collecting the transaction price from them, and all supporting activities, such as, designing, engineering, quality assurance and accounting.
2.	Investing	Firms invest the excess capital not required in the business outside the business. They also invest in other firms for trade benefits, such as, investment in a firm that is a customer or vendor. Investing activities relate to managing such investments.
3.	Financing	Firms arrange finances from investors and through borrowings to support other activities. Financing activities relate to managing the finance.

Operating activities are core business activities.

Financing activities relate to managing the finance.

Investing activities relate to managing investments in financial assets and investment properties.

1.1.3 Firm Structures

Entrepreneurs (promoters) assess the suitability of different firm structures by assessing the capital requirements and the degree of business risk of the underlying venture.

Limited, and unlimited liabilities of investors

Limited liability implies that the firm's creditors have no access to the personal wealth of investors (owners) and the firm cannot ask owners (shareholders in case of a company) to contribute more than their commitment. Unlimited liability implies that the firm's creditors can recover their dues from the personal wealth of the owners.

Sole proprietorship firm

Only an individual (called, the sole proprietor) contributes the equity capital. This structure is suitable for a low-risk venture that requires a small amount of capital. For example, this structure is suitable for a mom-and-pop store that serves the local community surrounding it. Such a store holds low inventory to cater to the demand of the members of the community to which the sole proprietor belongs.

BOX 1.1 SUPPLIERS OF FINANCIAL CAPITAL

(a) Investors (owners/deemed owners): Investors' investment is classified in the balance sheet as *equity capital*. They are called *residual claimants*, as they take the business risks, as their claim is residual. Their share in the surplus generated by the firm is net profit, which is calculated after deduction all expenses, finance cost and tax expense. In a situation of liquidation, the assets that remain after settling all other claims are distributed to investors.

In the U.S.A. and some other jurisdictions, equity share is called *common share*.

Book value (value in the balance sheet) of equity is called *net worth*.

(b) Lenders (debt capital): Firms finance a part of financial capital by borrowing funds from financial institutions and the public (by issuing bonds). Depending on the risk of the underlying venture, lenders decide the loan-to-value (LTV) ratio and the interest rate. Therefore, a firm's borrowing capacity depends on the amount of equity capital of the firm. Lenders take credit risk—the firm may fail to honour its commitment to repay the capital and interest.

(c) Mezzanine capital: Companies can issue preference shares. Claim of the holders of preference shares is senior to the claim of equity shareholders but subordinate to all other claims. They are entitled to a pre-specified dividend. Usually preference shares are cumulative in nature—unpaid dividends are accumulated and paid when the company earns profit. Redeemable preference shares are classified in the balance sheet as borrowings. Indian companies are not permitted to issue preference shares other than preference shares redeemable within ten years from the issue date.

(d) Operating creditors: Operating creditors, such as, suppliers of goods and services provide a part of working capital by extending credit to the firm. Working capital is the capital that supports day-to-day operations.

Capital structure

Capital structure refers to the proportion of equity and debt capital in the total capital invested in the firm. Finance supplied by operating creditors is not included in the total capital.

Investors who invest in the equity of the firm are called residual claimants

Lenders assume credit risk.

Capital structure refers to the proportion of equity and debt in the total capital invested in the firm.

Ordinary partnership firm

Ordinary Partnerships are governed by the Indian Partnership Act, 1938. A partnership firm cannot have more than 50 partners. The Companies Act 2013 permits the government to increase the limit to 100 partners. Every partner is jointly and severally liable for all obligations assumed by the firm. Internal governance (e.g., capital contribution, profit sharing and retirement) is regulated by the partnership agreement. Partnership structure is suitable for professional firms and other small business firms, which require a small amount of capital and the risk of the underlying venture is low.

Limited liability partnership (LLP)

An LLP is required to be registered with the government and is governed by the LLP Act, 2008. There is no limit on the number of partners. It is a legal entity separate from partners. It enjoys perpetual succession–change in partners does not affect its existence. Each partner is an agent of the LLP. The liability of the LLP is met out of the LLP's property. A partner is not liable for wrongful acts or omissions of other partners. An LLP is run like a general partnership and has a similar degree of management flexibility. It facilitates partnership among individuals who operate in different geographic locations and may not be closely known to each other. Most large professional firms of accountants, lawyers, etc. adopt the LLP structure.

Company

Limited liability companies are incorporated under the Companies Act, 2013 and are governed by that Act.

Companies enjoy perpetual succession—change in shareholders does not affect the company's existence.

A company is a juridical person.

Companies enjoy perpetual succession—change in shareholders does not affect the company's existence. This enables shareholders to freely trade in shares and transfer them to other investors.

A company is a juridical person. It can enter into contracts and can sue and be sued in its own name. It acts through its Board of Directors, which delegates some powers, particularly those related to day-to-day operation, to the Chief Executive Officer (CEO). Directors are elected by equity shareholders using their voting rights. Under the Indian Companies Act, with a single exception, one share has one vote. Memorandum of Association, which is the most important public document, specifies among other things, the objects that the company will pursue and the address of its registered office.

Internal governance of a company is guided by its Articles of Association.

Public limited companies, whose securities are listed in one or more recognised stock exchanges are called listed companies.

Company structure is the most preferred structure, as it allows the entrepreneur to venture into a risky business, as risks are shared by a large number of investors. Companies are classified into three categories—private limited company (also called closely-held company), public limited company and listed company (also called publicly held company). One-person company (OPC) is a private limited company.

Table 1.2 below presents the types of companies.

TABLE 1.2 Types of Companies

S. No.	*Company type*	*Description*
1.	Private limited company (Closely held company)	(a) A private limited company cannot invite public to invest in its equity capital. (b) Number of shareholders cannot exceed 200. (c) Usually, friends and members of the expanded family of the promoter invest in the equity of the company. (d) Private equity funds invest in start-ups, which usually adopt the private limited company structure.
2.	One person company	(a) It is a type of private limited company. (b) Only one investor invests in the equity capital. (c) The compliance cost is quite low, as it enjoys a large number of exemptions from complying with the provisions of the Companies Act, 2013. (d) It is suitable for a business which requires low capital, but the underlying venture is risky.
3.	Public limited company	(a) It can invite the public to contribute to its equity capital. (b) There is no limit on the number of shareholders. (c) The Companies Act, 2013 stipulates a large number of prescriptions, proscriptions, and disclosure requirements to protect the shareholders' interest.
4.	Listed company (Publicly traded company)	(a) Public limited company, whose securities are listed and traded in one or more recognised stock exchanges (such as, Bombay Stock Exchange and National Stock Exchange). (b) The Securities and Exchange Board of India (SEBI) is responsible for protecting shareholders' interest. (c) A listed company is required to comply with all the regulations issued by SEBI, in addition to the requirements under the Companies Act, 2013.

1.2 ACCOUNTING—AN INFORMATION SYSTEM

Accounting is the science and art of collecting and collating data and using them in communicating information in structured formats to facilitate decision-making. There are two distinct branches of accounting–Financial Accounting and Management Accounting, which subsumes cost accounting.

Table 1.3 below presents the nature of the two branches of accounting.

TABLE 1.3 Financial Accounting, Cost Accounting and Management Accounting

S. No.	*Accounting classification*	*Description*
1.	Financial accounting system	(a) The goal is to communicate information to investors (including potential investors), lenders, and other creditors, who are the primary users of financial statements. (b) It records transactions (buying and selling goods and services) entered into by the firm, and also the economic impact of events other than transactions (such as, loss due to natural calamity and loss due to embezzlement). (c) The data so recorded are used to communicate relevant information to the primary users. (d) The structured formats that are used to communicate information are called financial statements. (e) The principles and methods for preparing and presenting financial statements are governed by accounting standards. *Book keeping and accounting* The system for recording data is called book keeping. Firms use computer software for book keeping. Accounting is concerned with formulating accounting policy—the principles and methods for preparing and presenting financial statements are governed by accounting standards and preparing financial statements.
2.	Cost accounting system	(a) It collects and collates cost information to determine product cost for inventory valuation and submission to the government, if required. (b) Product costs that are submitted to government are determined using cost accounting principles codified in cost accounting standards.
3.	Management accounting system	(a) It collects and collates data, and uses data collected by the financial accounting and cost accounting systems to communicate information to managers for planning and control. (b) Planning is evaluating alternatives and choosing the activities to be performed in future for achieving the firm's goals, and implementing the decisions. (c) Control requires information on deviations of actual results from planned outcome, and also on whether employees are performing their tasks as desired. Management accounting system provides the feedback. (d) Managers require information at the granular level in the format desired by them.

The goal of financial accounting is to communicate information to investors, lenders, and other creditors.

The cost accounting system collects and collates cost information to determine product cost for inventory valuation.

The management accounting system collects and collates data to communicate information to managers for planning and control.

1.2.1 Users of Financial Statements

Primary users

Investors, lenders, and other creditors are the primary users of information communicated through financial statements. Investors use the information, along with information collected from other sources on the possible changes in the business environment, to predict the cash flows that the firm will generate in future. They use the predicted cash flows to value the enterprise and to decide whether to buy, sell, or hold investment in the firm.

Lenders and other creditors too predict the future cash flows to assess the risk of lending or extending credit to the firm. The risk is that the firm might fail to honour its commitment to repay the principal or pay the agreed interest on the principal, may be due to its weak financial health. This risk is called the credit risk.

Other users

Investors, lenders, and other creditors are the primary users of financial statements.

Information that is useful to primary users is also useful to other stakeholders who have an interest in the stability and growth of the firm.

Employees have an interest in the growth and stability of her employers, as her career growth and stability of employment depends on the same. Communities around which the firm operates have an interest in the growth and stability of the firm because their economic development and welfare depend on the same. For the same reason, federal and local governments, and politicians have interest in the growth and stability of the firm. Policy makers use the information to make policy decisions, such as, whether to provide incentives to firms operating in a particular industry.

The income tax department uses the information to assess the tax payable by the firm.

Internal users

Board of directors uses the information to evaluate the performance of subsidiaries and associates. A company is a subsidiary if the entity controls that company. A company is an associate if the firm has significant influence on the operating and financial decisions of that company. Employees and top management are also considered internal users of information communicated through financial statements. Investors, being the deemed owners of the firm, are also considered internal users of that information.

1.2.2 Accounting–Business Language

Accounting is called business language because business firms communicate results of their activities to investors, lenders and other creditors using accounting jargons and symbols exactly in the same way as members of different communities communicate among themselves using words and symbols. In the case of language, experts differ on what is good usage of words in constructing sentences. Similarly in accounting, experts differ on what are good accounting principles and what are bad accounting principles. In the case of language, the same word or symbol communicates different emotions and meanings in different communities. Similarly, in accounting, jargons communicate different meanings in different jurisdictions, although there are efforts to bring uniformity. Because of such similarities, accounting is aptly called the business language. Managers must learn that language to decipher the stories behind number presented in financial statements.

12.3 Components of Financial Statements

The complete set of financial statements consists of four primary financial statements, and notes to accounts.

Primary financial statements

Primary financial statements (balance sheet, statement of profit and loss, and cash flow statement) are summary statements.

Primary statements are summary statements. The following are the primary statements:

1. Balance sheet: Entities present in the balance sheet the amount and details of equity capital, assets and liabilities (including debt capital) as at the end of the accounting period, and thus, present its financial position;
2. Statement of profit and loss (income statement): Entities present in the statement of profit and loss the analyses of income and expenses and thus, reports the results of its operating, investing, and financing activities;
3. Statement of changes in equity: Entities present in the statement of changes in equity details of how each component of equity has changed during the accounting period;

4. Cash flow statement: Entities present in the cash flow statement, cash inflows and outflows arising from operating, investing and financing activities during the accounting period.

Notes: Entities disclose in the Notes the break-up of figures presented in primary financial statements, and information that cannot be presented in those statements, and also provide clarifications for better understanding of information presented in the primary financial statements.

1.3 ACCOUNTING CONVENTIONS

Accounting conventions are age-old conventions that underlie accounting principles.

1.3.1 Entity Concept

Financial statements are prepared for an entity, which defines the boundary of financial reporting. Usually, for stand-alone financial statements, the firm is the entity. Therefore, the stand-alone financial statements present the aggregated results of the activities performed by all the divisions and strategic business units (SBUs) operating within the boundary of the entity. For consolidated financial statements, the Group is considered a single economic entity. Group consists of parent and subsidiaries. According to the entity concept, the owner is an entity separate from the firm.

Financial statements are prepared for an entity, which defines the boundary of financial reporting.

1.3.2 Money Measurement

Economic phenomena are depicted in financial statements by description and value. A common measurement unit is necessary to add the value assigned to each economic phenomenon. A monetary unit (e.g., INR) is used as the common measurement unit. Consequently, only those items are presented in financial statements which can be measured in money.

1.3.3 Going Concern

Going concern is an accounting concept. An entity is said to be a going concern when it is unlikely that the entity will close down in the foreseeable future–voluntarily, or otherwise. Foreseeable future is usually defined as one year after the balance sheet date. Firms are often forced to close down due to weak financial position and inability to mobilise resources by issuing equity or borrowing. They are also forced to close down due to change in the government policy, such as, a policy to ban production of an item due to environmental considerations (such as, use of plastic) or health considerations (such as, chewing tobacco). When the management and the auditor of an entity conclude that the going concern assumption is not valid, the entity measures assets for the presentation in the balance sheet using principles, which are different from the measurement principles that are applied to measure assets of a going concern. For example, when a going concern assumption is not valid, items of property, plant, and equipment are measured at the liquidation value, while those assets for a going concern are measured at acquisition cost or fair value. If the management and auditor conclude that the entity is not a going concern, that is disclosed.

An entity is said to be a going concern when it is unlikely to close down in the foreseeable future

1.3.4 Cost

Traditionally, financial statements are prepared and presented on a historical cost basis. Assets are recorded at acquisition cost. Liabilities are recorded at the amount of proceeds received in exchange for an obligation. In some circumstances, e.g., income tax liabilities are recorded at the amount of cash expected to be paid to satisfy the liability in the normal course of business.

Traditionally, financial statements are prepared and presented on a historical cost basis.

With increase in complexity of transactions, and gradual shift from transaction-based accounting to event-based accounting, accounting practice is shifting its focus from the cost convention. For example, investments in equity shares issued by another entity are measured at fair value.

1.3.5 Realisation

According to Realisation convention, an asset should be recorded at historical cost, and any change in value should be recognised at the time the firm realises or disposes of the asset.

According to this convention, an asset should be recorded at historical cost, and any change in value should be recognised at the time the firm realises or disposes of the asset. An unrealised gain should not be recognised. For some assets and liabilities, the current accounting principles contravene this convention. For example, some assets, such as investments held for trading, are measured at fair value (FV) and change in FV is recognised as gain or loss.

1.3.6 Accrual

According to the accrual convention, income is recognised as it is earned and expenditure is recognised, either as an asset or as an expense, when it is incurred, without waiting for receipt or payment of cash. For example revenue (income from sale of goods and services) is earned when the entity fulfils its promise to the customer to transfer the goods or services and expects that the customer will fulfil its promise to pay in exchange for those good or service without waiting for realising the transfer price from the customer. Similarly, an expenditure is recognised when the entity receives and accepts the good or service and assumes the obligation to pay the transaction price without waiting for outflow of cash (or other asset).

According to the accrual convention, income is recognised as it is earned and expenditure is recognised, either as an asset or as an expense, when it is incurred.

Accrual includes long-term accruals, which requires allocating the cost of an asset (such as, a piece of equipment) that the entity intends to use for a number of years to those years in which the entity will use the asset.

1.3.7 Matching

According to the matching convention, in order to present a true and fair view of the operating result, income and expenses should be matched, to the extent possible. For example, the cost of goods sold should not include the cost of units purchased but remained unsold. With the shift in focus from the statement of profit and loss to the balance sheet, some expenses in the statement of profit and loss do not have a cause-and-effect relationship with the income recognised in the same statement. For example, research expenditure is recognised as expense for the period in which the expenditure is incurred.

According to the matching convention, income and expenses should be matched, to the extent possible.

1.3.8 Periodicity

Entities usually operate for a fairly long period. Investors and lenders need information periodically to predict the future cash flows, and also, to evaluate the management in its stewardship function. The convention is to issue a complete set of financial statements at an interval of 12 months. The 12–month period is called the fiscal year or the accounting year. As in most other countries, in India, publicly traded companies are required (by governing regulations) to publish abridged financial statements on a quarterly basis.

1.3.9 Conservatism (Prudence)

In a situation of significant uncertainty, it is preferable to understate profit and assets rather than overstating the same. The operating rule is that firms should recognise all estimated losses immediately and should not recognise gain until realised. The rule is in sync with good corporate governance practice, which requires disclosure of bad news immediately and disclosure of good news only when confirmed. The convention does not allow intentional overstatement of liabilities or understatement of assets.

EXAMPLE 1.1 (Inventory valuation)
The cost of goods sold is measured using the following formula,

Cost of goods sold = Opening stock + Purchases – Closing stock

Therefore, the cost of goods sold is a function of the valuation of the stock of the units in the year-end inventories. Higher the value of the closing stock, lower is the cost of goods sold, and higher is the reported profit.

Stock-in-trade is valued at the lower of cost and net realisable value. For example, if the cost is ₹10,000 and the entity expects to realise (net of direct costs) ₹12,000 by selling the goods in any subsequent period, the stock is measured at ₹10,000 and the expected gain is not recognised in the current fiscal year. On the other hand if it expects to realise (net of direct costs) ₹9,000, the stock is measured at ₹9,000, resulting in recognition of estimated loss in the current fiscal year.

EXAMPLE 1.2 (Onerous contract)
An executory contract is one, performance of which remains wholly or partly unperformed by both parties. Firms are required to recognise estimated loss on an executory contract in the current fiscal year. For example, if the firm estimates that by executing the contract in the next fiscal year, it will incur a loss of ₹20,000 and if declines to execute the contract, it will pay a penalty of ₹15,000, it recognises the loss of ₹15,000 in the current fiscal year, if decides not to execute the contract. If it decides to execute the contract, it should recognise the loss of ₹20,000 in the current year.

1.3.10 Accrual Accounting and Cash Basis of Accounting in Comparison

Accrual system of accounting is considered superior to the cash basis accounting, because by using this system the entities are able to correctly present the results of activities performed during the current year. Indian companies are required to use the accrual system.

Accrual system of accounting is considered superior to the cash basis accounting.

EXAMPLE 1.3 (Accrual accounting)
Fact pattern: In its first year of operation, a car dealer sold cars for ₹10 crore on credit and collected ₹8 crore from customers.

Discussion: Under the accrual accounting system, it will recognise revenue at ₹10 crore and recognise trade receivables in the balance sheet at ₹2 crore. Under the cash basis of accounting, ₹8 crore will be recognised as revenue and no asset will be recognised in the balance sheet.

It is obvious that the dealer using the accrual system will present the results of its operating activities fairly and will disclose important information, which is, even if it does not perform any activity in a subsequent accounting period, it will generate a cash flow of ₹2 crore.

1.4 QUALITATIVE CHARACTERISTICS OF FINANCIAL STATEMENTS

1.4.1 Relevance

Information should be relevant for the purpose for which it is used by primary users. Information that is useful for predicting the future performance and that is useful in evaluating past forecasts is relevant. For example, information on the composition of income earned during the current period, and the composition of assets and liabilities that the entity holds at the end of the accounting period are relevant in predicting the future cash flows. Usually, the information that is useful in predicting future performance is also useful in evaluating past forecasts.

Information is relevant if it is useful for predicting the future and evaluating the earlier forecasts.

Substance over form

In order to be relevant, financial statements should present economic phenomena correctly by looking into the economic substance of transactions piercing through the legal form.

Complete and neutral

Information should be complete and neutral.

Information should be complete and neutral. Neutrality implies that the information should be free from bias in the sense that it is not slanted, weighted, emphasised, deemphasised, or otherwise manipulated to increase the probability that users will receive the financial information favourably or unfavorably.

EXAMPLE 1.4 (Substance over form)

Fact pattern: M sells an asset to N for ₹1,00,000 with a promise to buy it back the same after a year for ₹1,10,000.

Discussion: Substance of the transaction is that N has lent 1,00,000 to M, who has promised to repay the amount with an interest of ₹10,000. Therefore, the transaction should be recorded as a financing transaction and not as a sale transaction, although the form of the transaction is that of a sale transaction.

1.4.2 Comparability

Information provided in financial statements of comparable entities should be comparable. Comparability is achieved through consistency.

Primary users evaluate the relative performance, cash flows and financial position of comparable firms. Therefore, information provided in financial statements of comparable entities should be comparable. Therefore, firms operating in a particular industry should apply the same accounting principles for accounting for like items.. This is achieved by regulating the firms' accounting policy through accounting standards, which codify the generally accepted accounting principles (GAAP). For example, the accounting policy for recognising revenue in real estate business should be the same for all the entities operating in the real estate sector. Primary users are also interested in comparing the performance of an entity over time in order to get an insight into the trend of financial position and performance, for example, of profitability. Therefore, information provided in financial statements of the same entity for different periods should be comparable.

Consistency

Comparability is achieved through consistency in applying the same accounting principles from period-to-period.

1.4.3 Verifiability

Many of the figures presented in financial statements are estimates. For example, the liability that might arise from oil leakage from an oil rig is an estimate. Estimates should be reliable. Reliability of an estimate is established when the management's estimate is verifiable by auditors independently. In general terms, an estimate is verifiable when different experts independently arrive at the same estimate or estimates that do not differ materially. Entities are required to disclose estimation uncertainties.

Information should be understandable to those users, who have a reasonable knowledge of business and economic activities.

1.4.4 Timeliness

Timeliness is an important quality, as delayed information loses usefulness.

1.4.5 Understandability

Those users, who have a reasonable knowledge of business and economic activities and who review and analyse the information diligently should be able to understand the information communicated through financial statements. Classifying, characterising, and presenting information clearly and concisely make it understandable.

1.5 ACCOUNTING STANDARDS, ACCOUNTING POLICIES AND ACCOUNTING ESTIMATES

1.5.1 Accounting Standards

Generally accepted accounting principles (GAAP) codifies acceptable accounting principles and methods. In India accounting standards sit at the top of the GAAP hierarchy. Just below that is Guidance Notes issued by the Institute of Chartered Accountants of India (ICAI). Other technical pronouncements issued by ICAI sit below the Guidance Notes. It implies that firms have to comply with accounting principles and methods stipulated in accounting standards and they should refer to Guidance Notes and then to technical pronouncements if they do not find guidance on the subject issue in accounting standards.

GAAP codifies acceptable accounting principles and methods. In India accounting standards sit at the top of the GAAP hierarchy.

India has two set of accounting standards—one that is fully converged with IFRS (called Ind AS), and the other that is based on IFRS, but not converged with IFRS (called AS). International Financial Reporting Standards (IFRS) are issued by the International Accounting Standards Board (IASB), an international body created to bring uniformity in GAAP being used by countries and territories across the globe in order to facilitate integrations of capital markets across the world. Non-finance companies other than those whose net worth is less than ₹250 crore, apply Ind AS. Shadow banks (called non-banking financial institutions), other than those whose net worth is less than ₹250 crore, apply Ind AS. Banks and insurance companies have deferred the application of Ind AS.

In India, accounting standards are issued by ICAI. The Ministry of Corporate Affairs notifies the accounting standards applicable to companies registered under the Companies Act.

1.5.2 Accounting Policies

Accounting policies are the specific principles, bases, conventions, rules, and practices, which an entity applies in preparing and presenting its financial statements. Accounting policies should be in conformity with the principles and methods stipulated in the GAAP. Firms cannot change accounting policies voluntarily. Once the firm makes a choice, it has to apply the accounting policy consistently from year to year. Thus, the GAAP is a deterrent to earnings management.

Accounting policies are the specific principles, bases, conventions, rules, and practices, which an entity applies in preparing and presenting its financial statements.

Earnings management

Earnings management is at the centre of corporate governance failures. Earnings management refers to bending accounting rules to match reported earnings with consensus forecasts by financial analysts, or to present a better than the real picture of financial position and performance. For example, a firm may understate or overstate assets and liabilities, or recognise income from sale of goods earlier or later than the point at which it should be recognised.

1.5.3 Accounting Estimates

Estimates change as new information flows in. For example, estimate of the amount recoverable from a customer going through the bankruptcy process changes as new information flows in.

The change in estimate gets reflected in the financial statements for the period in which the estimate is revised and in financial statements for the subsequent period.

Difference between accounting policy and accounting estimate

Accounting policy: Depreciation on depreciable assets will be estimated based on the estimated useful life, which is the period for which the entity intends to use the asset, and residual value, which is the amount that the entity expects to realise by disposing of the asset at the end of its useful life.

Accounting estimates: The management has estimated the useful life of the asset and its residual value at 10 years and zero respectively, and it allocates acquisition cost (net of residual value) uniformly to each year as covered by the useful life as depreciation.

EXAMPLE 1.5 (Accounting for accounting estimate)

Fact pattern: The acquisition cost a piece of equipment is ₹10 lakhs. The management has estimated the useful life and residual value at 10 years and zero. At the end of the fourth year, before charging depreciation, the entity revises the estimate of the useful life to 7 years.

Discussion: The depreciation charged in first three years:

Year 1: (10,00,000/10) or ₹1,00,000
Year 2: (10,00,000/10) or ₹1,00,000
Year 3: (10,00,000/10) or ₹1,00,000

Depreciation to be charged from the 4th year to 7th year:

Year 4: (7,00,000/4) or ₹1,75,000
Year 5: (7,00,000/4) or ₹1,75,000
Year 6: (7,00,000/4) or ₹1,75,000
Year 7: (7,00,000/4) or ₹1,75,000

The effect of revision of the useful life is given in the year of revision (year 4) and also in subsequent three years (year 5 to year 7).

1.6 MATERIALITY AND TRUE AND FAIR VIEW

Information is material if its omission, misstatement, or cluttering could influence the decisions.

Entities decide both qualitative and quantitative threshold for deciding the materiality of information.

1.6.1 Materiality

Information is material if its omission, misstatement, or cluttering could influence the decisions that users make on the basis of information communicated through financial statements. The materiality of an item is assessed in terms of its nature or amount. Entities decide both qualitative and quantitative threshold for deciding the materiality of information. An example of a quantitative threshold is reporting income from sale of a product separately if it is 10 per cent or more of the total income from sale of goods. An example of a qualitative threshold is reporting sales of a new product separately for initial three years, even if it does not meet the qualitative threshold. Entities use the materiality threshold to decide aggregation and disaggregation of items in the balance sheet and the statement of profit and loss.

1.6.2 True and Fair View

Financial statements provide a true and fair view only if it meets the minimum threshold of desired qualities.

Financial statements provide a true and fair view of the financial position, economic performance, and cash flows only if it meets the minimum threshold of desired qualities. Generally, a financial statement provides a true and fair view if it is

(a) free from material error or bias,
(b) prepared by applying the GAAP, and
(c) presented in the prescribed format.

Schedule III to the Companies Act prescribes the formats to be used by the companies, other than banking companies, insurance companies and electricity companies, in presenting financial statements. The Reserve Bank of India (RBI) prescribes the formats for banking companies, the Insurance Regulatory and Development Authority of India (IRDAI) prescribes the formats for insurance companies, and the Electricity Act, 2003 provides the format for electricity companies.

1.6.3 Events Occurring after the Balance Sheet Date

Estimation is at the centre of financial reporting. Management uses information collected with reasonable efforts to estimate different economic phenomena, such as, the likely obsolescence of a product or process to estimate how long it expects to use a piece of equipment or what would be the increase in the employees' compensation in the next round of negotiation. Management takes into consideration evidence (about the conditions at the balance sheet date) provided by the events unfolded after the balance sheet date but before approval of financial statements by the Board of Directors in estimating the assets, liabilities, income and expenses.

Adjusting and non-adjusting events

Events that occur after the balance sheet date are called adjusting if they provide additional evidence value of assets and liabilities on the balance sheet date, and others are called non-adjusting events.

Events that provide additional evidence are called adjusting events and other events are called non-adjusting events. Material non-adjusting events are disclosed in the board of director's report. However, if the non-adjusting event destroys the fulcrum of the business and invalidates the 'going concern' assumption, the assets and liabilities are measured based on the assumption that the entity was not a going concern at the balance sheet date.

The following are the examples of non-adjusting events which should be disclosed in the Board of Director's report:

1. Major business combination after the balance sheet date.
2. Announcing a plan to discontinue an operation.
3. Major purchase or disposal of assets, or acquisition of major assets by the government.
4. Commencement of a major restructuring.
5. Major change in exchange rates.
6. Major change in tax rates.
7. Issuance of significant guarantees on behalf of third parties.
8. Commencement of major litigation arising of events that occurred after the balance sheet date.

1.7 INTERNAL CONTROL, INTERNAL AUDIT AND EXTERNAL AUDIT

1.7.1 Internal Control

Internal control encompasses all types of controls to enhance the probability that the firm will achieve its goals.

Internal control encompasses all types of controls to enhance the probability that the firm will achieve its goals. Internal control cannot ensure that the firm will achieve its goals, because controls involve human interventions and possibility of human errors cannot be ruled out totally.

Some controls are preventive controls and others are detective controls.

Preventive controls

Preventive controls aim to prevent frauds, errors and wastes, and detective controls aim to detect the same.

Preventive controls aim to prevent frauds, errors, and wastage due to operational inefficiency or inappropriate decisions by managers operating at different levels. Examples of preventive controls are security check for visitors and employees, restrictions on employees to enter in some specified zones within the factory or office without prior permission of the top management, signing of cheques by two officers, evaluation of tenders by a committee of officers, and listing and rating of vendors by a committee of officers. Formulation of policies by the board of directors is also a part of preventive control.

Detective controls

Detective controls aim to detect frauds, errors, and wastage due to operational inefficiency or inappropriate decisions by managers operating at different levels. Examples of detective controls are physical verification of cash and inventories, surprise checks by higher level managers to check whether Standard Operating Procedures (SOP) are followed strictly.

1.7.2 Internal Check

Internal check is a part of internal control. Routine entries for transactions and other routine activities are handled by more than one employee in such a manner that the work of one employee is automatically checked against the work of another for detection of errors and irregularities. For example, a bank reconciliation statement is prepared by an employee other than the employee who handles bank transactions and maintains cash books. Signing of cheques by two officers is also an example of internal check.

Internal audit is an independent, objective assurance and consulting activity designed to add value, and improve an organisation's operations.

1.7.3 Internal Audit

Internal audit is an independent, objective assurance and consulting activity designed to add value, and improve an organisation's operations. Internal audit is being carried out by an internal department or by an external agency. In either case, the Head of the internal audit function reports to the board of directors. It is the third line of defence against fraud, errors, etc. First line of defence is the operating managers who follow the SOPs, and the second line of defence is surprise checks by senior managers. Internal audit provides assurance that internal controls are adequate and effective.

1.7.4 External Audit

It is mandatory for a company to appoint a practicing Chartered Accountant (CA) or a CA firm to audit the financial statements. The auditor is appointed by the body of shareholders. The auditor so appointed is called an external auditor. The external auditor reports to the shareholders. Financial statements with an audit report are presented before the body of shareholders for approval. Annual report of companies includes financial statements with the audit report. The annual report is available on the website of every listed company. Therefore, an audit report is a public document.

The auditor's responsibility is to:

(a) provide a reasonable assurance that financial statements present a true and fair view, and

(b) report fraud or suspected fraud detected in the course of audit.

The external auditor's responsibility is to provide a reasonable assurance that financial statements present a true and fair view, and report fraud or suspected fraud detected in the course of audit.

Qualified report

It issues a qualified report if it concludes that the financial statements are not communicating a true and fair view of the financial position, performance, and cash flows.

Disclaimer

If the auditor is unable to form an opinion on whether the financial statements are communicating a true and fair view, it issues a disclaimer.

Resignation

In extreme situations, the auditor resigns if it is unable to conduct the audit due to lack of cooperation from the management. Qualified audit report, disclaimer, or auditor's resignation signals that the governance of the company is weak.

Emphasis of matter

The external auditor might add an 'emphasis of matter' paragraph in his report. He/she adds the paragraph to draw attention to one or more notes to accounts, which he/she considers that those are fundamental to the users' understanding of the financial statements. An emphasis of the matter paragraph indicates that the auditor's opinion is not modified with respect to the matters emphasised.

NFRA regulates the auditing profession.

1.7.5 NFRA

National Financial Reporting Authority (NFRA), constituted by the government, regulates the auditing profession to ensure that the auditor forms independent judgement and is not negligent in performing its duties.

1.8 FAIR VALUE

Accounting Standards require certain assets and in some situations, liabilities to be measured at fair value. In measuring certain other assets, firms have the option to choose between historical cost or fair value. Therefore, it is important to understand the concept of fair value in an accounting context.

Definition

Fair value (FV) is the exit price.

FV of an asset is the price that would be received by selling the asset. FV of a liability is the price that would be paid to transfer the liability.

FV is determined by an *orderly transaction* between *market participants* in the *principal market* or in absence of a principal market in the *most advantageous market.*

Market participants: Market participants are knowledgeable and fully informed about the asset or liability.

Orderly transaction: Orderly transaction implies *arm's length transaction*. Arm's length implies that the transaction has been entered into freely without any duress.

Principal market: The principal market is the one with the greatest volume and level of activity for the asset or liability that can be accessed by the entity. For example, for listed shares either the Bombay Stock Exchange (BSE) or the National Stock Exchange (NSE) is the principal market.

Most advantageous market: The most advantageous market is the one, which maximises the amount that would be received for the asset or paid to extinguish the liability after transport and transaction costs. Often these markets would be the same.

In case of a non-financial asset, the market considers the best use of the asset in determining the price. For example, if the corner plot in an upcoming residential project is most suitable for commercial activity, the market will determine the price assuming commercial use, provided commercial activity within the residential project is legally permitted and feasible. Feasibility is important because residents might object to carry out commercial activity, although it is legally permitted.

Fair value does not fit into the 'marked-to-market' concept because fair value of an asset or liability that is not traded in the market can also be estimated by using an economic model with assumptions that market participants would have made.

Fair Value (FV) of an asset is the price that would be received by selling the asset and the same of a liability is the price that would be paid to transfer the liability.

FV is determined by an orderly transaction between market participants in the principal market or in absence of a principal market in the most advantageous market.

Reliability levels

Entities are required to disclose the level of reliability of the estimated fair value. The following are the three levels of reliability:

Level 1: Price at which the asset or liability is being traded in an *active market* is the most reliable estimate of FV. In an active market a large number of buyers and sellers trade regularly and information about the item of the asset or liability flows freely. For example, stock exchange is an active market for shares of listed companies.

Level 2: Estimated fair value has level 2 reliability if it is estimated using market inputs. For example, an equity share is thinly traded, and the last available price is six-month old. The valuer takes that price as the starting point and makes necessary adjustments for the events that occurred during the period between the date when it was last traded and the valuation date.

Level 3: Estimated fair value has level 3 reliability if it is estimated without using market inputs. For example, the fair value of a 100-year-old haveli (mansion).

Entities are required to disclose the level of reliability of the estimated fair value.

REVIEW PROBLEMS

R 1.1 Indicate whether the following statements are True or False:

(i) Investing activity is one of the core activities of the business.
(ii) Investors in the equity capital of a company are residual claimants.
(iii) Investment in the debt capital by a lender is exposed to business risks when the firm accumulates loss, year after year.
(iv) The personal wealth (not invested in business) of investors in sole proprietorship and general partnership firms, are exposed to business risks.
(v) The liability of a firm irrespective of its structure is limited to the value of assets that it holds.
(vi) Shares of listed companies are traded in stock exchanges only because companies enjoy perpetual succession.
(vii) Credit risk is that an individual or a firm might default in honouring its commitment to repay the loan and interest on loan wilfully.
(viii) Accounting policy of a company is regulated by the accounting standards applicable to it.
(ix) In a way, the external auditor monitors the board of directors, which is responsible for the governance and management of the company.
(x) When the external auditor agrees with the management that the company is a going concern, shareholders and other stakeholders are assured of the sustainability and growth of the company.
(xi) The principle of prudence ensures that the management discloses the bad news as early as possible and defer the disclosure of good news until confirmed.
(xii) In the context of valuation of assets, the terms fair value and replacement cost are used interchangeably.
(xiii) Consistency in applying accounting principles leads to comparability of financial statements of the same company over a number of financial years and comparable companies for the same financial year.
(xiv) Events that occur after the balance sheet date are not considered in valuation of assets and liabilities for depicting in the balance sheet.
(xv) Accounting standards deter earnings management.

ASSIGNMENTS

1. Indicate against each statement whether it is True or False:

(i) The financial report of a company is primarily targeted towards investors.
(ii) The liability of an equity shareholder of a private limited company is unlimited.
(iii) Interest-free credits do not form part of capital invested in a firm.
(iv) Publicly traded companies should necessarily be public limited companies.
(v) 'Decision usefulness' is the overriding principle in the preparation and presentation of financial statements.
(vi) Information is reliable only if it is free from material error or bias.
(vii) Materiality is determined with reference to the size of the item.
(viii) Contemporary financial accounting practice ignores inflation while measuring assets and liabilities at historical cost.
(ix) Only those expenses that are incurred to earn the revenue for the period are recognised in the statement of profit and loss for the current period.
(x) Application of the principle of prudence results in understatement of profit.
(xi) The threshold of reliability of information provided in footnotes is lower than the threshold of reliability of information provided in the balance sheet or the income statement.
(xii) Internal auditing is a part of the internal control system.

(xiii) Auditors of financial statements provide an absolute assurance that financial statements are providing a true and fair view of the financial position and operating performance of the company.

(xiv) An enterprise has the complete discretion to formulate its accounting policy.

2. Fill in the blanks:

(i) A private limited company is also known as a....................company.

(ii) Information is reliable only when it is ....

(iii) The terms 'equity' and...........are used interchangeably.

(iv) An enterprise classifies a debt as 'secured debt' only if it provides a .... as security.

(v) Financial statements are primarily aimed at ....

(vi) The equity capital, long-term debt and short-term debt of a company as at December 31, 2006 were ₹5,00,000, ₹3,00,000, and ₹2,00,000, respectively. The interest-free credit on that date was ₹1,00,000. The capital invested in the company as at December 31, 2006 was ₹..............

(vii) An assertion by the auditor that he could not form an opinion on whether the financial statements give a true and fair view is called ....

(viii) A change in accounting policy should be accounted for ....

(ix) A change in accounting estimate should be accounted for ....

3. Analytical questions:

(i) Explain why equity capital is called risk capital. If debt capital is 80% of the total capital employed in a firm, will it be correct to say that the debt capital is exposed to credit risk only?

(ii) Is the notion of 'safe debt level' appropriate for determining the capital structure?

(iii) "The photographic analogy for the balance sheet is a snapshot and for the profit and loss account and cash flow statement is a motion picture." Explain.

(iv) Elucidate the statement that "in the preparation and presentation of financial statements, accountants always balance between relevance and reliability."

(v) Do you believe that harmonisation of accounting practices across the globe is a prerequisite for the movement of capital across the globe? Present your views in the form of a note.

(vi) A firm is investigating a financial fraud. The investigation is not complete on the date on which the financial statements for the year 2005 were approved by the Board of Directors. The external auditor is in a dilemma whether he can assert in his audit report that the financial statements give a true and fair view of the financial position as at December 31, 2005 and operations of the firm for the 2005. Assume yourself in the position of the auditor. How will you resolve the dilemma?

(vii) An equity shareholder who is disappointed with the performance of the company comments "Why to make a fuss about internal control when an internal control system cannot ensure the success of the firm"? Is the shareholder expecting too much from an adequate and efficient internal control system?

(viii) "Politics is inherent to the accounting standard setting process." Explain.

CHAPTER

2

ACCOUNTING FUNDAMENTALS

CHAPTER OBJECTIVES

The objectives of this chapter is to introduce to readers the concepts of equity, assets, and liabilities and the relationship between them. In particular, the objective is developing and understanding of:

- Accounting equation—relationship between equity, assets, and liabilities;
- Concepts of assets, liabilities, income and expenses;
- Classification of assets and liabilities;
- Authorised capital, face value of shares, book value of shares, market value of shares, and market capitalisation.

2.1 ACCOUNTING EQUATION

Both the owners and outsiders to whom the firm promises to transfer economic resources (liabilities) have claim on the firm's assets. This is presented by the following accounting equation:

Assets = Equity + Liabilities

Assets = Equity + Liabilities

In order to emphasise that the owner's claim is residual, the accounting equation can also be written as,

Equity = Assets – Liabilities

Firms measure assets and liabilities on the last day of the accounting period (balance sheet date), and the difference between the two is equity (owners' claim).

EXAMPLE 2.1 (Equity)

Fact pattern: The amount of assets and liabilities in the balance sheet of Sulochana Limited (SL) as at March 31, 2019, was ₹1,00,00,000 and ₹40,00,000, respectively.

Discussion: The equity in the balance sheet was (₹1,00,00,000 – ₹40,00,000) or ₹60,00,000.

Table 2.1 presents the definitions and characteristics of assets and liabilities.

TABLE 2.1 Definitions and Characteristics of Assets and Liabilities

1. Asset	(a) Asset is any economic resource that is valuable to the firm. (b) An economic resource is valuable only if • it has potential to benefit the firm in future, and • the firm controls the same. (c) Control implies the right to direct the use of the resource, and to preclude others from enjoying the benefits embedded in that. For example, public road used by the firm is valuable to it, but it is not an asset of the firm, as the firm has no control over the same. (d) Asset arises from past events. This means that assets do not arise from executory contracts, on which neither party has fulfilled its promise. For example, commitment to purchase an asset does not result in recognition of the asset. Asset is recognised only when the control of the economic resources is transferred to the firm. *Examples of assets:* Land, building, machinery, furniture and fixture, product brand, inventories of stock-in-trade, etc., product brand, license, and computer software.
2. Liability	(a) Liability is an obligation, present at the balance sheet date. (b) Obligation arises when the firm promises to transfer economic resources to another entity. (c) They arise from past events, called obligating events. For example, an obligation to refund the loan arises because the firm borrowed funds in the past. (d) An obligation is present at the balance sheet date if the firm has no practical way to avoid transfer of the economic resource. In case of contractual obligations and statutory obligations the firm has no practical way to avoid transfer of the economic resources, as those are enforceable in the court of law. *Constructive obligation* • Constructive obligation arises from a custom being followed by the firm or from a specific assertion. • Such a custom or assertion create legitimate expectation among beneficiaries that the firm will fulfil its promise. *For example:* a promise to voluntarily clean the city where the factory is located gives rise to a constructive obligation if the firm asserted that promise publicly. • Constructive obligations are not enforceable in the court of law. Yet, in most situations, the firm has on practical way to avoid transfer of economic resources, as nonfulfillment of the promise results in loss of reputation and erosion of relationship capital causing a loss that is higher than the cost of fulfilling the obligation.

Asset is any economic resource that has potential to benefit the firm in future, and is controlled by the firm.

Liability is an obligation, present at the balance sheet date, that is, the firm has no practical way to avoid transfer of the economic resource to settle the obligation.

Net worth

Book value of equity (amount of equity on the balance sheet) is called net worth. The term net assets and net worth are used interchangeably.

For depicting in the balance sheet, assets are not measured at their realisable value. Therefore, in the situation of liquidation, the value that the assets will realise might be much different from the value at which they are depicted in the balance sheet.

Book value of equity is called net worth.

BOX 2.1 CURRENT AND NON-CURRENT CLASSIFICATION OF ASSETS AND LIABILITIES

Current assets and liabilities

The management expects to consume current assets or realise cash from them within 12 months after the balance sheet date or normal operating cycle if it is longer than 12 months. Management expects transfer of assets within 12 months after the balance sheet date or normal operating cycle if it is longer than 12 months to settle current liabilities.

Assets held for sale (such as finished goods and stock-in-trade) are classified as current assets and liabilities held for trading (such as shares taken on loan by a short seller) are classified as current liability even if they do not meet the above-mentioned criteria.

For example, in the balance sheet dated March 31, 2022 (the last date of the financial year 2021–2022), assets which are expected to be consumed or generate cash within the financial year 2022–2023 should be classified as current assets and liabilities which are expected to result in transfer of economic within the financial year 2022–2023 should be classified as current liabilities.

The management expects to consume current assets or realise cash from them within 12 months after the balance sheet date or normal operating cycle if it is longer than 12 months.

Non-current assets and non-current liabilities

Those assets and liabilities that cannot be classified as current are classified as non-current. Fixed assets and capital advance (advance paid to the supplier of an item of fixed asset) are classified as non-current assets. Bank balances which are not available to support current operation are non-current assets. For example, balance in escrow account with a bank that can be used only for the purchase of a piece of land, and margin money deposited with bank against letter of credit (LC) issued by the bank are non-current assets.

Examples of current assets: Trade receivables (amount due from customers), and inventories of raw materials and components, except those items that do not meet the criteria, are classified as current assets. Cash and cash equivalents, investments held for trading, inventories of finished goods and stock-in-trade are classified as current assets.

Examples of current liabilities: Short-term borrowing (borrowing to be repaid within 12 months from the date of borrowing), current portion of long-term borrowings are classified as current liabilities. Trade creditors and advance from customers, except those items that do not meet the criteria, are classified as current liabilities.

Management expects to settle current liabilities within 12 months after the balance sheet date or normal operating cycle if it is longer than 12 months.

Normal operating cycle

Operating cycle is the period which commences from the date of acquisition of assets that are sold with or without conversion and ends at the date when cash is collected from customers. Usually, operating cycle is expressed in terms of days or months. It is the total of raw material holding period, conversion period, finished goods (or merchandise) holding period and average collection period.

Example: An entity holds raw materials for 2 months, takes 5 months to convert the raw material into finished goods, holds finished goods for 1 month, and realises amount due from customers in 2 months. The operating cycle is 10 months.

Table 2.2 presents the classification of assets and liabilities.

TABLE 2.2 Classification of Assets and Liabilities

	Classification	*Criteria*	*Examples*
ASSETS			
1.	Fixed assets	(a) The firm should intend to use the asset for more than one annual period. (b) It should use it for producing goods and services, or for administration or for earning rent. (c) Firms do not sell items of fixed assets in the ordinary course of business or consume them in the production process.	(a) *Property, plant, and equipment (PP&E)* Tangible fixed assets owned by the firm. *Examples:* land, building, plant and machinery, furniture and fixtures and computer. (b) *Intangible assets* Examples are goodwill, product brand, patent, copy right, and computer software. (c) *Right-of-use assets* Items of PP&E taken on lease. (d) *Capital work-in-progress* Items of PP&E under construction or yet to be installed. (e) *Intangible assets under development* Costs accumulated during the development stage (at the stage of developing a prototype and testing before commercial use) of new products or processes.
2.	Inventories	Inventories are (a) inputs that the entities consume in the production process, and (b) items that they hold for sale.	Stock of raw materials and components, work-in-process, finished goods, stock-in-trade, and stock of stores and spares. Loose tools are also included in inventories.
3.	Investments	Capital that firms invest outside the business to earn a regular income (such as, rent, interest, and dividend) or to benefit from capital appreciation.	Investment in the equity shares and bonds issued by another company, investment in units of mutual fund, fixed deposits with bank, and loan to another company. Investment in property (land and building) is classified as *investment property*.
4.	Monetary assets	Amount realisable from a monetary asset is known or determinable using a formula in the contract with another entity.	Cash, trade receivables, loan to employees, and deposit with bank. Cash includes demand deposits with banks, which can be withdrawn without prior notice and without paying penalty.
5.	Non-monetary assets	Assets that cannot be classified as monetary assets.	Fixed assets, investments in equity, and investment in mutual fund units.
6.	Cash equivalents	(a) Highly liquid assets that can be easily converted into fixed amount of cash. (b) Investments in equity instruments and units of a mutual fund are not cash equivalents.	As a practice, the following are included in cash equivalents: (a) Investments in debt securities with a maturity of three months or less from the date of acquisition, (b) Term deposits with banks with original maturity of three months or less, and (c) Cheques, and demand drafts on hand.

Fixed assets are those assets which the firm intends to use for more than one annual period for producing goods and services, or for administration or for earning rent.

Monetary assets are those assets from which the amount realisable is known or determinable.

Cash equivalents are highly liquid assets that can be easily converted into fixed amount of cash.

(*Contd...*)

	Classification	Criteria	Examples
7.	Marketable securities	Marketable securities are unrestricted short-term investment in listed equity shares and debt instruments (usually, maturity period of one-year or less).	(a) Commercial papers, treasury bills issued by the government, and other money market instruments. (b) Units of mutual funds traded in stock exchange and equity shares of listed companies are marketable securities.
8.	Financial assets	It is a contractual right to receive cash or another financial asset.	Trade receivables, investment in corporate bond, investment in equity shares, loan given to another entity and deposit with another entity.
9.	Non-financial assets	Assets that cannot be classified as financial assets are non-financial assets.	Fixed assets, advance paid to vendors and income tax refund.
LIABILITIES			
10.	Creditors	Creditors represent claims received from a third party and accepted by the entity.	Trade creditors (claims from suppliers of goods and services received and accepted), outstanding borrowings, and advance received from customers.
11.	Accruals (also called outstanding liabilities)	Accruals are liabilities for goods and services received, but the supplier's claim is either not received or received but not accepted by the date the financial statements are approved by the Board of Directors.	(a) *Example:* Estimated liability for electricity consumed for which the electricity bill is not received. (b) Measurement of accruals involves estimation.
12.	Provision	(a) Provisions are the liabilities of uncertain timing and amount. (b) Provisions are measured at the management's best estimate.	(a) *Examples:* Liability for post-retirement benefits (e.g., specified pension benefits) to employees, and liability for product warranty. (b) Estimation uncertainties in case of provisions are much higher than those in case of accruals.
13.	Financial liability	Obligations to pay cash or another financial asset arising from contractual arrangements.	Trade payables, security deposit received from contractors, debentures issued by the company, and borrowings from banks and financial institutions.
14.	Non-financial liabilities	Liabilities, which cannot be classified as financial liabilities, are classified as non-financial liabilities.	Advance received from customers, deferred revenue, and income tax liability.

Marketable securities are unrestricted short-term investment in listed equity shares and debt instruments (usually, maturity period of one-year or less).

A financial asset is a contractual right to receive cash or another financial asset.

A financial liability is a contractual obligation to pay cash or another financial asset.

2.1.1 Income

Recall the accounting equation, which is,

Equity = Asset – Liabilities

Equity increases when total amount of assets increases without any change in liabilities. Similarly, equity increases when total amount of liabilities decreases without any change in assets. The total amount of assets increases when owners infuse capital in cash or other assets. That increase is not income. Increase in assets other than infusion of capital is income. Examples of income are income from sale of goods and services, interest income, dividend income, government grant, and waiver of a liability by the counter party.

EXAMPLE 2.2 (Income)

Fact pattern: Equity at the beginning of the accounting period was ₹200,000 and it has increased to ₹300,000. During the period, the owner infused fresh capital amounting to ₹40,000.

Discussion: During the period, equity increased by ₹10,00,000, of which through infusion of capital by the owner. Therefore, income for the period is (₹1,00,000 – 40,000) or ₹60,000.

Increase in equity other than by infusion of capital is income and reduction in equity other than by distribution of assets to equity holders is expense.

EXAMPLE 2.3 (Income on reduction of liability)

Fact pattern: The firm recognised a liability of ₹20,000 for accrued interest expense payable on borrowings from bank. The bank waived the interest liability.

Discussion: The waiver of a liability is recognised as income, as the total amount of liabilities decreases without any change in assets.

2.1.2 Expense

Expense is reduction in equity, other than by distribution to owners. Therefore, dividend is not an expense.

Examples of expense are purchase of stock-in-trade, purchase of raw materials, salary and wages to employees, electricity expense, power expenses, advertisement expense, research and development expense and training expense. Loss, such as loss due to embezzlement or accident, reduces equity and therefore, is recognised as expense.

Expenditure from which an asset is recognised is not expense. Accounting Standards stipulate accounting principle for recognition of assets.

EXAMPLE 2.4 (Expenditure incurred to acquire a piece of equipment)

Fact pattern: BB & Co. purchased a piece of equipment in a cash transaction for ₹5,00,000.

Discussion: The total amount of assets has not changed. Only the composition has changed. Therefore, expenditure incurred to acquire the piece of equipment is not an expense.

EXAMPLE 2.5 (Expenditure incurred to acquire a piece of equipment)

Fact pattern: BB & Co. purchased a piece of equipment for ₹5,00,000 on credit.

Discussion: The total amount of assets and also that of labilities have change by ₹5,00,000. Therefore, there is no change in the amount of equity. Therefore, expenditure incurred to acquire the piece of equipment is not an expense.

Depreciation is the systematic allocation of depreciable amount of an item of PP&E over its useful life.

Depreciation and impairment loss

Depreciation and impairment loss of assets are expenses. Depreciation is the systematic allocation of depreciable amount of an item of property, plant, and equipment over its useful life. Consequently, when depreciation of an asset is recognised, its carrying amount in the balance sheet is reduced. Depreciable amount is the difference between the acquisition cost and the residual value.

Impairment loss occurs when the firm reduces the carrying amount (book value) of the asset to the recoverable amount, which is lower than the carrying amount. Recoverable amount is the maximum amount of cash flow that the firm expects to generate either by using the asset or selling it.

Impairment loss occurs when the firm reduces the carrying amount of the asset to the recoverable amount, which is lower than the carrying amount.

EXAMPLE 2.6 (Impairment loss)

Fact pattern: The carrying amount of a machine is ₹40,000. The management estimates the recoverable amount at ₹30,000.

Discussion: The carrying amount of the asset is reduced to ₹30,000, resulting in the reduction of the total amount of assets by ₹10,000, without an change in liability. Thus equity is reduced by ₹10,000. Therefore, impairment loss of ₹10,000 is recognised. Expense includes loss.

2.2 FACE VALUE, BOOK VALUE AND MARKET VALUE OF EQUITY SHARES (COMMON SHARES OR ORDINARY SHARES)

This section is relevant to financial statements of companies registered under the Companies Act 2013.

2.2.1 Authorised Capital and Face Value

The authorised capital of a company is the maximum amount of share capital, measured at face value, that the company is authorised to issue to its shareholders.

The authorised capital may be increased with shareholders' approval at a general meeting, if permitted by the Articles of Association.

Face value (par value) of share is calculated by dividing the authorised capital by the number of parts in which it is divided by the company.

The authorised capital of a company is the maximum amount of share capital, measured at face value, that the company is authorised to issue to its shareholders. The Memorandum of Association, which is the constitutional document that a company submits to the government while filing the application for registration, mentions the amount of authorised capital. Part of the authorised capital can (and frequently does) remain unissued.

The authorised capital may be increased with shareholders' approval at a general meeting, provided this is permitted by the Articles of Association, which describes the internal regulation of a company.

Authorised capital has no economic significance. Higher the authorised capital, higher will be the registration fees and stamp duty. Usually, a company that has ambition to grow as a large company signals the ambition by mentioning high authorised capital in the Memorandum of Association.

Face value (also called par value) of share is calculated by dividing the authorised capital by the number of parts in which the authorised capital is divided by the company. It is at the discretion of the company to decide the face value.

EXAMPLE 2.7 (Face value)

Fact pattern: Both Ishita Limited (IL) and Jassi Limited (JL) have an authorised capital of ₹10,00,000. IL has decided to divide its authorised capital into 1,00,000 shares. JL has decided to divide its authorised capital into 10,000 shares.

Discussion:

Face value of share of IL: ₹10,00,000/1,00,000 = ₹10

Face value of share of JL: ₹10,00,000/10,000 = ₹100

Authorised capital does not limit the capacity of the company to mobilise equity capital from public. A company can issue shares at a premium. The issue price is usually determined through the book-building process.

EXAMPLE 2.8 (Share Premium)

Fact pattern: Both IL and JL in example 2.7 decide to issue all the shares to mobilise ₹1 crore from the market.

The issue prices of shares are as follows:

IL: (₹1,00,00,000/1,00,000) = ₹100; JL: (₹1,00,00,000/10,000) = ₹1,000

Discussion: Share premiums per share are as follows:

IL: ₹100 (Issue price) – 10 (Face value) = ₹90

JL: ₹1,000 (Issue price) – 100 (Face value) = ₹900

In the balance sheet of both the companies, the amount mobilised will be presented as follows:

Equity	
Share capital (Issued, subscribed, and paid up)	₹10,00,000
Reserves and surplus (Securities premium)	90,00,000
Total	**₹1,00,00,000**

2.2.2 Book Value

Book value per share is calculated by dividing the amount of equity in the balance sheet by the number of outstanding shares. The number of outstanding shares is the number of shares issued and subscribed less the number of shares bought back.

Book value per share is calculated by dividing the amount of equity in the balance sheet by the number of outstanding shares.

2.2.3 Market Value and Market Capitalisation

Market value per share refers to the price at which the shares are being traded in the capital market. It reflects the market (investors collectively) expectation about the future performance of the company. Market value of the equity is called market capitalisation. Share price may be perceived as market capitalisation divided by the number of outstanding shares. However, in practice, share price being observable, market capitalisation is calculated as follows:

Market capitalisation = Share price × No. of outstanding shares

EXAMPLE 2.9 (Market capitalisation)

Fact pattern: The share price is ₹120, and the number of outstanding shares is 5,00,000.

Discussion: The market capitalisation is: ₹120 × 5,00,000 = ₹6,00,00,000.

Intrinsic value and market capitalisation: Market capitalisation may not be the same as the intrinsic or the fundamental value of the equity. There can be many reasons for this. For example, market may not be confident of the outcome of the company's strategy (e.g., turnaround strategy of a sick company projected by its management). Moreover, in the short-term, the share price is affected by factors such as liquidity in the market and market sentiment. In the long-term, market capitalisation tends to converge to the intrinsic or fundamental value of the equity capital. Therefore, managers focus on improving the fundamental value of the company. However, they keep an eye on the market value because that provides an insight into market's evaluation of the company's strategy and operational efficiency.

Market value per share refers to the price at which the shares are being traded in the capital market.

Market value of the equity is called market capitalisation.

REVIEW PROBLEMS

R2.1 Indicate whether the following statements are True or False:

(i) Equity is the balancing figure in the accounting equation.
(ii) A company cannot have negative net worth.
(iii) Every economic resource that is valuable to an entity is the entity's asset.
(iv) In evaluating whether currently the an entity has the practical ability to avoid transfer of economic resources, its financial position should not be considered.
(v) Fixed assets are always classified as non-current asset.
(vi) The terms cash equivalents and marketable securities are used interchangeably.
(vii) The management has the discretion to decide the face value of shares.
(viii) The terms face value, nominal value and par value of shares are used interchangeably.
(ix) The terms cash equivalents and marketable securities are used interchangeably.
(x) Companies disclose authorised capital in the balance sheet, and it is not a part of book value of equity.
(xi) Entities do not own 'right-of-use' assets.

R2.2 Fill in the blanks:

(i) The balance sheet shows assets and liabilities at ₹5,00,000 and ₹3,00,000 respectively. The book value of equity at the balance sheet date is................
(ii) An asset that the entity does not intend to consume in the production process or hold for sale is a fixed asset if the entity intends to continue it for more than........................period.

(iii) Inventories of finished goods and stock-in-trade is classified as .... assets. [Choose between the words 'current' and 'non-current']

(iv) An entity has reported operating cycle at 10 months, and holding period of inventories, trade receivables, and work-in-process at 3 months, 3 months and 6 months respectively. The average credit allowed by supplier of goods and services is.............months.

(v) A company has decided to issue shares at a price of ₹150. The face value each share is ₹10. The share premium is ₹.............

(vi) The carrying amount, value in use, and fair value less cost to sell are ₹4,50,000, ₹4,20,000 and ₹4,00,000 respectively. The impairment loss is ₹..................

(vii) The price at which shares of company is trading in the capital market is ₹100 per share. The book value per share is ₹60. Number of outstanding shares is 10,000. The market capitalisation is ₹..............

CASE STUDY

Meera's Boutique

A couple of years ago, Meera was a perfect house wife with husband (Abhishek), a son (Amitabh), and mother-in-law (Sharmila). She still remembers those days when she had no space for herself, but life was full of satisfaction. She used to be busy the whole day with the growing Amitabh and the ageing Sharmila. She used to get break from household chores only in the weekend evenings when she used to go out with Abhishek either to watch movies or plays or for shopping. She suddenly felt a vacuum in her life when she lost her mother-in-law in the summer of 2002. She got frightened looking at the future when Amitabh would not require her company as much as he requires now. She decided to join a dress designing course to get her engaged. She enjoyed the first year: found new friends, enjoyed her own creativity and, more importantly, found her own space.

She had started a small venture on January 1, 2004 with full encouragement and support from Abhishek and Amitabh. That is how Meera's Boutique had come into existence. In 2004, Meera operated from home. She had to sell on credit although she purchased materials in cash and paid for all services like tailoring in cash. She was happy that the boutique had no liability at the year end. She was happy for another reason. On the last day of the year, her entire stock was purchased by Suprita, who lives in Washington. She liked the dresses so much that she purchased all the items to sell them in Washington to her Indian friends.

Meera scaled up her business in 2005. The following is the summary of her transactions in the year:

1. Meera borrowed ₹5,00,000 from Punjab National Bank on April 1, 2005 at an interest rate of 10% per annum compounded yearly.
2. The loan at (1) above is repayable in five equal annual instalments payable on 31 March every year.
3. Interest on the loan at (1) above is payable annually on 31 March.
4. Meera leased an accommodation in the marketplace on June 1, 2005, by paying a lump sum amount of ₹3,00,000. The lease is for 20 years, and monthly lease rent is ₹1,000. The lease rent will increase by 10% every year. The first lease rent was paid on June 1, 2005. As per the terms of the lease, subsequent lease rents are payable at the end of the previous month. For example, the lease rent for January 2006 was payable on December 31, 2005. Meera paid lease rents on due dates.
5. Meera renovated the space by spending ₹80,000. The renovation was complete on April 30, 2005.
6. Meera purchased furniture on May 1, 2005, for ₹1,00,000.
7. Meera estimates the useful life of furniture at 10 years. She uses the straight-line method of depreciation.
8. Meera paid an insurance premium of ₹2,000 on May 1, 2005. The premium covers all types of risks for one year.
9. Meera purchased materials for ₹5,00,000 on credit on different dates.

10. Meera paid ₹4,50,000 to her suppliers of materials.
11. Meera sold sarees, dress materials and dresses for ₹5,00,000 in cash.
12. Meera sold sarees, dress materials and dresses for ₹2,00,000 on credit.
13. Meera realised ₹1,50,000 from its customers.
14. Meera paid ₹1,50,000 towards tailoring charges and other office expenses. At the end of the year ₹10,000 is outstanding towards tailoring charges.
15. Meera sold an item of furniture (cost ₹2,400) on 31 December for ₹2,000.

Assignment

(a) Prepare a work sheet (in the format provided in Balance Sheet) for the preparation of financial statements of Meera's Boutique for 2005. Indicate increase by (+) and decrease by (–).

(b) Prepare the income statement for 2005 and balance sheet as at December 31, 2005.

(c) Prepare a statement showing cash flow from operations.

(d) Reconcile the profit as per the income statement with the cash flow from operations.

Use the following additional information provided by Meera about closing stock as at December 31, 2005:

Annexure I

Meera's Boutique

Balance Sheet as at December 31, 2005

	Amount ₹	*Amount ₹*
ASSETS		
Trade Receivables	50,000	
Cash and bank balance	1,00,000	1,50,000
EQUITY AND LIABILITIES		
Capital		1,50,000

Annexure II

WORK SHEET (Amount in ₹)

Transaction Number	*Cash*	*Current assets other than cash*	*Non-current assets*	*Current liabilities*	*Non-current liabilities*	*Equity (Capital)*
1.						
2.						
3.						
4.						
5.						
6.						
7.						
8.						
9.						
10.						
11.						
12.						
13.						
14.						
15.						

ASSIGNMENTS

1. Tick the correct answer:

(i) Neutrality is an ingredient of:

	Reliability	Relevance
(a)	Yes	Yes
(b)	Yes	No
(c)	No	Yes
(d)	No	No

(ii) What is the underlying concept that supports the immediate recognition of an estimated loss?
(a) Substance over form
(b) Consistency
(c) Matching
(d) Prudence

(iii) Which of the following is an essential characteristic of an asset?
(a) The claim to an asset's benefit is legally enforceable.
(b) An asset is tangible.
(c) An asset is obtained at a cost.
(d) An asset provides future benefits.

(iv) In the accounting equation:
(a) Equity and assets are dependent variables.
(b) Assets and liabilities are dependent variables.
(c) Equity and liabilities are dependent variables.
(d) None of the above

(v) The intangible assets are:
(a) Fictitious assets that will not result in flow of economic benefits to the enterprise
(b) Non-monetary assets without physical substance
(c) Non-monetary current assets without physical substance
(d) None of the above

(vi) Receivable, that is, the amount due from a customer is a:
(a) Monetary current asset
(b) Non-monetary current asset
(c) Fixed asset
(d) None of the above

(vii) An asset is classified as a non-current asset or current asset based on:
(a) The utility of the asset
(b) Whether the asset is movable or not
(c) Its intended use
(d) None of the above

(viii) Current assets are:
(a) Assets that are expected to be realised within 12 months of the balance sheet date.
(b) Assets that are expected to be realised or consumed in the normal course of the enterprise's operating cycle.
(c) Assets that are expected to be realised within 12 months of the balance sheet date, and also, assets that are expected to be realised or consumed in the normal course of the operating cycle of the enterprise.
(d) None of the above

(ix) Current liabilities are:
 (a) Liabilities that are due to be settled within 12 months of the balance sheet date.
 (b) Liabilities that are expected to be settled in the normal course of the operating cycle of the enterprise.
 (c) Liabilities that are due to be settled within 12 months of the balance sheet date, and also, liabilities that are expected to be settled in the normal course of the operating cycle of the enterprise.
 (d) None of the above

(x) A provision is a:
 (a) Liability of uncertain timing
 (b) Liability of uncertain timing and amount
 (c) Liability of uncertain amount
 (d) None of the above

(xi) An increase in current assets results in:
 (a) Increase in cash flow from operations
 (b) Decrease in cash flow from operations
 (c) Increase in cash flow from operations, if the operating result for the period is profit
 (d) None of the above

(xii) A decrease in working capital leads to:
 (a) Increase in cash flow from operations
 (b) Decrease in cash flow from operations
 (c) Decrease in cash flow from operations, if the operating result for the period is loss
 (d) None of the above

(xiii) Purchase of goods (for sale) for ₹10,000 results in:
 (a) Increase in equity by ₹10,000, if the purchase is on credit
 (b) Increase in equity by ₹10,000, if the purchase is on cash basis
 (c) Decrease in equity by ₹10,000
 (d) None of the above

(xiv) Sale of goods (stock-in-trade) for ₹10,000 leads to:
 (a) Decrease in equity by ₹10,000
 (b) Increase in equity by the difference between ₹10,000 and the cost at which the goods were purchased if the cost was lower than ₹10,000
 (c) Increase in equity by ₹10,000
 (d) None of the above

(xv) Payment of ₹5,000 towards salaries and wages results in:
 (a) Increase in equity by ₹5,000
 (b) Decrease in equity by ₹5,000
 (c) Decrease in equity by ₹5,000 if it does not include any advance payment of salaries and wages
 (d) None of the above

(xvi) Interest accrued but not due for payment leads to:
 (a) Decrease in equity
 (b) Decrease in both equity and assets
 (c) Decrease in equity and increase in liabilities
 (d) None of the above

(xvii) Prepaid insurance premium should be classified as a:
 (a) Current asset
 (b) Fictitious asset
 (c) Non-current asset
 (d) None of the above

(xviii) Payment of dividend by a company results in:
(a) Decrease in equity that represents a loss
(b) Decrease in equity that represents distribution to owners
(c) Decrease in equity that represents an expense
(d) None of the above

2. State whether the following statements are True or False:

(i) Usually, monetary assets are classified as current assets or investments.
(ii) Investments are necessarily assets that are held by an enterprise for the accretion of wealth through distribution or for capital appreciation.
(iii) Current assets are necessarily short-term assets.
(iv) Both the terms 'intangible asset' and 'fictitious asset' represent an asset that has no physical substance, and these two terms are used interchangeably.
(v) Non-current assets are those assets that are intended to be used either for production or for administrative purposes.
(vi) The current part of a long-term liability should be classified as a current liability.
(vii) The degree of uncertainty surrounding 'provision' is higher as compared to the degree of uncertainty surrounding 'accruals'.
(viii) Short-term bank borrowings should be classified as secured loans, and not current liabilities.
(ix) Any change in policy should be given effect retrospectively while the effect of any change in accounting estimate should be accounted for in the period of change or in subsequent periods.
(x) Profit on sale of machinery being used in production by an enterprise is an extraordinary income.
(xi) The profit measured as increase in net worth and the profit computed as excess of revenue over costs are not one and the same.
(xii) The fact that a liability is used to fund trading activities does make that liability one that is held for trading.
(xiii) Trade receivables is a financial instrument.
(xiv) An enterprise has the option to classify derivative instruments that are assets either as an 'asset held for trading' or as an 'asset available for sale'.

3. Selected balance sheet information of Jones Limited (JL) for the recent four years is presented as follows:

Jones Limited

Balance Sheet (Extract) for 2003–2006

Particulars	*Years*			
	2003	2004	2005	2006
Non-current assets	150	175	225	?
Shareholders' equity	?	250	300	360
Total assets	?	?	750	?
Current liabilities	200	225	?a	?b
Current assets	350	?	?a	?b
Non-current liabilities	100	?	?	180
Total liabilities and shareholders' equity	?	650	?	800

(a) Current assets − Current liabilities = 225
(b) Current assets − Current liabilities = 300

Required: Fill in the blanks.

4. The following transactions relate to a pharmaceutical company. Indicate whether or not each transaction immediately gives rise to an asset or a liability under the GAAP. If accounting recognises an asset or liability, state the account title and amount.

(i) The company sends a cheque of ₹10,00,000 to United India Insurance Company Limited for insurance of property, plant and equipment. The period of coverage begins next month.

(ii) The company places a purchase order on Alfa Laval Limited for a boiler for ₹20,00,000.

(iii) The company acquires chemicals for ₹8,00,000 on credit from Herdilia Chemicals Limited.

(iv) The company places a purchase order on HMT Limited for a special equipment for ₹30,00,000 and pays an advance of ₹6,00,000 to the vendor.

(v) The firm hires a well-known scientist to head its research and development activities. Employment begins next month; 1/2 of the annual salary of ₹1,20,00,000 is payable at the end of each month worked.

(vi) The company receives an order from East India Drug Stores for ₹10,00,000.

(vii) The company purchases 1,00,000 equity shares of Preetam Genetics Limited for 500,00,000, with an intention to establish long-term relationship with the company.

(viii) The company receives a bill from its attorney for ₹5,00,000 to cover services rendered in defending the company in a successful law suit.

(ix) The company receives a notice from its attorney that an individual who used one of its branded medicines has filed a suit claiming damage for its vocal cord for ₹25,00,000.

(x) The company issues equity shares for ₹3,00,00,000.

5. Group the following items into assets, liabilities, equity, income and expenses:

(i) Capital: ₹10,00,000
(ii) Withdrawal by the owner: ₹1,00,000
(iii) Land: ₹5,00,000
(iv) Building: ₹5,00,000
(v) Sales: ₹20,00,000
(vi) Purchases: ₹12,00,000
(vii) Railway siding: ₹2,00,000
(viii) Interest received: ₹50,000
(ix) Wages: ₹40,000
(x) Salaries: ₹1,20,000
(xi) Insurance claim receivable: ₹30,000
(xii) Furniture and fixtures: ₹1,50,000
(xiii) Depreciation for the year: ₹50,000
(xiv) Repairs and maintenance: ₹60,000
(xv) Interest on investment accrued but not due: ₹25,000
(xvi) Interest on loan accrued but not due: ₹30,000
(xvii) Trade receivables: ₹5,00,000
(xviii) Patent: ₹1,00,000
(xix) Copyright: ₹3,00,000
(xx) Prepaid expenses: ₹50,000
(xxi) Insurance premium: ₹1,00,000
(xxii) Loan: ₹5,00,000
(xxiii) Public deposit: ₹3,00,000
(xxiv) Conveyance charges: ₹34,000
(xxv) Travelling expenses: ₹1,50,000
(xxvi) Telephone charges: ₹2,00,000
(xxvii) Advance from customers: ₹5,00,000
(xxviii) Insurance claim: ₹3,00,000
(xxix) Bad debt: ₹20,000
(xxx) Discount received: ₹40,000
(xxxi) Closing stock of finished goods: ₹90,000
(xxxii) Goodwill: ₹5,00,000

(xxxiii) Brand: ₹45,00,000
(xxxiv) Discount allowed: ₹2,00,000
(xxxv) Research expenses: ₹10,00,000
(xxxvi) In-process research: ₹80,00,000
(xxxvii) Customers' list: ₹50,000
(xxxviii) Subsidy received from the government to meet expenses: ₹1,00,000
(xxxix) Subsidy received from the government to meet the cost of equipment: ₹1,00,000
(xl) Export incentives received: ₹2,00,000

6. Classify the following elements of financial statements into property, plant and equipment, intangible assets, investments, monetary current assets, non-monetary current assets, fictitious assets, current liabilities, long-term liabilities, equity, income, gains, expenses and losses.

	(Amount ₹)
(i) Land	1,00,00,000
(ii) Goodwill	50,00,000
(iii) Advertising expenses to the extent not written off	2,00,000
(iv) Salaries and wages	50,00,000
(v) Plant and machinery	5,00,00,000
(vi) Real estate (not being used in business)	5,00,00,000
(vii) Sales	10,00,00,000
(viii) Purchases	6,00,00,000
(ix) Bad debt	2,00,000
(x) Rents and rates	3,00,000
(xi) Receivables	1,00,00,000
(xii) Trade creditors	1,00,00,000
(xiii) Advances from customers	50,00,000
(xiv) Insurance claim received	2,00,000
(xv) Insurance premium	5,00,000
(xvi) Insurance premium paid in advance	20,000
(xvii) Freight inward	1,00,000
(xviii) Freight outward	10,00,000
(xix) Deposit with customs department	5,00,000
(xx) Excise duty paid	10,00,000
(xxi) Sales tax collected from customers	5,00,000
(xxii) Discount allowed to customers	5,00,000
(xxiii) Bank charges	2,00,000
(xxiv) Printing and stationery	3,00,000
(xxv) Closing stock of goods-in-trade	1,00,00,000
(xxvi) Depreciation	5,00,000
(xxvii) Dividend received on investment	8,00,000
(xxviii) Shares in B & Co. Ltd.	80,00,000
(xxix) Share capital	1,00,00,000
(xxx) Retained earnings	5,00,000
(xxxi) Loan from Industrial Development Bank of India	1,00,00,000
(xxxii) Cash credit from State Bank of India	50,00,000
(xxxiii) Railway siding	50,00,000
(xxxiv) Patent	5,00,000
(xxxv) Copyright	5,00,000
(xxxvi) Interest paid	10,00,000
(xxxvii) Loss from fire	2,00,000
(xxxviii) Discount received from suppliers	5,00,000
(xxxix) Bank fixed deposit	8,00,000
(xl) Cheques-in-hand	1,00,000
(xli) Repairs and maintenance	5,00,000
(xlii) Expenses of epoxy painting (ships are epoxy painted every five years)	5,00,000

(xliii)	Training expenses	1,00,000
(xliv)	Training expenses on special training with collaborators to the extent not written off	10,00,000
(xlv)	Bills receivable	8,00,000
(xlvi)	Bills payable	3,00,000
(xlvii)	Goods sent on approval lying with customers	6,00,000
(xlviii)	Power and fuel	5,00,000
(xlix)	Staff welfare expenses	2,00,000
(l)	Travelling expenses	8,00,000

7. Analytical questions

(i) A has entered into an irrevocable agreement to purchase machinery from B & Co. for ₹1,00,000. Should A recognise the asset and the corresponding liability?

(ii) A & Co. while launching its new product, 'Zoom' toothpaste, incurred expenditure of ₹1 million on advertisement. The Managing Director of the company proposes that the expenditure be shown as an asset on the balance sheet; however, the accountant disagrees. Who is right?

(iii) "Users of financial statements assume that the enterprise is a going concern." Comment on this statement.

(iv) The CESC has installed a transformer within the premises of the factory owned by Mr. A, who paid an amount of ₹50,000 to the CESC towards the cost of the transformer and installation charges. As per the agreement, the ownership of the transformer lies with CESC. Should this expenditure of ₹50,000 be treated as an asset?

(v) Human resource is not shown as an asset in the balance sheet though managers claim that it is the most important asset of an enterprise. What could be the reasons for not recognising human resource as an asset on the balance sheet?

(vi) An analyst asserts "If the normal operating cycle of a firm is significantly long, classification of assets into current and non-current does not provide any meaningful insight". Do you agree with this statement? Justify from answer.

(vii) Swaroop Limited (SL) manufactures and sells compressors of various capacities, including large compressors that are used in oil exploration. The auditor of the company argues that it has no well-defined normal operating cycle for the following reasons:

(a) Its collection period (i.e., the period between the dispatch of goods and collection of receivables) is erratic. It varies between two months and nine months.

(b) Its production cycle varies between 2 months to 18 months although the production cycle for each type of compressor is well-defined.

(c) The auditor proposes that the classification of assets into current or non-current should be based on the 12–month criterion. Do you agree? Explain your position on this issue.

(viii) On January 1, 2002, Damodaran Limited (DL) borrowed ₹1,00,00,000 from Universal Bank Limited (UBL). The loan is repayable on September 30, 2006. The company has approached the bank to roll over the loan for another period of two years. If the bank agrees to the proposal, the repayment date will be shifted to September 30, 2008. On the date of the board meeting, which is convened to consider and approve financial statements for 2005, the Board of Directors is informed that the Core Committee of the bank that considers the restructuring proposal has recommended acceptance of the proposal, and it is pending for approval by the Board of Directors. In the balance sheet dated December 31, 2005, DL classifies the borrowing as a non-current liability. Is DL right in classifying the liability as a non-current liability? Explain your views on this issue.

(ix) Mr. Nitin, a professional accountant, argues that it is difficult to believe that a firm cannot estimate the useful life of an asset, and therefore, the concept of intangible assets with indefinite life is not warranted. He believes that the concept is introduced to allow smoothing of profit. Do you agree with Mr. Nitin? Explain your opinion.

8. **Problems**

(i) Fill in the appropriate columns in the table (given below the points) against each of the following transactions entered by Ms. Manjula on January 2010:

- Manjula started business with ₹1,00,000 in cash.
- She deposited ₹90,000 in bank.
- Furniture for ₹30,000 was purchased on credit.
- Goods were purchased for ₹1,20,000 on credit.
- Manjula borrowed from bank ₹50,000, repayable within 12 months.
- The supplier of goods was paid ₹50,000 by cheque in part settlement of the amount due to it.
- Supplier of the furniture was paid ₹30,000 by cheque in full and final settlement of its claim.
- Manjula sold goods for ₹60,000 on credit.
- She sold goods for ₹20,000 in cash.
- She paid ₹68,000 to the supplier of goods in full and final settlement of its claim.
- Manjula paid ₹20,000 to employees.
- She paid ₹2,000 towards telephone charges.
- She sold goods for ₹40,000 on credit.
- Cheque for ₹60,000 was received from a customer in settlement of the amount due to the firm.
- Depreciation on furniture for the month of January was ₹300.
- Interest accrued on loan taken from the bank at the end of the month was ₹500.
- Stock at the end of the month was valued at ₹40,000.

Sl. No.	Cash and Bank		Current assets other than cash and bank		Non-current Assets		Current Liabilities		Non-current Liabilities		Equity	
	Dr.	Cr.	Dr.	Cr.	Dr.	Cr.	Dr.	Cr.	Dr.	Cr.	Dr.	Cr.

(ii) (a) Classify the following items into equity, liability, asset, income and expenses and indicate whether the balance in the account is debit or credit:

Sl. No.	Particulars	Amount ₹,000	Credit Balance (Amount)			Debit Balance (Amount)	
			Equity	Liability/Valuation Allowance	Income	Asset	Expense
1.	Capital	1,000					
2.	Reserves and surplus	3,000					
3.	Loan from SBI	500					
4.	Land	100					
5.	Machinery	500					
6.	Furniture and fixtures	50					
7.	Vehicle	100					
8.	Product brand	30					
9.	Telephone expenses	10					
10.	Advance from customers	30					
11.	Advance to employees	20					
12.	Loan to suppliers	40					
13.	Stock-in-trade (Opening)	500					
14.	Receivables	400					
15.	Advertising expenses	100					
16.	Employee compensation	200					
17.	Travelling expenses	100					
18.	Conveyance charges	20					
19.	Training expenses	50					
20.	Sales	2,500					
21.	Purchases	2,300					
22.	Accumulated depreciation	130					
23.	Interest income	10					
24.	Freight inward	40					
25.	Freight outward	50					
26.	Cash and bank balance	2,880					
27.	Interest expense	60					
28.	Interest accrued on loan	30					
29.	Trade creditors	350					
	Total	15,100					

(b) Assuming that the stock-in-trade at the end of the period was valued at ₹6,00,000 and the depreciation for the period amounted to ₹65, calculate the profit before tax for the period.

(c) Prepare the balance sheet at the end of the period. (Ignore income tax.) [**Answer:** (Amount ₹,000) (a) Equity: 4,000; Liabilities/Valuation allowance: 1,040; Income: 2,510; Assets: 4,620; and Expenses: 2,930.; (b) Loss: 385; (c) Balance sheet: Equity capital 3,615; Loan fund 500; PPE: 555; Intangible asset: 30; Current assets: 3,940; Current liabilities: 410.]

CHAPTER

3

BALANCE SHEET AND STATEMENT OF CHANGES IN EQUITY

CHAPTER OBJECTIVES

The objectives of this chapter is to introduce to readers the balance sheet structure and information communicated through balance sheet, and also to provide a brief overview of the statement of changes in equity. In particular, the objective is developing and understanding of:

- Balance sheet—purpose structure, and current and non-current classifications;
- Current tax asset and deferred tax asset;
- Marshalling of assets and liabilities;
- Equity—share capital, other equity, capital reserve, and revenue reserve;
- Consolidated financial statements—overview;
- Statement of changes in equity—overview;
- Bonus shares, right issue, and share buyback.

3.1 BALANCE SHEET

3.1.1 Purpose and Structure of Balance Sheet

Purpose

Balance sheet is a snapshot statement of the financial position of a company at the end of the accounting period. It communicates summarised information on equity, assets, and liabilities. Details are disclosed in notes to accounts.

Balance sheet is a snapshot statement of the financial position of a company at the end of the accounting period.

3.1.2 Balance Sheet Structure

Indian companies present financial statements in the format prescribed in Schedule III of the Companies Act, 2013. Schedule III has three divisions. Division I format should be used by the companies which apply the accounting principles and methods stipulated in AS. Division II formats are used by the companies which apply the accounting principles and methods stipulated in Ind AS. Division III formats are to be used by non-banking finance companies (NBFCs). We shall discuss general principles in the light of Schedule III, division II.

Companies present the balance sheet in a vertical format. Notionally there are two segments. Assets are presented in the upper segment. Equity and liabilities are presented in the lower segment. It mirrors the accounting equation. Table 3.1 below presents the format.

TABLE 3.1 Balance Sheet Format

	Current year	*Previous Year*
A. ASSETS		
B. EQUITY AND LIABILITIES		
Equity		
Liabilities		
Total of Equity and Liabilities		

Assets, liabilities, and equity are depicted in the balance sheet by description and value. The value at which an asset or liability is depicted is called its carrying amount. In the balance sheet assets and liabilities are classified into current and non-current categories. Further, under those two categories different types of assets and liabilities are presented as separate line items.

Criteria for classifying assets and liabilities into current and non-current categories and grouping of assets and liabilities were discussed in Chapter 2.

When assets are marshalled in order of liquidity, assets are listed in the descending order of liquidity.

3.1.3 Marshalling of Assets and Liabilities

Marshalling of assets and liabilities in the balance sheet refers to arranging assets and liabilities in the balance sheet in a specific order.

When assets are marshalled in order of permanence, assets are listed in descending order of permanence.

Marshalling in order of liquidity

Assets are marshalled in descending order of liquidity. The most liquid asset (cash) is listed first, and least liquid asset is placed last.

Marshalling in order of permanence

Assets are listed in descending order of decreasing permanence–the asset that stays longest with the company is listed first.

Marshalling of assets under the Companies Act

Schedule III requires presentation of assets in the following order:

Non-current assets are placed at the top and then comes current assets. Non-current assets are arranged in the following order: – PP&E, capital WIP, investment property, goodwill, other intangible assets, intangible assets under development, biological assets other than bearer plants, financial assets [(i) investments, (ii) trade receivables, (iii) loans, and (iv) others], deferred tax asset, and other non-current assets.

Current assets are arranged in the following order:

Inventories, financial assets [(i) investments, (ii) trade receivables, (iii) cash and cash equivalents,(iv) bank balances other than those included in cash and cash equivalents (v) loans and (iv) others], current tax asset, and other current assets.

Marshalling of liabilities under the Companies Act

The format prescribed in Schedule III of the Companies Act, 2013 requires companies to present liabilities in the following sequence and with the following details:

(a) Non-current liabilities are placed first and then comes the current liabilities.
(b) Non-current liabilities are arranged in the following sequence: financial liabilities [(i) borrowings, (ii) trade payables, (iii) other financial liabilities, other than those included in provision], provisions, deferred tax liabilities (net), other non-current liabilities.
(c) Current liabilities are arranged in the following sequence: financial liabilities [(i) borrowings, (ii) trade payables, (iii) other financial liabilities, other than those included in provision], other current liabilities, provisions, current tax liabilities (net).

Current tax asset and deferred tax assets are presented as separate line items. Current tax asset is classified as a current asset. Deferred tax asset is classified as a non-current asset. Contingent liabilities are disclosed in notes.

Current tax asset represents income tax paid in advance against the income tax obligation for the current period.

3.1.4 Tax Assets

Current tax asset

Current tax asset represents income tax paid in advance against the income tax obligation for the current period. For example, advance tax paid for the assessment year 2023–2024 (corresponding to the financial year 2022–2023) is recognised as current tax asset in the balance sheet as at March 31, 2022.

A deferred tax asset (liability) arises when the entity overpaid (underpaid) income tax due to temporary differences.

Temporary difference is the difference between the carrying amount of assets and liabilities in the balance sheet and the tax base, which reverse in future.

Deferred tax asset

A deferred tax asset (liability) arises when the entity overpaid (underpaid) income tax due to temporary differences between financial accounting and tax accounting. Tax accounting refers to the accounting principles that are applied for computing taxable income. The tax liability is assessed based on the taxable income. Temporary difference is the difference between the carrying amount of assets and liabilities in the balances sheet and the tax base. Tax base is the notional carrying amount of those items in income tax books. Temporary differences reverse over one or more future periods.

EXAMPLE 3.1 (Deferred tax asset and deferred tax liability)

Fact pattern: The cost of a machine is ₹1,000 and the estimated residual value is zero. The entity charges depreciation at 10% of the cost of the machine and the income tax law allows depreciation at the rate of 25% on the written down value (WDV).

Discussion: At the end of the first year, carrying amount of the asset in the balance sheet is (1000 – 100) or ₹900. The tax base is (1,000 – 250) or ₹750. The difference of (900 – 750) or ₹150 between the carrying amount of the machine and its tax base is temporary because over the life of the machine, the difference will be reduced to zero, as the cost of ₹1000 will be charged as depreciation both in financial accounting and tax accounting over the asset's life. It is correct to assume that the entity will recover as income at least ₹900 (carrying amount) from the use of the machine in future periods. It will allow deduction of only ₹750 (tax base) as depreciation in future years. In this way, it has underpaid income tax in the current year. If we assume the income tax rate at 40%, the entity should recognise a deferred tax liability of (₹150 × 0.40) or ₹60 in the balance sheet at the end of the first year.

Assume that the entity's trade receivables at the end of the current year are ₹1,000. The revenue earned from the customer has already been included in computing the taxable income of the current year. Therefore, the amount that the entity will realise from the customer in future will not be taxable. In a sense, the amount of trade receivables in tax book will be deductible from the amount that the entity will realise in computing the taxable income. The tax base is the same as the carrying amount of the trade receivables. However, if the entity estimates that it may not be able to recover ₹100 from customers, a temporary difference arises. The entity provides valuation allowance (provision for doubtful debts) of ₹100. Therefore, the carrying amount of the trade receivables in the balance sheet is (1,000 – 100) or ₹900. The tax department allows deduction for loss on account of bad debt only when the entity writes off the debt. In the tax books, valuation allowance is not recognised. Consequently, the tax base is ₹1,000. The temporary difference between the carrying amount is (1,000 – 900) or ₹100. In this case, the tax base is higher. The entity will realise ₹900 and a deduction of ₹1,000 will be allowed. Thus, on this account, a negative taxable income of ₹100 will arise, which will be adjusted against taxable income of the year in which the entity will realise the amount. In a sense, the entity has overpaid tax for the current year. This will be adjusted in future. If we assume tax rate of 40%, deferred tax asset of (100 × 0.40) or ₹40 should be recognised in the balance sheet prepared at the end of the current year.

The income tax law allows carry forward of unadjusted loss for eight years. Therefore, the entity will pay lower tax than the tax payable without adjustment for the loss carried forward. So, deferred tax asset is recognised for loss that will be carried forward for adjustment in future. For example, if the tax rate is 40% and the taxable income for the current period shows a loss of ₹1,000, the entity recognises deferred tax asset of (1,000 × 0.40) or ₹400, provided it expects enough taxable profits in future years against which the carry forward loss will be adjusted.

3.1.5 Contingent Liabilities

Contingent liabilities are liabilities existence of which is surrounded by uncertainties.

Contingent liabilities are not recognised in the balance sheet. Those are disclosed in notes. Types of contingent liabilities is presented in table 3.2 below.

TABLE 3.2 Types of Contingent Liabilities

Type	Example
1. Liabilities existence of which is surrounded by uncertainties	Performance guarantee issued on behalf of another entity, as the liability will arise only if that entity fails to perform.
2. Liabilities that exist at the balance sheet date, but the management expects that it is less than likely that economic resources will be transferred to settle the liability	(a) A customer's claim in arbitration and the management expects that the arbitration award will not result in the transfer of economic recourses (b) Income tax claim under appeal
3. Liabilities that exist at the balance sheet date, but the management is unable to estimate the value of the resources to be transferred to settle the liability	The compensation payable for the damage caused to the members of the neighbouring community, and environment due to gas leakage from the plant, occurred in the last quarter of the fiscal year.

Contingent liabilities include liabilities that exist at the balance sheet date, but the management expects that it is less than likely that economic resources will be transferred to settle the liability.

Contingent liabilities are disclosed in notes to accounts.

Commitments

Companies are required to disclose commitment to purchase assets. This information is relevant to users, as most of those commitments results in recognition of assets and liabilities within a short period after the balance sheet date.

Companies are required to disclose commitment to purchase assets.

For example, at the close of the current accounting year (2022–2023), vendor on which an order is placed for the purchase of a piece of equipment is yet to execute the same. The price of the equipment is ₹50 lakhs. The scheduled delivery date is June 15, 2023. As per the terms of the contract payment shall be made by September 30, 2023. The entity is required to disclose this information in a note below the balance sheet. This information is relevant, as, had the liability and asset been recognised, the current liability and fixed assets would have increased by ₹50 lakhs. Neither the asset nor the liability is recognised, as GAAP does not permit recognition of assets and liabilities from executory contracts.

Derivative instruments

Derivative instruments (e.g., forward contract to buy foreign exchange, call and put options, and currency swaps) are recognised as assets when movement of fair value is favourable to the entity, and as a liability when movement of the fair value is unfavourable to the entity.

EXAMPLE 3.2 (Derivative Instruments)

Fact pattern: SS & Co. had entered into a forward contract on March 1, 2022, to purchase USD 1,00,000 on May 30, 2022, at the exchange rate of USD 1 = ₹65 in order to pay to a supplier (of material) located in U.S.A. On March 31, 2022, the forward exchange rate for purchasing USD on May 30, 2022, was US $ 1 = ₹66.

Discussion: From the perspective of SS & Co., it is a favourable movement because the firm will purchase US $ at ₹65 per USD, while the price for purchasing USD has moved upwards. In the balance sheet as of March 31, 2022, the forward contract should be recognised as an asset measured at (1,00,000 × ₹1) of ₹1,00,000.

3.2 EQUITY

3.2.1 Difference Between Equity and Liabilities

In case of liability, the entity has no discretion but to transfer economic resources as promised. In case of equity, the entity has unconditional discretion to decide whether to repay the capital or pay a return on capital.

Equity has two components: Share capital and other equity.

In case of liability (such as, borrowings), the entity has no discretion but to transfer economic resources as promised. In case of equity, the entity has unconditional discretion to decide whether to repay the capital or pay a return on capital. In case of a company, the body of shareholders decide whether to buy back shares or to pay dividend.

Components of equity

Equity has two components:

- Share capital–total face value of outstanding shares, and
- Other equity–profit earned and retained over the life of the company.

Some other items are included in other equity, such as, cash received for which the company has no obligation to refund the amount and items arising the application of some accounting principles (such as, hedge accounting).

Share application money to the extent not refundable

Companies invite public to subscribe to a specified number of shares at the Initial Public Offering (IPO) or follow-up offering (FPO). Often they receive applications for a greater number of shares than on the offer. The Companies Act 2013 and SEBI Regulations prescribe the process for allocating shares. Application money received for shares in excess of the application money required, is adjusted against the money payable by the applicant on allotment. Application money is refunded to those applicants to whom shares are not allotted. Share application money received and not refundable is a component of the other equity because once shares are allotted the money will be transferred to the share capital. Share application money that is refundable is a liability.

Equity component of compound financial instruments

Debenture is a type of corporate bond that companies issue to borrow money from public. There are three types of debentures–non-convertible debentures (NCD), debentures compulsorily convertible into equity shares (CCD), and debentures optionally convertible into equity shares (OCD). NCDs are classified as borrowings. CCDs are classified as equity, as the company has no obligation to repay the amount received. OCD is a compound instrument, which has the components of equity and borrowings. The GAAP requires splitting of the two components and provides guidelines for splitting the amount received on issue of the debenture. The equity component is included in other equity.

There are three types of debentures–non-convertible debentures (NCD), debentures compulsorily convertible into equity shares (CCD), and debentures optionally convertible into equity shares (OCD).

3.2.2 Reserves and Surplus

'Reserves and surplus' is the total of the securities premium and net profit retained in the company over the period of its existence. A part of the retained profit is appropriated to various reserves for meeting future requirements.

Capital reserve and revenue reserve

Reserves and surplus are classified into capital reserve and revenue reserve. Generally, revenue reserve is created out of net profit earned by the company from its operating and investing activities. Capital reserve is created out of capital profit. Capital reserve is not available for distribution to shareholders. A revenue reserve that is created for a specific purpose is also not available for distribution to shareholders.

Revenue reserve is created out of net profit earned by the company from its operating and investing activities.

EXAMPLE 3.3 (Capital profit from reissue of forfeited shares)

Fact pattern: A company issued shares at ₹120 per share and a shareholder failed to pay the last call of ₹60. The company forfeited the share and It reissued the same at ₹110.

Discussion: The company, for the share forfeited and received ₹60 from the original allottee and ₹110 on reissue. In total, it received ₹170 while on other shares it had received 120. Thus, it earned a capital profit of (170 – 120) or ₹50.

Securities premium reserve

Securities premium is the difference between the issue price of shares and their face value. The Companies Act, 2013 (Section 78) restricts the use of securities premium reserve. For example, it cannot be used for the payment of dividend, but can be used for issuing bonus shares and buying back own shares.

3.2.3 Types of Revenue Reserves

Free reserve (also called, general reserve)

It is available for distribution as dividend. Free reserve does not include unrealised profit, such as, gain from the change of the fair value of investments held for trading.

Capital redemption reserve

It is a statutory reserve. The Companies Act, 2013 requires companies to create the reserve when preference shares are redeemed out of profit and when the company buys back shares out of free reserves. The Companies Act, 2013 restricts the use of capital redemption reserve. For example, it cannot be used for payment of dividend, but it can be used for issuing bonus shares.

Capital reserve is created out of capital profit. Capital reserve is not available for distribution to shareholders.

Debenture redemption reserve

It is a statutory reserve. Companies Act, 2013 requires companies to create the reserve when they issue debentures. On redemption of the debentures for which the reserve is created, it is no longer necessary to retained in this account and the balance should be transferred to the General Reserve.

Share option outstanding account

Companies grant stock options (ESOP) to employees as part of compensation to their employees. It is the right to purchase company's shares at a specified price on or before a specified price before a specified date. The fair value of ESOP at the grant date is recognised as employee benefits over the vesting period. The grant date is the date of granting the option. Vesting period is the period for which the employee has to render the services in order to be entitled to the option. It is assumed that the employees pay the option premium, which is the price for buying the right, by rendering services. When a company writes a call option on its own share, the premium earned is not refundable. Therefore, it is in the nature of equity. When the option is exercised, the amount lying in the credit of share option outstanding account is transferred to share capital (to the extent of face value of shares issued) and securities premium account. If the option is not exercised, the amount lying in the credit of share option outstanding account is transferred to General Reserve.

Retained earnings

Retained earnings represent the profit that the company has earned till date from the date of its formation, and not distributed to shareholders as dividend or buy-back of shares, and not appropriated to any specified reserve. A negative amount of retained earnings, which is the amount of loss accumulated over the life of the company, is reported as accumulated deficit and presented as a deduction from reserves and surplus.

Other comprehensive income are those which the GAAP does not allow to be included in profit or loss for the period. They are accumulated in equity.

Other comprehensive income

The GAAP does not allow certain types of income to be included in profit or loss for the period. These are presented as other comprehensive income in the statement of profit and loss and accumulated in equity. Items of other comprehensive income that are presented as separate line items in other equity are as follows:

1. Debt instruments through other comprehensive income;
2. Equity instruments through other comprehensive income;
3. Effective portion of cash flow hedge arising from hedge accounting;
4. Revaluation surplus arising from revaluation of a class of PP&E; and
5. Exchange difference on translating the financial statements of a foreign operation whose functional currency is different from that of the reporting company.

Money received against share warrant

Share warrant is a type of call option, which are usually issued to promoters.

Share warrant is a type of call option. Companies usually issue share warrants to their promoters. The money received against share warrant is not refundable. Therefore, it is in the nature of equity. When the option is exercised, the amount lying in the credit of 'money received against share warrant' is transferred to share capital (to the extent of face value of shares issued) and securities premium account. If the option is not exercised, the amount lying in the credit of 'money received against share warrant' is transferred to General Reserve.

When an investor controls the investee, the investee is a subsidiary of the investor, called parent.

3.3 CONSOLIDATED FINANCIAL STATEMENTS

3.3.1 Subsidiary, Associate and Joint Venture

Subsidiary

When an investor controls the investee, either by holding majority of voting right or otherwise, the investee is a subsidiary of the investor, called parent.

Associate

When an investor significantly influences the operating and financing decisions of an investee, the investee is an associate of the investor. If the investor holds 20% or more, but less than 50% of the voting rights of the investee, it is assumed that the investee is an associate of the investor.

Joint venture

In a joint venture, irrespective of the share holding of each joint venture partner, critical decisions are taken through consensus among partners by virtue of an agreement between them.

3.3.2 Preparation of Consolidated Financial Statements

Consolidated financial statements are prepared considering the Group as a single economic entity. The parent and its subsidiaries constitute the Group.

In consolidated financial statements, the carrying amounts of items is the aggregate of the carrying amount of those items in the standalone financial statements of the parent and its subsidiaries, adjusted for transactions between the group companies (parent and its subsidiaries). For example, revenue in the consolidate statements of profit and loss does not include revenue from sale-purchase transactions between group companies. The claims between the group companies are eliminated. For example, if ₹50,000 is due from a subsidiary to the parent on account of a purchase-sale transaction, ₹50,000 is reduced from total carrying amount (parent plus subsidiaries) of both trade creditors and trade debtors. Unrealised gain or losses on assets purchased from group companies are also eliminated. For example, if the parent is holding raw materials stock purchased from a subsidiary, on which the subsidiary earned a profit of ₹10,000, the inventory value is reduced by ₹10,000.

In the consolidated balance sheet investment in subsidiaries does not appear.

In case the parent is not holding 100 per cent of outstanding shares, the share of non-controlling interest in the subsidiary's equity is presented in the consolidated balance sheet as a separate line item in the consolidated balance sheet.

In the consolidated balance sheet, investment in an associate (joint venture) is presented at the acquisition cost plus the investor's share in the increase in the net worth of the associate (joint venture), reduced by dividend received. In the statement of profit and loss, dividend received from the associate (joint venture) is eliminated and investor's share in the associate's (joint venture's) profit or loss is presented as a separate line item. Investor's share in transactions between the associate (joint venture) is eliminated.

Detailed discussion on the consolidation process is outside the scope of this text.

When an investor significantly influences the operating and financing decisions of an investee, the investee is an associate of the investor.

In a joint venture, critical decisions are taken through consensus among partners by virtue of an agreement between them.

3.4 STATEMENT OF CHANGES IN EQUITY

Statement of changes in equity presents movements in each component of equity during the current year. For example, share capital changes due to issue of new shares or on account of buy-back of shares. Similarly, in a particular year, the debenture redemption reserve has been transferred to free reserve after redeeming the debentures during the current year.

Consolidated financial statements are prepared considering the Group as a single economic entity.

3.5 BONUS SHARES, RIGHT ISSUE, AND SHARE BUY BACK

3.5.1 Bonus Share

Issue of bonus shares is a process of capitalisation of retained profit. It does not change the amounts of assets and liabilities in the balance sheet and consequently, the amount of shareholders' fund. The number of outstanding shares increases. This is like dividing a cake into two or more pieces. It facilitates selling the cake in pieces, and thus, attracts buyers who cannot afford to buy the whole cake. Therefore, issue of bonus shares adds to the attractiveness of the company's stock, which represents the collection of shares. This is reflected in marginal increase in market capitalisation of the company.

Market capitalisation also increases marginally because investors take issue of bonus shares as a 'good news'. By issuing bonus shares, companies transfer a portion of the retained profit (which was available for distribution) to capital, which cannot be distributed to shareholders. Therefore, issue of bonus share signals management's confidence in the growth of the company.

Issue of bonus shares is a process of capitalisation of retained profit. It does not change the amount of shareholders' fund.

EXAMPLE 3.4 (Issue of bonus shares)

Fact pattern: The following are the details of shareholders' fund of Sumedha Limited (SL) as at March 31, 2009:

Capital: Issued, subscribed, and paid up

Share capital–issued, subscribed, and paid up	1,00,000 shares of ₹10 each	₹10,00,000
Reserves and surplus		₹40,00,000
Total Equity		₹50,00,000

On April 1, 2009, the company issued bonus shares in the ratio of 1:1. Before the issue of bonus shares, Ms. Shefali was holding 10,000 shares. The share price before issue of bonus share was ₹150 per share.

Discussion: The following is the composition of shareholders' fund after issue of bonus shares:

Capital: Issued, subscribed, and paid up

Share capital–issued, subscribed, and paid up	2,00,000 shares of ₹10 each	₹20,00,000
Reserves and surplus		₹30,00,000
Total Equity		₹50,00,000

Before the issue of bonus shares, Shefali held 10,000 shares with a book value of (₹50,00,000/1,00,000) or ₹50 each. Therefore, the book value of 10,000 shares held by Shefali was ₹50 × 10,000 or ₹5,00,000. After the issue of bonus shares, the book value comes to (₹50,00,000/2,00,000) or ₹25 each. After the issue of bonus shares Shefali holds 20,000 shares. The book value of 20,000 shares held by Shefali is ₹25 × 20,000 or ₹5,00,000. Although the book value per share is reduced to ₹25 from ₹50, the total book value of shares held by Shefali remains the same. Market capitalisation before the bonus issue was (₹150 × 1,00,000) or ₹1,50,00,000.

If we ignore marginal increase in capitalisation due to increased liquidity of shares and good news communicated to the capital market by issue of bonus share, market capitalisation after bonus issue remains at ₹1,50,00,000. In the absence of any new information, the price at which the shares of the company should trade in the capital market is (₹1,50,00,000/2,00,000) or ₹75 per share. Wealth of Shefali in terms of market value will remain the same at ₹15,00,000.

Right issue refers to the issue of shares to the existing shareholders..

Unless the Articles of association of the company otherwise provide, the offer for rights issue is deemed to include a right to renounce the shares in favour of any other person.

Right Issue

Section 62 of the Companies Act, 2013 provides a pre-emptive right to the existing shareholders to subscribe to further issue of capital by the company. Unless the Articles of association of the company otherwise provide, the offer for rights issue is deemed to include a right to renounce the shares in favour of any other person. On expiry of the specified period within which the offer for rights issue is to be accepted or the right to renounce is to be exercised, the Board of Directors may dispose of the shares in such manner as they think most beneficial to the company. Market value of a share with *rights*-on contains the value of the right. Therefore, the offer price should be lower than the market price at the expiration date. If the offer price is equal to the market price at the expiration date, the right to subscribe, which is traded in the market, will have zero value. Moreover, a rational investor will only subscribe to the rights offering if the offer price is below the market price at the expiration date.

EXAMPLE 3.5 (Right issue)

Fact pattern: 'A' Ltd. decides to issue right shares at a time when the prevailing market price is ₹48 per share. It decides to issue one right share at ₹37 each for every 10 shares held.

Discussion: The stock holding before rights issue is ₹48 × 10, or ₹480. If the shareholder subscribes to the rights issue, the value of 11 shares increases to ₹480 + ₹37, or ₹517. The price after the rights issue should be (517/11) or ₹47. The only difference between the old (right-on) share price of ₹48 and the new (ex-rights) share price of ₹47 is that the former carried rights to subscribe to the issue. The difference of ₹1 is the price of one right. Someone who does not hold shares in A Ltd. may acquire ten rights and then exercise them at a further cost of ₹37. The total cost would be (₹1 × 10) + ₹37, or ₹47. The alternative is that he or she can purchase ex-right share from the market at ₹47. It should be appreciated that the rights issue does not enhance the productivity of assets in place, and thus, does not change the expected cash flow stream. Therefore, the issue price is irrelevant as long as the rights are exercised.

Share buy-back and treasury stock

Companies buy back their own shares to:

- distribute surplus cash to shareholders; or
- enhance the share price in the capital market by reducing the number of floating shares; or
- for restructuring capital structure by reducing the proportion of equity; or
- increase the proportion of promoter's holding.

In India, shares bought back are to be extinguished within seven days from the last day of completion of the buy-back. In U.S.A., reissue of the bought-back shares is permitted under relevant statutes. 'Treasury stock' (shares bought back and held for reissue) is presented as a deduction from the share capital.

Companies buy back shares to distribute surplus cash to shareholders or enhance the share price or restructure the capital structure or increase the proportion of promoter's holding.

In India, shares bought back are to be extinguished within seven days from the last day of completion of the buy-back.

In U.S.A., reissue of the bought-back shares (treasury stock) is permitted.

REVIEW PROBLEMS

R3.1 Indicate whether the following statements are True or False:

(i) In the context of deferred tax, temporary differences reverse over one or more future periods.
(ii) Balance sheet presents the stock of assets and liabilities on the balance sheet date.
(iii) Law requires existing shareholders either to subscribe to issue right issue or reject the offer, they cannot sell the right to subscribe to the right issue.
(iv) Issue of 'bonus shares' reduces the book value of equity.
(v) Share buyback is a process of returning excess cash to shareholders.
(vi) Securities premium reserve is a capital reserve.
(vii) Debenture redemption reserve is a capital reserve.
(viii) Total of revenue reserves should match with the amount of cash and cash equivalents that the company holds on the balance sheet date.
(ix) An investee is classified as a subsidiary of the investor only if the investor holds majority of voting rights in the investee.
(x) The essence of joint ventures is that the venturers agree to take key operating and financing decisions jointly irrespective of their respective voting rights in the joint venture firm.

R3.2 Fill in the blanks:

(i) 'A' Ltd. decides to issue right shares at a time when the prevailing market price is ₹150 per share. It decides to issue one right share at ₹128 each for every 10 shares held. The price for each right is ₹.............
(ii) Marshalling in order of permanence requires assets to be presented in the balance sheet in the ....order of permanence.

(iii) SS & Co. had entered into a forward contract on March 1, 2022, to purchase USD 1,00,000 on May 30, 2022, at the exchange rate of USD 1 = ₹78.00 in order to pay to a supplier (of material) located in U.S.A. On March 31, 2022, the forward exchange rate for purchasing USD on May 30, 2022, was US $ 1 = ₹76.

In the balance sheet as of March 31, 2022, SS & Co should recognise the forward contract as an ....measured at ₹....................

ASSIGNMENTS

1. Indicate against each statement whether it is True or False:

(i) If the proportion of debt in the capital structure of an entity is higher than the ideal debt-equity ratio for entities operating in the industry, the company is exposed to higher financial risks.

(ii) Share capital in the balance sheet of an Indian company represents the amount of capital originally contributed by shareholders.

(iii) Issue of bonus shares is a process of distribution of profit to shareholders.

(iv) Market capitalisation of a listed company increases significantly on announcement of the issue of bonus shares.

(v) Profit prior to incorporation of a company is capital profit.

(vi) Capital redemption reserve is created on buy-back of equity shares.

(vii) General reserve is also called free reserve.

(viii) Usually, public deposits obtained by companies are unsecured loan.

(ix) Amount borrowed for a period longer than one year is classified as long-term loan.

(x) Provisions should always be classified as current liabilities.

(xi) Contingent liabilities represent possible obligations.

(xii) The amount of net current asset represents investment in working capital.

(xiii) Asset intensity ratios of different firms operating in the same industry might differ because of their different business models.

(xiv) Firms invest outside the business to earn a regular return or to gain from capital appreciation and not for anything else.

(xv) Loans and advances to employees and suppliers are always classified as current assets.

(xvi) The terms 'non-controlling interests' and 'minority interests' are often used interchangeably.

(xvii) The concept of treasury shares is not relevant in India.

(xviii) When the normal operating cycle is not clearly identifiable, it is assumed to be 12 months.

(xix) Fair value of an asset is the entry price in the sense that it represents the price at which the entity can purchase a similar asset which has been used for the purpose for which the asset under consideration is used and has been used for the same number of years for which the asset under consideration is used.

(xx) Current assets and current liabilities may be viewed as short-term assets and short-term liabilities.

2. Indicate which of the following represents change in accounting policy (indicate by writing P), which represents change in accounting estimate (indicate by writing AE), and which represents correction of error (indicate by writing E)

(i) A change in the cost accounting formula (from FIFO to weighted average method) being used for valuation of inventories.

(ii) Revision in the estimate of arrears pay to employees made in the previous year on conclusion of the wage agreement in the current year.

(iii) A change in the depreciation method (e.g., straight line method to the written down value method).

(iv) A fraud occurred in one of the earlier years and detected in the current year.

(v) An appeal against penalty imposed by the revenue department was decided against the company in the previous year, but no liability could be provided due to lack of information.

(vi) A provision for doubtful debts against receivables created in the previous year is revised upward at the end of the current year on receipt of fresh information about the financial health of a major customer.

(vii) Change from the cost model to the revaluation model for the measurement of property, plant, and equipment.

(viii) Revision in the estimate of the useful life of an item of property, plant, and equipment.

(ix) Revision in the cost of an asset constructed internally due to the correction of an error in calculation in the worksheet.

(x) Revision in the estimate of service tax liability for services rendered in the previous year based on the legal opinion (on a provision of the service tax law) obtained in the current year.

3. Fill in the blanks:

(i) The total carrying amount of assets less the amount of current liabilities in the balance sheet is ₹1,000, and the amount of outstanding loan at the balance sheet is ₹200. The net worth of the company at the balance sheet date is ₹..........

(ii) The number of outstanding shares immediately before the issue of bonus shares in the proportion of 2 : 1 was 10,000, and the amount of equity in the balance sheet was ₹10,00,000. Immediately after issue of bonus shares, the equity in the balance sheet will be ₹..........

(iii) The market capitalisation of a company immediately before the issue of bonus shares in the ratio of 4 : 1 was ₹100,00,000. Immediately after the issue of bonus shares, the market capitalisation will be ₹........... (ignore the signalling effect of issuance of bonus shares).

(iv) A reserve created to comply with requirements of income tax law should be classified as..........reserve.

(v) The carrying amount of fixed assets at the beginning of the current year was ₹10,000 and the same at the end of the current year was ₹12,000. During the current year, the company earned revenue of ₹30,000. The fixed assets intensity ratio is ....

(vi) A company purchased an item of PP&E on April 1, 2008 for ₹100,000. It charges depreciation on similar assets at the rate of 10% per annum. The company uses the straight line method of depreciation and estimates residual value of zero for such assets. The income tax law allows depreciation at the rate of 25% on the written down value. The tax base of the asset as at March 31, 2010 was ₹..........

(vii) Considering the facts in (vi) above and assuming the income tax rate of 40 per cent, the deferred tax liability as at 31 March 2010 was ₹..........

(viii) Considering the facts in (vi) and (vii) above, the amount of deferred tax expense recognised in the profit and loss account for the year ended on March 31, 2010 was ₹.........

(ix) A company provides the following information:
Raw material holding period: two months; work-in-progress holding period: eight months; finished goods holding period: one month; average receivables collection period: three months; and average payment period to suppliers of raw materials: three months. The normal operating cycle is........ months.

(x) A company, which fabricates specialised non-standard steel structures, provides the following information:
Raw material holding period: 2–5 months; work-in-progress holding period: 8–13 months; finished goods holding period: one month; average receivables collection period: 3–8 months; and average payment period to suppliers of raw materials: three months. The normal operating cycle is.........months.

(xi) At the close of accounting year 2009–2010, an entity, engaged in merchandising business, is holding stock-in-trade, which it expects to sell in 2011–2012. The stock of goods should be classified as .... asset. [Select from the words 'current' and 'non-current'.]

(xii) An item of PP&E should be classified as asset. [Select from the words 'current' and 'non-current'.]

(xiii) Trade investments should be classified as assets. [Select from the words 'current' and 'non-current'.]

(xiv) Advance received from customers against orders to be executed after 24 months after the balance sheet date, by a company whose operating cycle is 18 months, should be classified as .... liability. [Select from the words 'current' and 'non-current'.]

(xv) Pre-paid rent is a .... asset. [Select from the words 'monetary' and 'non-monetary'.]

(xvi) Advance paid to a supplier against a purchase order is a......... asset. [Select from the words 'monetary' and 'non-monetary'.]

(xvii) Investment in equity shares issued by another entity is a....... asset. [Select from the words 'monetary' and 'non-monetary'.]

(xviii) Receivables from customers are.............. asset. [Select from the words 'monetary' and 'non-monetary'.]

(xix) On January 1, 2010, a company operating in capital goods industry received ₹1,00,000 from a customer towards advance against an order to be executed after 24 months. The incremental borrowing rate for the company at that point in time was 15%. The advance should initially be recorded at ₹..........

(xx) An entity should....... a constructive obligation present on the balance sheet date. [Select from the words 'recognise' and 'disclose'.]

CHAPTER

4

INCOME STATEMENT

CHAPTER OBJECTIVES

The objectives of this chapter is to introduce to readers the income statement structure and information communicated through that statement. In particular, the objective is developing and understanding of:

- Purpose and format of the income statement;
- Income and expenses classification;
- Discontinued operation and non-current assets held for sale;
- Earnings per share—Basic EPS, and diluted EPS;
- Profit hierarchy.

In India, the income statement is called the statement of profit and loss, and net income is called net profit.

4.1 PURPOSE, AND FORMAT OF THE STATEMENT OF PROFIT AND LOSS

4.1.1 Purpose

The purpose of the statement of profit and loss is to communicate the result of the operating, investing, and financing activities performed during the reporting period.

The statement of profit and loss also presents an analysis of income and expenses.

The purpose of the statement of profit and loss is to communicate the result of the operating, investing, and financing activities performed during the reporting period, and also to present an analyses of income and expenses.

4.1.2 Format

Table 4.1 below presents the format of the statement of profit and loss provide in Schedule III of the Companies Act 2013:

TABLE 4.1 Format of the Statement of Profit and Loss

		Note No.	*Figures for the current reporting period*	*Figures for the previous reporting period*
	INCOME			
(I)	Revenue from operations			
(II)	Other income			
(III)	Total income (I + II)			
(IV)	**EXPENSES**			
	Cost of materials consumed			
	Purchase of stock-in-trade			
	Changes in the inventories of finished goods, stock-in-trade, and work-in-process			
	Employee benefit expense			
	Finance costs			
	Depreciation and amortisation expense			
	Other expenses			
	Total expenses (IV)			
(V)	**Profit/(loss) before exceptional items and tax (I–IV)**			
(VI)	Exceptional items			
(VII)	**Profit/(loss) before tax (V–VI)**			
(VIII)	Tax expense (i) Current tax (ii) Deferred tax			
(IX)	**Profit/(loss) for the period from continuing operation (VII–VIII)**			
(X)	Profit/(loss) from discontinued operations			
(XI)	Tax expense of discontinued operations			
(XII)	Profit/(loss) from discontinued operations after tax (X – XI)			
(XIII)	**Profit/(loss) for the period (IX + XII)**			

(Contd...)

		Note No.	*Figures for the current reporting period*	*Figures for the previous reporting period*
(XIV)	Other comprehensive income A (i) Items that will not be reclassified to profit/(loss) (ii) Income tax relating to items that will not be reclassified to profit/(loss) A (i) Items that will be reclassified to profit/(loss) (ii) Income tax relating to items that will be reclassified to profit/(loss)			
(XV)	Total comprehensive income for the period (XIII + XIV)			
(XVI)	Earnings per equity share (for continuing operation) 1. Basic 2. Diluted			
(XVII)	Earnings per equity share (for discontinued operation) 1. Basic 2. Diluted			
(XVIII)	Earnings per equity share (for discontinued and continuing operation) 1. Basic 2. Diluted			

Methods for calculating earnings per shares (EPS) will be discussed in Chapter 15.

4.2 INCOME AND EXPENSES CLASSIFICATION

4.2.1 Income

Table 4.2 below presents types of income and expenses.

Revenue is the income from the ordinary business activities (selling of goods and services) of the firm.

Income from operating activates incidental to producing and selling goods and services is classified as other operating income.

TABLE 4.2 Types of Income and Expenses

	Type	*Description*
INCOME		
1.	Revenue	(a) Income from the ordinary business activities of the firm. (b) In case of non-finance companies, revenue is the income from the sale of goods and services. (c) In case of finance companies interest income and income from investments should be classified as revenue. (d) In case of insurance companies, insurance premium earned and income from investments should be classified as revenue.
2.	Other operating income	(a) Income from operating activates incidental to producing and selling goods and services. (b) Example: Income from the sale of scrap generated in the manufacturing process.

(*Contd...*)

	Type	Description
3.	Other income	(a) For non-finance companies: Income from investing activities (interest, dividend, and gain or loss from change in the fair value of investments measured at fair value) (b) Income that cannot be classified as revenue or other operating income. Examples: Gain from the sale of items of property, plant and equipment (PP&E) and sale of investments, and government subsidy
EXPENSES		
4.	Cost of materials consumed	This line items appears in the statement of profit and loss of manufacturing companies. It is calculated as, Cost of material consumed = Purchase of inputs – Increase in the inventories of inputs Inputs are those that are used in producing goods, mostly raw materials and components.
5.	Finance costs	Finance cost is the total of interest expense and other expenses related to borrowings, such as, bank charges for issuance of Letter of Credits (LC), and bank guarantees.
6.	Other expenses	Other expenses includes all operating expenses–selling, distribution, and administrative expenses. It also includes research expenses and development expenses, to the extent not capitalised.

Natural classification model for analysing expenses requires analyses of expenses by their nature.

Functional classification model for analysing expenses requires presenting expenses by functions.

4.2.2 Analyses of Expenses

The following are the two models for analysing expenses in the statement of financial statements:

(a) Natural classification–analysing expenses by their nature, such as: purchases, depreciation, employee benefits, and advertisement expenses; and
(b) Functional classification–analysing expenses by functions, such as: cost of goods sold, administrative expenses, and selling and distribution expenses.

Indian companies are required to analyse expenses using natural classification. Companies in the U.S.A. and many other jurisdictions analyse expenses using functional classification.

4.2.3 Exceptional Items

Companies are required to present exceptional items separately in the statement of profit and loss.

Exceptional items are the expenses and/or incomes, which arise from normal operations of the entity, but either do not occur regularly or are not within the normal range (in terms of the amount of the item). Analysts exclude exceptional items from profit or loss to measure the performance of the company, as those are non-recurring items. The following are the examples of exceptional items:

Exceptional items are the expenses and/or incomes, which arise from normal operations of the entity, but either do not occur regularly or are not within the normal range.

1. Write-down of inventories to net realisable value or of property, plant, and equipment to recoverable amount, as well as reversals of such write-down;
2. Restructuring of the activities of an entity and reversals of any provisions for the costs of restructuring;
3. Disposals of items of property, plant, and equipment, which do not occur in the normal course of operation;
4. Disposals of investments; and
5. Litigation settlements.

4.2.4 Total Comprehensive Income and Other Comprehensive Income

Total comprehensive income has two components:

- net profit for the period, and
- other comprehensive income (OCI).

OCI includes those items of income that are considered in calculating net profit. The GAAP lists nine items that are to be included in other comprehensive income. Most items of OCI are those income that do not arise from operating decisions. However, there is at least one item of gain or loss for which the company has a choice either to treat it as an item of OCI or to include it in profit or loss. It is the gain or loss arising from the change in the fair value of investment in equity. However, this option is not available for investments in equity held for trading.

Total comprehensive income has two components: net profit for the period, and other comprehensive income (OCI).

The GAAP lists nine items that are to be included in OCI.

Examples of OCI are revaluation gain arising from the revaluation of items of PP&E, difference arising from remeasurement of liability arising from post-retirement benefits under scheme where the benefits are defined in the scheme (such as, the formula in the scheme to determine the amount of pension payable to employees after retirement) and fair value gains and losses arising from measurement investment in debts cash flow from which meets specified criterion.

Analysts, analyse economic performance of companies considers net profit and not total comprehensive income.

4.2.5 Discretionary Expenses

Expenses that has no cause and effect (input-output) relationship with revenue earned for the accounting period are called discretionary expenses because the management can reduce those expenses without impacting the revenue, and consequently, the profit for the reporting period. Examples are research and development expenses, advertisement expenses, training expenses, and expenses on (preventive) repair and maintenance. Inadequate discretionary expenses impact the long-term earning capacity of the firm. Decision impact the future earning capability of the entity. For example, cutting down training expenses might reduce the capability of the entity to adapt new generation technology. Similarly, cutting down advertising expenses might dilute the product brand.

Expenses that has no cause and effect (input-output) relationship with revenue are called discretionary expenses.

4.3 DISCONTINUING OPERATION AND NON-CURRENT ASSETS HELD FOR SALE

Companies are required to disclose the profit or loss from discontinued operation separately in the statement of profit and loss. This disclosure is important for users who forecast future cash flows from the company's operations.

Non-current assets held for sale

Non-current assets (such as, items of property, plant and equipment) are classified as 'non-current assets held for sale' when the company decides to generate cash from those assets by sale and not from use and expects to complete the sale transaction within a year from the date of classification.

Discontinuing operation

The entity classifies the segment as discontinued operation or non-current assets as held for sale when it actively searches for buyers and expects to sell the business within one year from the date of such classification.

Operation: Operation in this context is a segment of business which can be identified separately and whose income and expenses can be separated from continuing operations.

EXAMPLE 4.1 (Discontinued operation)

Fact pattern: An entity which is in the business of selling designing, manufacturing, and selling women's clothing, fashion accessories decides to discontinue the accessory business

Discussion: The entity should classify the segment as discontinued operation when it actively searches for buyers and expects to sell the business within one year.

EXAMPLE 4.2 (Discontinued operation)

Fact pattern: An entity decides to reduce production capacity be selling one of the factories that produce the same product.

Discussion: The factory should not be classified as a discontinuing operation, as it cannot be identified separately and its income and expenses cannot be separated from continuing operations.

However, the assets of the factory is classified as non-current assets held for sale.

Measurement

Assets of a discontinuing operations and assets held for sale are measured at the lower of the carrying amount, and fair value less costs to sell. The carrying amount immediately before classifying the operation as discontinuing operation or assets held for sale is considered for comparing with the FV less costs to sell.

Profit or loss consists of profit or loss from operation, and gain or loss from the sale of the assets of the operation.

Gross Profit = Sales – Cost of goods sold
Cost of goods sold includes the purchase price (cost or production) and costs incurred to bring the goods to the location and condition of sale.

EBITDA = Gross Profit– Operating Expenses, excluding depreciation and Amortisation EBITDA is used as a proxy for cash profit.

4.4 PROFIT HIERARCHY

Profit is calculated at different levels to better understand the company's performance. In this section we shall discuss some common measures of profit.

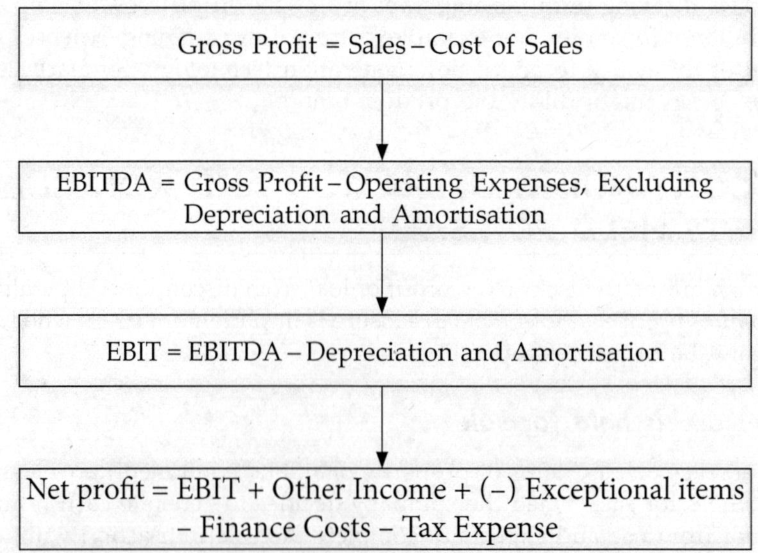

Figure 4.1 Profit hierarchy

EBIT = EBITDA – Depreciation and Amortisation

4.4.1 Gross Profit

The terms of cost of sales and cost of goods sold are used interchangeably.

Cost of sales includes the purchase price of stock-in-trade and costs incurred to bring the goods to the location and condition of sale. In the case of a manufacturing company, cost of sales is the cost of production and costs incurred to bring the goods to the location and condition of sale.

$$\text{Gross profit margin} = \frac{\text{Gross Profit}}{\text{Revenue}} \times 100$$

Gross profit margin measures the procurement efficiency of a merchandising company. Also, measures the procurement and manufacturing efficiency of a manufacturing company.

Gross profit margin = (Gross Profit ÷ Revenue) × 100

4.4.2 Earnings Before Interest, Tax, Depreciation and Amortisation (EBITDA)

EBITDA is used as a proxy for cash profit.

$$\text{EBITDA Margin} = \frac{\text{EBITDA}}{\text{Revenue}} \times 100$$

EBITDA margin of comparable companies of different ages are comparable, as depreciation and amortisation depend on the investment in fixed assets. Different amount of investment is required to create the same production capacity at different points in time. Companies endeavour to earn a decent EBITDA margin to stay afloat during difficult times. EBITDA margin is an effective measure of performance in capital intensive industries such as power generation companies and companies providing mobile connectivity and internet services, which do not require replacement of fixed assets frequently. Often investors calculate value of such companies using EBITDA multiple. Depreciation and amortisation are real expenses, and therefore, should not be excluded in measuring performance over a long period of time.

EBITDA margin = (EBITDA ÷ Revenue) × 100

4.4.3 Earnings Before Interest and Tax (EBIT)

$$\text{EBIT Margin} = \frac{\text{EBIT}}{\text{Revenue}} \times 100$$

Some analysts consider EBIT as operating profit.

4.4.4 Net Profit

Net profit is available for distribution to owners (investors in equity capital).

4.4.5 Operating Profit

Operating profit is the profit before interest, after tax. It is referred to as net operating profit after tax (NOPAT). It is also called net operating profit less adjusted tax (NOPLAT).

$$\text{NOPAT} = \text{Net profit} \pm \text{Exceptional items} \times (1 - t) - \text{Other Income} \times (1 - t) + \text{Finance cost} \times (1 - t)$$

Here, t represents marginal tax rate. There is only single corporate tax rate applicable to Indian companies, and, in that context, t refers to that tax rate.

Net operating profit after tax (NOPAT) = Net profit ± Exceptional items × (1 – t) – Other Income × (1 – t) + Finance cost × (1 – t), where 't' stands for the tax rate.

$$\text{Operating profit margin} = \frac{\text{Operating profit}}{\text{Revenue}} \times 100$$

Operating profit margin is used to measure the operating efficiency.

REVIEW PROBLEMS

R 4.1 Indicate whether the following statements are True or False:

(i) The cost of goods sold is lower than the cost of purchases when the value inventories of stock-in-trade results increases during the financial year.
(ii) For a non-finance company, revenue is the income from sale of goods and services.
(iii) For a finance company, interest and dividend income from investments are classified as other income.
(iv) Exceptional items are non-recurring income and expenses.
(v) Total comprehensive income is the difference between the opening and closing book value of equity.
(vi) When the management cuts discretionary expenses to improve current period's profit, quite likely that the long-term earning capacity of the firm is impaired.
(vii) Functional classification of expenses in the income statement provides an opportunity to unscrupulous managers to misrepresent how the revenue and profit was earned during the reporting period.
(viii) It is incorrect to consider EBIT as operating profit.
(ix) Analysts use EBITDA as proxy for cash profit, although it does not measure cash flows from operating activities.
(x) Gross profit can be increased by increasing the sales promotion expenses.

R 4.2 Fill in the blanks:

(i) An entity has decided to sell one of the four production facilities which are used to produce the same product. The estimated profit or loss from operating that factory during the current period should be included in the profit or loss from................ operation. [Select one of the two words, 'continuing' and 'discontinuing'.]
(ii) An entity provides the following information: Net profit: ₹5,00,000; Other income: ₹50,000; Finance costs: ₹60,000; and exceptional income: ₹20,000. Assuming marginal tax rate of 40 per cent, the operating income is ₹................
(iii) Training expense is a ....expense. [Select one of the two words, 'discretionary' and 'non-discretionary'.]

CASE STUDY

God Bless Bipasha and John

Bipasha is a good looking, intelligent and smart lady with a pleasant personality in her early 20s. She always wanted to do something of her own. Every year, she visits places endowed with natural beauty and places of historical interest. Immediately after graduating with a BBA degree, she identified tourism as her passion and started the tourism business on January 1, 2004. She arranged a bank loan of ₹10,00,000, which was 50% of the total capital required by the firm. Bipasha contributed balance 50%. The bank sanctioned the loan against the personal guarantee of Bipasha under a special scheme to support young entrepreneurs. The rate of interest was 10% per annum to be compounded annually. A moratorium of one year was fixed on payment of interest. Interests for the years 2004 and 2005 were payable on January 1, 2006. The loan was to be repaid in five equal annual instalments starting from January 1, 2006.

Bipasha started working in the firm named Bipasha & Co. (BC). She works with corporate clients only. Her business model is quite simple. She arranges group tours for employees of her clients. She has entered into memorandum of understanding (MOU) with tourism departments of different state governments, which allow 20% discount over published rates to Bipasha. She pays 50% in advance for all bookings. The advance is non-refundable in case of cancellation of a trip. Bipasha allows group discount, which varies between 5% and 15%, depending on the size of the group, and collects 50% of the estimated cost at the commencement of the tour. She directly arranges visits to places not covered in tour packages.

In addition, Bipasha arranges conducted tours jointly with Modern Transporters Co. (MTC), which operates inter-state bus services.

The year 2004 was a good year for Bipasha. She earned a small profit in the very first year of the business. She submitted the following balance sheet as at December 31, 2004 to the bank from which she borrowed money.

Balance Sheet of BC as at December 31, 2004

	Amount ₹	*Amount ₹*
ASSETS		
Office Building	10,00,000	
Less Accumulated Depreciation	50,000	9,50,000
Advance to the Tourism Department		2,00,000
Deposit with Electric Supply Company		50,000
Trade Receivables		3,00,000
Bank balance		6,50,000
Cash balance		50,000
		22,00,000
EQUITY AND LIABILITIES		
Capital		10,50,000
Bank loan	10,00,000	
Interest accrued but not due	1,00,000	11,00,000
Trade creditors (Amount due to transport operator)		50,000
		22,00,000

The year 2005 was an eventful year for Bipasha. It was not that everything went well. There was no problem in her business. She maintained excellent relationship with her clients and the business picked up well. However, she got so involved with the business that she could not pay attention to herself. She never realised until the second half of December 2005 that she had messed up her relationship with John, who was Bipasha's classmate in school and then again in the college. It was not just a coincidence that they joined the same college to study BBA. They planned it like that. They were going steady in their relationship and started believing that they are made for each other. John is a handsome guy, presently working with a call centre. Truly speaking, Bipasha and John together is a perfect match, perhaps the best couple in the city in terms of their physical attractiveness, warmth in behaviour, and commitment to friendship, not only with each other, but with all friends. However, after BBA, Bipasha and John seldom met except on public holidays because both were busy in building their career.

Bipasha first realised that John was emotionally upset when she proposed that they should spend the New Year eve together. John was not ready. He accused her of ignoring him. Bipasha tried everything to correct the situation. She could make John to agree to take a break from work in the last week of December and to spend a few days together in a resort. Those days were real fun for both. Both realised that one should take break from work to rejuvenate oneself. Bipasha learned that every relationship is to be nurtured at every stage. She had to defer some tours and cancel bookings, but she felt no regret.

God bless Bipasha and John and let them live happily ever after.

The cashbook of Bipasha & Co. (BC) and notes are placed in Annexure I. The bank requires that the balance sheet as at December 31, 2005 should present current and non-current assets and liabilities separately.

Assignment

Prepare financial statements of Bipasha & Co. (BC) for 2005.

Annexure I

Bipasha & Co.

Cash Book: For the year 2005 (Amount in ₹)

Receipts		Amount	Assets		Amount
To opening balance			By purchase of car		6,00,000
Bank	6,50,000		By payments to state tourism department		20,00,000
Cash	50,000	7,00,000			
To realisation from customers		35,00,000	By payments to railways and airlines towards cost of tickets		5,00,000
To commission received from railways/airlines		50,000	By tour expenses on tours other than package tours		3,00,000
To interest received on investment		70,000	By electricity charges		20,000
To sale of investments		2,00,000	By telephone charges		30,000
			By stationery expenses		5,000
			By salaries and wages		2,45,000
			By insurance premium		10,000
			By other office expenses		50,000
			By purchase of investments		6,00,000
			By closing balance		
			Bank	1,10,000	
			Cash	50,000	1,60,000
		45,20,000			45,20,000

Bipasha & Co. provided the following information:

1. BC purchased car on January 1, 2005.
2. BC uses straight-line method of depreciation.
3. BC charges depreciation at the rate of 5% on office building and 25% on the car.
4. Payments to state tourism departments include payment of advances for bookings cancelled subsequently amounting to ₹50,000.
5. Insurance premium was paid on July 1, 2005 to cover risks for one year.
6. Advances with the state tourism department as at December 31, 2005 was ₹1,50,000.
7. Trade receivables as at December 31, 2005 was ₹2,00,000.
8. The cost of investments sold during 2005 was ₹1,50,000.

Outstanding investments include 10% corporate bonds with face value of ₹2,00,000. The interest on those bonds is payable annually on 30 June. The bonds were purchased on July 1, 2005 in the secondary market at ₹2,30,320. The maturity date of the bond is June 30, 2009.

Outstanding investments include 90 days treasury bills issued by the government on December 1, 2005. The treasury bills were purchased on the date of issue at the face value of ₹1,00,000. The coupon rate is 5% per annum. Interest will be paid by the government along with principal on maturity.

ASSIGNMENTS

1. Multiple choice questions:

(i) Which of the following formulas is most appropriate for computing expenses?
  (a) Payments + Beginning prepaid + Ending outstanding.
  (b) Payments + Beginning prepaid + Ending outstanding – Ending prepaid – Beginning outstanding.
  (c) Payments + Ending outstanding – Beginning outstanding.
  (d) Payments + Beginning prepaid – Ending prepaid.

(ii) Which of the following statements is correct?

(a) An expense represents the expenditure incurred during the period and from which no asset could be recognised.

(b) An expense represents the portion of an asset allocated to the current period.

(c) An expense represents an element of cost of goods or services sold during the period.

(d) An expense represents either the expenditure incurred during the period and from which no asset could be recognised, or the portion of an asset allocated to the current period, or an element of cost of goods or services sold during the period.

(iii) Which of the following statements is correct?

(a) Extraordinary items are distinguished by their unusual nature and by the infrequency of their occurrence.

(b) Extraordinary items are distinguished by their unusual nature.

(c) Extraordinary items are distinguished by the infrequency of their occurrence.

(d) Extraordinary incomes are distinguished by their magnitude relative to other items of income of similar nature and extraordinary expenses are distinguished by their magnitude relative to other items of expense of similar nature

Note: IFRS do not recognise the concept of extraordinary item.

(iv) Which of the following statements is correct?

(a) Prior period item arises due to difference in actual amount and the estimated amount of an expense or income recognised in one of the earlier years based on that estimate.

(b) Prior period item arises due to revision of estimate of an expense or income recognised in one of the earlier years based on that estimate due to unfolding of new information.

(c) Prior period item arises due to a fundamental error in calculation or in interpretation of a law or a contract, etc., which occurred in one of the earlier years.

(d) Prior period item arises due to a fundamental error in calculation, which occurred in one of the earlier years.

2. State whether the following statements are True or False:

(i) Increase in equity due to fresh contribution from owners represents income for the period.

(ii) Discretionary expenses recognised in the income statement usually do not have any direct cause and effect relationship with revenue recognised in the income statement.

(iii) Revenue represents income from core activities of the enterprise.

(iv) Profit from sale of an item of fixed assets is included in revenue.

(v) Usually, recognition of revenue results in simultaneous recognition of one or more current assets.

(vi) For a commission agent, only the commission earned is revenue.

(vii) Interest earned on loans and advances by a financial institution is recognised as other income.

(viii) Advertisement expenditure is usually considered as deferred revenue expenditure.

(ix) The amount of equity and the amount of net profit of an entity, which holds long-term investments, determined under IFRS, are likely to be different from those determined under the Indian GAAP.

(x) Revaluation gain is an item of other comprehensive income.

(xi) Each item of expense recognised in the profit and loss account for a particular period has cause and effect relation with the revenue recognised in that profit and loss account.

(xii) Asset-liability measurement approach recognises the concepts of deferred revenue expenditure and fictitious asset.

(xiii) IFRS require that preliminary expenses should be amortised over a reasonable period.

(xiv) IFRS require that share issue expenses should be deducted from equity.

(xv) The terms 'revenue' and 'turnover' are used interchangeably.

(xvi) Profit on sale of an item of PP&E should be recognised as other income in the profit and loss account.

(xvii) EPS is calculated by dividing net profit for the year (reduced by the preference dividend payable to preference shareholders) by the number of shares outstanding at the end of the period.

(xviii) Non-current assets of a discontinued operation are measured in the balance sheet at the lower of cost and fair value less costs to sell.

(xix) NOPLAT is not affected by the capital structure of the entity.

(xx) EPS is not affected by the capital structure of the entity.

3. Selected income statement information of Zubeda Limited (ZL) for recent four years is presented below:

(Amount, ₹)

Particulars	Year			
	2003	2004	2005	2006
Sales	10,000	?	15,000	30,000
Cost of goods sold	7,000	8,000	?	?
Gross profit	?	4,000	5,000	?[a]
Marketing and administrative expenses	1,000	?	1,500	1,500
Operating profit (PBIT)	?	2,800	?	?
Interest expense	600	?	700	750
Income tax expense	560	800	1,120	?[b]
Net profit	?	1,350	?	?

Notes:

[a] Gross profit is 25% on cost of goods sold.

[b] Income tax expense is 40% of net profit.

Required: Fill in the cells with '?'.

4. Fill in the blanks:

(i) The amount of equity in the balance sheet is ₹20,000; the carrying amount of liabilities in the balance sheet is ₹5,000; the carrying amount of assets is ₹........

(ii) During a particular period, a company incurred an expenditure of ₹100,000 to promote a new product launched in the market during that period. The management estimates that the expenditure would benefit the company for five years (including the current year). The amount of sales promotion expense to be recognised in the profit and loss account for the period is ₹........

(iii) During a particular period, the value of goods sold (based on the list price) by an entity was ₹10,00,000. It allowed a trade discount of ₹2,00,000 and also allowed cash discount amounting to ₹20,000 to those customers who had paid the amount due within 10 days. The company should recognise revenue on the profit and loss account at ₹........

(iv) A company was incorporated on April 1, 2010. During 2010–2011, the company issued 10,000 shares with face value of ₹10 for ₹100 per share. During the year, the company reimbursed ₹20,000 towards preliminary expenses to its promoters. In the profit and loss account for 2010–2011, the company should recognise preliminary expenses at ₹........

(v) A business enterprise operates as a travel agent. It purchases air tickets against request from customers. On every ticket, it gets a commission (from the airlines) of 2% of the cost of the ticket. It pays to the airlines as per the payment terms agreed with airlines. Payment to airlines is not related to the realisation of the cost of the ticket from the customer. During 2010–2011, the firm purchased tickets from airlines for ₹1,00,00,000. In the profit and loss account for 2010–2011, the firm should recognise revenue at ₹.........

(vi) During 2010–2011, a firm sold an item of equipment for ₹10,00,000. The acquisition cost and accumulated depreciation on the date of the transaction were ₹50,00,000 and ₹45,00,000, respectively. The profit on the sale of the item was ₹.........

(vii) A company is in the merchandising business. During the year ended on March 31, 2011, it earned revenue of ₹1,00,00,000. It purchased goods for ₹65,00,000 and incurred logistic expenses of ₹7,00,000 to bring the goods to the central stores. It incurred logistic expenses of ₹1,00,000 to transport goods from the central warehouse to different stores. The company incurred home-delivery expenses of ₹ ₹20,000. It reported increase in the value of stock-in-trade during the year at ₹2,00,000. The gross profit ratio for the year was ....per cent.

(viii) A company reported the following numbers for the year ended March 31, 2011: Revenue ₹1,00,00,000; gross profit ₹30,00,000; EBITDA ₹20,00,000; EBIT: ₹15,00,000; and net profit ₹9,00,000. During 2010–2011, the company earned a cash profit margin of...... per cent.

(ix) Research and development expense is a .... expense. (Choose from the words 'discretionary' and 'non-discretionary').

5. Analytical questions:

5.1 A & Co., while launching its new product, Zoom toothpaste, incurred expenditure of ₹10 lakhs on advertisement. The Managing Director of the company proposes that the expenditure be shown as an asset on the balance sheet, with which the accountant disagrees. Who is right?

5.2 "Users of financial statements assume that the enterprise is a going concern." Elaborate the statement.

6. Problems:

6.1 Analyse the following transactions entered into by A & Co. during January 2006, using the format given at the end of this question. Determine the operating results of A & Co. during the reporting period, and also, the amount of cash flow generated through operations during that period.

(a) Started business with furniture valued at ₹12,000.
(b) Owners introduced ₹1,00,000 in cash.
(c) Purchased goods for sale, in cash, for ₹50,000.
(d) Purchased goods for sale for ₹50,000 from B & Co. on credit.
(e) Lost goods purchased at ₹10,000 due to fire, no insurance claim admitted.
(f) Sold goods costing ₹20,000 at ₹25,000 on cash basis.
(g) Sold goods costing ₹40,000 to C & Co. for ₹48,000 on credit.
(h) Paid ₹1,000 towards freight inward.
(i) Paid ₹1,000 towards freight outward.
(j) Paid ₹2,000 towards salary and wages.
(k) Obtained an overdraft of ₹50,000 from State Bank of India.
(l) Received a loan of ₹1,20,000 from Industrial Development Bank of India payable over five reporting periods commencing from the current reporting period.
(m) Interest accrued but not due on the balance sheet's date on the loan received from IDBI ₹1,000.
(n) Paid ₹12,000 towards insurance premium to cover a risk period of 12 months ending after 11 months from the balance sheet date.
(o) Realised ₹47,000 from C & Co. in full and final settlement of the claim against sale of goods.
(p) Charged depreciation on furniture ₹100.
(q) Discount received on the purchase of goods ₹5,000.

(r) Bank charges debited by bank ₹300.
(s) Conveyance charges paid to the staff ₹500.
(t) Purchased machinery for ₹30,000 in cash.
(u) Paid ₹2,000 towards printing and stationery.

Format for Analysing Transactions

Transaction Sl. No,	Non-current assets	Current assets other than cash	Cash	Non-current liabilities	Current liabilities	Equity (Capital)
(a)						
(b)						
(c)						
(d)						
(e)						
(f)						
(g)						
(h)						
(i)						
(j)						
(k)						
(l)						
(m)						
(n)						
(o)						
(p)						
(q)						
(r)						
(s)						
(t)						
(u)						
Total						

Note: Indicate increase by (+) and decrease by (–).

6.2 The following is the balance sheet of B & Co. Ltd. as on January 1, 2006:

Particulars	Amount (₹)	Amount (₹)
ASSETS		
Furniture and fixture	1,00,000	
Less: Accumulated Depreciation	20,000	80,000
Prepaid insurance		10,000*
Trade Receivables (Sharma Limited)		60,000
Cash balance		50,000
Total		2,00,000
EQUITY AND LIABILITIES		
Equity		50,000
Long-term loan		50,000
Short-term borrowings		50,000
Trade payables (Alpha Limited)		50,000
Total		2,00,000

*Prepaid insurance represents premium that will cover the next 10 months.

Analyse the following transactions entered into by B & Co. Ltd. during January 2006 using the format given at the end of the previous question.

Determine the operating results of B & Co. Ltd. for January 2006, and also, the cash flow generated through operations during that period. Draw the balance sheet as of January 31, 2006.

List of transactions

(a) Purchased goods for ₹40,000 in cash.
(b) Purchased goods on credit from Alpha Ltd. for ₹60,000.
(c) Paid freight inward for ₹2,000.
(d) Sold goods purchased for ₹8,000 at ₹10,000 on cash basis.
(e) Sold goods, purchased for ₹50,000 at ₹75,000 on credit to Gamma Ltd.
(f) Paid freight outward for ₹5,000.
(g) Paid ₹5,000 towards rent of a godown.
(h) Realised ₹58,000 from Sharma Ltd., allowed a discount of ₹2,000.
(i) Paid ₹48,000 to Alpha Ltd. towards full and final settlement for goods supplied prior to January 1, 2000.
(j) Realised ₹60,000 from Gamma Ltd.
(k) Paid ₹7,000 towards salaries and wages.
(l) Interest accrued but not due as on January 31, 2000, ₹500.
(m) Outstanding liabilities as on January 31, 2000, ₹1,000.
(n) Change in depreciation ₹1,000.

CHAPTER

5

THE ACCOUNTING CYCLE: RECORDING TRANSACTIONS

CHAPTER OBJECTIVES

The objectives of this chapter is to introduce to readers the income statement structure and information communicated through that statement. In particular, the objective is developing and understanding of:

- Accounting cycle;
- Double entry book keeping system—debit-credit rules, general ledger, cash book, books of prime entries, journal proper, and subsidiary ledgers; and
- Trial balance—balancing of general ledger, structure of trial balance, and errors not detected by trial balance.

5.1 THE ACCOUNTING CYCLE

Accounting cycle starts with recording of opening entries (balances carried forward from the previous reporting period) in the general ledger and ends with the preparation of financial statements. The following steps are involved in the preparation of financial statements:

Accounting cycle starts with recording of opening entries in the general ledger and ends with the preparation of financial statements.

1. Recording of opening entries in the general ledger.
2. Recording of transactions and events in the journal (Journalisation).
3. Posting journal entries in appropriate accounts in the general ledger.
4. Balancing the accounts in the general ledger.
5. Preparing the trial balance.
6. Recording adjustment entries.
7. Preparing adjusted trial balance.
8. Recording closing entries to prepare financial statements.

Accounting cycle ends at the end of the current accounting period and begins immediately at the start of the next accounting period.

We shall discuss all the element of the accounting cycle in this and next chapter.

BOX 5.1 VOUCHER AND ACCOUNTING CODE

Voucher

Every entry in the books of accounts is supported by a voucher. Voucher is a written document which provides evidence for some facts about the transaction. Vouchers are serially numbered and describe the transaction or other event. They bear the accounting code for correct recording of transactions and other events. They are supported by original documents such as invoice from the supplier of goods or service and invoice preferred on a customer.

Accounting code

In order to ensure correct bookkeeping, a code is assigned to each account head. For example, accounting code assigned to an item of fixed asset indicates that it is an item of fixed asset, it belongs to a particular type of fixed asset (PP&E and intangible asset), it belongs to a particular class of fixed asset (e.g., land, building and plant and machinery), its nature (e.g., factory building or office building) and its location (e.g., corporate office and factory located in Hosur). Accounting codes help in aggregation and disaggregation of different items of assets, liabilities, equity, income, and expenses for presenting in financial statements.

5.2 DOUBLE ENTRY BOOKKEEPING

Double entry bookkeeping principle is that every debit should have a credit.

5.2.1 Double Entry Bookkeeping Principle

Universally, the double entry bookkeeping rules are applied for recording transactions and other events.

Double entry bookkeeping principle is that *every debit should have a credit.*

Books of accounts

General ledger is the depository of data.

General ledger is the depository of data. All transactions are recorded first in books of primary entries and then posted in the general ledger. All account heads are maintained in that ledger. We shall discuss the books of accounts in greater details in subsequent sections.

Debit side and credit side

In the general ledger transactions are recorded in T Account. It is called T Accounts, because of its shape like the English alphabet T. Conventionally, left side of the T Account is called *Debit side* and the right side is called the *Credit side.* The following is the format of T Account:

Account Name...

DEBIT SIDE	CREDIT SIDE

5.2.2 Double Entry Bookkeeping Rules

Double entry bookkeeping rule is derived from the accounting equation, which is:

$$\text{Equity} = \text{Assets} - \text{Liabilities}$$

Equity is the residual figure in the accounting equation.

Increase (decrease) in the total amount of assets results in either increase (decrease) in liabilities or increase (decrease) in equity

Increase (decrease) in the total amount of liabilities results in either decrease (increase) in assets or decrease (increase) in equity.

BOX 5.2 EFFECTS OF CHANGES IN THE TOTAL AMOUNT OF ASSETS AND LIABILITIES

1. Increase in the total amount of assets results in either increase in liabilities or increase in equity.
2. Decrease in the total amount of assets results in either decrease in liabilities or decrease in equity.
3. Increase in the total amount of liabilities results in either decrease in assets or decrease in equity.
4. Decrease in the total amount of liabilities results in either increase in assets or increase in equity.

EXAMPLE 5.1 (Purchase of a piece of equipment in cash)

Fact pattern: An entity purchased a piece of equipment for ₹50,000 in a cash transaction.

Discussion: The transaction has changed the composition of assets that the entity holds. It has not changed the total amount of assets, total amount of liabilities, and the equity.

EXAMPLE 5.2 (Purchase of a piece of equipment on credit)

Fact pattern: An entity purchased a piece of equipment for ₹50,000 on credit.

Discussion: This transaction results in increase in the total amount of assets and increase in the total amount of liabilities.

EXAMPLE 5.3 (Decrease in liabilities)

Fact pattern: An entity paid the supplier of a piece of equipment ₹50,000 to settle the amount due to it against purchase a piece of equipment on credit.

Discussion: The transaction has resulted in the decrease in both the total amount of assets and total amount of liabilities.

Conventionally, asset account is debited for increase in asset.

Bookkeeping rules

Conventionally, asset account is debited for increase in asset. This is the starting point in developing the bookkeeping rules. The rules are presented in Table 5.1 below:

TABLE 5.1 Debit Credit Rules

Sl. No.	*Particulars*	*Increase*	*Decrease*
1.	Assets	Debit	Credit
2.	Liabilities	Credit	Debit
3.	Equity	Credit	Debit
4.	Income	Credit	Debit
5.	Expense	Debit	Credit

Income increases equity. Therefore, income is credit. Expense decreases equity. Therefore, expense is debit.

Asset Account

DEBIT	CREDIT
Increase	**Decrease**

Assets: Debit the account for increase and credit the account for decrease.

Liability Account

DEBIT	CREDIT
Decrease	**Increase**

Liabilities and Equity: Debit the account for decrease and credit the account for increase.

Equity Account

DEBIT	CREDIT
Decrease	**Increase**

Income Account

DEBIT	CREDIT
Decrease	**Increase**

Income: Debit the account for decrease and credit the account for increase.

Expense: Debit the account for increase and credit the account for decrease.

Expense Account

DEBIT	CREDIT
Increase	**Decrease**

EXAMPLE 5.4 (Application of Debit Credit Rules)

	Transaction	Effect	Debit		Credit	
			Account Head	Amount ₹	Account Head	Amount ₹
1.	The owner introduced capital in the form of cash ₹50,000	Increase in assets and increase in equity	Cash A/c *(Asset)*	50,000	Capital A/c *(Equity)*	50,000
2.	Deposited ₹25,000 in bank	Change in the composition of assets	Bank A/c *(Asset)*	25,000	Cash A/c *(Asset*	25,000
3.	Purchased furniture on credit from BB& Co. for ₹10,000	Increase in assets and increase in liabilities	Furniture A/c *(Asset)*	10,000	Sundry Creditors – BB &Co. *(Liability)*	10,000
4.	Purchased stock-in-trade on credit for ₹20,000 from KK & Co.	Increase in expense and increase in liabilities	Purchase A/c *(Expense)*	20,000	Trade Payables –KK &Co. *(Liability*	20,000
5.	Paid ₹500 towards carriage inward for bringing the stock-in-trade	Decrease in assets and increase in expense	Carriage Inward A/c (Expense)	500	Cash A/c . *(Asset)*	500
6.	Sold stock-in-trade on credit to RR & Co. for ₹30,000	Increase in assets and increase in income	Trade Receivables A/c-RR & Co. *(Asset)*	30,000	Sales *(Income)*	30,000
7.	Purchased stock-in-trade on credit from TT & Co. for ₹50,000	Increase in expense and increase in liabilities	Purchase A/c *(Expense)*	50,000	Trade Payables –TT &Co. *(Liability*	50,000
8.	Received ₹28,000 from RR & Co. (customer) in full and final settlement by transfer to the bank account	Decrease in assets, increase in expense, and increase in liabilities	Bank A/c *(Asset)* Discount Allowed A/c *(Expense)*	28,000 2,000	Trade Receivables A/c-RR & Co. *(Asset)*	30,000
9.	Withdrew ₹20,000 from bank for office expenses	Change in the composition of assets	Cash A/c *(Asset)*	20,000	Bank A/c *(Asset)*	20,000
10.	Paid salary in cash ₹10,000	Decrease in assets, increase in expense	Salary A/c *(Expense)*	10,000	Cash A/c *(Asset)*	20,000
11.	Owner withdrew cash ₹5,000 for personal use	Decrease in assets and equity	Drawings A/c *(Equity)*	5,000	Cash A/c *(Asset)*	5,000
12.	Sold stock-in-trade on credit to PP & Co. for ₹40,000	Increase in asset and income	Trade Receivables A/c-RR & Co. *(Asset)*	40,000	Sales *(Income)*	40,000

	Transaction	Effect	Debit		Credit	
			Account Head	Amount ₹	Account Head	Amount ₹
13.	PP & Co. returned goods sold to him (at Sl. No. 12 above) valued ₹5,000	Decrease in asset and income	Sales Return *(Income)*	5,000	Trade Receivables A/c-PP & Co. *(Asset)*	5,000
14.	Paid carriage outward (transport charges for delivering goods to customers) in cash ₹3,000	Decrease in assets and increase in expense	Carriage Outward A/c *(Expense)*	3,000	Cash A/c *(Asset)*	3,000
15.	Paid ₹46,000 to TT & Co. (refer transaction at serial number 7) in full and final settlement by transfer to the banak account	Decrease in assets, decrease in liabilities, and increase in income	Trade Payables –TT &Co. *(Liability*	50,000	Bank A/c *(Asset)* Discount Received (Income A/c)	46,000 4,000
16.	Paid electricity bill for ₹4,000 by transfer to the bank account of the utility company	Decrease in assets and increase in expense	Electricity Charges A/c *(Expense)*	4,000	Bank A/c *(Asset)*	4,000
17.	Received a cheque for ₹35,000 from PP & Co. (Refer the transactions at Sl.No.12 and 13) towards amount due from it.	Change in the composition of assets	Bank A/c *(Asset)*	35,000	Trade Receivables A/c-PP & Co. *(Asset)*	35,000
18.	Cheque received from PP & Co. (Refer transaction at serial number 17) is dishonoured and the bank levied a charge of ₹200 for returning the cheque.	Change in the composition of assets (Assuming that the bank charges will bo rocovored from the customer)	Trade Receivables A/c-PP & Co. *(Asset)*	35,200	Bank A/c *(Asset)*	35,200
19.	Cheque received from PP & Co. (Refer transaction at serial number 17) is dishonoured and the bank levied a charge of ₹200 for returning the cheque.	Change in the composition of assets with decrease and increase in expense (Assuming that the bank charges will be borne by the entity)	Trade Receivables *(Asset)* Bank charges A/c *(Expense)*	35,000 200	Bank A/c *(Asset)*	35,200
20.	Received a fresh cheque for ₹35,200 from PP & Co. (Refer the transactions at Sl.No.18) in *lieu of the dishonored cheque.*	Change in the composition of assets	Bank A/c *(Asset)*	35,200	Trade Receivables A/c-PP & Co. *(Asset)*	35,200

5.2.3 Alternative Debit-Credit Rules

Table 5.2 below presents the alternative debit-credit rules.

Real Account: Debit what comes in and credit what goes out.

Personal Account: Debit the receiver and credit the giver.

Nominal Account: Debit expense account for increase and credit income account for increase.

TABLE 5.2 Alternative Debit-Credit Rules

Classification of accounts	*Nature and Examples*	*Debit-credit rules*
Real Account	**Account of things** Examples: Items of property plant and equipment, Items included in inventories, investments in financial assets, and investment property	Debit what comes in, and credit what goes out
Personal Account	**Account of entities** Examples: Trade receivables (amount that customer owes to the firm), Trade creditors (amount that entity owes to suppliers of inputs), shareholders, bond holders, lenders, bank, and insurance company	Debit the giver, and credit the receiver
Nominal Account	**Account of income and expenses** Examples: sales, employee benefit expenses, interest income, and interest expense	Debit expenses, and credit income

It is not easy to remember these rules. However, it is important to remember the classification, as it helps in communicating with accountants.

Normal balances

Normally the balances (debit or credit) in different types of accounts are as follows:

	Account Type	Normal balance (Debit)	Normal balance (Credit)
1.	Assets	✓	
2.	Liabilities		✓
3.	Equity		✓
4.	Income		✓
5.	Expenses	✓	

Note: The normal balance is debit if the type of account is debited for increase and the normal balance is credit if the type of account is credited for increase.

5.2.4 General Ledger

In general ledger accounts for each account head is maintained in the form of T Accounts. No transaction is posted directly in the general ledger. Those should be routed through the books of prime entry. Only control accounts are maintained in the general ledger, except for those accounts where the number of transactions is small, to avoid cluttering of information.

A control account, which maintained in the general ledger, is a summary account.

Control account

A control account is a summary account. For example, Trade Receivable is a control account, which presents the aggregate of amounts that customers owe to the entity. Details of every customer is maintained in a subsidiary ledger. Maintaining control accounts in the general ledger avoids cluttering of information. It is also a control mechanism. The total of the subsidiary ledger should agree with the balance in the control account.

Each T Account takes the following form:

Account Name..................

Dr.				Cr.			
Date	Particulars	LF	Amount	Date	Particulars	LF	Amount

LF stands for Ledger Folio. Reference to the Ledger Folio in which the corresponding account is debited or credited is useful for cross referencing.

5.2.5 Books of Prime Entry

We shall discuss four important books of prime entry – Cash book, purchase day book, sales day book, and journal proper.

Cash book

Cash and bank transactions are recorded directly in the 'cash book'. A cash book is primarily a journal. It also serves the purpose of a ledger account, and therefore, the cash account and bank account are not maintained in the general ledger. Balances in the cash book are taken directly to the trial balance that lists balances in various account heads in the general ledger. Thus, a cash book serves the dual purpose of maintaining a journal to record cash and bank transactions, and also, maintaining cash and bank accounts in the general ledger. The following are the different types of cash books that are being maintained by enterprises:

A cash book, which is primarily a journal, also serves the purpose of a ledger account.

1. **Single-column cash book:** It records only cash receipts and cash payments.
2. **Double-column cash book:** It provides additional information on discount received and discount allowed.
3. **Triple-column cash book:** It has an additional column to record bank transactions.

Single-column cash book records only cash receipts and cash payments.

Double-column cash book provides additional information on discount received and discount allowed.

Illustration 5.1 (Single column cash book)
Record the following cash transactions entered into by A & Co. in January 2019 in a single-column cash book.

2019		₹
Jan. 1	Cash-in-hand	1,000
Jan. 6	Received from B & Co.	600
Jan. 10	Paid rent	500
Jan. 15	Sold goods for cash	2,000
Jan. 27	Purchased furniture for cash	1,200
Jan. 31	Paid salaries	800

Solution:

Dr.	Receipts				Payments		Cr.
Date	Particulars	LF	Amount (₹)	Date	Particulars	LF	Amount (₹)
2019							
Jan. 1	To balance b/d		1,000	Jan. 10	By rent A/c		500
Jan. 6	To B & Co. A/c		600	Jan. 27	By furniture A/c		1,200
Jan. 15	To sales A/c		2,000	Jan. 31	By salaries A/c		800
				Jan. 31	By balance c/d		1,100
			3,600				3,600
Feb. 1	To balance b/d		1,100				

Illustration 5.2 (Double column cash book)

A & Co. commenced business on January 1, 2019 with a cash balance of ₹2,000 as capital. It had the following cash transactions for January 2010. Prepare the cash book.

2019		₹
Jan. 1	Purchased furniture	200
Jan. 2	Purchased goods	300
Jan. 4	Sold goods	400
Jan. 6	Paid to B & Co.	500
	Allowed discount	20
Jan. 15	Received from C & Co.	600
	Allowed discount	30
Jan. 20	Purchased calculator	200
Jan. 31	Paid salaries	500

Solution:

A & Co.: Cash Book

Dr.	*Receipts*				*Payments*				*Cr.*
Date	*Particulars*	*LF*	*Discount (₹)*	*Cash (₹)*	*Date*	*Particulars*	*LF*	*Discount (₹)*	*Cash (₹)*
2019									
Jan. 1	To capital A/c			2,000	Jan. 1	By furniture A/c			200
Jan. 4	To sales A/c			400	Jan. 2	By purchases A/c			300
Jan. 15	To C & Co. A/c		30	600	Jan. 6	By B & Co. A/c		20	500
					Jan. 20	By calculator A/c			200
					Jan. 31	By salaries A/c			500
					Jan. 31	By balance c/d			1,300
Total			30	3,000	**Total**			20	3,000
2019									
Feb. 1	To balance b/d			1,300					

Illustration 5.3 (Triple column cash book)

A commenced business as A & Co. on January 1, 2019, with a cash balance of ₹2,000. Record the transactions for January 2010 in a cash book with discount and bank columns.

2019		₹
Jan. 1	Deposited cash with bank	1,500
Jan. 4	Received cheque from B & Co.	1,000
Jan. 5	C & Co. is paid by cheque. He allowed a discount of ₹20.	330
Jan. 6	Received cheque from M & Co. after allowing a discount of ₹50	450
Jan. 10	Goods sold in cash to R & Co.	500
Jan. 12	Cash drawn for office use	500
Jan. 15	Paid for office expenses in cash	500
Jan. 25	Paid salaries for January in cash	500
Jan. 25	Cheque received from Y & Co.	400
Jan. 31	Cheque received from Y & Co. returned unpaid by bank	400

Solution:

Dr. Receipts						Payments					Cr.
Date	Particulars	LF	Discount (₹)	Cash (₹)	Bank (₹)	Date	Particulars	LF	Discount (₹)	Cash (₹)	Bank (₹)
2019						2005					
Jan. 1	To capital			2,000		Jan. 1	By cash			1,500	
Jan. 1	To bank	C			1,500	Jan. 5	By C & Co.		20		330
Jan. 4	To B & Co.				1,000	Jan. 12	By cash	C			500
Jan. 6	To M & Co.		50		450	Jan. 15	By office expenses			500	
Jan. 10	To sales			500		Jan. 25	By salaries			500	
Jan. 12	To bank	C		500		Jan. 31	By Y & Co.				400
Jan. 25	To Y & Co.				400	Jan. 31	By balance c/d			500	2,120
			50	3,000	3,350				20	3,000	3,350
Feb. 1	To Balance b/d			500	2,120						

'C' denotes "Contra", i.e., there is a corresponding entry on the other side in the bank/ cash column.

Petty cash book

As a matter of convenience, an imprest (a predetermined amount of cash) is sanctioned to some individuals authorised to make payments of small amounts of high frequency. Examples of such payments are postage, conveyance, carriage, and stationery. The individual so authorised maintains a cash book known as a *petty cash book*. The individual periodically recoups his imprest by submitting an account of payments released to him during the period. A petty cash book usually has multiple columns to accommodate different types of payments.

As a matter of convenience, an imprest is sanctioned to some individuals authorised to make payments of small amounts of high frequency.

The imprest holder maintains the petty cash book.

Purchase day book

In view of a large number of transactions, a separate journal entitled, 'purchase day book', is maintained by enterprises to record credit purchases. However, credit purchases, other than purchases of stock-in-trade or materials being used in the manufacturing process, are not recorded in the purchase day book. Similarly, cash transactions are not recorded in this journal.

Entities also maintain a 'purchase return book' to record return of goods to suppliers.

Illustration 5.4 (Purchase day book)

A & Co. deals in ladies garments. The rough book of the firm shows the following transactions for the month of January 2019:

Jan. 1 Purchased from B & Co. on credit:
10 cotton salwar suits @ ₹500 per suit
10 silk salwar suits @ ₹1,500 per suit

Less: Trade discount @ 10%

Jan. 10 Purchased in cash from C & Co. 2 cotton salwar suits @ ₹150 per suit

Jan. 15 Purchased a calculator for office use from D & Co. on credit for ₹500

Jan. 20 Purchased from Y & Co. on credit: 10 cotton sarees @ ₹600 per saree
10 silk sarees @ ₹2,000 per saree

Less: Trade discount @ 10%

Jan. 31 Purchased 10 cotton suit lengths @ ₹300 per suit length from Z & Co. on credit.

Prepare the purchase day book of A & Co. for the month of January 2005.

Solution:

A & Co.: Purchase Day Book

Date	Particulars	Ledger Folio	Amount (₹)	Net Amount (₹)
2010				
Jan. 1	M/s B & Co.			
	10 cotton salwar suits @ ₹500		5,000	
	10 silk salwar suits @ ₹1,500		15,000	
			20,000	
	Trade discount @ 10%		(2,000)	18,000
Jan. 20	M/s Y & Co.			
	10 cotton sarees @ ₹600		6,000	
	10 silk sarees @ ₹2,000		20,000	
			26,000	
	Trade discount @ 10%		(2,600)	23,400
Jan. 31	M/s Z & Co.			
	10 cotton suit lengths @ ₹300			3,000
		Total		44,400

Total is posted in the general ledger periodically through journal proper. Journal proper is discussed below. Details of the suppliers are maintained in the subsidiary ledger.

Sales day book

Firms record credit sales of stock-in-trade in a sales day book. The mechanics of posting entries from the sales day book to the general ledger and the subsidiary ledger for debtors are similar to those of posting from the purchase day book.

Entities also maintain a 'sales return book' to record return of goods by customers.

Illustration 5.5 (Sales day book)

A & Co. deals in ladies' garments. The rough book of the firm shows the following transactions for January 2019:

Jan. 2 Sold to Alpha & Co. on credit:
- 5 cotton salwar suits @ ₹600 per suit
- 5 silk salwar suits @ ₹1,800 per suit
- *Less:* Trade discount @ 10%

Jan. 3 Sold old furniture to M & Co. for ₹100 on credit

Jan. 8 Sold to Beta & Co. on credit:
- 5 cotton salwar suits @ ₹600 per suit
- 5 silk salwar suits @ ₹1,800 per suit
- *Less:* Trade discount @ 10%

Jan. 15 Sold two silk sarees to M/s. Beauty for ₹2,500 in cash

Jan. 31 Sold to Gamma & Co. on credit:
- 5 cotton sarees @ ₹800 per saree
- 10 silk sarees @ ₹2,500 per saree
- *Less:* Trade discount @ 10%

Required:

Prepare the sales day book of A & Co. for January 2019.

Solution:

Date	Particulars	LF	Amount (₹)	Amount (₹)
2019				
Jan. 2	M/s Alpha & Co.			
	5 cotton salwar suits @ ₹600		3,000	
	5 silk salwar suits @ ₹1,800		9,000	
			12,000	
	Trade discount @ 10%		(1,200)	10,800
Jan. 8	M/s Beta & Co.			
	5 cotton salwar suits @₹600		3,000	
	5 silk salwar suits @ ₹1,800		9,000	
			12,000	
	Trade discount @ 10%		(1,200)	10,800
Jan. 31	M/s Gamma & Co.			
	10 cotton sarees @₹800		8,000	
	10 silk sarees @ ₹1,800		25,000	
			33,000	
	Trade discount @ 10%		(3,300)	29,700
	Total			51,300

5.2.6 Journal Proper

Journal proper is used record other transactions for which no specific book of prime entry is maintained, and for recording entries to rectify mistakes in books of accounts. It is also used for recording adjustment entries (discussed in chapter 6). We present the format of a journal proper by using the figures of the Purchase Day book and Sales Day book in illustrations 5.4 and 5.5.

Journal proper is used record transactions for which no specific book of prime entry is maintained, and for recording rectification entries and adjustment entries.

Entry in journal proper for the illustration at 5.4:

Date	Particulars		Ledger Folio	Amount (₹)
	Purchases A/c	Dr.	44,400	
	To Trade Payables A/c	Cr.		44,400
	(Being credit purchases of stock-in-trade on credit in the month of January 2019)			

Entry in journal proper for the illustration at 5.5:

Date	Particulars		Ledger Folio	Amount (₹)
	Trade Receivable A/c	Dr.	51,300	
	To Sales A/c	Cr.		51,300
	(Being credit sales of stock-in-trade on credit in the month of January 2019)			

The sentence in the bracket below the entries is called *narration*, as it briefly describes the transaction, adjustment, etc. The transactions, etc. are posted in the general ledger through the journal proper.

5.2.7 Subsidiary Ledgers

Subsidiary ledgers are memorandum books.

Subsidiary ledgers are memorandum books that are not part of the double-entry bookkeeping system. Those ledgers are maintained to record the details of the entities with whom the entity has transacted during the accounting period and the amount due to or due from them. For example, in the subsidiary ledger for Trade Receivables, details transaction with each customer is recorded–the amount for which goods sold, amount received and balance after each transaction. The total of the balances in the accounts of all the customers should agree with the balance in the Trade Receivables Account in the general ledger. Usually, subsidiary ledgers are maintained for trade receivables, trade payables, advances to employees, advance received from customers, and sundry creditors.

Entities also maintain a fixed asset register with details of acquisition cost, accumulated depreciation, accumulated impairment loss and carrying amount.

5.3 TRIAL BALANCE

Trial balance is the list of debit and credit balances in various account heads in the ledger

The total of the debit balances should agree with the credit balances.

Transactions are recorded in the T Account opened for every Accounts Code developed by the entity. The T accounts are balanced at the end of every period, usually a month. After the balancing process, a list is prepared for debit and credit balances. The list is called the trial balance. The total of the debit balances should agree with the credit balances, as entity applies the double-entry bookkeeping principle–every debit has a corresponding credit.

The trial balance forms the basis of preparing the statement of profit and loss and the balance sheet.

5.3.1 Balancing the General Ledger

We shall explain the balancing process with hypothetical entries in some hypothetical T Accounts.

The trial balance forms the basis of preparing the statement of profit and loss and the balance sheet.

EXAMPLE 5.5 (Balancing the T Accounts)
The following is the T Account for the Capital contributed by the owner.

Capital A/c (Amount in ₹)

Dr.					*Cr.*
Date	*Particulars*	*LF Amount (₹)*	*Date*	*Particulars*	*LF Amount (₹)*
Jan 1			Jan 1	By Bank A/c	50,000

In the month of January, only one transaction is recorded in the credit side of the Capital Account. Therefore, at the month-end, there is a credit balance of ₹50,000. Accountants present that as follows:

Capital A/c (Amount in ₹)

Dr.					*Cr.*
Date	*Particulars*	*LF Amount (₹)*	*Date*	*Particulars*	*LF Amount (₹)*
Jan 31	To balance c/d *(Balancing figure)*	50,000	Jan 1	By Bank A/c	50,000
	Total	50,000		Total	50,000
			Jan 31	By Balance b/d	50,000

c/d stands for carried down and b/d stands for brought down.

The process is simple. The following steps are involved:

(i) Total the debit and credit sides of the T Account.
(ii) Calculate the difference.
(iii) If the total of the debit side is greater than the total of the credit side, the T account has the debit balance, which is the difference between the total amount of the debit side and that of the credit side. Similarly, if the total of the credit side is greater than the total of the debit side, the T account has the credit balance.

(iv) Enter the difference in that side, the total of which is smaller than the other side. Record the difference as balance c/d (carried down).

(v) Total both the sides. Now the totals are equal.

(vi) Enter the amount of the balance c/d in the side in which the total before the balancing process was greater and describe the entry as balance b/d (brought down)

EXAMPLE 5.6 (Balancing the T Account)

Trade Receivables A/c (Amount in ₹)

Dr.							*Cr.*
Date	*Particulars*	*LF*	*Amount (₹)*	*Date*	*Particulars*	*LF*	*Amount (₹)*
Jan 1	To balance b/f		50,000	Jan 6	By Bank A/c		50,000
Jan 1	By Sales A/c		50,000	Jan 25	By Bank A/c		40,000
Jan 5	By Sales A/c		80,000		By Discount Allowed		2,000
Jan 15	By Sales A/c		50,000	Jan 31	To Balance c/d *(Balancing figure)*		1,38,000
	Total		230,000		**Total**		230,000
Jan 31	To Balance b/d		1,38,000				

b/f stands for brought forward from the previous period.

The trial balance fails to disclose errors of omission, errors of commission, clerical errors, compensating errors and errors of principle.

5.3.2 Trial Balance

The following is the trial balance format presented with hypothetical figures:
Trial Balance of .... (Name of the entity) as of .... (Date)

Particulars	*LF*	*Dr (₹)*	*Dr (₹)*
Capital A/c			27,000
Cash A/c		1,900	
Bank A/c		24,050	
Stock of goods a/c		4,000	
Machinery A/c		20,000	
Furniture A/c		4,700	
Roy & Co. A/c		950	
Loan from SBI A/c			10,000
Patel & Co. A/c			2,000
Loan from New Age Inv. Co. A/c			20,000
Purchases A/c		5,000	
Sales A/c			3,500
Discount A/c		100	
Profit on sale of furniture A/c			50
Repairs to machinery A/c		200	
Freight inward A/c		100	
Municipal taxes A/c		100	
Advertisement A/c		500	
Sales of newspapers A/c			50
Rent A/c		500	
Salaries A/c		500	
Total		62,600	62,600

Matching of the debit side total with the credit side total of the trial balance is not a conclusive proof of the correctness of books of accounts.

5.3.3 Errors not Detected by Trial Balance

Matching of the debit side total with the credit side total of the trial balance is not a conclusive proof of the correctness of books of accounts. The trial balance fails to disclose errors that do not affect the agreement of the trial balance. Following are the examples of errors not disclosed by the trial balance:

1. **Errors of omission:** These comprise omission in recording a transaction or other event in books of original entry. If only one aspect of the transaction is recorded, the partial omission throws the trial balance out of agreement.
2. **Errors of commission:** These pertain to incorrect recording of a transaction or other event in books of original entry. For example, a purchase of ₹10,000 is recorded as a purchase of ₹1,00,000. If recording of a transaction is partially incorrect, it throws the trial balance out of agreement.
3. **Clerical errors:** These errors relate to posting of an entry in a wrong account with the correct amount, and the correct side does not throw the trial balance out of agreement. For example, a credit purchase of ₹1,000 from Shyam is credited wrongly to the account of Shyam Lal.
4. **Compensating errors:** A compensating error is one that is counterbalanced by another error or errors of the same amount either in the same account or other accounts. For example, omission of posting an entry of ₹1,500 on the debit side is compensated by under posting of ₹1,500 on the credit side.
5. **Errors of principle:** An error of principle arises by reason of a transaction being recorded in a fundamentally incorrect manner. For example, conversion of a temporary shed into a permanent building is recorded as repair and maintenance of building.

REVIEW PROBLEMS

R5.1 Indicate whether the following statements are True or False:

(i) Cash book is both a general ledger and a book of prime entry.
(ii) Subsidiary ledgers are not a part of double entry bookkeeping.
(iii) Only control accounts are maintained in the general ledger.
(iv) Asset accounts normally show a credit balance.
(v) Bank account is classified as real account.
(vi) The totals of debit side and credit side of the trial balance agrees only if no error occurred in recording transactions.
(vii) All credit purchases are recorded in purchase day book.
(viii) All cash expenditures reduce equity.
(ix) In the subsidiary ledger for trade receivables details of credit transactions entered with each customer is maintained.
(x) Fixed assets register is a subsidiary ledger.

R5.2 Fill in the right column in the following table to indicate which account (s) is to be debited and which account (s) should be credited against each transaction listed in column 2.

	Transaction	*Account to be debited*	*Account to be credited*
1.	The owner introduced capital in the form of cash		
2.	The owner introduced capital in the form of stock-in-trade		
3.	The owner introduced capital by transferring the amount to the firm's bank account		
4.	Cash is withdrawn from bank		
5.	Purchased stock-in-trade on credit		
6.	Purchased stock-in-trade by cash		
7.	Purchased a piece of equipment on credit		
8.	Sold stock-in-trade to a customer on credit		
9.	Sold stock-in-trade to a customer on cash		
10.	Goods sold returned by a customer		
11.	Goods purchased returned to the suppliers		
12.	Stock-in-trade issued to the owner for personal use		
13.	Stock-in-trade distributed as free samples		
14.	Carriage inwards paid in cash		

	Transaction	Account to be debited	Account to be credited
15.	Carriage outwards paid in cash		
16.	Insurance premium paid by cheque		
17.	Stock-in-trade lost by fire		
18.	Amount received from customers by cheque against the amount due against credit sales		
19.	Discount allowed to a customer		
20.	Discount received from a supplier		
21.	Cheque received from a customer is dishonoured		
22.	Amount due to a supplier of stock-in-trade paid by cheque		
23.	Deposited cash in bank		
24.	Amount borrowed form bank and the amount is transferred by the bank to the entity's bank account		
25.	Amount invested in mutual fund units		
26.	Interest earned on investments in bond		
27.	Dividend received on investment in equity		
28.	Interest paid to the lender		
29.	Loan disbursed to employees by cheques		
30.	Maintenance charges for the maintenance of plant and machinery paid in cash		

ASSIGNMENTS

1. Tick the correct answer:

(i) A cash book:
(a) is a journal.
(b) is a ledger account.
(c) serves the dual purpose of journal and ledger account.
(d) none of the above.

(ii) A purchase day book is used:
(a) to record only credit purchases.
(b) to record only credit purchases of stock-in-trade and materials being used; in manufacturing activities.
(c) to record credit as well as cash purchases.
(d) for none of the above.

(iii) Dishonouring of cheques and other negotiable instruments received are taken in books through:
(a) sales day book.
(b) journal proper.
(c) journal proper or cash book.
(d) none of the above.

(iv) A government grant received by a company results in:
(a) increase in liability.
(b) increase in asset.
(c) increase in asset and equity.
(d) none of the above.

(v) Sale of goods, purchased for ₹8,000, on credit for ₹10,000 results in:
(a) a gain of ₹2,000 and increase in current assets and equity by ₹2,000.
(b) a gain of ₹2,000 and increase in current assets and liability by ₹2,000.
(c) an increase in asset and liability by ₹2,000.
(d) none of the above.

(vi) A trial balance fails to disclose:
(a) Errors in casting the books of subsidiary records.
(b) Errors in balancing the account.
(c) Errors in posting from the book of subsidiary record to the ledger
(d) None of the above.

2. State whether the following statements are True or False:

(i) A bank account is a real account.
(ii) A prepaid insurance account is a nominal account.
(iii) A cash account is a real account.
(iv) A capital account is a personal account.
(v) An asset account should be credited for increase in its carrying amount.
(vi) Journals record transactions in chronological order while entries in general ledger are analytical.
(vii) Debtors' account can never be credited.
(viii) A trial balance discloses all types of errors.
(ix) A credit purchase of plant should be recorded in the purchase day book.
(x) Purchase of goods (stock-in-trade) is usually recorded as an asset.
(xi) Cash book is both a journal and a ledger.

3. Against each item in the following list, indicate whether it should usually show a debit balance or a credit balance. If it shows a debit balance, indicate by marking 'D' against it and if it shows a credit balance, indicate by marking 'C' against it. Also, classify each item into current asset (CA), non-current asset (NCA), current liability (CL), non-current liability (NCL), valuation allowance (V), income (I), and expense (E).

Sl. No.	Account Head	Sl. No.	Account Head
(i)	Share capital	(xxi)	Penalty paid
(ii)	Share premium	(xxii)	Power expenses
(iii)	Land	(xxiii)	Advertisement expenses
(iv)	Salaries and wages	(xxiv)	Depreciation
(v)	Sales	(xxv)	Training expenses
(vi)	Telephone charges	(xxvi)	Research expenses
(vii)	Conveyance	(xxvii)	Goodwill
(viii)	Travelling expenses	(xxviii)	Bad debt
(ix)	Purchases	(xxix)	Accumulated depreciation
(x)	Provident fund contribution	(xxx)	Provision for doubtful debts
(xi)	Prepaid insurance	(xxxi)	Provision for income tax
(xii)	Advances from customers	(xxxii)	Loan from bank
(xiii)	Sales return	(xxxiii)	Interest due but not paid
(xiv)	Purchase return	(xxxiv)	Trade debtors
(xv)	Discount allowed	(xxxv)	Trade creditors
(xvi)	Building	(xxxvi)	Loss by fire
(xvii)	Interest income	(xxxvii)	Investment in a subsidiary company
(xviii)	Royalty received	(xxxviii)	Investment in 180–day treasury bills
(xix)	Land development	(xxxix)	Cash-in-hand
(xx)	Interest paid	(xL)	Bank overdraft

4. Analytical question: Do you agree that the concept of subsidiary ledgers has helped in allocation of duties and analysis and scrutiny of accounts in the general ledger? Explain your views on the issue.

5. Problem:

1. The following are the transactions entered into by Mr. A during April 2000:

   April 1 Opening balances:

   Stock-in-trade: ₹1,000.

   Amount due from Alpha & Co.: ₹2,000.

   Cash-in-hand: ₹500.

   Cash at bank: ₹1,000.

   Amount due to B & Co.: ₹2,000.

2. The following are the transaction details:
    1. A brought in cash, ₹10,000.
    2. A deposited ₹8,000 in the bank.
    3. A purchased goods for ₹2,000 on credit from Y & Co.
    4. A purchased goods for ₹1,000 on credit from B & Co.
    5. A purchased furniture for ₹3,000 on credit from R & Co.
    6. A purchased goods for ₹3,000 on credit from C & Co.
    7. A sold goods to Alpha & Co. for ₹2,000 on credit.
    8. A received a cheque for ₹20,000 from New India Investment Co., towards loan.
    9. A purchased goods for ₹500 in cash.
    10. A paid ₹100 towards conveyance charges.
    11. A purchased electrical fittings for ₹500.
    12. A withdrew ₹1,000 from the bank for office use.
    13. A purchased goods for ₹3,000 from M & Co. on credit.
    14. A paid ₹500 towards office expenses.
    15. A sold goods for ₹3,000 to Gamma & Co. on credit.
    16. A paid ₹1,950 by cheque to Y & Co. Y & Co. allowed a discount of ₹50.
    17. A paid ₹100 towards cartage inward.
    18. A purchased goods for ₹8,000 from Y & Co. on credit.
    19. A purchased furniture for ₹15,000 from R & Co. on credit.
    20. A paid ₹3,000 to R & Co. by cheque.
    21. A received a cheque for ₹1,950 from Alpha & Co. He allowed a discount of ₹50.
    22. A sold goods for ₹8,000 to Delta & Co. on credit.
    23. A paid ₹100 towards freight outward.
    24. A paid ₹200 towards conveyance charges.
    25. A withdrew ₹1,000 from the bank towards personal expenses.
    26. A paid ₹200 towards travelling expenses.
    27. A paid ₹1,000 to B & Co. by cheque.
    28. A received a cheque of ₹3,000 from Gamma & Co.
    29. The bank informed that the cheque received from Gamma & Co. was returned unpaid by his banker. The banker levied a service charge of ₹20.
    30. A received a bank demand draft of ₹2,900 from Gamma & Co. towards full and final settlement of the amount due from them.
    31. A purchased goods for ₹2,000 on credit from B & Co.
    32. A received a cheque of ₹7,900 from Delta & Co. A discount of ₹100 was allowed.
    33. A sold goods for ₹500 to Mr. Z on cash basis.
    34. A sold goods for ₹2,000 to Delta & Co. on credit.
    35. A paid Y & Co. ₹7,900 by cheque. A discount of ₹100 was allowed.
    36. A withdrew ₹2,000 for office use.
    37. A purchased goods for ₹3,000 from Y & Co. on credit.
    38. A paid ₹15,000 to R & Co. by cheque.
    39. A paid insurance premium of ₹1,200 by cheque.
    40. A paid rent of ₹2,000 by cheque.
    41. A sold goods for ₹3,000 to Alpha & Co. on credit.
    42. A sold goods for ₹2,000 to Beta & Co. on credit.
    43. A paid ₹200 towards conveyance charges.
    44. A sold goods for ₹500 to Mr. Z on cash basis.
    45. A purchased goods for ₹1,000 from X & Co. on cash basis.
    46. A received ₹2,950 from Alpha & Co. by cheque. A discount of ₹50 was allowed.
    47. 31 A paid ₹1,000 in cash towards wages.
    48. A paid ₹1,500 in cash towards salaries.

Required: Record the above transactions appropriately in the cash book (with discount and bank columns), purchase day book, sales day book and journal proper. Also, prepare the trial balance after posting the transactions in the general ledger.

CHAPTER 6

COMPLETION OF THE ACCOUNTING CYCLE: PREPARATION OF THE BALANCE SHEET AND INCOME STATEMENT

CHAPTER OBJECTIVES

The objectives of this chapter is to introduce to readers the mechanics of preparing financial statements starting from trial balance prepared after balancing the general ledger. In particular, the objective is developing and understanding of:

- ❖ Steps in preparing financial statements—rectification of errors, accrual accounting adjustment;
- ❖ Gain or loss from sale of items of PP&E;
- ❖ Bank reconciliation statement;
- ❖ Preparation of manufacturing account, trading account, and profit and loss account.

6.1 STEPS IN PREPARING FINANCIAL STATEMENTS

The following are the steps involved in preparing the income statement and balance sheet:

Step 1: Rectification of errors in the trail balance extracted after balancing the T Accounts in the general ledger.

Step 2: A trial balance is extracted after incorporating rectification entries (usually called unadjusted trial balance).

Step 3: Pass adjustment entries to adjust figures in the unadjusted trial balance for applying the principles of accrual accounting.

Step 4: Extract the trail balance (usually called, adjusted trial balance) after incorporating adjustment entries.

Step 5: Prepare income statement using the data in the adjusted trial balance.

Step 6: Prepare balance sheet using the data in the adjusted trial balance and profit reported in the income statement.

Step 7: Pass closing entries to close the nominal accounts.

6.1.1 Rectification of Errors

Suspense account

Pending rectification of errors, the difference between the total of debit balances and those of credit balances are placed in the Suspense Account. If the difference is not material, the balanced sheet and the profit and loss account can be prepared without rectifying the errors to publish financial statements on or before the target date. If the difference is material, the balance sheet and the profit and loss account should not be prepared without rectifying the errors, because that distorts the information communicated to the users of financial statements.

Pending rectification of errors, the difference between the total of debit balances and those of credit balances are placed in the Suspense Account..

If the difference is material, financial statements should not be prepared without rectifying the errors.

Rectification entries

Necessary entries are recorded in journal proper to rectify the errors.

EXAMPLE 6.1 (Error in recording transaction)

Error: A sale of goods for ₹6,000 to Ms. Rajani was entered in the purchase day book.

Result of the error: The sale transaction was incorrectly recorded as a purchase transaction, resulting in overstatement of purchases and trade payables, and understatement of sales and trade receivables.

Correction entries: The following are the correction entries:

Date	*Particulars*		*LF*	*Dr.* (₹)	*Cr.* (₹)
March 31	Trade Payables (Rajni) A/c	Dr.		6,000	
	Trade Receivables (Rajni) A/c	Dr.		6,000	
	To Purchases A/c	Cr.			6,000
	To Sales A/c	Cr.			6,000
	(Being rectification of the error occurred by recording a sales transaction as purchase transaction)				

EXAMPLE 6.2 (Mis-classification of expenditure)

Error: Legal charges of ₹10,000 paid on purchase of building debited to legal expenses a/c.

Result of the error: The error in classifying the expenditure has resulted in understatement of the building cost and overstatement of legal charges.

Correction entries: The following are the correction entries:

Date	Particulars	LF	Dr. (₹)	Cr. (₹)
March 31	Building A/c Dr. To Legal charges A/c Cr. (Being rectification of error in classifying expenditure incurred towards legal charges related to the purchase of a building)		10,000	10,000

EXAMPLE 6.3 (One-side error)
₹1,000 written off as depreciation on plant and machinery was credited to the machinery account, but was not debited to the depreciation account.

Error: Recording in the depreciation account is omitted:

Result of the error: Depreciation account is understated, resulting in disagreement of the trial balance. Presumably, the difference was recorded in Suspense Account

Correction entries: The following are the correction entries:

Date	Particulars	LF	Dr. (₹)	Cr. (₹)
March 31	Depreciation A/c Dr. To Suspense A/c Cr. (Being rectification of error caused by omission in recording depreciation in the depreciation account)		1,000	1,000

Contemporary practice (Ind AS) is that when errors are detected in a subsequent reporting period, the comparative figures of the previous year's balance sheet–general reserve, assets and liabilities are restated.

If the error occurred in a period earlier than the previous period, three balance sheets are presented.

EXAMPLE 6.4 (Error of commission, compensating error)
Discount allowed of ₹240 had been posted to the credit of discount received account as ₹420.

Error: Recording in the discount allowed is recorded as discount receives; and ₹240 is recorded as ₹420.

Result of the error: Discount allowed is understated by ₹240, and correspondingly, trade receivables is overstated by the same amount; and discount received is overstated by ₹420 and corresponding trade payables is understated by the same amount.

Correction entries: The following are the correction entries:

Date	Particulars	LF	Dr. (₹)	Cr. (₹)
March 31	Discount Received A/c Dr. Discount Allowed Dr. To Trade Payables A/c Cr. To Trade Receivables Cr. (Being rectification of error caused by recording discount allowed at ₹240 as discount received at ₹420).		420 240	 420 240

If we assume that trade receivables and trade payables were correctly recorded, the rectification entry should be as follows:

Date	Particulars	LF	Dr. (₹)	Cr. (₹)
March 31	Discount Received A/c Dr. Discount Allowed Dr. To Suspense A/c Cr. (Being rectification of error caused by recording discount allowed at ₹240 as discount received at ₹420).		420 240	 660

Errors detected in a subsequent period

Earlier practice (Prior period adjustment account): When errors were detected in a subsequent reporting period, adjustments in nominal accounts were debited or credited to the 'prior period adjustment A/c' in the current year's statement of profit and loss. However, adjustments in assets or liabilities accounts were debited or credited to the concerned accounts.

Contemporary accounting practice (Ind AS): The comparative figures of the previous year's balance sheet–general reserve (for effect on profit of the previous period), assets and liabilities are restated. If the error occurred in a period earlier than the previous period, three balance sheets are presented—current year's balance sheet, restated comparative figures of the previous year's balance sheet, and the balance sheet at the commencement of the previous period with corrected figures of the general reserve, assets, and liabilities. For example, if the error occurred in 2017–2018 is detected in the year 2021–2022, three balance sheets will be presented—balance sheet as of March 31,2022, balance sheet as of March 31,2021, and balance sheet as of March 31, 2020.

6.1.2 Accrual Accounting Adjustments

In order to apply the accrual accounting principles, at the end of the accounting period, adjustments are required in the balances appearing in the unadjusted trial balance.

The transactions are recorded in a routine manner based on the account head recorded in the voucher. Therefore, in order to apply the accrual accounting principles, at the end of the accounting period, adjustments are required in the balances appearing in the unadjusted trial balance.

Adjustments to revenue and other income

Accounting principle: Entities should recognise revenue when it fulfills the performance obligations specified in the contract with the customer and expects that the customer will fulfill its obligation by paying the transaction price in exchange of the goods and services.

The unbilled revenue should be included in the current period's revenue.

Unbilled revenue: In certain situations, the entity fulfills the obligation and defer preferring the claim on the customer. For example, a company, like Airtel, which provides internet and telephony services decides the billing cycle for different groups of customers. Assume that the billing cycle for a group of customers is from 15th of a month to the 14th of the next month. Therefore, as on 31st March (the last day of the current financial year), services rendered from 15th March to 31st March remains unbilled. However, to present the true and fair view of the operation, the unbilled amount should be included in the current period's revenue.

Assuming unbilled revenue of ₹50,000, the following adjustment entry is passed:

Date	*Particulars*		*LF*	*Dr.* (₹)	*Cr.* (₹)
March 31	Unbilled Revenue A/c	Dr.		50,000	
	To Revenue A/c	Cr.			50,000
	(Being recognition of unbilled revenue.)				

Recognition of the revenue that is allocated to the unfulfilled obligation should be deferred.

The result of the above journal entry is to increase the revenue by ₹50,000. Unbilled Revenue of ₹50,000 to be recognised in the balance sheet as an asset.

Deferred Revenue: Before preparing the income statement, it is assessed how much of the performance obligations against the amount received as revenue and recorded as such has remained unfulfilled till the last date of the accounting period. For example, a company publishing magazines receive subscription for 12 monthly issues. Delivery of the magazine starts from the month next to the month when the subscription is received. For example, against subscription received in September, delivery will commence in October. Therefore, part of obligation remains unfulfilled for subscription received in the current year, which begins on April 1.

Assuming deferred revenue of ₹80,000, the following journal entry is passed:

Date	*Particulars*		*LF*	*Dr.* (₹)	*Cr.* (₹)
March 31	Revenue A/c	Dr.		80,000	
	To Deferred Revenue A/c	Cr.			80,000
	(Being recognition of deferred revenue.)				

The result of the above entry is to reduce the current year's revenue by ₹80,000. Deferred Revenue of ₹80,000 should be recognised as a liability.

Accrued income is recognised as an asset in the balance sheet and is added to the concerned income account.

Accrued Income: Some income accrues evenly over time. An example is the interest income. For example, on an investment in a bond made on October 1, 2021, interest is payable annually on September 30. Therefore, the entity would receive the first year's interest on September 30, 2022. As the interest accrues evenly over the period, it has earned interest for the period 1st October, 2021 to 31st March, 2022 in the current year, although cash will be received only on September 30, 2022. This interest income should be recognised in the statement of profit and loss for the year 2021–2022. The following adjustment entry is passed to recognise the interest income accrued from 1st October, 2021 to 31st March, 2022, assuming the accrued interest income is ₹20,000:

Date	*Particulars*		*LF*	*Dr.* (₹)	*Cr.* (₹)
March 31	Accrued Interest Income A/c	Dr.		20,000	
	To Interest Income A/c	Cr.			20,000
	(Being recognition of interest income accrued on investment in bond issued by..............on October 1, 2021.)				

Accrued interest income is recognised as an asset in the balance sheet

Dividend income does not accrue evenly over the period of time.

Dividend income: An entity becomes entitled to the dividend income on investment in equity shares issued by another company only when the body of shareholders of that company approves the payment of dividend in the Annual General Meeting (AGM). Therefore, dividend income does not accrue evenly over the period of time.

Adjustment entries passed in the previous accounting period are reversed at the commencement of the current accounting period.

Reversal entries: Adjustment entries passed in the previous accounting period are reversed at the commencement of the current accounting period. Therefore, revenue and other income figures in the adjusted trial balance are adjusted for deferred revenue, unbilled revenue, and accrued income of the previous accounting period.

Let us take the example of deferred and unbilled revenue. The reversal entries are:

Date	*Particulars*		*LF*	*Dr.* (₹)	*Cr.* (₹)
April 1	Revenue A/c	Dr.		50,000	
	To Unbilled Revenue A/c	Cr.			50,000
	(Being reversal of unbilled revenue.)				

Date	*Particulars*		*LF*	*Dr.* (₹)	*Cr.* (₹)
March 31	Deferred Revenue A/c	Dr.		80,000	
	To Revenue A/c	Cr.			80,000
	(Being recognition of deferred revenue.)				

As a result of reversal entries, at the commencement of the current year, before recording sales transaction for that year, the revenue account will show the following entries:

Revenue Account

DEBIT	*Amount ₹*	*CREDIT*	*Amount ₹*
To Unbilled amount	50,000	By Deferred Revenue	80,000

Unbilled amount was included in the revenue of the previous year, but the invoice will be raised in the current year. Therefore, the unbilled revenue will be included in the revenue recorded during the current year. The reversal entry will reduce the revenue recorded in the current year. Similarly, no invoice will be raised for deferred revenue in the current year. Therefore, revenue that will be recorded in the current year will not include revenue not recognised in the previous account period and deferred to the current year. The reversal entry increases the revenue of the current accounting period.

Table 6.1 below summarises the adjustment entries to adjust revenue and other income for applying the principles of accrual accounting:

TABLE 6.1 Adjustment Entries for Revenue and Other Income

	Nature of adjustment	*Adjustment entry*	*Revenue for the current year*	*Balance sheet presentation*
1.	*Deferred Revenue* Amount received is recorded as revenue, part of the performance against that has remained unfulfilled.	Debit: Revenue A/c Credit: Deferred Revenue A/c	Revenue in the unadjusted trial balance – Closing Deferred Revenue	Recognise Deferred Revenue as a liability
2.	*Unbilled Revenue* Performance in the contract with the customer is fulfilled, but invoice is not preferred on the customer.	Debit: Unbilled Revenue A/c Credit: Revenue A/c	Revenue in the unadjusted trial balance + Closing Unbilled Revenue	Recognise Unbilled Revenue as an asset
3.	*Accrued Income* Income (such as, interest income) accrued, but cash not received.	Debit: Accrued Income A/c Credit: Revenue A/c	Revenue in the unadjusted trial balance + Closing Accrued Income	Recognise Accrued Income as an asset

Expenses

While preparing financial statements, it is necessary to analyse whether services would be received in a subsequent period for the payment made in the current period (called prepaid expenses) and whether for some services received during the current period the payment would be made in a subsequent period (called, accrued expenses). Adjustment entries are passed for prepaid expenses and accrued expenses.

Prepaid expenses

Pre-paid expense is recognised as an asset in the balance sheet and is deducted from the concerned expense account.

Examples of prepaid expenses are rent paid in advance or insurance premium paid for a year, which will end in the next accounting year.

Assuming that ₹12,000 is paid towards the insurance premium for the period 1st October 2021 to 30th September 30, 2022, the following adjustment entry is passed on 31st March 2022.

Date	*Particulars*		*LF*	*Dr.* (₹)	*Cr.* (₹)
March 31	Pre-paid Insurance Premium A/c	Dr.		6,000	
	To Insurance Premium Expense A/c	Cr.			6,000
	(Being recognition of prepaid insurance premium on insurance policy No........)				

When insurance premium was paid, ₹12,000 was recorded as insurance premium. The result of the above entry is to reduce the insurance premium by ₹6,000. The pre-paid insurance premium is recognised as an asset in the balance sheet..

When claims for services received is either not received or accepted, adjustment entry is required to recognise the expense and the corresponding liability.

Accrued expenses

When a claim for services received is accepted, a liability is recognised. However, when claims for services received is either not received or accepted, adjustment entry is required to recognise the expense and the corresponding liability. Assuming accrued electricity expense of ₹30,000, the following adjustment entry is passed:

Date	*Particulars*		*LF*	*Dr.* (₹)	*Cr.* (₹)
March 31	Electricity Expense A/c	Dr.		30,000	
	To Accrued Electricity Expense A/c	Cr.			30,000
	(Being adjustment for the electricity consumed in March, for which bill is not received.)				

The result of the above entry is to increase the electricity expense for the year by ₹30,000. Accrues electricity expense is recognised in the balance sheet as a liability.

The above entries are reversed immediately at the commencement of the next accounting period.

Table 6.2 below summarises the adjustment entries to adjust expenses for applying the principles of accrual accounting:

TABLE 6.2 Adjustment Entries for Revenue and other Income

	Nature of adjustment	*Adjustment entry*	*Revenue for the current year*	*Balance sheet presentation*
1.	*Pre-paid Expense* Expense recorded in the current accounting period for which benefits will be received in a subsequent accounting period	Debit: Pre-paid Expense A/c Credit: Expense A/c	Expense in the unadjusted trial balance – Closing Pre-paid expense	Recognise Pre-paid expense as an asset.
2.	*Accrued Expense* Income (such as, interest income) accrued, but liability not recognised, or cash not paid	Debit: Expense A/c Credit: Accrued Expense A/c	Revenue in the unadjusted trial balance + Closing Accrued Income	Recognise Accrued expense as a liability

6.1.3 Depreciation and Amortisation

The term depreciation is used in the context of items of PP&E. The term amortisation is used in the context of intangible assets.

Entities disclose in the balance sheet gross block of the asset, the accumulated depreciation, and the accumulated impairment loss.

The term depreciation is used in the context of items of property, plant, and equipment (PP&E). The term amortisation is used in the context of intangible assets. The adjustment entries are same for both.

Entities disclose in the balance sheet gross block (acquisition cost) of the asset, the accumulated depreciation, and the accumulated impairment loss as follows:

	Amount (₹)
Gross block	****
Less: Accumulated Depreciation	****
Less: Accumulated Impairment Loss	****
Net block	****

Valuation allowance

Accumulated depreciation is recorded in the account head, "Provision for depreciation". Provision for depreciation is not a liability. It is valuation allowance, which is reduction in the asset value.

Assuming depreciation is ₹20,000 to be provided on machinery, the following adjustment entry is passed:

Provision for depreciation is a valuation allowance, and not a liability.

Date	*Particulars*		*LF*	*Dr.* (₹)	*Cr.* (₹)
March 31	Depreciation on machinery A/c	Dr.		20,000	
	To Provision for Depreciation on machinery A/c	Cr.			20,000
	(Being depreciation for the current year on machineries.)				

The result of the above entry is to recognise depreciation for the current accounting period and increase the provision for depreciation.

6.1.4 Provision for Doubtful Debts and Bad Debt

Nature of provision for doubtful debts and bad debts

Firms often fail to recover the full amount that customers owe to it. Therefore, they provide for impairment loss of trade receivables. They create a valuation allowance to recognise the estimated loss arising from non-recovery of the trade receivables. The valuation allowance is accumulated in the Provision for Doubtful Debts. Firms continue their efforts to recover the doubtful debts. However, at some point in time they decide not to make further efforts to recover doubtful debts. At that point, they recognise the amount recoverable as bad debt and write off the amount due from the customer.

Firms provide for the estimated impairment loss of trade receivables and create a valuation allowance.

Provision for doubtful debt is a valuation allowance, while bad debt is a loss.

Accounting entries

Usually, provision for doubtful debt is created through the following *closing entry*, assuming that the management requires a provision of INR 20,000:

Date	*Particulars*		*LF*	*Dr.* (₹)	*Cr.* (₹)
March 31	Profit and Loss A/c	Dr.		20,000	
	To Provision for Doubtful Debts A/c	Cr.			20,000
	(Being provision created for doubtful debts)				

Provision for doubtful debts can also be recorded through the following adjustment entry:

Date	*Particulars*		*LF*	*Dr.* (₹)	*Cr.* (₹)
March 31	Impairment Loss on Trade Receivables A/c	Dr.		20,000	
	To Provision for Doubtful Debts A/c	Cr.			20,000
	(Being provision created for doubtful debts)				

Firms recognise the amount not recoverable from customers as bad debt and write off the amount due from the customer.

The 'Impairment loss on trade receivable' appears in the adjusted trial balance and is recognised in the statement of profit and loss.

Bad debt

Bad debt is recorded through the following adjustment entry, assuming bad debt of INR 5,000:

Date	*Particulars*		*LF*	*Dr.* (₹)	*Cr.* (₹)
March 31	Bad Debt A/c	Dr.		5,000	
	To Trade Receivables A/c	Cr.			5,000
	(Being provision created for doubtful debts)				

Bad debt is identified with a particular customer. That customer's account is taken out of the subsidiary ledger.

The opening balance of the provision for doubtful debts appears in the unadjusted trial balance.

Topping up the provision

If the firm is in operation from an earlier period, the opening balance of the provision for doubtful debts appears in the unadjusted trial balance. That balance is first adjusted for the bad debt recorded in the books by passing the following adjustment entry, assuming the bad debt of INR 5,000 already recorded in the books:

Date	Particulars		LF	Dr. (₹)	Cr. (₹)
March 31	Provision for doubtful debts A/c	Dr		5,000	
	To Bad Debt A/c	Cr.			5,000
	(Being adjustment of the provision created for doubtful debts for bad debt recorded during the period)				

The accounting entry is required for topping up the provision.

EXAMPLE 6.5 (Provision for doubtful debts)

The opening balance in the provision for doubtful debts was INR 30,000. It is to be adjusted for bad debt ₹5,000, and at the year-end provision required is INR 35,000 is required. The closing or the adjustment entry should be passed for topping up the provision by (35,000 – (30,000 – 5,000)) or INR 10,000.

Assume that, in the above example, the year-end provision required is INR 20,000. In that case the excess provision of ((30,000 – 5,000) – 20,000) or INR 5,000 is written back. The following is the journal entry:

Date	Particulars		LF	Dr. (₹)	Cr. (₹)
March 31	Provision for Doubtful Debts A/c	Dr.		5,000	
	To Impairment Loss on Trade Receivables A/c	Cr.			5,000
	(Being reversal of the impairment loss on trade receivables)				

The contemporary practice (Ind AS/IFRS) requires that all estimated discounts, including cash discounts should be adjusted against revenue.

The amount of discount is estimated by applying a per cent on the amount of trade receivables, reduced by the provision for doubtful debts.

Provision for discount to be allowed to customers

The contemporary practice (Ind AS/IFRS) requires that all estimated discounts, including cash discounts should be adjusted against revenue.

The amount of discount is estimated by applying a per cent on the amount of trade receivables, reduced by the provision for doubtful debts, as discount will be allowed to only those customers who will pay the amount due to the firm.

EXAMPLE 6.6 (Provision for discount)

The balance in trade receivables is ₹5,00,000 and the year-end provision required is ₹40,000. The provision for discount to be allowed will be estimated by applying the percentage on (5,00,000 – 40,000) or ₹4,60,000. Assume that the estimated discount is 2 per cent, the estimated provision for discount is (4,60,000 × 0.02) or ₹9,200.

The following adjustment entry is required:

Date	Particulars		LF	Dr. (₹)	Cr. (₹)
March 31	Revenue A/c	Dr.		9,200	
	To Provision for Discount to customers A/c	Cr.			9,200
	(Being adjustment for estimated discount to be allowed to customers)				

Traditionally, the provision is created through the *closing entry*, as follows:

Date	Particulars		LF	Dr. (₹)	Cr. (₹)
March 31	Profit and Loss A/c	Dr.		9,200	
	To Provision for discount to customers A/c	Cr.			9,200
	(Being Provision for discount to be allowed to customers)				

6.1.5 Closing Stock

Transactions for the purchase of stock-in-trade, and raw material, etc. are recorded as an expense—Purchase Account is debited and Cash Account or Trade Payables Account is credited. Inventories of those items are counted physically and valued for carrying in the balance sheet. Closing stock is recorded through a *closing entry*. Similarly, the closing stock of finished goods and work-in-progress are also recorded through a closing entry.

Transactions for the purchase of stock-in-trade, and raw material, etc. are recorded as an expense—Purchase.

Inventories of those inputs, finished goods and work-in-progress are recorded through a closing entry.

Assuming closing stock of ₹80,000, the following entry is passed:

Date	Particulars		LF	Dr. (₹)	Cr. (₹)
March 31	Closing Stock A/c	Dr.		80,000	
	To Trading A/c	Cr.			80,000
	(Being recording of the closing stock)				

The closing stock of the previous year appears in the unadjusted trial balance as the opening stock. Closing stock does not appear in the trial balance.

Closing stock in the trial balance

Closing stock appears in the unadjusted trial balance when it is recorded by adjusting the purchases through the following journal entry.

Date	Particulars		LF	Dr. (₹)	Cr. (₹)
March 31	Closing Stock A/c	Dr		80,000	
	To Purchases A/c	Cr.			80,000
	(Being Provision for discount to be allowed to customers)				

This is not the practice. However, if the closing stock appears in the trial balance, in calculating the cost of material consumed or cost of goods sold, the closing stock should not be deducted.

EXAMPLE 6.7 (Cost of goods sold)

***Alternative** 1(Appropriate accounting)*

The unadjusted trial balance shows the opening stock and purchases of stock-in-trade at ₹50,000 and ₹6,00,000 respectively. The closing stock of the stock-in-trade is valued at ₹70,000.

The cost of goods sold = Purchases – (Closing stock – Opening Stock)

The cost of goods sold = ₹6,00,000 – (70,000 – 50,000) = ₹5,80,000

***Alternative** 2(Inappropriate accounting)*

The unadjusted trial balance shows the opening stock, purchases, and closing stock-in-trade at ₹50,000, ₹5,30,000, and ₹70,000 respectively.

The cost of goods sold = Purchases + Opening Stock

The cost of goods sold = ₹5,30,000 + 50,000 = ₹5,80,000

***Alternative** 3(Inappropriate accounting)*

Both the opening stock and closing stock are adjusted against purchases. Therefore, the unadjusted trial balance shows neither the opening stock nor the closing stock. In that case the figure against the Purchase Account, adjusted for the opening and closing stock presented in the unadjusted trial balance is the cost of goods sold.

6.2 GAIN OR LOSS ON DISPOSAL OF ITEMS OF PP&E

The gain or loss from the sale of in item of PP&E is the difference between the sale proceeds and the carrying amount (also called, written down value) of the asset.

Firms dispose items of property, plant, and equipment (PP&E) when they retire those permanently from use either by sale or otherwise. If they sale the retired items, they recognise gain or loss.

The gain or loss from the sale is the difference between the sale proceeds and the carrying amount (also called, written down value) of the asset. For example, if the sale proceed is ₹1,00,000 and the WDV is ₹80,000, the gain from the sale of the asset is ₹20,000. The accounting is explained in the Example 6.8 below:

EXAMPLE 6.8 (Gain or loss from the disposal of items of PP&E)

The following information is available:

The Machine Account is showing a balance of ₹10,00,000 and Provision for Depreciation Accounting is showing a balance of ₹6,00,000; Acquisition cost of the machine: ₹2,00,000; Accumulated depreciation on the machine ₹1,60,000, and sale proceed ₹60,000.

The journal entries and T accounts are presented below:

Journal entries

Date	*Particulars*		*LF*	*Dr.* (₹)	*Cr.* (₹)
	Cash A/c	Dr.		60,000	
	To Sale of Machine A/c	Cr.			60,000
	(Being sale of machine No.......................)				

Date	*Particulars*		*LF*	*Dr.* (₹)	*Cr.* (₹)
	Sale of Machine A/c	Dr.		2,00,000	
	To Machine A/c	Cr.			2,00,000
	(Being transfer of the acquisition cost of machine No....)				

Date	*Particulars*		*LF*	*Dr.* (₹)	*Cr.* (₹)
	Provision of depreciation A/c	Dr.		1,60,000	
	To Sale of machine A/c	Cr.			1,60,000
	(Being transfer of accumulated depreciation on machine No.............)				

Date	*Particulars*		*LF*	*Dr.* (₹)	*Cr.* (₹)
	Sale of Machine A/c	Dr.		20,000	
	To Gain/loss on Sale of machine A/c	Cr.			20,000
	(Being gain on the sale of machine No.............)				

T Accounts

Sale of Machine A/c

Particulars	*Dr. Amount* (₹)	*Particulars*	*Cr. Amount* (₹)
To Machine A/c	2,00,000	By Cash A/c (Sale of the machine)	60,000
To Gain/Loss on sale of machine A/c	20,000	By Prov. for Depreciation on Machine A/c	1,60,000
	2,20,000		2,20,000

Machine A/c

Dr.			*Cr.*
Particulars	*Amount (₹)*	*Particulars*	*Amount (₹)*
To Balance b/d	10,00,000	By Sale of Machine A/c	2,00,000
To balance b/d	10,00,000	By Balance c/d	8,00,000
	800,0000		10,00,000

Provision for Depreciation A/c

Dr.			*Cr.*
Particulars	*Amount (₹)*	*Particulars*	*Amount (₹)*
To Sale of Machine A/C	1,60,000	By Balance b/d	6,00,000
To balance /cd	4,40,000	By Balance b/d	6,00,000
	6,00,000		4,40,000

Gain/Loss on Sale of Machine A/c

Dr.			*Cr.*
Particulars	*Amount (₹)*	*Particulars*	*Amount (₹)*
		By Sale of Machine A/c	20,000

The gain will be transferred to the statement of profit and loss. After recording the transaction for the sale of machine the Machine Account balance is the cost of machines that the firm holds after sale of the machine and Provision for Depreciation Account balance is the accumulated depreciation on those machines.

6.3 BANK RECONCILIATION STATEMENT

The debit balance in the bank account in the general ledger of the entity is an asset because the entity has the right to receive cash from the bank. The right of the entity to receive cash from the bank is an obligation of the bank to pay cash to the entity as per contractual terms. Therefore, entity's account in the bank's general ledger shows credit balance of the same amount. A bank statement, which is the copy of the entity's account maintained in the bank's books, provides a mirror image of the bank account being maintained in the general ledger or cash book of the entity.

Bank reconciliation statement is prepared, as a part of the internal control system, to locate the reasons for the difference between the bank balance as per the firm's book and that as per the bank's book.

Adjustment entries are passed for errors committed by bank, and for transaction not recorded in the entity's books.

Usually, the debit (credit) balance in the bank account in the entity's general ledger should agree with the credit (debit) balance in the entity's account in the bank's general ledger. More often they do not agree. The following are the most common reasons:

1. Amount transferred electronically by another entity not credited in the entity's account;
2. Cheques issued are not presented for payment, and cheques deposited are not collected;
3. Collections and payments directly by the bank not recorded in the entity's books of accounts;
4. Bank charges, etc. recorded in the entity's account maintained by the bank not recorded in the entity's books of account.
5. Errors in recording transactions by the bank.

Bank reconciliation statement is prepared to locate the differences. This is a component of the internal control system, as differences might arise from fraud perpetrated by entity's employees or bank's employees or a third party. Moreover, unless adjustment entries are passed for errors committed by bank, and for transaction not recorded in the entity's books, entity's financial statements will not communicate the true and fair view of the financial position, financial performance, and cash flows.

Illustration 6.1 (Bank reconciliation statement)

On December 31, 2019, the bank column of the cash book of A & Co. shows a debit balance of ₹5,000, while the bank statement shows a credit balance of ₹4,850.

On examination of the cash book and bank statement, it is found that:

1. A cheque of ₹2,000 deposited with the bank on December 1, 2019, is yet to be collected on that date.
2. Cheques amounting to ₹3,000 issued and recorded in the cash book are yet to be presented to the bank for payment.
3. A cheque for ₹500 has been dishonoured prior to December 31, 2019, but not recorded in the cash book.
4. A dividend of ₹200 collected by the bank directly has not been recorded in the cash book.
5. Bank charges of ₹50 have not been recorded in the cash book.
6. A cheque of ₹800 drawn by Mr. A has been wrongly debited by bank in A & Co.'s account.

Required:

(i) Prepare a bank reconciliation statement,
(ii) Make appropriate adjustments in the cash book, and
(iii) Prepare a bank reconciliation statement after adjustments.

Solution: (i)

A & Co.: Bank Reconciliation Statement as on December 31, 2019

Balance as per cash book			₹5,000
Add:	Cheques issued not yet presented	₹3,000	
	Dividend collected not yet recorded in the cash book	200	3,200
			8,200
Less:	Cheques deposited not yet collected	₹2,000	
	Cheque dishonoured not yet recorded in the cash book	500	
	Bank charges not yet recorded in the cash book	50	
	Cheque wrongly debited by bank	800	₹3,350
	Balance as per bank statement		₹4,850

(ii)

A & Co.: Cash Book, Bank Column (incomplete)

Dr.	*Receipts*			*Payments*	*Cr.*
Date	*Particulars*	*Amount (₹)*	*Date*	*Particulars*	*Amount (₹)*
2019			2019		
Dec. 31	To balance b/d	5,000	Dec. 31	By trade debtors	
	To dividend			(Cheque dishonoured)	500
	received A/c	200		By bank charges	50
				By balance c/d	4,650
2020		5,200			5,200
Jan. 1	To balance b/d	4,650			

(iii)

A & Co.: Final Bank Reconciliation Statement as on December 31, 2019

Particulars		*Amount (₹)*	*Amount (₹)*
Balance as per cash book			4,650
Add:	Cheques issued not yet presented		3,000
			7,650
Less:	Cheques deposited not yet collected	2,000	
	Cheque wrongly debited by bank	800	2,800
	Balance as per bank statement\		4,850

Illustration 6.2 (Bank reconciliation statement)

On investigation, it is found that:

(a) a cheque for ₹3,000 was deposited with the bank, but not yet collected.
(b) a cheque for ₹5,000 was issued, but not yet presented.
(c) a dividend of ₹700 directly collected by the bank has not been recorded in the cash book.
(d) bank charges of ₹500 have not been recorded in the cash book.
(e) a cheque of ₹1,000 had been dishonoured by the bank, but no entry has been made in the cash book.

Required:

(i) Prepare a bank reconciliation statement.
(ii) Make appropriate adjustments in the cash book.
(iii) Prepare a bank reconciliation statement after adjustments at (ii) above.

Solution: (i)

Bank Reconciliation Statement as on December 31, 2019

Balance as per cash book (overdrawn)		₹3,000
Add: Cheques deposited but not collected	3,000	
Bank charges not yet recorded in the cash book	500	
Cheque dishonoured not yet recorded in the cash book	1,000	4,500
		7,500
Less: Cheques issued but not yet presented	₹5,000	
Dividend directly collected by bank	700	5,700
Balance as per bank statement (overdrawn)		₹1,800

Trading account presents income and expenses up to the gross profit level.

Profit and loss account communicates operating expenses and net profit.

(ii)

Cash Book, Bank Column (incomplete)

Dr.	*Receipts*			*Payments*	*Cr.*
Date	*Particulars*	*Amount (₹)*	*Date*	*Particulars*	*Amount (₹)*
2019			2019		
Dec. 31	To dividend received A/c	700	Dec. 31	By balance b/d	3,000
	To balance c/d	3,800		By trade debtors (Cheque dishonoured)	1,000
				By bank charges	500
		4,500			4,500
				By balance c/d	3,800

(iii)

Final Bank Reconciliation Statement as on December 31, 2019

Balance as per cash book (overdrawn)	₹3,800
Add: Cheques deposited but not yet collected	3,000
	6,800
Less: Cheques issued but not yet presented	5,000
Balance as per bank statement (overdrawn)	1,800

6.4 MANUFACTURING, TRADING AND PROFIT AND LOSS ACCOUNT

Trading account present income and expenses up to the gross profit level and profit and loss account shows operating expenses and net profit.

6.4.1 Trading Account

Gross profit = Sales – Cost of goods sold

Trading account presents revenue (sales) and expenses that are included in the cost of goods sold. Cost of goods sold includes the purchase price of the merchandise and costs incurred to bring the goods to the location and condition of sale. Purchase price include taxes that are not refundable. Other costs include the cost of converting the goods bought in bulk into saleable units and labelling, etc. Conventionally, the compensation to employees who are involved in the process of conversion is termed as *wages* to distinguish the compensation to employees involved in marketing, sales, distribution, and administration. Compensation to those employees are termed as *salaries*.

Conventionally, depreciation is considered operating expenses.

6.4.2 Abnormal Loss

Abnormal losses should be excluded from cost of goods sold to measure gross profit correctly.

Abnormal losses should be excluded from cost of goods sold to measure gross profit correctly.

Cost of goods sold = Purchases – (Closing Inventories – Opening Inventories)

Inventories are physically counted at the end of the accounting period and valued in accordance with the accounting principles stipulated in the GAAP. Therefore, increase or decrease in inventories include decrease in inventories due to abnormal loss, for example, loss by fire. It is necessary to recognise gross loss in the trading account and net loss (gross loss less insurance claim) in the profit and loss account.

EXAMPLE 6.9 (Loss by fire)

Gross loss by fire: ₹50,000, Insurance Claim accepted by the insurance company: ₹40,000, and net loss ₹10,000

The following journal entries are passed to record loss by fire, insurance claim and net loss by fire.

Date	*Particulars*	*LF*	*Dr.* (₹)	*Cr.* (₹)
	Loss by fire A/c Dr. To Cost of goods sold A/c Cr. (Being loss of stock-in-trade due to fire occurred in the premises on ....)		50,000	50,000

Date	*Particulars*	*LF*	*Dr.* (₹)	*Cr.* (₹)
	Insurance Claim A/c Dr. To Loss by fire A/c Cr. (Being Insurance claim accepted for the loss of stock-in-trade in fire occurred in the premises on........................)		40,000	40,000

The T Account of Loss by Fire, Cost of goods sold and Insurance Claim will be as follows:

Loss by Fire A/c

Dr. *Cr.*

Particulars	*Amount* (₹)	*Particulars*	*Amount* (₹)
To Cost of goods sold A/c	50,000	By Insurance Claim A/c	40,000
		By Balance c/d	10,000
Total	50,000		50,000
To balance b/d	10,000		

Insurance Claim A/c

Dr. *Cr.*

Particulars	Amount (₹)	Particulars	Amount (₹)
To Loss by Fire A/c	40,000	By Balance c/d	40,000
Total	40,000		40,000
To balance b/d	10,000		

Cost of Goods Sold A/c

Dr. *Cr.*

Particulars	Amount (₹)	Particulars	Amount (₹)
To Balance c/d	50,000	By Loss by Fire A/c	50,000
Total	50,000		50,000
		To balance b/d	50,000

The loss by fire account is closed by transferring the balance to the profit and loss account. Cost of goods sold account is closed by transferring balance to the trading account. Insurance claim, if not received by the end of the accounting period, is recognised as an asset in the balance sheet. When insurance claim is received cash or bank account is debited and the insurance claim account is credited, resulting in closure of the insurance claim account.

In examination question paper, usually, information on loss by fire is presented as additional information. Presentation in financial statements is illustrates in the illustration 6.5.

Presentation

Trading, and profit and loss account can be presented either in the vertical form or in the T form. The current practice is to present those account in the vertical form. Therefore, we shall use the vertical form in illustrations below. However, in order to illustrate the T form, in Illustrations 6.3 and 6.4, we shall present the trading account and profit and loss account in both the vertical form and the T form.

Trading, and profit and loss account can be presented either in the vertical form or in the T form.

The current practice is to present those account in the vertical form.

Illustration 6.3 (Trading Account)

The following particulars have been extracted from the books of a trader for the year ended March 31, 2019.

Particulars	Amount (₹)
Sales	10,02,000
Sales returns	2,000
Purchases	7,03,000
Purchases returns	3,000
Stock of merchandise (April 1, 2018)	80,000
Stock of merchandise (March 31, 2019)	60,000
Freight and duty	40,000
Carriage inwards	20,000
Carriage outwards	25,000
Wages	50,000

Required: Prepare trading account for the year ended on March 31, 2019.

Solution:

T Form

Trading Account for the year ended on March 31, 2019

Dr. *Cr.*

Expenditures	*Amount* (₹)	Income	*Amount* (₹)
To Opening Stock	80,000	By Sales less returns	10,00,000
To Purchase less returns	7,00,000	By Closing stock	60,000
To Freight and duty	40,000		
To Carriage inwards	20,000		
To Wages	50,000		
To Gross profit	1,70,000		
Total	10,60,000	**Total**	10,60,000

Vertical Form

Trading Account for the year ended on March 31, 2019

Dr. *Cr.*

Particulars	*Amount* (₹)	*Amount* (₹)
I. **INCOME**		
Sales	10,02,000	
Sales return	(2,000)	10,00,000
II. **EXPENSES**		
Purchases	7,03,000	
Purchase return	(3,000)	7,00,000
Change in inventories of stock-in trade		20,000
To Freight and duty		40,000
To Carriage inwards		20,000
To Wages		50,000
Total II		8,30,000
III. Gross Profit (I–II)		1,70,000

Illustration 6.4 (Trading and profit and loss account)

From the following details extracted from the books of a trader for the year ended March 31, 2019, prepare trading and profit and loss account:

Particulars	*Amount* (₹)
Purchases	15,00,000
Opening stock	3,70,000
Sales	27,00,000
Returns outward	2,00,000
Returns inward	3,00,000
Wages	2,50,000
Salaries	1,50,000
Carriage inward	30,000
Carriage outward	20,000
Duty and clearing charges	5,000
Factory rent	25,000
Office rent	15,000
Fuel and power	10,000
Travelling and conveyance	9,500

(*Contd...*)

Particulars	Amount (₹)
Rent, rates and taxes	24,500
Interest received	5,400
Discount allowed	6,000
Discount received	4,600
Insurance charges	5,000
Bad debts	6,500
Trade expenses	2,000
Advertisement	9,000
Depreciation on plant	12,500
Depreciation on furniture	3,000
Closing stock	5,50,000

Solution:

T Format

Trading and Profit and Loss Account for the Year ended March 31, 2019

Dr. *Cr.*

Expenses	Amount ₹	Income	Amount ₹
To Opening stock	3,70,000	By Sales, less returns and discount allowed	23,94,000
To Purchases less returns	13,00,000	By Closing stock	5,50,000
To Wages	2,50,000		
To Carriage inward	30,000		
To Duty and clearing charges	5,000		
To Factory rent	25,000		
To Fuel and power	10,000		
To Gross profit c/d	9,54,000		
Total	29,44,000	**Total**	29,44,000
To Salaries	1,50,000	By Gross profit b/d	9,54,000
To Carriage outward	20,000	By Interest received	5,400
To Office rent	15,000	By Discount received	4,600
To Travolling and conveyance	9,500		
To Rent, rates and taxes	24,500		
To Insurance charges	5,000		
To Bad debts	6,500		
To Trade expenses	2,000		
To Advertisement	9,000		
To Depreciation on plant	12,500		
To Depreciation on furniture	3,000		
To Net profit transferred to Capital A/c	7,07,000		
Total	9,64,000	**Total**	9,64,000

Notes:

(i) Depreciation on plant is considered as an expense charged against gross profit. This is how depreciation of plant is treated in most textbooks. This is not correct, as depreciation on plant is an expense that is incurred to convert merchandise in saleable package. It is similar to factory rent.

(ii) Tax expense is not recognised in the profit and loss of the business in a sole–proprietorship firm because the sole-proprietor pays the tax on his/her income.

(iii) Ind AS (IFRS) requires all discounts (including cash discounts) should be deducted from revenue (sale of goods and services).

Vertical Format

Particulars	Amount (₹)	Amount (₹)
I. INCOME		
Sales	27,00,000	
Return inwards	(3,00,000)	
Discount allowed	(6,000)	23,94,000
II. COST OF SALES		
Purchases	15,00,000	
Return outward	2,00,0000	13,00,000
Increase in the inventories of stock-in-trade		(1,80,000)
To Wages		2,50,000
To Carriage inward		30,000
To Duty and clearing charges		5,000
To Factory rent		25,000
To Fuel and power		10,000
Total II		14,40,000
III. GROSS PROFIT (I–II)		9,54,000
IV. OPERATING EXPENSES		
To Salaries	1,50,000	
To Carriage outward	20,000	
To Office rent	15,000	
To Travelling and conveyance	9,500	
To Rent, rates and taxes	24,500	
To Insurance charges	5,000	
To Bad debts	6,500	
To Trade expenses	2,000	
To Advertisement	9,000	
To Depreciation on plant	12,500	
To Depreciation on furniture	3,000	
Total IV		2,57,000
V. OPERATING PROFIT (III–IV)		6,97,000
VI. OTHER INCOME		
Interest received	5,400	
Discount received	4,600	
Total VI		10,000
Net profit transferred to Capital Account		7,07,000

Companies that manufacture goods might prepare the manufacturing account that communicates the cost of manufacturing the goods sold.

Balance sheet lists the equity (capital), assets, and liabilities.

6.5 MANUFACTURING ACCOUNT

Companies that manufacture goods might prepare the manufacturing account that communicates the cost of manufacturing the goods sold. Manufacturing account does not present any income. The elements that get into the cost of manufacturing are—cost of inputs, and conversions costs. Conversion costs are wages (cost of direct labour) and expenses incurred in converting the inputs into finished goods.

6.6 BALANCE SHEET

Balance sheet lists the equity (capital), assets, and liabilities. We discussed the balance sheet structure in Chapter 3. Nominal accounts (income and expenses) in the adjusted trial balance are transferred to the manufacturing, trading, and profit and loss account. The balances in the equity (capital), assets, and liabilities accounts are presented in the balance sheet, after adjusting the capital for the profit reported in the profit and loss account.

Illustration 6.5 (Manufacturing, trading, and profit and loss account, and balance sheet)

The following is the trial balance of A & Co. as on March 31, 2019:

Sl. No.	*Particulars*	*Dr. Amount (₹)*	*Cr. Amount (₹)*
1.	Mr. A's capital a/c		10,00,000
2.	Mr. A's drawing a/c	20,000	
3.	Purchases of raw materials less return	6,00,000	
4.	Purchases of finished goods less return	14,00,000	
5.	Freight inward for finished goods	20,000	
6.	Wages	1,20,000	
7.	Salaries	1,50,000	
8.	Rates and taxes	30,000	
9.	Electric power	60,000	
10.	Electricity charges for lights and fans	25,000	
11.	Office rent	30,000	
12.	Reserve account		50,000
13.	Travelling expenses	1,00,000	
14.	Insurance premium	1,80,000	
15.	Advertisement expenses	40,000	
16.	Sales less return		30,00,000
17.	Bad debts written off	10,000	
18.	Discounts (debit balance)	5,000	
19.	General expenses	36,000	
20.	Postage and telegram	15,000	
21.	Opening stock as on April 1, 2018:		
	Raw materials	50,000	
	Work-in-progress	80,000	
	Finished goods	2,00,000	
22.	Factory land	80,000	
23.	Factory building	60,000	
24.	Plant and machinery	5,00,000	
25.	Furniture and fixtures	1,05,000	
26.	Sundry creditors		2,00,000
27.	Sundry debtors	6,00,000	
28.	Cash in hand	20,000	
29.	Cash in bank	14,000	
30.	Provision for depreciation of factory building		20,000
31.	Provision for depreciation of plant and machinery		2,50,000
32.	Provision for depreciation of furniture and fixtures		30,000
		45,50,000	45,50,000

Additional information:

1. Closing stock as on March 31, 2019

   Raw materials ₹60,000
   Work-in-progress ₹85,000
   Finished goods ₹2,20,000

2. Provide depreciation at 15% on plant and machinery, 10% on furniture and fixtures and 5% on factory buildings. The enterprise uses the straight-line method of depreciation.
3. Provide 2% discount on debtors and create provision of 5% for doubtful debts.

4. Sundry creditors include ₹2,000 realised from A & Co., a customer, whose account had been written off two years back.
5. Insurance premium was paid for the period from July 1, 2018 to June 30, 2019.
6. One machine whose cost in the books as on April 1, 2018 stood at ₹86,000 was disposed of on September 30, 2018 for ₹16,000 in part exchange for a machine costing ₹30,000. The transaction was recorded at the net amount of ₹14,000. The provision for depreciation on the machine as on April 1, 2018 was ₹66,000. No depreciation need be provided on machinery disposed of during the year.
7. During the year, a fire broke out in the godown of finished goods causing a loss of ₹20,000. The insurance company has admitted a claim of ₹18,000 only. This event has not been recorded in the books.
8. The following expenditure was outstanding for which no provision has been made in the books: Audit fees: ₹10,000, Advertisement: ₹2,000

Solution:

The first step is to adjust the balances in the trial balance for the additional information. No journal entries are required in the examination situation.

We are presenting the results of the adjustments in the working notes below:

Working notes:

1. No adjustment is required for information at (1). It will be used to calculate the cost of production and cost of goods sold.
2. (a) We have calculated depreciation after adjusting the cost of the asset based on the information provided at (6). The adjusted cost of the plant and machinery is ₹4,30,000 – old items: ₹4,00,000, and new machine acquired on September 30, 2018: ₹30,000. Depreciation on the old machine: ₹4,00,000 × 0.15 = ₹60,000. Depreciation on the new machine for half-year: ₹30,000 × 0.50 × 0.15 = ₹2,250. Total depreciation ₹62,250. The provision for depreciation is increased to (₹1,84,000 + 62,250) = ₹2,46,250.

   (b) Depreciation on furniture and fixtures: ₹1,05,000 × 0.10 = ₹10,500. Provision for depreciation is increased to (₹30,000 +10,500) = ₹40,500.

   (c) Depreciation on factory buildings: ₹60,000 × 0.05 = ₹3,000. Provision for depreciation is increased to (₹20,000 + 3,000) = ₹23,000.
3. (a) Provision for doubtful debts: (₹6,00,000 × 0.05) = ₹30,000

   (b) Provision for discount: (6,00,000 – 30,000) × 0.02 = ₹11,400
4. Sundry creditors in the trial balance is ₹2,00,000. By mistake, ₹2,000 realised from a customer, whose account was already written off, was credited to sundry creditors A/c. Therefore, sundry creditors account should be reduced to (₹2,00,000 – 2,000) = ₹1,98,000. Recovery of bad debt of ₹2,000 should be recognised as a gain in the profit and loss account.
5. Insurance premium expense in the trial balance is ₹1,80,000. The premium covers three months of the next financial year. Therefore, ₹45,000 should be recognised as pre-paid expenses in the balance sheet and insurance premium expense of (₹1,80,000 – 45,000) or 1,35,000 should be recognised in the statement of profit and loss.
6. The following adjustments are required:

   (a) The machine purchased in exchange of the old machine and payment of cash of ₹14,000 is recorded at 14,000, instead of ₹30,000. Therefore, the amount of plant and machinery appearing in the trial balance at ₹500,000 should be increased by (₹30,000 – 14,000) or 16,000. Thus, it comes to 5,16,000. This includes the cost of the machine disposed of by exchanging for the new machine. Therefore, the cost should be reduced by the cost of the machine disposed. This will reduce the plant and machinery balance to (₹5,16,000 – 86,000) or ₹4,30,000.

(b) The provision for depreciation on plant and machinery in the trial balance at ₹2,50,000 includes the amount of accumulated depreciation disposed by exchanging that for a new machine. Therefore, the provision for depreciation is to be reduced to (₹2,50,000 – 66,000) or ₹1,84,000.

(c) Gain/Loss from the disposal of the machine is not recorded. Therefore, an adjustment is required. The WDV of the machine disposed was (₹86,000 – 66,000) or ₹20,000. The amount realised, that the value assigned in the exchange transaction was ₹16,000. Therefore, the loss on the disposal of the machine was (₹20,000 – 16,000) or ₹14,000.

7. Gross loss by fire: ₹, 20,000, Insurance claim: ₹18,000 ad net loss is (₹20,000 – 18,000) or ₹2,000. Gross Loss will be recognised in the trading account, net loss will be recognised in the profit and loss account, and insurance claim will be recognised as an asset in the balance sheet.

8. (a) Audit fee is not appearing in the trial balance. Therefore, audit fee expense of ₹10,000 should be recognised in the profit and loss account, and accruals (liability) of the same amount should be recognised in the balance sheet.

(b) The trial balance shows advertisement expenses at ₹40,000. Advertisement expenses should be increased to (₹40,000 + 2,000) or ₹42,000.

Manufacturing, Trading, and Profit and Loss Account

For the Year ended on March 31, 2019

Particulars	Amount (₹)	Amount (₹)
I. INCOME		
Sales less return	30,00,000	
Discount allowed	(5,000)	
Provision for discount to customers	(11,400)	29,83,600
II. COST OF GOODS MANUFACTURED		
Purchases of raw materials less return		6,00,000
(Increase)/Decrease in inventories of raw materials (60,000 – 50,000)		(10,000)
(Increase)/Decrease in inventories of WIP (85,000 – 80,000)		(5,000
Wages		1,20,000
Electric power		60,000
Depreciation:		
Factory building	62,250	
Plant and machinery	3,000	65,250
Total II		8,30,250
III. COST OF GOODS SOLD		
Purchases of finished goods less return		14,00,000
(Increase)/Decrease in finished goods inventories (2,20,000 – 2,00,000)		(20,000)
Freight inward for finished goods		20,000
Goods lost by fire		(20,000)
Total III		22,10,250
IV. GROSS PROFIT (I–III)		7,73,350
V. OTHER INCOME		
Loss on sale of machinery		(4,000)
VI. OPERATING EXPENSES		
Salaries		1,50,000
Rates and taxes		30,000
Electricity charges for lights and fans		25,000
Office rent		30,000
Travelling expenses		1,00,000
Insurance premium		1,35,000
Advertisement expenses		42,000
Bad debts written off		10,000
Bad debt recovered		(2,000)
Provision for doubtful debts		30,000
General expenses		36,000

(Contd...)

Particulars	Amount (₹)	Amount (₹)
Postage and telegram		15,000
Depreciation on furniture and fixture		10,500
Loss by fire		2,000
Audit fee		10,000
Total (VI)		6,23,500
Operating Profit (IV + V – VI)		1,45,850

Balance sheet of A & Co. as on March 31, 2019

Particulars	Amount (₹)	Amount (₹)
ASSETS		
Non-current Assets		
Factory land		80,000
Factory building	60,000	
Provision for depreciation	(23,000)	37,000
Plant and Machinery	4,30,000	
Provision for depreciation	(2,46,250)	1,83,750
Furniture and fixtures	1,05,000	
Provision for depreciation	(40,500)	64,500
Total non-current assets		3,65,250
Current Assets Inventories:		
Raw materials	60,000	
Work-in-progress	85,000	
Finished goods	2,20,000	3,65,000
Sundry debtors	6,00,000	
Provision for doubtful debts	(30,000)	
Provision for doubtful debts	(11,400)	5,58,600
Insurance claim		18,000
Prepaid expenses		45,000
Cash-in-hand		20,000
Cash-in-bank		14,000
Total current assets		10,20,600
Total Assets		13,85,850
EQUITY AND LIABILITIES		
Capital		
Opening balance	10,00,000	
Drawings	(20,000)	9,80,000
Reserves	50,000	
Profit for the year	1,45,850	1,95,850
Total		11,75,850
Liabilities		
Non-current liabilities		Nil
Current Liabilities		
Sundry creditors		1,98,000
Outstanding liabilities (Accruals)		12,000
Total liabilities		2,10,000
Total equity and liabilities		13,85,850

Closing entries transfer balances in nominal accounts appearing in the adjusted trial balance to the manufacturing account, trading account and profit and loss account.

The closing entries close nominal accounts in the general ledger.

6.7 CLOSING ENTRIES

Closing entries are entries that are passed to transfer balances in nominal accounts appearing in the adjusted trial balance to the manufacturing account, trading account and profit and loss account. The closing entries close nominal accounts in the general ledger. The remaining accounts represent either assets or liabilities. Those are presented in the balance sheet. The following illustration shows closing entries.

Illustration 6.6 (Closing Entries)

The following are the closing entries for illustration 6.5 above:

Date	Particulars	LF	Dr. Amount (₹)	Cr. Amount (₹)
2005				
March 31	Manufacturing A/c		9,10,000	
	To Stock of raw material A/c			50,000
	To Stock of working progress A/c			80,000
	To Purchases of raw material A/c			6,00,000
	To Wages A/c			1,20,000
	To Electric power A/c			60,000
	(Being the accounts in the trial balance to be transferred to the manufacturing a/c, debit side)			
March 31	Manufacturing A/c		65,250	
	To Provision for depreciation on plant and machinery A/c			62,250
	To Provision for depreciation on factory building			3,000
	(Being provision for depreciation on plant and machinery at the rate of 15% and on building at the rate of 5%)			
March 31	Stock (closing) of raw material A/c		60,000	
	Stock (closing) of working progress A/c		85,000	
	To Manufacturing A/c			1,45,000
	(Being the value of a stock in hand as on March 31, 2000)			
March 31	Trading A/c		8,30,250	
	To Manufacturing A/c			8,30,250
	(Being the transfer of cost of goods manufactured during the accounting period)			
March 31	Trading A/c		16,20,000	
	To Stock of finished goods A/c			2,00,000
	To Purchases of finished goods A/c			14,00,000
	To Freight inward A/c			20,000
	(Being the accounts in the trial balance transferred to the trading A/c, debit side)			
March 31	Sales A/c		30,00,000	
	Goods lost by fire A/c		20,000	
	To Trading A/c			30,20,000
	(Being the accounts in the trial balance transferred to the trading a/c, credit side)			
March 31	Stock (closing) of finished goods A/c		2,20,000	
	To Trading A/c			2,20,000
	(Being the value of stock in hand as on March 31, 2000)			
March 31	Profit and loss A/c		5,94,000	
	To Salaries A/c			1,50,000
	To Rates and taxes A/c			30,000
	To Electricity charges A/c			25,000
	To Office rent A/c			30,000
	To Travelling expenses A/c			1,00,000
	To Insurance premium A/c			1,35,000
	To Advertisement expenses A/c			42,000

(Contd...)

Date	Particulars	LF	Dr. Amount (₹)	Cr. Amount (₹)
	To Bad debts A/c			10,000
	To Discount A/c			5,000
	To General expenses A/c			36,000
	To Post and telegram A/c			15,000
	To Loss by fire A/c			2,000
	To Loss on sale of plant and machinery			4,000
	To Audit fees			10,000
	(Being the various expense accounts transferred to the profit and loss A/c)			
March 31	Bad debt recovered A/c		2,000	
	To Profit and loss A/c			2,000
	(Being the bad debts recovered A/c transferred to the profit and loss A/c)			
March 31	Profit and loss A/c		51,900	
	To Provision for depreciation on furniture and fixtures A/c			10,500
	To Provision for doubtful debts A/c			30,000
	To Provision for discount A/c			11,400
	(Being various provisions created for the accounting year ending March 31, 2000 as per details below: Depreciation on F&F @10% Provision for doubtful debts @5% Provision for discount @2%)			
March 31	Profit and loss A/c		1,45,850	
	To Capital A/c			1,45,850
	(Being the transfer of net profit to the capital a/c)			

The profit and loss appropriation account shows the appropriation of profit brought forward from the previous period and profit (loss) earned incurred during the period.

Appropriation takes the form of transfer to reserves, interest on capital and distribution to owners.

6.8 PROFIT AND LOSS APPROPRIATION ACCOUNT

The profit and loss appropriation account shows the appropriation of profit brought forward from the previous period and profit (loss) earned incurred during the period. Appropriation takes the form of transfer to reserves, interest on capital and distribution to owners such as payment of dividend in case of a limited liability company.

REVIEW PROBLEMS

R6.1 Indicate whether the following statements are True or False:

(i) Closing stock of stock-in-trade is usually recorded in the books through a closing entry.

(ii) Both adjustment entries and closing entries are passed before drawing the financial statements.

(iii) Pre-paid expense is an asset.

(iv) Drawings of cash for personal use by the sole-proprietor is an equity transaction.

(v) Depreciation is a valuation allowance.

(vi) There is no difference in the characteristics of advance from customers and deferred revenue.

(vii) After preparation of the financial statements, nominal accounts are closed by transferring to the manufacturing account, trading account, and profit and loss account.

(viii) Provision for doubtful debts is a liability.

(ix) Unbilled revenue is presented in the balance sheet as a current liability.

(x) Distribution expenses are not included in the cost of goods sold.

R6.2 Fill in the blanks:

(i) The adjusted trial balance of an entity provides the following information: Opening stock of stock-in-trade: ₹50,000; Purchases: ₹6,00,000; Sales: ₹15,00,000; Wages: ₹60,000; Carriage inward: ₹10,000; Carriage outward: ₹20,000; Salaries: ₹1,00,000; Operating expenses (other than salaries and depreciation): ₹1,00,000 ; Finance Cost; ₹10,000; Capital: ₹2,00,000; Assets: ₹10,00,000; Liabilities: ₹2,50,000. Following additional information is provided: (a) Depreciation for the year: ₹80,000; (b) Goods lost by fire: ₹30,000 against which insurance claim of ₹20,000 is accepted by the insurance company (amount yet to be received); (c) Closing Stock ₹60,000 Gross Profit: ₹................, Net profit ₹................

(ii) An entity, which is in the merchandising business, has provided the following information: Sales less return: ₹10,00,000; Purchases less return: ₹6,00,000; Carriage inward: ₹20,000; Carriage outward: ₹30,000; wages: ₹50,000; salary ₹1,00,000; Other operating expenses ₹1,10,000; increase on the inventories of stock-in-trade ₹40,000; and Loss of stock-in-trade by fires: ₹60,000; and insurance claim received against that loss from fire: ₹50,000. The gross profit is ₹................

(iii) The unadjusted trial balance shows Plant and Machinery (Gross Block) at ₹5,00,000 and accumulated depreciation at ₹300,000.
The following additional information is provided: An item of Plant and Machinery was sold for ₹60,000 on the first day of the financial year. The cost of that item was ₹1,50,000 and accumulated depreciation on the date of sale was ₹1,10,000. Sale proceeds were credited directly to the plant and machinery account. No other adjustment was made for this transaction. Depreciation is to be provided at 10 per cent on the gross block. Before making the adjustments for the above, the net profit, using the data in the unadjusted trial balance, was reported at ₹2,00,000. After correcting the recording of the transaction and providing for depreciation, the net profit is ₹................

(iv) The following information is provided by an entity: Balances in un adjusted trial balance: Revenue: ₹10,00,000; Deferred Revenue (Opening balance): ₹75,000; and Unbilled revenue (opening balance): ₹55,000. The management estimated that at the year end, deferred revenue is ₹80,000 and unbilled revenue is ₹30,000. [Assume that the adjustment entries for the previous year was not reversed.] Revenue for the year is ₹................

(v) The trial balance shows revenue at ₹5,00,000. The unearned revenue at the end of the previous year was ₹10,000. However, the year-end trial balance does not show that figure. The entity estimates unearned revenue at the end of the current year at ₹15,000. The revenue for the current year to be recognised in the profit and loss account is ₹................

(vi) The trial balance shows the following figures: Trade receivables: ₹5,00,000; Provision for doubtful debts: ₹8,000; and Bad debt: ₹2,000. The entity presents bad debt as a separate line item in the statement of profit and loss. It maintains provision for doubtful debts at 2 per cent of trade receivables. The provision for doubtful debts to be recognised in the profit and loss account is ₹................

(vii) An entity, which follows the financial year from April 1 to March 31 of the following year, paid annual insurance premium of ₹24,000 on July 1, 2021. The prepaid insurance premium to be recognised as an asset in the balance sheet is ₹................

(viii) An entity has investment in the equity shares issued by a company. The notice for annual general meeting (AGM) of that company shows that the board of directors of that company has proposed a dividend of 10 per cent on the face value of shares. The aggregate face value of the shares held by the entity is ₹500,000. The AGM of that company is scheduled on September 20, 2022. The Board meeting of the entity in which the financial statements for 2021–2022 will be placed for approval is scheduled on September 5, 2022. The dividend income to be recognised in the statement of profit and loss for the year 2021–2022 is ₹................

(ix) In the current year, an entity purchased a machine for ₹500,000. It paid cash ₹400,000 and an old machine. The old machine acquired few years back at a cost of ₹200,000 and accumulated depreciation on the date of acquisition the new machine was ₹180,000. The transaction was recorded by debiting the plant and machinery account by the amount of cash paid for acquiring the new machine. The trial balance shows machinery account at ₹2,000,000 and accumulated depreciation at ₹800,000. The company provides full depreciation on the items of plant and machinery it holds of the balance sheet date at the rate of 10 per cent on gross block. The plant and machinery (net block) should be carried in in the balance sheet at ₹................

(x) The trial balance shows trade receivables at ₹800,000. The subsidiary ledger shows as credit balance of ₹100,000 against a customer. On investigation it is found that the customer paid excess amount which is refundable. The company maintains 2 per cent of amount outstanding against customers at the balance sheet date as provision for doubtful debts. The trial balance does not show provision of doubtful debts. The provision for doubtful debts to be created is ₹................

R 6.3 On April 1, 2018, Suraj acquired a business as a going concern from Chandni for a sum of ₹28,000. He took stock valued at ₹2,400, furniture and fittings valued at ₹2,540, building valued at ₹12,000 and trade debtors ₹2,560. He undertook to pay trade creditors amounting to ₹2,560.

In addition to the sum paid for the business, Suraj paid ₹2,000 into a business bank account.

At the end of the year (March 31, 2019), in addition to the balances arising from the above, the following balances were extracted from Suraj's books:

Particulars	*Amount* (₹)
Sales	86,980
Purchases	55,230
Carriage inward	1,250
Wages and salaries	8,700
Advertising	4,680
Rates and insurance	1,950
Electricity	870
Sundry office expenses	420
Debtors	6,580
Creditors	2,160
Cash-in-hand and balance at bank	560
Drawings	10,400
Discounts allowed to customers	560

Prepare Suraj's trading and profit and loss account for the year ended March 31, 2019 and a balance sheet as at that date, after taking into account the following additional information:

(i) Stock as at March 31, 2019 was valued at ₹4,560.
(ii) Building is to be depreciated by 5% and furniture and fittings by 20% of book value.
(iii) Wages and salaries ₹450 were outstanding.
(iv) Rates ₹300 were prepaid
(v) Provision for doubtful debts is to be made at 5% on sundry debtors.

R 6.4 A bookkeeper has submitted to you the following trial balance as at March 31, 2019 wherein the totals of debit and credit balances are not equal:

Particulars	*Debit amount* (₹)	*Credit amount* (₹)
Creditors	10,000	
Bills payable		560
Long-term loan from bank	5,000	

(Contd...)

Particulars	*Debit amount (₹)*	*Credit amount (₹)*
Capital account	45,400	
Sales		63,000
Purchase returns	500	
Discount earned	100	
Bad debt recovered	350	
Interest on investments	300	
Fixed assets	30,000	
Opening stock	7,500	
Trade receivables		20,500
Bills receivables	1,000	
Investments	5,000	
Cash-in-hand	500	
Cash-in-bank	1,000	
Drawings		900
Purchases	52,500	
Sales returns		1,000
Carriage inward	140	
Freight outward		200
Duty paid on purchases		160
Primary packing expenses	200	
Rent paid		300
Insurance paid	360	
Office and administrative expenses	1,320	
Discount allowed		200
Bad debts	500	
Interest on loan from bank		250
Delivery expenses	660	
Selling and distribution expenses	1,000	
Income tax paid	100	
Value added tax (VAT) collected	200	
Loose tools	200	
Apprentice premium received		50
Commission received		30
Total	1,63,830	87150

Required:

(i) Redraft the trial balance correctly as at March 31, 2019

(ii) Prepare a trading and profit and loss account for the year ended March 31, 2019, and balance sheet as at March 31, 2019, after considering the following adjustments:

(a) Closing stock was valued at ₹4,000

(b) Rent outstanding for March 2016: ₹60

(c) Insurance unexpired on March 31, 2016: ₹90

(d) Accrued interest on investment amounted to ₹150

(e) One-third of the commission received in respect of work to be done next year

(f) ₹125 is due for interest on bank loan

(g) Loose tools are valued at ₹80

(h) Provide for depreciation on fixed assets @10% per annum.

ASSIGNMENTS

1. Tick the correct answer:

(i) A suspense account is opened

(a) when the debit side total does not agree with the credit side total of the trial balance.

(b) when the debit side total does not agree with the credit side total, and the error could not be located till the preparation of the trial balance.

(c) when the debit side total and credit side total of the trial balance agree due to compensating error.

(d) when an error has occurred in adding up balances appearing in the trial balance.

(ii) Closing stock is recorded in the books of accounts through

(a) an adjustment entry.

(b) a closing entry.

(c) a closing entry or by adjusting purchases through an adjustment entry.

(d) an opening entry.

(iii) Accruals are recorded in the books of accounts through

(a) an adjustment entry.

(b) a closing entry.

(c) an opening entry.

(d) either a closing entry or an opening entry.

(iv) While making the trading and profit and loss accounts

(a) only nominal accounts are transferred to the trading and profit and loss accounts.

(b) only nominal accounts and opening stock are transferred to the trading and profit and loss accounts.

(c) all nominal and real accounts are transferred to the trading and profit and loss accounts.

(d) only real accounts are transferred to the trading and profit and loss accounts.

(v) The balance sheet should show the

(a) bank balance as per the bank statement.

(b) bank balance as per the cash book.

(c) bank balance either as per the bank statement, or as per the cash book, at the discretion of the management.

(d) bank balance as per the cash book, adjusted for cheques deposited but not collected till the balance sheet's date.

2. Indicate whether following sentences are True or False:

(i) Wages should be debited to the trading account.

(ii) Freight outward should be debited to the trading account.

(iii) Loss of stock by fire, before adjustment for insurance claims, should be credited to the trading account.

(iv) Prepaid expenses are a part of current assets.

(v) Closing stock, when appearing in the trial balance, should be taken directly to the balance sheet.

(vi) Prior-period adjustment should be taken directly to the balance sheet.

(vii) Provision for doubtful debts is a liability.

(viii) No depreciation should be charged if an item of depreciable has not been used during the reporting period.

(ix) Gross profit measures the performance of the enterprise in the market place.

(x) A change in depreciation method is a change in accounting estimate.

3. Fill in the blanks:

(i) The balance sheet dated December 31, 2005 shows expenses accrued (outstanding liability) on account of travelling expenses at ₹20,000. The balance in the travelling expenses account in the general ledger for the year 2006 shows a debit balance of ₹5,00,000. The management estimates expenses accrued (outstanding liability) on account of travelling as at December 31, 2006 are ₹30,000. The amount of travelling expenses to be recognised as an expense in the income statement for the year 2006 is ₹.................

(ii) Sunny Limited (SL) pays insurance premium for the manufacturing facility on 1 April every year. The insurance policy covers a period of one year. During the years 2005 and 2006, SL paid ₹24,00,000 and ₹30,00,000 towards insurance premium. SL should recognise ₹................ as insurance expense in the income statement for the year 2006 and should recognise ₹............... as.....................in the balance sheet as at December 31, 2006.

(iii) The balance sheet dated December 31, 2005 of Ruksha Limited (RL) shows receivables (gross) and provision for doubtful debts at ₹5,00,000 and ₹25,000, respectively. During the year 2006, RL has written off ₹5,000 as bad debt against the provision for doubtful debts. The balance as at December 31, 2006 in the receivables A/c in the general ledger is ₹8,00,000. RL, as a policy, maintains a provision for doubtful debts at 5% of the balance in the receivables A/c. RL has decided that from the year 2006, it will provide for discount (that it allows to customers for payment before the due date) at 1% of the balance in receivables A/c without violating the accounting convention. The income statement of RL for the year 2006 should be debited by ₹..........for provision for doubtful debts and by ₹.............for provision for discount.

(iv) Mona Limited (ML) is in merchandising business. There was no stock of goods at the beginning of the year 2006. During the year 2006 it purchased 1,00,000 units of goods in which it trades for ₹20,00,000. It incurred ₹40,000 towards freight inward and ₹2,00,000 towards wages to make the goods ready for sale. At the end of the year, 5,000 units were in stock. The closing stock of 5,000 units should be valued at ₹................

(v) Yashmin Limited (YL) is in merchandising business. The stock of goods at the beginning of the year 2006 was valued at ₹1,20,000. During the year 2006, it purchased 1,00,000 units of goods in which it trades for ₹30,00,000. It incurred ₹50,000 towards freight inward, ₹2,00,000 towards wages to make the goods ready for sale and ₹30,000 towards freight outward during the year 2006. At the end of the year, 5,000 units were in stock. During the year, 5,000 units were lost by fire for which the insurance company has accepted a claim of ₹1,50,000. The revenue for the year is recognised at ₹40,00,000. The gross profit for the year 2006 is ₹................

(vi) Diya Limited (DL) manufactures small motors for farm use. On July 1, 2006, it sold a machine that was purchased on January 1, 2000. The cost of the machine was ₹10,00,000. DL follows straight-line method of depreciation. The depreciation rate for plant and equipment is 10%. The income statement for the year shows that DL incurred a loss of ₹20,000 on the sale of the machine. DL sold the machine for ₹................

(vii) The bank reconciliation statement for the year 2006 shows cheques issued but not presented ₹1,50,000, cheques received but not credited 1,00,000, cheques deposited but dishonoured ₹20,000, dividends directly collected by bank ₹10,000, and bank charges not recorded in the cash book ₹5,000. The bank balance (credit balance) as at December 31, 2006, as per cash book, is ₹5,00,000. The bank balance of ₹............... should be shown as a..................... in the balance sheet as at December 31, 2006.

(viii) Mallika Limited (ML) assesses its tax liability for the year 2006 at ₹10,00,000. It estimates the deferred tax liability as at December 31, 2006 at ₹2,50,000 as against the deferred tax liability of ₹2,15,000 recognised in the balance sheet as at December 31, 2005. ML should recognise the tax expense in the income statement for the year 2006 at ₹................

4. Analytical questions:

4.1 The finance director of a large company was not quite agreeable to the Audit Committee's suggestion that bank reconciliation statements should be prepared fortnightly instead of the present practice of preparing bank reconciliation statement quarterly. What should be the appropriate frequency for the preparation of the bank reconciliation statement? Prepare a note explaining your position.

4.2 Withdrawal of the concept of 'extraordinary items' is a sharp shift from an age old accounting practice. Prepare a note explaining the possible reason for this change in approach.

4.3 According to an analyst "Deferred tax liability is nothing but an accrual. Therefore, it should be treated as a debt in analysing financial statements". Do you agree? Explain your position on this issue.

5. Problems:

5.1 Pass journal entries to rectify the following errors:

(a) A cheque of ₹1,000 received for loss of stock by fire had been deposited in the proprietor's bank account.

(b) An item of purchase of ₹236 was entered in the purchase day book as ₹326.

(c) The cost of a motor car purchased for ₹1,50,000 had been debited to the purchase account.

(d) ₹1,200 received from a debtor was debited to the sundry debtors account.

(e) The sales day book was undercast by ₹500.

(f) Discount of ₹200 allowed to a customer was debited to the sundry debtors account.

(g) Wages of ₹10,000 paid towards construction of a building for internal use was debited to the wages account.

(h) ₹500 spent on repairs to machinery was debited to the plant and machinery account.

(i) ₹325 paid for freight on machinery was debited to the freight account for ₹532.

5.2 The cash book of Alpha Ltd. shows a bank balance of ₹25,800, which is not in agreement with the balance appearing in the bank statement issued by the bank. An examination of the cash book and bank statement disclosed the following:

(a) Cheques deposited amounting to ₹5,000 not yet collected.

(b) Cheques issued amounting to ₹7,500, not yet presented for payment.

(c) A cheque for ₹1,200 received from a customer, returned by the bank but not recorded in the cash book.

(d) Dividend amounting to ₹750 collected directly by the bank.

(e) Bank charges of ₹500 debited by the bank.

(f) A cheque for ₹2,500 issued by Alpha & Co. wrongly debited by the bank.

(g) A bill amounting to ₹2,000 discounted, subsequently dishonoured by the bank but not recorded in the cash book.

Required:

(i) Prepare the bank reconciliation statement.

(ii) Pass necessary adjustment entries.

(iii) Prepare the bank reconciliation statement after adjustment.

5.3 The bank statement issued by the bank shows an overdraft of ₹10,000 in the account of Gamma Ltd. This balance is not in agreement with the balance as per the cash book. An examination of the cash book and bank statement disclosed the following:

(a) Cheques deposited amounting to ₹6,000 not yet collected.
(b) Cheques issued amounting to ₹8,000 not yet presented.
(c) Dividend amounting to ₹1,200 collected directly by the bank.
(d) Bank charges of ₹400 debited by the bank.
(e) A cheque of ₹1,500 received from a customer, returned by the bank but not recorded in the cash book.

Required:

(i) Prepare the bank reconciliation statement.
(ii) Pass necessary adjustment entries.
(iii) Show the bank balance that appears in the balance sheet.

5.4. From the following trial balance, prepare (a) manufacturing account; (b) trading and profit and loss account; and (c) balance sheet:

Trial Balance as at March 31, 2019

Particulars	*Dr.* (₹)	*Cr.* (₹)
Wages	20,000	
Opening stock—raw materials	5,710	
Purchases	88,274	
Carriage inward	3,686	
Repairs	6,000	
Salaries—factory	2,100	
Salaries—general	1,000	
Rates and taxes	2,240	
Travelling expenses	3,550	
Insurance—factory	700	
Insurance—general	80	
Bad debts	410	
General expenses	2,942	
Carriage outward	9,424	
Other assets	1,13,884	
Drawings	1,000	
Opening stock—finished goods	56,000	
Opening stock—work-in-progress	1,000	
Sales		1,74,000
Opening profit and loss account balance		12,000
Capital		1,31,000
Sale of scrap		1,000
	3,18,000	3,18,000

Closing stocks: Raw materials: ₹5,272; Finished goods: ₹34,324; Work-in-progress: ₹10,000

5.5 The following is the trial balance of Anindita as on March 31, 2019:

Particulars	*Debit amount* (₹)	*Credit amount* (₹)
Fixed assets	54,000	
Depreciation on fixed assets	6,000	
Cost of goods sold	1,11,600	

(*Contd...*)

Particulars	*Debit amount (₹)*	*Credit amount (₹)*
Closing stock	8,400	
Trade debtors	40,000	
Trade creditors		19,400
Bills payable		1,120
Bills receivables	2,000	
12% investments (Purchased on July 1, 2015)	10,000	
Interest on investments		900
Accrued interest on investments	300	
Interest	500	
Loan from bank		800
Cash-in-hand	1,000	
Cash-at-bank	2,000	
Drawings	2,000	
Interest on drawings		200
Interest on capital	8,000	
Capital		87,800
Sales		1,46,000
Return inward	2,000	
Carriage outward	400	
Discount allowed	400	
Discount received		200
Bad debts	1,300	
Rent	720	
Outstanding rent		120
Insurance	540	
Prepaid insurance	180	
Other office and administrative expenses	2,640	
Selling and distribution expenses	8,980	
Provision for doubtful debts		5,300
Provision for discount on debtors		1,120
Total	2,62,960	2,62,960

Required: Prepare a Trading and Profit and Loss Account and Balance Sheet.

5.6 Mr. A, a shopkeeper, had prepared the following trial balance from his ledger as on March 31, 2006:

Particulars	*Dr. (₹)*	*Cr. (₹)*
Purchases	3,10,000	
Sales		4,15,000
Stock of goods as on April 1, 2005	50,000	
Cash-in-hand	2,100	
Cash-in-bank	12,000	
Mr. A's capital		2,88,600
Drawings	4,000	
Rates and taxes	5,000	
Salaries	32,000	
Postage	11,500	
Salesmen's commission	35,000	
Insurance	9,000	
Advertising	17,000	
Furniture and fittings	22,000	
Printing and stationery	3,000	

(Contd...)

Particulars	Dr. (₹)	Cr. (₹)
Motor car	48,000	
Bad debts	2,000	
Cash discounts	4,000	
General expenses	14,000	
Carriage inwards	10,000	
Carriage outwards	22,000	
Wages	20,000	
Outstanding liability for expenses	11,000	
Sundry creditors		40,000
Sundry debtors	1,00,000	
	7,43,600	7,43,600

Additional information:

(a) Cost of goods in stock as on March 31, 2006: ₹1,45,000.

(b) Mr. A had withdrawn goods worth ₹5,000 during the year.

(c) Printing and stationery expenses of ₹11,000 relating to the 2004–2005 accounting year had not been provided in that year, but were paid in this year by debiting outstanding liabilities.

(d) Purchases include purchase of furniture worth ₹10,000.

(e) Debtors include ₹5,000 bad debts.

(f) Creditors include a balance of ₹4,000 to the credit of LM Corporation in respect of which it has been decided and settled with the party to pay only ₹1,000.

(g) Sales include goods worth ₹15,000 sold out to SM & Co. on approval and remaining unsold as on March 31, 2006. The cost of the goods was ₹10,000.

(h) Provision for bad debts is to be created at 5% of sundry debtors.

(i) Depreciate furniture and fittings by 10% and the motor car by 20%.

(j) Salesmen are entitled to a commission of 10% on total sales.

Required: Prepare the trading and profit and loss accounts for the year ended on March 31, 2006 and the balance sheet as on that date.

5.7 The following balance amounts on March 31, 2019, are extracted from the books of Mr. Amritlal, a manufacturer-cum-trader:

Particulars	Amount (₹)
Stock of raw materials, April 1, 2018	25,500
Stock of work-in-progress, April 1, 2018	30,700
Stock of finished goods, April 1, 2018	40,500
Stock of stores (factory), April 1, 2018	2,100
Cash-in-hand	1,600
Cash-in-bank	32,800
Purchase of raw materials	3,12,000
Purchase of finished goods	1,27,400
Purchase of factory stores	12,300
Factory wages	2,94,600
Salary of works manager	15,000
Office salaries and wages	86,400
Carriage inwards (raw materials)	32,300
Carriage inwards (finished goods)	10,600
Carriage outwards	3,700
Rent and rates (factory)	2,800
Rent and rates (general)	2,400
Electric charges (factory)	3,800

(Contd...)

Particulars	Amount (₹)
Electric charges (general)	1,700
Insurance (factory)	2,100
Insurance (general)	700
Travelling expenses	4,300
Brokerage on purchases (raw materials)	3,100
Commission on sales	2,600
Advertisement	12,400
Sales	10,36,500
Return outward (finished goods)	12,200
Return inwards (finished goods)	23,700
Repairs and renewals (factory)	8,500
Trade expenses	10,200
Provision for bad debts	2,600
Bad debts	1,800
Plant and machinery	3,26,400
Furniture and fixtures	57,300
Sundry trade debtors	65,800
Sundry trade creditors	1,53,400
Loose tools	8,400
Bills receivable	4,600
Bills payable	5,400
Loan on mortgage (October 2018 @6% p.a.)	1,20,000
Income tax (for 2017–2018 financial year)	10,000
Income tax (in advance for 2018–2019 financial year)	8,000
Amritlal's capital	2,80,000
Amritlal's drawings	22,000

In addition, you are given the following information and particulars:

1. Closing stock on March 31, 2019:

Raw materials	₹28,700
Work-in-progress	₹33,300
Finished goods	₹43,800
Factory stores	₹2,900

2. Purchase of finished goods for ₹500 utilised for private use of Amritlal has not been duly adjusted.
3. Two bills receivable for ₹200 and ₹300, respectively has been dishonoured and await adjustment.
4. A quarter of advertisement represents payment in advance to advertising agents.
5. Depreciation on plant and machinery and furniture and fixture @10% and loose tools @20% to be provided.
6. Provision for bad debts should be maintained at 5% of the debtors.
7. Interest on mortgage for 6 months to be provided.

Required: Prepare a manufacturing account, trading and profit and loss account for the year ending March 31, 2019 and the balance sheet as at that date.

5.8 From the following trial balance of Manorama, prepare the manufacturing, trading and profit and loss account for the year ended March 31, 2016, and a balance sheet as on that date after giving effect to the adjustments given below:

Trial balance as on March 31, 2019

Particulars	Debit amount (₹)	Credit amount (₹)
Capital account as at April 1, 2018		36,600
Drawings account	5,000	
Purchases	1,05,250	

(Contd...)

Particulars	*Debit amount (₹)*	*Credit amount (₹)*
Rates and taxes	1,250	
Salaries	5,000	
Carriage	1,000	
Fuel and cool	700	
Factory insurance	300	
Advertisement	1,000	
Factory power	800	
Bad debt written off	500	
Cash discount allowed	100	
Sundry expenses	175	
Opening stock—raw materials	3,000	
Opening stock—finished goods	2,500	
Patents	600	
Postage and telegrams	650	
Wages	1,750	
Cash discount received		750
Factory buildings	10,000	
Furniture and fixtures	2,575	
Plant and Machinery	4,750	
Sundry debtors	9,350	
4% government promissory notes (subscribed on April 1, 2018)	1,000	
Sundry creditors		5,250
Sales		1,26,650
Cash-in-hand	2,275	
Cash-at-bank	9,725	
Total	1,69,250	1,69,250

Note: Closing stock as at March 31, 2019:

Raw materials: ₹2,500
Finished goods: ₹2,000

Adjustments:

(i) Depreciation/amortisation to be provided at the following rates:

Plant and machinery: 10% Patents: 10%
Building: 2.5% Furniture: 5%

(ii) Provide 2.5% on debtors for doubtful debts.

(iii) Purchase invoice aggregating ₹1,250 were omitted to be entered in the purchase day book.

(iv) Debtors include ₹250 due from the proprietor.

(v) The amount of ₹250 received in respect of a private loan advanced by the proprietor was wrongly credited to sundry debtors account.

(vi) Purchase invoices of the value of ₹3,750 were entered in the purchase day book on March 29, 2019, but the goods in respect thereof were received on April 3, 2019.

(vii) An amount of ₹175 received from a debtor was wrongly credited to sales account.

(viii) The annual interest on government promissory notes accrued due on March 31, 2019 but was collected only in April 2019.

(ix) Carriage includes ₹400 towards outward charges.

5.9 Mr. X, a trader, has extracted the following trial balance from his books as on March 31, 2019:

Sl. No.	Particulars	Dr. Amount (₹)	Cr. Amount (₹)
1.	Purchases	4,00,000	
2.	Sundry debtors	1,50,000	
3.	Cash-in-hand	4,000	
4.	Cash-in-bank	8,000	
5.	Rent, rates and taxes	3,000	
6.	Insurance premium	9,000	
7.	Salaries	42,000	
8.	Carriage outward	21,000	
9.	Carriage inward	18,000	
10.	Sundry creditors		50,000
11.	Claim recoverable	5,000	
12.	Advertisement expense	9,000	
13.	Furniture and fixtures	23,000	
14.	Deposit with supplier	6,000	
15.	Office equipment	10,000	
16.	Bills receivable	6,000	
17.	Bad debts	4,000	
18.	Sales		7,00,000
19.	Opening stock	30,000	
20.	Electricity expenses	2,000	
		7,50,000	7,50,000

The following additional information is provided:

1. A purchase invoice for ₹15,000, received from a sundry creditor, has not been entered through oversight.
2. The claim recoverable has been settled with the insurance company for ₹2,000.
3. Depreciation is to be provided on the straight-line method on furniture and fixtures and office equipment at 5%. The original costs were:
   Furniture and fixtures ₹30,000
   Office equipment ₹15,000
4. Goods costing ₹5,000 were dispatched on 29 March. The sale, however, took place on April 2, 2019, when an invoice for ₹7,500, was raised against the customer.
5. Insurance premium includes a prepaid amount of ₹1,000.
6. The deposit with a supplier was made on October 1, 2018. It carried interest @12% p.a.
7. Two bills receivable from customers of ₹700 and ₹1,300 were dishonoured on March 30, 2019. These had earlier been discounted with the bank.
8. Provide 2% on sundry debtors for doubtful debts.
9. Physical stock of goods in hand on March 31, 2019, at cost was ₹1,00,000.

Required: Prepare the trading and profit and loss accounts and balance sheet from the given information.

5.10 Hari Singh has extracted the following trial balance from his books as on March 31, 2019:

Sl. No.	Particulars	Dr. Amount (₹)	Cr. Amount (₹)
1.	Drawing	16,000	
2.	Cash	6,760	
3.	Petty cash	1,000	
4.	Leasehold land	20,000	

(Contd...)

Sl. No.	Particulars	Dr. Amount (₹)	Cr. Amount (₹)
5.	Opening stock at market value	50,000	
6.	Salary	12,000	
7.	Sundry debtors	50,000	
8.	Wages	40,000	
9.	Bank	21,000	
10.	Capital		34,000
11.	Rent	9,000	
12.	Electricity	6,000	
13.	Motor car	10,240	
14.	Advertising	9,000	
15.	Sundry creditors		35,000
16.	Purchases	4,00,000	
17.	Postage and telephone	3,000	
18.	Sales		6,00,000
19.	Discounts	11,400	
20.	General charges	4,000	
21.	Petty cash expenses	9,600	
22.	Suspense		10,000
		6,79,000	6,79,000

Additional information:

1. Closing stock at market value as on March 31, 2019 was ₹80,000 (cost ₹75,000). Stock is being valued on a consistent basis of cost or market price, whichever is lower.
2. The petty cash balance represents the month-end imprest amount. As on the closing date, the petty cashier had vouchers totalling ₹400 for which he had not received reimbursement from the main cashier.
3. Discounts allowed amounting to ₹1,000 had been posted to the debit of sundry debtors.
4. Cash withdrawn from bank ₹4,000 had not been entered in the bank column of the cash book.
5. The sales account had been undercast on the credit side by ₹4,000.
6. The motor car which had been purchased in 2015–2016 was being depreciated at 20% on the reducing balance method. The original cost of the car is ₹20,000. The management estimates the useful life at 17 years (approx.) from the date the car was ready for use. It is now decided to charge depreciation at 6% on the straight–line method and to make this change effective from the year of purchase of the car.
7. Leasehold land was purchased during the year. On the date of purchase, the unexpired period of the lease was five years.
8. No entry had been passed in the books for stock withdrawn from the business by the proprietor valued at ₹10,000.
9. Telephone bills amounting to ₹1,000 remain unpaid.

Required: Prepare the trading, profit and loss account and balance sheet of the business of Hari Singh for the year ended on March 31, 2019.

5.11 After making necessary adjustments given below, prepare trading and profit and loss account for the year ending December 31, 2019, and the balance sheet as on that date from the following trial balance extracted from the books of Prem Jaipuria:

Trial balance as on December 31, 2019

Particulars	Amount (₹)	Particulars	Amount (₹)
Drawings	6,300	Capital	1,50,000
Cash-in-hand	3,870	Discount received	2,985
Bills receivables	1,860	9% loan account	15,000
Land and building	30,000	Purchase returns	1,455
Depreciation on land and building	2,580	Sales	2,81,505
Furniture	5,130	Provision for bad debts	4,650
Wages	46,875	Sundry creditors	18,675
Discount	3,960		
Office expenses	6,525		
Stock on December 31, 2018	60,255		
Purchase (adjusted)	1,35,375		
Stock on December 31, 2019	63,705		
Carriage	5,175		
General expenses	7,680		
Sales returns	1,920		
Plant	18,600		
Depreciation on plant	3,000		
Taxes	3,630		
Debtors	65,745		
Bad debts	1,380		
Insurance	705		
	4,74,270		4,74,270

Adjustments:

(i) Stock at the end includes stock received on consignment ₹3,500.

(ii) Depreciation on plant was calculated at 10% p.a. on the straight-line method instead of the written down value method.

(iii) Debtors included:

(a) Amount due from Sound Ltd. ₹3,745 considered as definitely good

(b) Amount due from Hopeless Ltd. ₹2,000 considered as definitely bad

(c) Amount due from Rambharose Ltd. ₹100 considered definitely doubtful.

(iv) It was decided to make provision for doubtful debts at 5% on debtors.

(v) Stock of ₹10,000 was burnt by fire on 20th December; claim of ₹4,000 is acceptable by the insurance company.

(vi) Loan of ₹4,000 was repaid on June 30, 2019, and ₹5,000 was repaid on September 30, 2019.

(vii) Depreciate furniture at 5% p.a.

CHAPTER 7

FIXED ASSETS

CHAPTER OBJECTIVES

The objectives of this chapter is to introduce to readers the nature and accounting for fixed assets. In particular, the objective is developing and understanding of:

- Recognition of property, plant and equipment (PP&E);
- Initial measurement of property, plant and equipment (PP&E);
- Subsequent expenditure on an existing item of property, plant and equipment (PP&E);
- Subsequent measurement of property, plant and equipment (PP&E);
- Measurement of right-of-use assets;
- Intangible assets—nature, recognition and measurement;
- Natural resources—nature, accounting for exploration costs.

7.1 PP&E: RECOGNITION PRINCIPLES

7.1.1 Recognition Criteria

Characteristics of PP&E

An asset that is classified as property, plant, and equipment (PP&E) is:

- A tangible asset that is owned by the firm,
- It is used for more than one annual accounting period,
- It is used for production, administration or for earning rent, and
- It is not consumed during production or sold in the ordinary course of business.

Examples are land, factory and office building, furniture and fixtures, plant and machinery, vehicle, and computer hardware.

Safety and environmental equipment

Items of PP&E may be acquired for safety or environmental reasons. The acquisition of such an item although does not directly increase the future economic benefits of the existing items of PP&E, it qualifies for recognition as an asset because it enables an entity to derive future economic benefits from related assets in excess of what could be derived had those items not been acquired.

An item of PP&E is a tangible asset owned by the firm, which the firm uses for more than one annual accounting period for production, administration or for earning rent.

An item of PP&E is recognised as an asset, if and only if, it is probable that future economic benefits will flow to the entity and the cost of the item can be measured reliably.

EXAMPLE 7.1 (Safety and environment equipment)

Fact pattern: A chemical manufacturer installs new chemical handling processes to comply with environmental requirements for the production and storage of dangerous chemicals.

Discussion: Related plant enhancements are recognised as an asset because without them the entity is unable to manufacture and sell chemicals.

Stores and spares

Spare parts and servicing equipment are usually classified as inventory. The cost of these items is recognised as expense in the statement of profit and loss when consumed. However, major spare parts and stand-by equipment qualify as PP&E when the entity expects to use them for more than one accounting period. For example, a pump used in an item of equipment qualifies as PP&E if, the entity expects to use it for more than one accounting period. Similarly, if the spare parts and servicing equipment can be used only in connection with an item of PP&E, they are accounted for as PP&E. Those spare parts are usually called insurance spares. Although they are normally acquired along with the item of equipment, they may also be acquired later.

Recognition criteria

An entity recognises the cost of an item of PP&E as an asset if and only if:

(a) it is probable that future economic benefits associated with the item will flow to the entity; and
(b) the cost of the item can be measured reliably.

Firms apply the above criteria in evaluating expenditures incurred:

(a) initially to acquire or construct an item of PP&E; and
(b) subsequently to add or replace parts (or an item), or service it.

7.1.2 Unit of Measure

It may be appropriate to aggregate individually insignificant items such as moulds, tools and dies, and to apply the recognition criteria to the aggregate value. Entities often decide to recognise cost of small items of PP&E (say, costing ₹5,000 or less) as expenses in the accounting period in which the asset is acquired.

Entities apply judgement in deciding which of the items of PP&E should be aggregated.

EXAMPLE 7.2 (Unit of measure)

Fact pattern: An entity has constructed a connecting road from highway to the factory for easy movement of goods and people. The local government has given permission for constructing the road subject to the condition that the entity would transfer the control of the road to the local government.

Discussion: The entity has no control on the road. Therefore, it cannot recognise the road as its asset. Recognising the expenditure as expense for the period in which it is incurred would distort the operating results and financial position presented in financial statements. Therefore, the expenditure should be capitalised and allocated to the assets that constitute the project.

7.1.3 Component Accounting

An entity should allocate the cost of an item of PP&E to its significant parts and recognise them separately.

An entity should allocate the cost of an item of PP&E to its significant parts and recognise them separately. The objective is to improve the accuracy of the depreciation accounting and replacement accounting. For example, it may be appropriate to recognise the airframe and engines of an aircraft as separate items and to depreciate them separately. Usually, a component is considered significant if its cost exceeds 10% of the total cost of the asset. A significant part of an item of property, plant and equipment may have a useful life and a depreciation method that are the same as those of another significant part of that same item. Such parts may be grouped in determining the depreciation charge.

7.2 PP&E: INITIAL MEASUREMENT

Initial measurement refers to the measurement while recording an asset immediately after acquisition.

7.2.1 Measurement Principle

At initial recognition, items of PP&E should be measured at the acquisition cost.

At initial recognition items of PP&E should be measured at the acquisition cost.

7.2.2 Cost Elements

The cost of an item of PP&E comprises of the purchase price, directly attributable costs, and the initial estimate of the dismantling costs.

The cost of an item of PP&E comprises of:

- Purchase price, including import duties and non-refundable purchase taxes, after deducting trade discounts and rebates.
- Any costs directly attributable to bringing the asset to the location, and the condition necessary for it to be capable of operating in the manner intended by the management.
- The initial estimate of the costs of dismantling and removing the item and restoring the site on which it is located.

7.2.3 Purchase Price

The purchase is the *cash price equivalent* at the recognition date.

If the supplier usually charges a lower price for cash sales, that lower price is the purchase price even if the entity has purchased the asset on credit by paying a price higher than the cash sales price. The difference between the price payable to the supplier and the cash sales price is recognised as interest over the credit period using the effective interest rate method.

Liquidated damages and penalty: The amount of liquidated damage should be recognised as 'Other Income' in the statement of profit and loss and should not be deducted from the cost of the asset. However, if an enterprise recovers compensation from the supplier for lower performance as compared to the promised or standard performance, the amount should be deducted from the purchase price of the equipment.

Time barred payment: Liability ceases to exist when an unclaimed amount that is lying against a supplier of equipment becomes time barred under the law. The amount of the liability so extinguished should be recorded as a reduction in the purchase price of the item of fixed asset.

A cost is directly attributable to the acquisition of an item of PP&E if it could be avoided had the entity not acquired the asset.

7.2.4 Directly Attributable Costs

A cost is directly attributable if it could be avoided had the entity not acquired the asset.

Table 7.1 blow lists examples of costs that are directly attributable and those that are not directly attributable.

TABLE 7.1 Examples of Costs that are Directly attributable and those that are not Directly Attributable

Directly Attributable	*Not Directly Attributable*
1. Costs of employee benefits arising directly from the construction or acquisition of the item of PP&E	1. Costs of opening a new facility
2. Costs of site preparation	2. Costs of introducing a new product or service (including costs of advertising and promotional activities)
3. Initial delivery and handling costs	3. Costs of conducting business in a new location or with a new class of customer (including costs of staff training)
4. Installation and assembly costs	4. Costs to train employees to operate the new piece of equipment
5. Costs of testing before putting into use	5. Administration and other general overheads
6. Professional fees	6. Abnormal loss incurred during the construction of the asset.
7. Directly attributable borrowing costs only for the construction period	7. Directly attributable borrowing costs after completion of the construction

Cost of testing: Costs of testing after deducting the net proceeds from selling any items produced while getting the asset ready for use is included in the cost of the item of PP&E.

A revision in the accounting for cost of testing is proposed. It is likely that the concerned IFRS will be revised. The revision requires that the sale proceeds of the items produced during testing should be recognised as revenue and the cost of production (excluding the depreciation of the asset which is under testing) should be recognised as the cost of sales of the items produced and sold.

Directly attributable borrowing costs are included in the cost of an item of PP&E if, it takes substantial period of time to get the item ready for intended use.

Cost of developing the land for making it suitable for intended use should be included in the cost of the land.

Borrowing costs: Directly attributable borrowing costs–interest and other costs incurred to arrange the borrowing, are included in the cost of an item of PP&E if, it takes substantial period of time (usually, one year or more) to get the item ready for intended use. Borrowing costs for the period of construction should be capitalised. It is not necessary that the borrowing should be specific to the acquisition of the asset. The true test is whether the borrowing could be avoided had the asset not been acquired.

Costs not to be added to the carrying amount of an existing asset:

Following costs are not added to the carrying amount of an existing asset:

- Costs incurred while an item capable of operating in the manner intended by management has yet to be brought into use or is operated at less than full capacity.
- Initial operating losses such as those incurred while demand for the output of the item builds up.
- Costs of relocating or reorganising part or all of an entity's operations.

Land development cost

Cost of developing the land for making it suitable for intended use should be included in the cost of the land.

Allocation of composite cost

Where several fixed assets are purchased for a consolidated price, the consideration should be apportioned to the various assets on a fair basis as determined by a competent valuer. For example, the cost of land and building purchased together should be allocated to land and building in proportion to their fair value (FV) unless the FV of the land is immaterial or by appraisal method.

Where several fixed assets are purchased for a consolidated price, the consideration should be apportioned to the various assets on a fair basis as determined by a competent valuer.

Cessation of accumulating cost against an item of PP&E

The accumulation of costs commences when the management commits to the acquisition of the item of fixed asset. It ceases when the asset is substantially ready for use. For example, when only some modification of the interior decoration of a building is left, it is deemed to be substantially complete and capitalisation of expenses on the building should be ceased.

The accumulation of costs commences when the management commits to the acquisition of the item of fixed asset and ceases when the asset is substantially ready for use.

EXAMPLE 7.3 (Cost of building)

Fact pattern: Baidehi Limited (BL) has purchased a building for ₹2 crore (20 million). It incurred the following additional expenditures to make the building ready for the intended use:

(a) Amount paid to an advocate to search the title of the land and building: ₹20,000
(b) Amount paid towards registration charges: ₹20 lakh (2 million)
(c) Amount paid to 'vastu' expert to suggest modifications in the building: ₹1,00,000
(d) Amount paid to an architect to design and supervise modifications: ₹10,00,000
(e) Cost of demolishing a part of the building for reconstruction: ₹1,00,000
(f) Cost of modifications: ₹40,00,000

The fair value (at the date of acquisition) of the land on which the building is constructed is estimated at ₹1.2 crore (12 million).

Discussion: The acquisition cost of the building is

Cost Elements	*Amount (₹)*
Purchase price (2.00 – 1.2) crores	80,00,000
Cost of searching the title [₹20,000 × (80/200)]	8,000
Cost of registration [20,00,000 × (80/200)]	8,00,000
Amount paid to Vastu expert	1,00,000

Cost of dismantling is included in the cost of the building as dismantling was necessary to make the building ready for intended use.

EXAMPLE 7.4 (Modification cost)

Fact pattern: Vasudevan Ltd. (VL) had purchased an old building for ₹10,00,000. The company intended to use it as a training centre. It incurred ₹4,00,000 to modify the building to make it suitable for the intended use.

Discussion: The cost of modification should be included in the cost of the building, as the expenditure is incurred to make the building ready for intended use. Accordingly, VL should record the asset at ₹14,00,000.

EXAMPLE 7.5 (Abnormal loss)

Fact pattern: Parthiv Patel Limited (PPL) had purchased a building with land for ₹25,00,000. It allocated the cost between land and building using appraisal method. The company recognised land at ₹15,00,000 and building at ₹10,00,000. Immediately after purchase, it received a notice from the Ahmedabad Municipal Corporation (AMC) advising the company to demolish the unauthorised extension. PPL incurred an expenditure of ₹10,000 for demolishing the unauthorised extension. The management estimates that the company paid ₹1,00,000 for the unauthorised portion to be demolished.

Discussion: The demolition was not contemplated at the time of acquisition. Therefore, the cost incurred for demolishing the unauthorised portion of the building is in the nature of abnormal loss. PPL should recognise the cost of demolition (₹10,000) as an expense in the statement of profit and loss for the year in which the expenditure is incurred. In addition, it should write down the carrying amount of the building by estimated cost of the demolished portion (₹1,00,000) and recognise the impairment loss in the statement of profit and loss.

EXAMPLE 7.6 (Abnormal loss)

Fact pattern: Shruti Limited (SL) purchased a second-hand car for office use. At the time of purchase, the company estimated that it would incur an additional expenditure of ₹1,00,000 to make the car ready for use. The actual expenditure incurred was ₹2,50,000. The details of repair bill show that ₹1,30,000 were incurred to repair an accidental damage which was camouflaged so well that it was not detected during the pre-purchase inspection.

Discussion: The repair of the accidental damage was not contemplated at the time of the purchase of the second-hand car. Therefore, an expenditure of ₹1,30,000 attributed to repair the accidental damage is similar to abnormal loss. Therefore, it should not be included in the cost of the car. It should be recognised as an expense in the profit and loss account in which the expenditure was incurred. The balance amount of ₹1,20,000) should be included in the cost of the car, as it was incurred for repair and modifications contemplated at the time of purchase of the car to make it ready for the intended use The original estimate of ₹100,000 has no bearing on the accounting for the acquisition cost, although that had a bearing on the decision to purchase the car.

EXAMPLE 7.7 (Relocation cost)

Fact pattern: Lakshita Limited (LL) is engaged in manufacturing leather products. Its factory is located at Topsia in Kolkata. The state government, as a policy, has decided to shift leather units to the outskirts of the city and has developed a leather complex. In order to comply with the government's directive, LL has decided to shift its manufacturing facility to the leather complex.

Discussion: The relocation cost should not be added to the carrying amount of the assets of the factory, as it will not benefit LL in terms of either increase in revenue or decrease in cost. The expenditure should be recognised as an expense for the period in which it is incurred. Drawing analogy from recognising safety and environmental equipment, it can be argued that the relocation cost should be recognised as an asset, as LL would not be allowed to operate the factory at its present location. However, capitalisation of the expenditure on relocating an item of PP&E is not considered as good accounting practice.

EXAMPLE 7.8 (Relocation cost)

Fact pattern: Ishika Limited (IL) has incurred an expenditure of ₹5 million to change the plant layout. The objective is to improve the flow of material from one workstation to another. It is expected that the modification will reduce the synthetic time (number of hours to produce one unit of the product) of production and will also reduce the material handling cost.

Discussion: The expenditure should be recognised as expense in the statement of profit and loss of the period in which the expenditure is incurred. The expenditure is not expected to increase economic benefits embedded in the items of PP&E.

EXAMPLE 7.9 (Relocation cost)

Fact pattern: The manufacturing facility of Sayantani Limited (SL) was located in an area which is a victim of flood every year. As a result, the facility could be used only for ten months in a year. In the current year, SL has relocated the factory in another district to ensure that the facility can be used for all the 12 months of the year. It incurred an expenditure of ₹4 million (excluding the cost of land and building in the new location) to relocate the factory.

Discussion: The expenditure should be recognised as expense in the statement of profit and loss for the period in which the expenditure is incurred. The expenditure is not expected to increase economic benefits embedded in items of PP&E.

EXAMPLE 7.10 (Testing cost)

Fact pattern: Hina Printers Limited (HPL) has imported a sophisticated printing machine. The machine requires adjustments to achieve the printing quality desired by customers with minimum waste, using the papers available in India. During test run, it has incurred cost of ₹1,00,000 and earned income of ₹10,000 through sale of the printed material as waste.

Discussion: As per the current accounting practice (₹100,000 – 10,000) or ₹90,000 should be included in the cost of the printing machine. However, if the concerned IFRS is revised based on the proposed revision, ₹10,000 should be recognised as revenue and ₹1,00,000 should be recognised as cost of sales.

EXAMPLE 7.11 (Testing cost)

Fact pattern: Nandini Cables Limited (NCL) imported equipment to produce cables. After installation, the equipment could not produce cables of intended quality and size. NCL started negotiating with the supplier to rectify or replace the equipment. This turned into a long-drawn dispute. In order to mitigate the financial loss, the firm started producing and marketing sub-quality cables, until a settlement with the supplier could be reached. The production and sale of sub-standard wires resulted in loss because the direct cost of production was higher than the sales realisation.

Discussion: NCL started commercial production when it started production and sale of sub-standard cables because it had produced quantity much higher than what is usually produced during the test run. Expenses incurred after the commencement of commercial production should not be capitalised. Therefore, the loss incurred on sale of low-quality cables should not be included in the cost of the equipment.

EXAMPLE 7.12 (Start-up cost)

Fact pattern: Laboni Hotels Limited (LHL) has constructed a hotel in a newly developed township called Kolkata Riverside. The hotel has 200 rooms and 50 service apartments. The construction of the hotel was complete in time. However, the township project is yet to be ready, and the industrial park has been delayed by a year. As a result, the occupancy rate of the hotel is abysmally low. The hotel has incurred considerable loss during the current year.

Discussion: The loss incurred by the hotel cannot be classified as start-up cost, as it has not resulted from activities that are necessary to make the hotel ready for use. Therefore, the loss should not be included in the cost of the hotel.

EXAMPLE 7.13 (Cessation of accumulation of cost)

Fact pattern: Sohail Limited (SL) constructed a multiplex in Chandigarh. Although the construction was completed on March 31, 2021, the multiplex could not be opened before January 1, 2022, due to delay in obtaining statutory clearances from the state government. SL incurred an expenditure of ₹0.5 million to maintain the multiplex during the intervening period.

Discussion: The multiplex was ready for the intended use (commercial production) on March 31, 2021. Therefore, capitalisation of cost should cease on that date. Costs incurred between April 1, 2021 and December 31, 2021 should be recognised as expense in the profit and loss account for the accounting period 2022–2023.

Illustration 7.14 (Cessation of accumulation of cost)

Fact pattern: The construction of a plant for manufacturing a special type of paint was completed on April 1, 2021. However, the production could not commence from that date because the High Court stayed the production on the petition of an activist group fighting for the protection of the environment. The final decision of the Court went in favour of the firm. The company started commercial production from January 1, 2022. It incurred expenses of ₹50,00,000 for the period from April 1, 2021 to December 31, 2021 on the maintenance of the plant.

Discussion: The firm should recognise expense of ₹50,00,000 in the profit and loss for the accounting year 2021–2022, as the expenditure was incurred after the asset was ready for use.

7.2.5 Asset Retirement Obligation

Asset Retirement Obligation (ARO) is the obligation to dismantle and remove the asset and restore the site. ARO is recognised in the balance sheet as a liability and the amount so recognised is added to the cost of the asset. For example, if the ARO is estimated at ₹10 lakhs, the liability is recognised at that amount and the same amount is added to the cost of the asset. The liability is measured at the present value (PV) of the estimated cost.

Asset Retirement Obligation (ARO) is the obligation to dismantle and remove the asset and restore the site.

Increase in the carrying amount of the provision for ARO due to the passage of time is recognised as borrowing cost.

Unwinding of the discount rate

Increase in the carrying amount of the provision due to the passage of time is recognised as borrowing cost. Change in the provision due to any other reason, such as, change in the estimated amount or the discounting rate should be adjusted to the carrying amount of the asset.

EXAMPLE 7.15 (Unwinding of discount rate)

Fact pattern: The entity has acquired an item of PP&E on April 1, 2021. The management estimates that it will incur an expenditure of ₹1,000 to fulfill the ARO at the end of the useful life of the asset, which is 10 years.

Discussion: The appropriate discount rate is 8% per annum. Immediately on the capitalisation of the asset on April 1, 2021, the entity should recognise a provision of [$(1{,}000/(1.08)^{10}$] or ₹463 and include the same in the acquisition cost of the asset. At the end of the accounting period, on March 31, 2022, the provision should be recognised at [$(1{,}000/(1.08)^9$] or ₹500. The increase in the amount of provision by ₹37 is due to the unwinding of the discount. It should be included in the borrowing costs for the year 2021–2022.

7.2.6 Assset Acquired Through Government Grant

When the government grant is in the form of non-monetary assets such as land or other items of PP&E, the entity has a choice either to measure both the asset and the grant at fair value or to measure both at a nominal amount.

When the government grant is in the form of non-monetary assets, the entity has a choice either to measure both the asset and the grant at fair value or at a nominal amount.

If the grant meets only a part of the cost of the item of PP&E, the entity has a choice to either recognise the grant a deferred income or deduct the grant from the acquisition cost of the asset.

If entity recognises a government grant related to a depreciable asset as a deferred income, it should allocate the grant over the useful life of the asset on a systematic and rational basis. If the grant relates to a non-depreciable asset, such as, land, the amount should be recognised immediately as income.

7.2.7 Expenditure During Construction Period

When an entity construction a new production facility, it incurs expenditures that at are not directly attributable to the acquisition or construction of the items of property, plant and equipment that are installed in the project, but are directly attributable to the project. Those expenditures are capitalised and allocated to the assets that are installed in the project proportionately, based on their respective acquisition cost.

Following are the examples of expenditures that are capitalised:

- General administration and office expenditure at the construction site.
- Expenditure on running of vehicles.
- Expenditure in connection with temporary structures and service facilities
- Depreciation of fixed assets used.

Expenditures that are not attributable to the construction activity should not be capitalised. Examples of such expenditure are expenditure on staff training, expenditure related to work for preparing for production activities, advance publicity campaign, costs involved in borrowing for the purpose of working capital, preliminary corporate expenditure, and corporate expenses.

Income during construction period

Some operations occur in connection with the construction and development of an item of property, plant, and equipment, but are not necessary for construction activities. The income and related expenses of incidental operations should be recognised as profit or loss for the period. However, income from operations that are necessary for construction activities should be deducted from construction cost.

EXAMPLE 7.16 (Income during construction period)

Fact pattern: Aparajita Limited (AL), during the construction of its factory, had constructed temporary quarters at the site and rented them to contractors for providing accommodation to their workers and employees. It received rent of ₹0.50 million from the contractors. The temporary quarters were demolished on completion of the construction activities.

Discussion: The cost of construction and demolition of temporary quarters should be included in the indirect cost of construction. Rent received from the contractors should be deducted from the total indirect cost of construction. The net indirect cost should be allocated to items of PP&E constructed during the construction period.

Indirect expenditures incurred during the construction period of a project are capitalised.

EXAMPLE 7.17 (Income during construction period)

Fact pattern: During the progress of the construction work, a part of the building site was allowed to be used as car parking space. The entity earned the parking fees and incurred expenditure on employees engaged to supervise the car parking operation.

Discussion: The operation was incidental to the construction activity and was not necessary for the same. Therefore, the car parking fees earned, and related expenses incurred should be recognised in profit or loss for the period in which the income is earned.

7.2.8 Exchange Transactions

The cost of an item of PP&E acquired in exchange for non-monetary assets or a combination of monetary and non-monetary assets should be measured at fair value.

If an enterprise is able to determine reliably the fair value of either of the asset received or the asset given up, then the fair value of the asset given up should be used to measure the cost of the asset received, unless the fair value of the asset received is more clearly evident. The principle is consistent with the accounting principle that an asset should initially be measured at the acquisition cost, which included purchase price. In an exchange transaction, the asset given is the purchase consideration.

The asset received in exchange is measured at the carrying amount of the asset given up if:

(a) the exchange transaction lacks commercial substance, or
(b) the fair value of neither the asset received, nor the asset given up is reliably measurable.

The cost of an item of PP&E acquired in exchange for non-monetary assets should be measured at fair value.

The asset received in an exchange transaction is measured at the carrying amount of the asset given up if the transaction lacks commercial substance, or the FV is not measurable reliably.

Commercial substance

An exchange transaction has commercial substance if:

1. the configuration (risks, timing, and amount) of the cash flows of the assets received differs from the configuration of the cash flows of the asset transferred;
2. the entity-specific value of the portion of the entity's operation affected by the transaction changes as a result of the exchange; or
3. the difference in (1) or (2) is significant relative to the fair value of the assets exchanged.

For the purpose of determining whether an exchange transaction has commercial substance, the entity-specific value of the portion of the entity's operation affected by the transaction shall reflect post-tax cash flows. An enterprise need not have to make detailed calculations if the result of these analyses is clear.

In most situations, an exchange of similar assets does not have a commercial substance. Therefore, in exchange of similar assets, no gain or loss is recognised.

EXAMPLE 7.18 (Exchange transaction)

Fact pattern: Girish Limited (GL) entered into an agreement with Williams Limited (WL) to exchange an item (C–101) of plant and machinery (carrying amount: ₹100,000) with an item (D–201) of plant and machinery (carrying amount: ₹800,000) being held by WL. Assume that the fair value of C–101 is ₹12,00,000 and the fair value of D–201 is ₹11,50,000.

Discussion: Consider the following two situations separately:

(i) C–101 and D–201 are similar, but D–201 will be more productive in the location in which the manufacturing facility of GL is located and C–101 will be more productive in the location in which the manufacturing facility of WL is located. However, the benefit is not significant as compared to the fair value of the asset exchanged. Therefore, the transaction lacks commercial substance.

(ii) C–101 and D–201 are similar, but D–201 will be more productive in the location in which the manufacturing facility of GL is located, and C–101 will be more productive in the location in which the manufacturing facility of WL is located. The benefit to GL and WL from the exchange transaction is significant as compared to the fair value of the asset exchanged. Therefore, the transaction has commercial substance.

In situation (i), neither GL nor WL will recognise any profit or loss from the exchange transaction. Both will record the asset received at the carrying amount of the asset given up.

In situation (ii), both GL and WL will recognise the new asset at the fair value of the asset given. Accordingly, GL will recognise the new asset at ₹12,00,000 and will recognise a gain (on disposal of a fixed asset) of (₹12,00,000 – 10,00,000) or ₹2,00,000 in the statement of profit and loss for the period in which the assets are exchanged. Similarly, WL will recognise the new asset at ₹11,50,000 and will recognise a gain (on disposal of a fixed asset) of (₹11,50,000 – 800,000) or ₹3,50,000 in the statement of profit and loss for the period in which the assets are exchanged.

7.3 PP&E: SUBSEQUENT EXPENDITURE

7.3.1 General Principles

Recognition criteria for the initial recognition of an item of PP&E should be applied in deciding whether the expenditure on an existing item of PP&E should be capitalised.

The cost of an item of PP&E is recognised as an asset if and only if (a) it is probable that future economic benefits associated with the item will flow to the entity; (b) the cost of the item can be measured reliably; and (c) the expenditure will provide benefits for more than one period.

If the expenditure fulfills the criteria, either the carrying amount of the item of the PP&E is adjusted or it is recognised as a separate component of the asset. An expenditure that fails to meet the recognition criteria should be recognised as an expense in the statement of profit and loss for the period in which the expenditure is incurred.

Recognition criteria for the initial recognition of an item of PP&E should be applied in deciding whether the expenditure on an existing item of PP&E should be capitalised.

An expenditure that fails to meet the recognition criteria should be recognised as an expense.

7.3.2 Examples of Costs that are Usually Capitalised

The following are the examples of expenditure which are usually adjusted to the carrying amount of an item of PP&E:

- Costs of modification of an item of PP&E to extend its remaining useful life.
- Costs of modification of an item of PP&E to increase its capacity.
- Costs of upgrading machine parts to achieve a substantial improvement in the quality of output.
- Costs for the development of a new production process enabling substantial reduction in operating costs.

EXAMPLE 7.19 (Subsequent expenditure)

Fact pattern: Sameera Limited (SL) has incurred an expenditure of ₹1 million to convert a garage into a showroom.

Discussion: The expenditure is expected to provide benefits, in terms of increase revenue, for more than one period. The cost can be measured reliably. Therefore, it should be adjusted to the carrying amount of the existing asset (garage).

EXAMPLE 7.20 (Subsequent expenditure)

Fact pattern: Neetu Limited (NL) has incurred an expenditure of ₹1.5 million to convert a temporary building into a permanent building.

Discussion: The expenditure is expected to provide benefits, in terms of increase in the useful life, for more than one period. The cost can be measured reliably. Therefore, the expenditure should be adjusted to the carrying amount of the existing asset.

EXAMPLE 7.21 (Subsequent expenditure)

Fact pattern: Smitha Limited (SL) has incurred an expenditure of ₹2 million to convert a machine into a CNC machine. The modification is expected to reduce waste and downtime and will also increase productivity.

Discussion: The expenditure is expected to provide benefits, in terms of reduced costs and higher revenue, for more than one period. The cost can be measured reliably. Therefore, the expenditure should be adjusted to the carrying amount of the existing asset.

Expenditure on routine repair and maintenance

The costs of the day-to-day servicing of the item of PP&E are recognised in profit or loss as incurred. Costs of day-to-day servicing are primarily the costs of labour and consumables and may include the cost of small parts. The purpose of these expenditures is often described as for the "repairs and maintenance" of the item.

The costs of the day-to-day servicing of the item of PP&E are recognised as expenses.

An entity recognises in the carrying amount of an item of PP&E the cost of the new part and derecognise the carrying amount of the part that is replaced.

Replacement of parts

Parts of some items of PP&E may require replacement at regular intervals. For example, a furnace may require relining after a specified number of hours of use, or aircraft interiors such as seats and galleys may require replacement several times during the life of the airframe. Items of PP&E may also be acquired to make a less frequently recurring replacement, such as replacing the interior walls of a building, or to make a non-recurring replacement. An entity recognises in the carrying amount of an item of PP&E the cost of replacing a and derecognise (write off) the carrying amount of the part that is replaced. If the cost of the part is material and its useful life does not terminate with the useful life of the principal equipment, the part should be recognised as a separate item of PP&E.

EXAMPLE 7.22 (Replacement of a part)

Fact pattern: The roof of a factory building of Barbara Limited (BL) was extensively damaged by hailstorm. BL replaced the roof completely. The cost of the new roof is ₹10 million.

Discussion: The cost of the new roof (₹10 million) should be adjusted to the carrying amount of the building. The estimated carrying amount of the old roof should be derecognised. The gain or loss on disposal of the roof that is replaced should be recognised in the profit or loss.

The cost of periodical inspection or overhaling is capitalised.

Periodical replacement and overhaul

A condition of continuing to operate an item of PP&E (e.g., an aircraft) may require regular major inspection. When each major inspection is performed, its cost is adjusted to the carrying amount of the item of PP&E as a replacement, if the recognition criteria are satisfied. Any remaining carrying amount of the cost of the previous inspection (as distinct from physical parts) is derecognised.

EXAMPLE 7.23 (Periodical inspection cost)

Fact pattern: Somalis Shipping Limited (SSL) owns some ships. A ship requires overhaul and inspection at an interval of five years.

Discussion: SSL should estimate the cost of 'overhaul and inspection' to allocate the composite acquisition cost of a new ship between the two assets, namely, the ship and the overhaul and inspection. Assume that the cost of overhaul and inspection is ₹10,00,000 approximately. SSL should recognise overhaul and inspection as a separate item of assets and should depreciate it over a period of five years.

EXAMPLE 7.24 (Overhauling)

Fact pattern: Koena Limited (KL), which uses calendar year as its fiscal year, overhauls the special equipment of its factory every five years. It last overhauled the equipment on January 1, 2018 for ₹5 million. However, in 2021, it has overhauled it again due to sudden decrease in its productivity. It incurred an expenditure of ₹6 million.

Discussion: KL should recognise the overhauling cost of ₹6 million incurred in 2021 as a separate component of the equipment. It should be depreciated over a period of five years. The written value of the overhauling cost capitalised in 2018 should be written off. It should be recognised as an expense in the statement of profit and loss for 2021. Ignoring the depreciation for 2021, the written down value comes to ₹2 million [(5/5) × 2].

7.4 SUBSEQUENT MEASUREMENT OF PP&E

Subsequent measurement refers to measuring the asset subsequent to acquisition for depicting the value of the asset (carrying amount) in the balance sheets prepared post-acquisition.

An entity can choose either the cost model or the revaluation model for the subsequent measurement of items of PP&E.

Entities can choose the revaluation model only for those items of PP&E, the fair value of which can be measured reliably.

Accounting policy choice: An entity can choose either the cost model or the revaluation model as its accounting policy. Entities can choose the revaluation model only for those items of PP&E, the fair value (FV) of which can be measured reliably. Once the choice is made, that policy should be applied consistently to an entire class of PP&E.

Examples of separate classes of assets are land, building, plant and machinery, and vehicles. Most companies use the cost model for subsequent measurement of items of PP&E.

7.4.1 Cost Model

An item of PP&E is carried in the balance sheet at its cost *less* any accumulated depreciation and any accumulated impairment losses.

7.4.2 Revaluation Model

Accounting principle

Under the revaluation model items of PP&E, the entity ensures that the carrying amount does not differ materially from the FV.

Items of PP&E are carried at a revalued amount, being its FV at the date of the revaluation *less* any subsequent accumulated depreciation and subsequent accumulated impairment losses. Items of PP&E should be revalued with sufficient regularity to ensure that the carrying amount does not differ materially from the FV at the end of the reporting period.

Frequency of revaluation

The frequency of revaluations depends on the frequency of changes in FV of the items of PP&E being revalued. When the fair value of a revalued asset differs materially from its carrying amount, a further revaluation is required.

Revaluation gain or loss

Revaluation gain or loss is the difference between the revalued amount and the carrying amount at the revaluation date. Revaluation gain is recognised in other comprehensive income (OCI) and accumulated in equity under the heading of 'Revaluation Reserve'. Revaluation loss is recognised in profit or loss.

The revaluation gain is recognised in profit or loss to the extent that it reverses a revaluation loss (of the same asset) that was previously recognised in profit or loss. Similarly, revaluation loss is recognised in OCI to the extent of any credit balance existing in the revaluation reserve in respect of that asset.

Revaluation gain is recognised in OCI and accumulated in equity under the heading of 'Revaluation Reserve'.

Revaluation loss is recognised in profit or loss.

Revaluation reserve

The revaluation reserve should be transferred directly to the retained earnings when the asset is derecognised. However, some of the revaluation reserve may be transferred to the retained earnings as the asset is used by an entity. In such a case, the amount of the surplus transferred would be the difference between depreciation based on the revalued carrying amount of the asset and the depreciation based on the asset's original cost. Transfers from revaluation surplus to retained earnings should not be routed through profit or loss.

The revaluation reserve should be transferred directly to the retained earnings when the asset is derecognised.

Tax effect

The effects of taxes on income, if any, resulting from the revaluation of PP&E are recognised and disclosed separately.

EXAMPLE 7.25 (Revaluation gain)

Fact pattern: A machine with carrying amount of ₹1,000 is revalued at ₹1,500.

Discussion: The asset's carrying amount in the balance sheet should be re-stated at ₹1,500. Revaluation gain of ₹500 should be recognised in other comprehensive income and should be accumulated in equity under a separate line item – 'revaluation reserve'.

EXAMPLE 7.26 (Revaluation gain)

Fact pattern: A machine, whose book value was ₹1000, was revalued at ₹800 and the revaluation loss of ₹200 was recognised in the statement of profit and loss. The current book value (₹800 minus depreciation accumulated after revaluation) of the asset is ₹500. The asset is revalued at ₹750.

Discussion: Revaluation has resulted in the revaluation gain is ₹250. Out of this, ₹200 should be recognised in the statement of profit and loss to reverse the revaluation loss of ₹200 recognised in profit and loss in an earlier period. The balance ₹50 should be recognised in OCI and should be presented in the balance sheet as revaluation reserve.

EXAMPLE 7.27 (Revaluation loss)

Fact pattern: A piece of land with carrying amount of ₹1,000 was revalued at ₹1,500 and revaluation gain of ₹500 was accumulated in equity under revaluation reserve of ₹500. The same piece of land is now revalued at ₹1,200.

Discussion: The revaluation loss of (₹1,500 – 1,200) or ₹300 should be recognised in OCI resulting in decrease in the balance in the revaluation reserve in the balance sheet by ₹300 to ₹200.

7.4.3 Non-current Assets Held for Sale

An item of non-current asset (e.g., an item of PP&E) as 'Held for Sale' if the entity decides to recover its carrying amount principally through sale rather than through continuing use, and it is expected that the sale transaction shall be completed within one year from the date of classification. An entity continues to classify the asset as held for sale if the events or circumstances that have extended the period to complete the sale beyond one year are not within the control of the entity.

Measurement

An entity measures an item of non-current asset classified as 'Held for Sale' at the lower of its carrying amount and fair value *less* costs to sell. The gain or loss arising from measurement of the asset at each balance sheet date should be recognised as gain or loss in the statement of profit and loss.

An entity measures an item of non-current asset classified as 'Held for Sale' at the lower of its carrying amount and fair value less costs to sell.

Presentation

An entity presents an item of non-current assets classified as 'Held for Sale' separately from other assets in the balance sheet.

7.5 RIGHT OF USE ASSETS

Right of used assets (ROU) are items of PP&E acquired through a lease contract.

Right of used assets (ROU) are items of PP&E acquired through a lease contract.

ROUs are initially measured at the total of the lease liability recognised in the balance sheet and cost directly attributable to the acquisition of the asset.

ROUs are subsequently measured using the cost model if items in the same class of PP&E are measured using the cost model. They are subsequently measured using the revaluation model if items in the same class of PP&E are measured using the revaluation model.

The items of ROU assets are depreciated using the same deprecation method and rate that is used to depreciate similar items of PP&E.

7.6 INTANGIBLE ASSETS

7.6.1 Nature of Intangible Assets

Intangible assets are non-monetary assets which are either separately identifiable, or protected by legal or contractual rights.

Intangible assets are fixed assets without physical substance. They provide economic benefits to the entity only in combination with other assets being used for the business. They enhance the *service potential* of other assets. Intangible assets provide enduring benefits to the entity. For example, a branded product earns a premium over the generic product of the same quality. A patent protects the right to exclude other from producing the product developed by the entity.

Entities frequently expend resources, or incur liabilities, on the acquisition, development, maintenance, or enhancement of intangible resources such as scientific or technical knowledge, design and implementation of new processes or systems, licences, intellectual property, market knowledge and trademarks (including brand names and publishing titles). Common examples of items encompassed by these broad headings are computer software, patents, copyrights, motion pictures, customer lists, mortgage servicing rights, fishing licences, import quotas, franchises, customer or supplier relationships, customer loyalty, market share, and marketing rights. From the entity's perspective all those items are complementary assets, as they enhance the financial productivity of tangible assets. However, from the accounting perspective, many of those resources are not assets, as the entity does not have sufficient control over those resources, or there is significant measurement uncertainty or there is significant uncertainty on whether the resource will benefit the entity.

7.6.2 Definition of Intangible Assets

Intangible assets are non-monetary assets which are,

- either separately identifiable, or
- protected by legal or contractual rights.

Monetary assets like trade receivables, loan and deposits are not intangible assets.

Separately identifiable

An intangible asset is separable if the entity could rent or dispose of the asset without also disposing of the business in which it is used. For example, a product brand is separately identifiable, as it can be sold separately without selling the business. Similarly, computer software is separately identifiable, as it can be sold, or the entity can rent it by giving another entity license to use the same.

Assets protected by contractual or legal rights

A product patent being held by a pharmaceutical company, and a copyright held by a publisher are intangible assets, as those are protected by legal right. License held by an airline to use the facilities of an airport is an intangible asset, as it is protected by contractual right.

GAAP does not permit recognition of internally generated intangible assets.

7.6.3 Recognition and Measurement

Recognition and measurement principles are similar to those applicable to PP&E.

Intangible assets acquired separately

Entities recognise intangible assets acquired separately or in a business combination transaction because they meet the recognition criteria—potential to benefit the entity, entity has control over the asset, and the cost or value can be measured reliably. Fair value (FV) is the cost of the assets acquired in a business combination.

Internally generated intangible assets

Contemporary accounting practice is not to recognise internally generated intangible assets, except computer software, as they fail to meet the recognition criteria. Specifically, expenditures on research, advertising, and training are recognised as expenses for the period in which those are incurred, even if the management expects to benefit from the same for more than one accounting period.

Development expenditure

Development phase starts at the end of the research phase. Examples of activities in the development phase are development of the prototype and testing the same before commercial use of the new product or process developed during the research phase.

Entities recognise the development expenditure as an asset (usually labeled as 'intangible assets under development') only when the entity demonstrates its intention and capabilities to complete the development project, and economic viability of the new product or process.

Development expenditure is recognised as an asset only when the entity demonstrates its intention and capabilities to complete the project, and economic viability of the new product or process.

No looking back: Usually, entities cannot demonstrate economic viability of the new product or process in the initial stage of the development project. Therefore, expenditure incurred before the economic viability is demonstrated are recognised as expense for the period in which the expenditure is incurred. Entities should not include the expenditure recognised as expense in one or more prior periods in the cost of 'intangible assets under development'.

7.6.4 PP&E used in R&D Activities

An item of PP&E, which is purchased and being used in research activities, and has alternative uses, is accounted for as any other item of PP&E. For example, a building in which research facilities are located should be accounted for as an item of PP&E if it can be used for purposes other than research.

7.6.5 Goodwill

Goodwill is the pre-eminent unidentifiable intangible asset that an entity creates in the course of its operation.

Goodwill is an amorphous asset that an entity creates in the course of its operation. It arises from business connections, trade name, regular customers, good reputation, and efficient management. It subsumes intangibles like corporate brand (e.g., highly respected company), product brand, organisation culture, knowledge, high employee morale, and customer relationship. It is the *pre-eminent unidentifiable* intangible asset.

GAAP does not permit recognition of the internally generated goodwill.

Contemporary accounting practice is not to recognise internally generated goodwill.

Goodwill is recorded only from a business combination transaction if the purchase consideration is higher than the fair value of identifiable assets, net of liabilities acquired. The excess of the purchase consideration is recognised as goodwill.

EXAMPLE 7.28 (Goodwill)

Fact pattern: M pays ₹1,00,000 to acquire 60% of N and the fair value of the 60% of the net assets (assets–liabilities) of N is ₹80,000,

Discussion: M recognises goodwill at ₹20,000 in the consolidate balance sheet. If P pays ₹2,00,000 to acquire 100% of R, which is dissolved after acquisition by P, and the fair value of the net assets of R is ₹1,70,000, P recognises goodwill at ₹30,000 in its stand-alone balance sheet.

Gain from bargain purchase: Occasionally, an acquirer makes a bargain purchase, which is a business combination in which the amount of the purchase consideration is less than the fair value of identifiable assets (net of the liabilities acquired) acquired in the transaction. The acquirer recognises the excess of the fair value over the purchase consideration in the balance sheet as capital reserve.

The excess of the purchase consideration paid over the FV of net assets acquired in a business combination is recognised as goodwill.

7.7 NATURAL RESOURCES

Nature of natural resources

Natural resources are wasting assets like oil, gas, and minerals. Their reserve depletes as those are extracted from the oil or gas reserves and mines.

Exploration cost

Entities obtain right to extract natural resources from the government. The right is like any other intangible asset. However, before acquiring such right entities obtain the right to explore whether natural resource is available under the parcel of land or sea. Two broadly acknowledged principles for accounting for exploration and evaluation costs are 'successful efforts method' and 'full cost method'.

Successful efforts method

Under the successful efforts method, cost of exploration and evaluation is either capitalised or expensed 'field-by-field' basis. If the reserve is not found, the expenditure is expensed. If the economically viable reserve is found, the expenditure is capitalised.

Full cost method

Under the full cost method cost of exploration over a vast geographical area, usually a country, is accumulated and capitalised. The capitalised cost is allocated to the economically viable reserves.

Impairment testing

The capitalised exploration and evaluation cost (exploration and evaluation asset) is tested for impairment immediately.

REVIEW PROBLEMS

R7.1 Indicate whether the following statements are True or False:

(i) Fixed assets are non-movable assets held by the business firm.

(ii) A tangible asset that the firm intends to use in production, administration, and rent are classified as property, plant, and equipment (PP&E) for a period of 12 months or more is classified as property, plant, and equipment.

(iii) Items of PP&E are initially measured at cost and not at fair value (FV).

(iv) Leased assets are not classified as PP&E.

(v) The purchase price of an item of PP&E is the cash price and not the price paid by the firm.

(vi) Relocation costs are not included in the acquisition cost of an item of PP&E.

(vii) Borrowing costs are included in the cost of item of PP&E production of which takes 12 months or more only if the amount was borrowed specifically for the acquisition of the assets.

(viii) Borrowing costs for the period that commences after the construction of the asset is complete should not be included in the acquisition cost.

(ix) Costs incurred for the upkeep of an item of PP&E (that is ready for use) before commencement of its commercial use should be included in the cost of that item only if commencement of the commercial production is delayed for reasons beyond the firm's control.

(x) Internally generated intangible assets, except computer software, are not recognised in the balance sheet.

(xi) The principle of component accounting aims to improve the accounting for depreciation.

(xii) A firm has an option to choose either the cost model or the revaluation model for estimating the carrying amount of an item of PP&E.

(xiii) An item of PP&E that is measured using the revaluation model is not depreciated.

(xiv) Cost incurred to overhaul an item of PP&E periodically is capitalised.

(xv) Items of PP&E taken on lease are not depreciated.

R7.2 Fill in the blanks:

(i) Tangible fixed assets taken on lease are classified as ....

(ii) Usually the composite cost incurred to purchase land and building is allocated between the piece of land and building based on their respective ....

(iii) A company has acquired another company paying a purchase consideration of ₹20,00,000. The fair value of assets acquired (net of liabilities assumed) is estimated at ₹18,00,000. The firm should recognise the goodwill at ₹................

(iv) A firm estimates that it will incur ₹20,00,000 to dismantle a piece of equipment after its useful life, which is estimated at 20 years. The appropriate discount rate is 10 per cent per annum. ₹................ should be included in the acquisition of the asset.

(v) The term depletion is associated with ....

(vi) A firm has revalued an asset resulting in revaluation gain of ₹2,00,000. The same asset was revalued earlier and a revaluation loss of ₹1,40,000 was recognised in the profit and loss. ₹................ should be recognised on Other Comprehensive Income and accumulated in equity as Revaluation Reserve.

(vii) A firm incurred ₹100 lakhs in the promoting a new innovative product in the current year. The management expects that the expenditure will benefit the firm in the current financial year and next three financial years. In the statement of profit and loss ₹................ lakhs should be recognised as product promotion expense.

(viii) A firm has purchased a piece of land For ₹40,00,000 with an intention to build an office building on the same. It incurred the following additional cost on the land before commencement of the building construction activities: Registration charges: 20,000; Legal fees to search the title of the land: ₹10,000; Demolishing the dilapidated building ₹2,00,000; and Cost of excavation, grading and filling the land: ₹1,50,000. It earned income of ₹20,000 by selling the debris. The acquisition cost of the land is ₹................

ASSIGNMENTS

1. Tick the correct answer:

(i) Deferred revenue expenditure is expenditure:

(a) that should be recognised as an asset.
(b) that, though benefiting more than one reporting period, does not pass the tests of asset recognition.
(c) that does not pass the test of asset recognition, but recognition of the same as an expense is deferred to match revenue with expenses.
(d) that is in the nature of revenue expenditure, but recognition of the same as an expense is deferred as a matter of prudence.

(ii) Events other than transactions entered into by an enterprise:

(a) do not result in recognition or derecognition of assets or liabilities.
(b) might result in recognition or derecognition of assets or liabilities or change in their carrying amount.
(c) might result in recognition or derecognition of assets, but never result in recognition or de-recognition of liabilities.
(d) might result in recognition or derecognition of liabilities.

(iii) Evidence that supports recognition of an asset or a liability:

(a) should necessarily be external evidence.
(b) should not necessarily be external evidence, but external evidence is considered superior to internal evidence.
(c) should necessarily be internal evidence.
(d) can either be an external evidence or internal evidence.

(iv) Control of the enterprise over a resource is an essential requirement for recognising it as an asset, and such control:

(a) should necessarily be supported by legal protection.
(b) should not be supported by any evidence—that management's perception is enough for recognising the asset.
(c) should not necessarily be supported by legal protection, though legal protection provides a strong evidence of control.
(d) comes from ownership rights only.

(v) Recognition of an asset or liability requires resolution of uncertainties as to the future inflow or outflow of economic benefits to or from the enterprise. The uncertainty gets resolved at an acceptable level:

(a) for both asset and liability, if it is probable (more likely than not) that economic benefit will flow to or from the enterprise.
(b) for both asset and liability, if it is sufficiently certain that economic benefit will flow to or from the enterprise.
(c) for the asset, if it is sufficiently certain that economic benefit will flow to the enterprise, and for the liability, if it is probable that the economic benefit will flow from the enterprise.
(d) for both asset and liability, if there is any possibility that economic benefit will flow to or from the enterprise.

(vi) In recognising assets or liabilities, accountants:
   (a) balance relevance and reliability.
   (b) assign greater importance to relevance than reliability.
   (c) assign greater importance to reliability than relevance.
   (d) place importance on reliability and ignore relevance.

(vii) Under historical cost basis of measurement, an item of property, plant and equipment:
   (a) is always carried at acquisition cost.
   (b) is carried at fair value as on the balance sheet's date.
   (c) is carried at fair value on the date of acquisition, adjusted for depreciation and impairment loss.
   (d) is carried at acquisition cost, adjusted for depreciation and impairment loss.

(viii) In selecting the appropriate basis for measuring assets and liabilities, the thumb rule is:
   (a) if both the historical cost measure and the current value measure are reliable, historical cost is the better measure.
   (b) if both the historical cost measure and the current value measure are reliable, current value measure is the better measure.
   (c) if both the historical cost measure and the current value measure are reliable, the better measure to use will be the one that is the most relevant.
   (d) if only one of the measures available is reliable, that should be used even if it is not relevant.

(ix) As a general rule, the cost of an item of property, plant and equipment:
   (a) always includes expenditure on start-up and commissioning.
   (b) does not include expenditure on start-up and commissioning.
   (c) includes only the expenditure on commissioning.
   (d) Includes expenditure on start-up and commissioning only if the asset is incapable of operating at normal level without such a start-up or commissioning period.

(x) A limited liability company in India should charge depreciation:
   (a) in accordance with rates provided in Schedule XIV to the Companies Act, 1956.
   (b) on the basis of estimated useful life and estimated residual value of the asset.
   (c) on the basis of estimated useful life and estimated residual value of the asset, but it should not be lower than the amount calculated at the rates provided in Schedule XIV to the Companies Act, 1956.
   (d) on the basis of the rates provided under the Income Tax law.

(xi) The useful life of a depreciable asset:
   (a) cannot exceed the economic life of the asset.
   (b) can exceed the economic life, but cannot exceed the technical life of the asset.
   (c) can neither exceed the economic life nor the technical life of the asset.
   (d) is equal to the economic life of the asset.

(xii) Under the Indian GAAP, goodwill:
   (a) should not be recognised in the balance sheet.
   (b) should be recognised in the balance sheet.
   (c) except internally generated goodwill, may be recognised in the balance sheet and should be amortised over a period to be decided by the management.
   (d) except internally generated goodwill, may be recognised in the balance sheet and should be amortised over its useful life, which should generally not exceed five years.

(xiii) Under the International Accounting Standards, goodwill:

(a) should not be recognised in the balance sheet.

(b) should be recognised in the balance sheet.

(c) except when it is internally generated, may be recognised in the balance sheet and should be amortised over a period to be decided by the management.

(d) except when it is internally generated, may be recognised in the balance sheet and should be amortised over its useful life, which should generally not exceed five years.

(xiv) Mallika Limited (ML) purchased a machine for ₹20,00,000 for its manufacturing operation and paid transportation charge of ₹10,000. In addition, ML spent ₹50,000 towards testing and preparing the machine for use. The cost of the machine should be recorded at:

(a) ₹20,60,000 (b) ₹20,10,000

(c) ₹20,50,000 (d) ₹20,00,000

(xv) On December 1, 2006, Shipra Limited (SL) purchased a piece of land for ₹40,00,000 for a factory site. SL razed an old structure and sold the material salvaged from the old structure. The company incurred additional costs and realised salvage proceeds during December 2006 as follows:

Demolition of old building	₹70,000
Legal fees	₹50,000
Registration charges	₹4,00,000
Proceeds from sale of salvaged material	₹15,000

In its December 31, 2006 balance sheet, SL should carry the land at:

(a) ₹44,50,000 (b) ₹45,20,000

(c) ₹45,05,000 (d) ₹40,00,000

(xvi) In 2006, Anuj Limited (AL) had purchased an old building on a free hold land for ₹80,00,000. The fair value of the land was estimated at ₹40,00,000. AL paid ₹10,00,000 towards registration charges and it incurred ₹50,000 towards legal expenses for documentation and registration. When renovation of the building was in progress, AL received a notice from the local municipal corporation for demolition of the building as the building plan was not approved by the municipality. AL appointed a lawyer to deal with the issue. A settlement was reached, according to which AL had to pay penalty of ₹5,00,000 and it had to demolish a part of the building. The cost of demolition was ₹100,000. The lawyer was paid ₹20,000. An architect estimated that the part demolished constituted 5% of the original building in terms of its value. The building should be carried (gross block) in the balance sheet as at December 31, 2006 at:

(a) ₹45,25,000 (b) ₹51,45,000

(c) ₹42,98,750 (d) ₹48,87,750

(xvii) Nisha Limited (NL) began constructing a building for its own use in January 2006. During 2006, NL incurred an interest of ₹60,000 on the amount specifically borrowed for construction of the building, and ₹20,000 on other borrowings. Interest computed on the weighted average amount of accumulated expenditures for the building during the year 2006 was ₹35,000. NL should capitalise interest amounting to:

(a) ₹60,000 (b) ₹35,000

(c) ₹80,000 (d) ₹20,000

(xviii) On April 20, 2007, Preeti Limited (PL) exchanges a car for 1,000 equity shares of Indian Oil Corporation Limited (IOCL). On that date, the written down value of the car was ₹3,50,000 and its fair value was ₹4,50,000. On that date, the share price of IOCL in the Bombay Stock exchange (BSE) was ₹395 per share. PL intends to hold the share for long term. PL should record the cost of investment at:

(a) ₹3,50,000 (b) ₹3,95,000
(c) ₹4,50,000 (d) ₹4,00,000

(xix) Omkara Limited (OL) participated in an auction of a 'haveli' (manson), which was put on auction by the revenue department of the government. OL purchased the haveli for ₹2 crore. The most popular and respected business daily reported that the government could not realise the fair value of the property as Mr. Omkara participated in the auction. The daily estimates the fair value at ₹4 crore. The newspaper daily alleges that the reserve price was set at ₹2 crore to facilitate OL's acquisition of the property at a discount. OL should record the haveli as an asset at:

(a) ₹2 crore (b) ₹4 crore
(c) ₹3 crore (d) None of the above

2. Indicate against each statement whether it is True or False:

(i) The concept of deferred revenue expenditure is not relevant in the asset–liability measurement approach.

(ii) In accounting, external evidence is considered superior to internal evidence.

(iii) Historical cost is always a better measure as compared to the fair value measure.

(iv) An attribute cannot be considered unreliable, solely because it is subjective.

(v) The estimated cost of dismantling and removing an asset and restoring the site should not be included in the cost of tangible fixed assets.

(vi) Borrowing costs should not be included in the cost of an item of property, plant and equipment unless the fund is borrowed specifically for the asset.

(vii) The cost of an item of property, plant and equipment should be adjusted for change in the carrying amount of the related liability, denominated in foreign currency, due to change in exchange rates.

(viii) It is the management's discretion to decide the periodicity of subsequent revaluation of revalued fixed assets.

(ix) Revaluation reserve is not available for distribution to shareholders either as dividend or as bonus shares.

(x) An item of property, plant and equipment temporarily retired from active use should be stated at the lower of their net book value and net realisable value.

(xi) An item of property, plant and equipment, classified as 'held for sale', should be carried at the lower of its net book value and 'fair value less costs to sell'.

(xii) Acquisition of a group of assets purchased from another enterprise might result in recognition of goodwill.

(xiii) An enterprise is usually precluded from recognising an intangible asset purchased as a part of business acquisition if it is not traded in an active market.

(xiv) Major stores and spare parts may qualify for recognition as items of PP&E.

(xv) The cost of an item of property, plant and equipment is the cash price equivalent at the recognition date.

(xvi) The carrying amount of the fixed asset should be adjusted for exchange difference arising on settlement or restatement of a liability, denominated in a foreign currency, assumed on acquisition of the item of PP&E.

(xvii) Administration and other general overhead costs allocated to activities related to the construction of a building internally by an entity are directly attributable to the construction of the building and should be included in its acquisition cost.

(xviii) Borrowing costs incurred on borrowings, which are directly attributable to the construction of a project, up to the commencement of commercial use of the facility should be capitalised.

(xix) Increase in the provision for asset retirement obligation during a particular period should be adjusted to the carrying amount of the asset.

(xx) Expenditure incurred to bring the fixed asset to its working condition should not be capitalised if the same was not contemplated at the time of acquisition of the asset.

3. Fill in the blanks:

(i) An equipment imported from the USA on deferred credit basis during the reporting period (calendar year) was recorded at ₹4,00,000 ($1 = ₹40). On the balance sheet's date the exchange rate is $1 = ₹45. The asset should be carried in the balance sheet at ₹.................. (ignore depreciation).

(ii) The carrying amount of a machine as on January 1, 2006 was ₹1,00,000. The enterprise revalues the asset on that date at ₹1,40,000. The asset was first revalued in 2003, and a revaluation loss of ₹10,000 was recognised. Revaluation reserve should be recognised at ₹.............

(iii) The gross book value and accumulated depreciation of an asset as on January 1, 2006 are ₹1,50,000 and ₹90,000, respectively. On June 30, 2006, the asset is sold at ₹70,000. The gain/(loss) on sale of the asset is ₹........ (ignore depreciation for 2006).

(iv) During the reporting period (calendar year) 2005, an enterprise incurred an expenditure of ₹4,00,000 on development of a new product. Out of the total expenditure, ₹3,50,000 were incurred till November 30, 2005. The expenditure met the criteria for recognition of an intangible asset on December 1, 2005. The recoverable amount of the know-how is estimated at ₹1,00,000. During 2006, expenditure incurred is ₹10,00,000. On the balance sheet's date, the recoverable amount is estimated at ₹9,50,000. In the balance sheet as at December 31, 2005, the intangible asset was recognised at ₹....... The cost of the intangible asset till December 31, 2006 is ₹...........The intangible asset should be recognised in the balance sheet as at December 31, 2006 at ₹.............

4. Analytical questions:

(i) The factory of Aman Limited, located at Naini near Allahabad, faced a hailstorm in the year 2005, causing serious damage to the roof of the factory building. The company incurred an expenditure of ₹1 million to put a new roof on the building. Should the expenditure be capitalised?

(ii) A Limited borrows funds to finance large projects. The lending institution releases funds in agreed instalments. Usually, funds are released at the interval of six months to meet the requirements for the next six months. AA Limited parks the funds released by the lending institution in treasury bills of different maturity. Should the interest earned on investments in treasury bills be deducted from the amount of interest paid to the lending institution to arrive at the borrowing cost to be capitalised?

(iii) Charlie Limited purchased a 'BMW', a luxury car, for use by its Chief Executive Officer (CEO). The car met with an accident while driving to the factory immediately after taking delivery from the showroom. The car had no insurance cover.

The firm incurred an expenditure of ₹0.3 million to repair the car, which includes the cost of a new engine to replace the engine damaged in the accident. Should the expenditure be capitalised?

5. Problem:

India Cables Limited commissioned a plant imported from Germany at a cost of ₹50 million on January 1, 2005. Initially, due to a technical snag, the output produced by the machine did not meet the specifications and the quality guaranteed by the supplier. It could produce cables shorter than the standard length and of low quality. A team of engineers from the firm that supplied the machine visited the plant on January 31, 2005, but could not rectify the defect. Another team visited the plant on March 30, 2005. They could not fully rectify the defect, but they could make the machine capable of producing high quality cable although of shorter length.

The company decided to continue to operate the plant.

From April 15, 2005, India Cables Limited, in order to reduce losses, produced and sold sub-quality shorter length cables as seconds. After prolonged negotiations, the supplier firm agreed to refund ₹15 million.

India Cables Limited proposes to capitalise ₹40 millions of expenditure incurred by it on salaries, wages and other overhead expenses during the period January 1, 2005–April 14, 2005, which constitute start-up and commissioning costs.

Required: Advise whether the company should capitalise the expenditure. Also, advise whether the amount refunded by the supplier should be deducted from the cost of the machine.

CHAPTER 8

CURRENT ASSETS

CHAPTER OBJECTIVES

The objectives of this chapter is to introduce to readers the nature and accounting for assets whose natural classification is current assets, and are classified as non-current assets if they do not meet the criteria for classifying an asset as current asset. In particular, the objective is developing and understanding of:

- Inventories—nature, components, and valuation;
- Trade receivables and contract assets;
- Loans;
- Other current assets—advances and pre-paid expenses, marketable securities, and cash and cash equivalents.

8.1 INVENTORIES

8.1.1 Definition

Table 8.1 below list the items that are included in inventories.

TABLE 8.1 Items that are Included in Inventories

	Nature of the item	*Examples*
1,	Assets held for sale in the ordinary course of business	Stock of merchandise, finished goods and apartments that real estate developers hold for sale
2.	Assets that are in the process of production of goods for sale in the ordinary course of business	Work-in-process
3	Inputs that are used in the production process	Raw materials, components, stores and spares, loose tools

8.1.2 Inventory Valuation Principle

Inventories are measured at the lower of cost and net realisable value.

General principle

Inventories are measured at the *lower* of:

- Cost; and
- Net realisable value (NRV).

BOX: 8.1 EXCLUSIONS TO THE GENERAL PRINCIPLES

This general principle applies to all inventories, except the following: Work-in-progress arising from construction contracts, including directly related service contracts; Financial instruments; and biological assets related to agricultural activity and agricultural produce at the point of harvest.

This principle does not apply to the measurement of inventories held by the following:

1. Agricultural and forest products, agricultural produce after harvest, and minerals and mineral products, to the extent that they are measured at net realisable value in accordance with well-established practices in those industries. (When such inventories are measured at net realisable value, changes in that value are recognised in profit or loss in the period of change.)
2. Commodity broker-traders who measure their inventories at fair value *less* costs to sell. (When such inventories are measured at fair value less costs to sell, changes in fair value less costs to sell are recognised in profit or loss in the period of change.)

8.1.3 Costs

The cost of inventories comprises costs of purchase, costs of conversion, and other costs incurred in bringing the inventories to their present location and condition.

The cost of inventories comprises:

- Costs of purchase (e.g., cost of merchandise, raw materials and components).
- Costs of conversion (e.g., direct employee cost and manufacturing overheads).
- Other costs incurred in bringing the inventories to their present location and condition.

Costs of transporting an item of finished goods to the location where it is usually being sold should be included in the cost of finished goods and stock-in-trade inventories.

Costs which are excluded from the cost of inventories

1. Storage costs, unless those costs are necessary in the production process before a further production stage
2. Administrative overheads that do not contribute to bringing inventories to their present location and condition
3. Selling and distribution costs.
4. Abnormal costs, such as demurrage and abnormal loss in the course of production

8.1.4 Cost of Purchase

Purchase price should exclude the implicit interest cost when the credit period extended by the vendor exceeds 12 months.

The costs of purchase of inventories comprise the purchase price, import duties and other taxes (other than those subsequently recoverable by the entity from the taxing authorities), and transport, handling, and other costs directly attributable to the acquisition of finished goods, raw materials, and services. Trade discounts, rebates and other similar items are deducted in determining the costs of purchase.

Interest included in the purchase price: If the credit extended by the supplier is longer than the normal credit period, and the credit allowed is for a period of 12 months or more, it is assumed that the purchase price includes interest charged for the credit period. The amount of interest included in the purchase price should be recognised separately as interest expense. Purchase price should be adjusted for the interest element.

8.1.5 Conversion Costs

In merchandising business, the retailer converts goods purchased in large quantity into salable units. A manufacturer converts raw materials, and components into finished goods. Conversion costs are included in the cost of inventories.

Elements of conversion cost is presented in table 8.2 below:

TABLE 8.2 Costs that are Included in the Cost of Inventories.

	Elements of conversion cost	*Accounting principle*
1.	Direct material cost	Material costs that can be traced directly to the units of finished goods produced are included in the cost of units produced.
2.	Direct labour cost	Labour costs that can be traced directly to the units of finished goods produced are included in the cost of units produced.
3.	Variable production overheads	Variable production overheads are allocated to each unit of production on the basis of the actual use of the production facilities.
4.	Fixed production overheads	(a) Fixed production overheads are allocated to the costs of conversion based on the normal capacity. (b) Overhead absorption rate is calculated by dividing the fixed overheads by the estimated normal production capacity. That rate is applied for assigning fixed production overheads to each unit of production. (c) If in any year the production is significantly higher than the normal capacity, actual production volume is used for allocation production overheads to the units produced.
5.	Borrowing cost	(a) Borrowing costs are usually not included in the cost of inventory. (b) Borrowing costs may be included in the cost of inventory of items such as, wine, or seasoned woods, because the seasoning process takes a substantial period of time (usually more than 12 months). (c) Borrowing costs for the period for which inventories are held in stock should not be included in the cost of inventories.

Fixed production overheads are allocated to the costs of conversion based on the normal capacity.

Borrowing costs are usually not included in the cost of inventory.

Overheads

Overheads are the indirect costs that cannot be traced directly to the units produced.

Indirect costs incurred during the production process are classified as production or manufacturing overheads. Similarly, indirect costs related to administrative activities are classified as administration overheads and those related to selling and distribution activities are classified as selling and distribution overheads. Examples of production overheads are depreciation and maintenance of the production facility, compensation to the production manager and supervisors, depreciation of equipment, and compensation of unskilled workers.

Fixed and variable overheads: Overheads that increase or decrease in direct proportion to the increase or decrease in the production volume are called variable overheads. Overheads that remain unchanged with the change in the production volume are called fixed production overheads.

Normal capacity

Normal capacity is the production expected to be achieved on average over a number of periods or seasons under normal circumstances, taking into account the loss of capacity resulting from planned maintenance.

Normal capacity is the production expected to be achieved on average over a number of periods or seasons under normal circumstances, taking into account the loss of capacity resulting from planned maintenance. Usually, the period of three to five years is considered by entities in estimating the normal capacity. Some accountants estimate the normal capacity without taking into consideration the expected market demand, while others consider the secular market demand. It is advisable to consider the secular market demand.

EXAMPLE 8.1 (Allocation of fixed production overheads)

Fact pattern: The management of an entity has estimated the normal capacity at 1,00,000 units. In a particular accounting year, it could produce only 60,000 units of the product as it could not procure the required quantity of inputs for variety of reasons. The fixed production overheads incurred during the year was ₹10,00,000.

Discussion: Production was lower than the normal capacity. Therefore, fixed production overheads should be assigned to each unit produced on the basis of normal capacity. Thus, the rate of (10,00,000/1,00,000) or ₹10 per unit should be assigned to each unit produced. The same rate should be used for calculating both the cost of units sold and units included in the year-end inventories.

EXAMPLE 8.2 (Allocation of fixed production overheads)

Fact pattern: The management of an entity has estimated the normal capacity at 100,000 units. In a particular accounting year it produced 125,000 units due to sudden surge in demand. The fixed production overhead incurred during the year was ₹2,00,00,000.

Discussion: Production during the year was significantly higher than normal. Therefore, fixed production overheads should be assigned to each unit produced on the basis of actual production. Thus, the rate of (2,00,00,000/1,25,000) ₹160 per unit should be assigned to each unit produced. The same rate should be used for calculating both the cost of units sold and units included in the year-end inventories.

Joint product and by-product

Joint costs are allocated between the joint products on a rational and consistent basis.

A production process may result in more than one product being produced simultaneously. This is the case, for example, when joint products are produced or when there are one or more main products and by-products. Products are classified into main product and by-product based on their relative sale value. The conversion costs of each product are not separately identifiable. They are allocated between the products on a rational and consistent basis. The allocation may be based, for example, on the relative sales value of each product, either at the stage in the production process when the products become separately identifiable, or at the completion of production. Most by-products, by their nature, are immaterial. When this is the case, they are often measured at net realisable value and this value is deducted from the cost of the main product. As a result, the carrying amount of the main product is not materially different from its cost.

EXAMPLE 8.3 (Allocation of joint costs)

Fact pattern: An entity produces a variety of chemicals for industrial use. The core process produces three joint products A, B and C. These products are further processed to produce a variety of chemicals required by the rubber industry. The cost of operating the core process in 2021 was ₹10,20,000. Realisation from sale of by-products was ₹20,000. Net realisable values (NRVs) of A, B and C at the point of separation were ₹3,00,000, ₹2,50,000 and ₹1,50,000 respectively. The NRV at the point of separation is calculated by deducting from the final sales value the total of the cost of further processing and estimated profit on the further processing cost.

Discussion: The joint cost, net of realisation from the sale of by-products, should be allocated to A, B and C in proportion to their respective NRV at the separation point. Net joint cost was ₹10,00,000. This amount should be allocated as follows:

A: 10,00,000 × (300/700) = ₹4,28,571; B: 10,00,000 × (250/700) = ₹3,57,143; C: 10,00,000 × (150/700) = ₹2,14,286

8.1.6 Techniques for Cost Measurement

Techniques for measuring the cost of inventories, such as the standard cost method or the retail method, may be used for convenience if the results approximate the cost.

Techniques for measuring the cost of inventories, such as the standard cost method or the retail method, may be used for convenience if the results approximate the cost.

Standard cost

Standard costs consider normal levels of materials and supplies, labour, efficiency, and capacity utilisation. They are regularly reviewed and, if necessary, revised in the light of current conditions.

Retail method

The retail method is often used in the retail industry for measuring inventories of large numbers of rapidly changing items with similar margins for which it is impracticable to use other costing methods. The cost of the inventory is determined by reducing the sales value of the inventory by the appropriate percentage gross margin. The percentage used takes into consideration inventory that has been marked down to below its original selling price. An average percentage for each retail department is often used.

8.1.7 Cost Formulas

Cost formulas are presented in Table 8.3 below:

TABLE 8.3 Cost Formulas

	Cost formula	*Method*
1.	Specific identification method	Each item in the inventories is tracked individually. For example, steel castings specifically bought for a particular compressor to be manufactured are not interchangeable and; therefore; can be tracked individually. Similarly, compressors tailor made for customers can be tracked to customers.
2.	First-in-first out (FIFO)	The FIFO method assumes that materials received first are issued first. Similarly, in the context of determination of cost of goods sold, it assumes that items purchased or produced first are sold first.
3.	Last-in-first-out (LIFO)	The LIFO method assumes that materials received last are issued first. Similarly, in the context of determination of cost of goods sold, it assumes that items purchased or produced last are sold first. Therefore, inventory costs of raw material, components, stores and spares and finished goods are computed using the cost of the oldest units purchased or produced.

(*Contd...*)

	Cost formula	Method
4.	Weighted average cost formula	Under the weighted average cost formula, raw materials and components issued to production are valued at the weighted average purchase price of all units in hand at the time of issue. Similarly, for computing the cost of the inventories of raw materials, components, stores and spares and finished goods are computed at the weighted average purchase price or production cost of all units in hand at the balance sheet date.

Choosing the formula

An entity should use specific identification method for determining the cost of items that are not ordinarily interchangeable or for items that have been segregated for specific projects. For the items that are interchangeable either FIFO or weighted average formula should be used. Use of the last-in-first-out (LIFO) formula is not permitted.

An entity should use specific identification method for determining the cost of items that are not ordinarily interchangeable or for items that have been segregated for specific projects.

Effect of cost formula in profit and assets

Use of the FIFO formula results in the earliest costs materials used in production or stock-in-trade is included in the cost of goods sold and inventories are valued at the recent costs. Use of the LIFO formula results in the recent cost materials used in production or stock-in-trade is included in the cost of goods sold and inventories are valued at the earliest costs. In an inflationary economy, the reported profit when LIFO formula is used is lower than the reported profit under the FIFO formula. It can be said that use of LIFO results in hidden profit, as in a competitive market, change in the selling price track change input prices, of course with a lag. Therefore, use of the LIFO formula violates the concept of 'true and fair view'. Weighted average formula smoothens the changes in the price of inputs.

For the items that are interchangeable, either FIFO or weighted average formula should be used.

Selection of the cost formula

An entity should select the cost formula based on the judgement about which method gives the *fairest possible approximation* of the cost incurred in bringing the items of inventory to their present location and condition. For example, FIFO is the most appropriate formula for use in industries where there is a high correlation between costs of raw materials and components, and prices of finished products such as crude oil refining and agriculture-based industries. The weighted average cost formula is preferable for other industries because it smoothens the fluctuations in the prices of inputs.

An entity should select the cost formula based on the judgement about which method gives the fairest possible approximation of the cost incurred in bringing the items of inventory to their present location and condition.

Perpetual and periodic inventory system

In the absence of any indication, it can be assumed that the entity uses the perpetual inventory system.

Perpetual inventory system: Under the perpetual inventory system, the entity changes and makes the stock record up to date with each physical addition to or withdrawal from the stock of goods. The record shows the physical quantity and the rupee valuations after each purchase or issue of the material. The entity explicitly computes the cost of goods sold and calculates the cost of ending inventory based on the stock record. It compares the computed amount of ending inventory with the actual amount of ending inventory as a control devise to measure the loss due to natural shrinkages, wastages, or theft, etc. Entities usually support the perpetual inventory system by continuous physical verification of stock.

Under the perpetual inventory system, the weighted average formula to determine the cost of inventory becomes the moving average formula.

Periodic inventory system: Under this system, the enterprise uses data on beginning inventory, additions to inventory, and ending inventory to find the cost of withdrawal from inventory and the cost of ending inventory.

EXAMPLE 8.4 (Inventory valuation)

Fact pattern:

Opening stock:

March 1: Stock on hand 400 units @ ₹7.50 each

Purchases:

March 5: 600 units @ ₹8 each;
March 15: 500 units @ ₹9 each;
March 25: 400 units @ ₹8.50 each; and
March 30: 300 units @ ₹9.50 each

Issues:

March 3: 300 units
March 10: 500 units
March 17: 400 units
March 26: 500 units
March 31: 200 units

Discussion: Closing stock using different cost formulas

FIFO Formula:

Under periodic inventory method:

300 units × ₹9.50 = ₹2,850

Under perpetual inventory method:

Issues:

March 3: 300 units; total from the opening stock of 400 units
March 10: 500 units; 100 from the opening stock + 400 units from purchase on March 5
March 17: 400 units; 200 from purchase on March 5 + 200 from purchase on March 15
March 26: 500 units; 300 from purchase on March 15 + 200 from purchase on March 25
March 31: 200 units; total from purchase on March 25

Closing stock

300 units × ₹9.50 = ₹2,850

LIFO Formula:

Under periodic inventory method:

300 units × ₹7.50 = ₹2,250

Under perpetual inventory method:

Issues:

March 3: 300 units; total from the opening stock of 400 units
March 10: 500 units; total from purchase of 600 units on March 5
March 17: 400 units; total from purchase of 500 units on March 15
March 26: 500 units; 400 from purchase on March 25 + 100 from purchase on March 15
March 31: 200 units; total from purchase of 300 units on March 30

Closing stock

(100 units × ₹7.50) + (100 units × ₹8) + (100 units × ₹9.50) = ₹2,500

Weighted Average Formula:

Under periodic inventory method:
March 1: Stock on hand 400 units @ ₹7.50 each = ₹3,000

Purchases:

March 5: 600 units @ ₹8 each = ₹4,800
March 15: 500 units @ ₹9 each = ₹4,500
March 25: 400 units @ ₹8.50 each = ₹3,400
March 30: 300 units @ ₹9.50 each = ₹2,850
Total cost: ₹18,550; Total units: 2,200
Weighted average cost = (₹18,550/2,200) = ₹8.432 per unit
Value of closing inventory: 300 units × ₹8.432 = ₹2,529.60

Under perpetual inventory system

Date	Purchases			Issues			Closing stock		
March	Qty.	Rate (₹)	Value(₹)	Qty.	Rate(₹)	Value(₹)	Qty.	Rate(₹)	Value(₹)
Opening stock	400	7.50	3,000				400	7.50	3,000
3				300	7.50	3,000	100	7.50	750
5	600	8.00	4,800				700	7.929	5,550
10				500	7.929	3,965	200	7.929	1,585
15	500	9.00	4,500				700	8.693	6,085
17				400	8.693	3,477	300	8.693	2,608
25	400	8.50	3,400				700	8.583	6,008
26				500	8.583	4,292	200	8.583	1,716
30	300	9.50	2,850				500	9.132	4,566
31				200	9.132	1,826	300	9.132	2,740

Value of the ending inventory: ₹2,740.

8.1.8 Net Realisable Value

Net realisable value (NRV) is the estimated selling price in the ordinary course of business *less* the estimated costs of completion and the estimated costs necessary to make the sale.

Net realisable value (NRV) is the estimated selling price in the ordinary course of business less the estimated costs of completion and the estimated costs necessary to make the sale.

Estimation of NRV

Estimates of NRV are based on the most reliable evidence available at the time the estimates are made, taking into consideration fluctuations of price or cost directly relating to events occurring after the balance sheet date to the extent that such events confirm conditions existing at the end of the period.

The NRV of the quantity of inventory held to satisfy firm sales or service contracts should be based on the contract price. If the sales contracts are for less than the inventory quantities held, the NRV of the excess is based on general selling prices.

Comparison of NRV with cost

The comparison of NRV with cost should be carried out on an item-by-item basis. However, if this is impracticable, groups of similar items may be considered together. Comparison of the total NRV of all stocks with their total purchase price or production cost is precluded.

The comparison of NRV with cost should be carried out on an item-by-item basis.

EXAMPLE 8.5 (Estimation of NRV)

Fact pattern: An entity manufactures equipment against firm orders. The typical contract terms require the entity to deliver the equipment at the customers' site. The entity has inventory of five pieces of equipment. The aggregate selling price of those items is ₹5,00,000. The entity estimates the delivery expenses at 2 per cent of the selling price.

Discussion: The NRV of those items are (₹5,00,000 – .02 × 5,00,000) or ₹4,90,000.

EXAMPLE 8.6 (Estimation of NRV of WIP)

Fact pattern: Job No. E–101 was incomplete at the balance sheet date. Cost incurred on that job till that date was ₹5,50,000. The entity estimates that it will incur further ₹100,000 to complete the job. The contract price is ₹800,000 and the estimated selling expense is ₹10,000.

Discussion: The NRV is (₹8,00,000 – ₹10,000 – ₹1,00,000) or ₹6,90,000. The NRV being higher than the cost, the job E–101 (work-in-process) should be carried in the balance sheet at ₹5,50,000, as a part of the inventory.

EXAMPLE 8.7 (Estimation of NRV)

Fact pattern: A pharmaceutical company produces a medicine named *Nemoxin*. The cost of production per unit is ₹50. The list price of the product as at March 31, 2022 was ₹48 per unit. In May 2022, before the approval of financial statements for 2021–2022, the company reduced the selling price to ₹45 per unit.

Discussion: The NRV is ₹45 per unit. The stock of *Nemoxin* as at March 31, 2022 should be valued at ₹45 per unit, which is lower than the cost of production of ₹50 per unit.

EXAMPLE 8.8 (Estimation of NRV)

Fact pattern: An entity produces woolen garments. It has 1,000 numbers of executive quality *Beautiful* brand pullovers in its stock as at March 31, 2022, the last day of the accounting year. In summer, the enterprise sells its product at a discount of 20% on the list price at which the product is being sold in the winter season. The management estimates that 200 units will be sold in summer and balance quantity will be sold in winter. The listed price is ₹1,000 per piece.

Discussion: The NRV of 200 units is ₹800 per unit and balance 800 units is ₹1,000 per unit.

NRV of raw materials, components and other supplies

Materials and other supplies held for use in the production of inventories are usually valued at cost.

Materials and other supplies held for use in the production of inventories are usually valued at cost. However, when a decline in the price of materials indicates that the cost of the finished products exceeds the NRV, the materials are written down to the NRV. In such circumstances, the replacement cost of the materials may be the best available measure of their net realisable value.

EXAMPLE 8.9 (Valuation of raw material)

Fact pattern: 10,000 units of raw material A was in stock at the balance sheet date. It was purchased at ₹20 per unit and the replacement cost at the balance sheet date was ₹15 per unit. One unit of A is required to produce one unit of B. The entity estimates the cost and the net realisable value of B at the balance sheet date at ₹100 and ₹98 respectively.

Discussion: A should be valued at its replacement cost, which is ₹15 per unit, as the management estimated that the NRV of the finished product (B) is lower than the cost by ₹2. The estimated amount of loss on the finished product is not a factor in determining the carrying amount of the raw material. If a loss is estimated on sale of the finished product, the raw material should be carried at the replacement cost.

8.2 TRADE RECEIVABLES

Trade receivables are measured at the transaction price. If the credit period extended to a customer is 12 months or more, it is assumed that the transaction price includes financing element.

'Trade receivables' represent the amount that customers owe to the entity. It is a financial asset. Those that meet the criteria for classifying as current assets are classified as current assets, and others are classified as non-current asset.

Measurement

Financial assets are initially recognised at fair value (FV). This accounting principle is applicable to trade receivables also.

Usually, FV is the transaction price to which the entity is entitled. However, if the credit period extended to a customer is 12 months or more from the date of transfer of the control of goods or delivery of services, it is assumed that the transaction price includes financing element. Both the revenue and the trade receivable are remeasured at the present value (PV) of the transaction price. PV is determined by discounting the amount receivable from the customer by the interest rate at which the customer could borrow from the market at the same terms and conditions at which the credit is granted to the customer.

The interest element should be recognised separately as interest income.

The interest element should be recognised separately as interest income.

EXAMPLE 8.10 (Financing element in transaction price)

Fact pattern: The transaction price of ₹1,20,000 is payable by the customer after 12 months from the date of delivery of the goods. The entity estimates that customer with its present credit rating could borrow the amount from market for 12 months at the interest rate of 10 per cent per annum.

Discussion: Revenue and trade receivables should be recognised at [₹1,20,000/(1,10)] or ₹1,09,091. Interest income should be recognised at (₹1,20,000 ₹1,09,091) or ₹10,909.

Impairment

Impairment loss occurs when the entity fails to recover the total amount due from the customer. Trade receivables are measured at the amount that is receivable from the customer reduced by the estimated impairment loss. Entities estimate the impairment loss based on the historical default rates over the expected life of the trade receivables and is adjusted for forward-looking estimates. This estimate is called *life-time expected credit loss.* Impairment loss is estimated for each class of customers separately using a provision matrix. Provision for the impairment loss is presented in the balance sheet as a deduction from the gross amount of trade receivables. The provision for impairment loss is also called *valuation allowance.* Earlier the provision for impairment loss was called the provision for doubtful debts.

Trade receivables are measured at the amount that is receivable from the customer reduced by the estimated impairment loss.

Table 8.4 presents an example of provision matrix.

TABLE 8.4 Example of Provision Matrix

	Current	*1–30 days past due*	*31–60 days past due*	*61–90 days past due*	*91 days or more past due*
Default rate (A)	0.5%	1.5%	3.0%	5.0%	10%
Gross carrying amount in ₹	20,000	10,000	5,000	3,000	1,000
Lifetime expected credit loss ₹	100	150	150	150	100

Contract asset

A contract asset arises when an entity has fulfilled the performance obligation to deliver the goods or services to the customer and recognised as revenue but not yet issued an invoice or received payment, because the amount is payable by the customer on fulfilment of some other conditions. For example, as per the contractual terms and conditions, the entity would issue the invoice when all the goods included in the contract would be delivered.

Contract assets are tested for impairment.

8.3 LOAN

Loan disbursed to another entity is a financial asset.

Loans that meet the criteria for classifying as current assets are classified as current assets, and others are classified as non-current assets.

Loan is initially recognised at the fair value (FV). It is subsequently measured at amortised cost using the effective interest rate method. A provision of impairment loss is recognised using the expected credit loss method.

Measurement

Loan is initially recognised at the fair value (FV). It is subsequently measured at amortised cost using the *effective interest rate method.* A provision of impairment loss is recognised using the expected credit loss method.

FV is different from the amount of loan if, the loan is granted at an interest rate different from the interest rate at which the borrower could borrow from the market at the same terms and conditions. Sometimes, entities provide loans to employees and vendors at concessional rates. It is very rare that entities lend money to a borrower at an interest rate higher than the market rate of interest. If the loan is provided at a concessional rate, the fair value should be lower than the amount of loan. The difference in the fair value and the amount of loan is recognised as an expense in the statement of profit and loss under an appropriate expense head.

Nominal and effective interest rate

The nominal rate is the interest rate as stated is usually compounded more than once per year. The effective rate (or effective annual rate) is a rate that, compounded annually, gives the same interest rate as the nominal interest rate. If two interest rates have the same effective rate, we say they are equivalent.

To find the effective rate (f) of a nominal rate (j) compounded m times per year, we can use the formula:

$$f = \left(1 + \frac{j}{m}\right)^m - 1$$

EXAMPLE 8.11 (Nominal and effective interest rate)

Fact pattern: Nominal rate is 12 per cent per annum, compounded quarterly.

Discussion: Effective interest rate = $\left(1 + \frac{0.12}{4}\right)^4 - 1 = 0.1255$ or 12.55 per cent

Impairment

Expected credit loss method should be used to estimate impairment of loans. It requires estimating the impairment loss before the loss event, such as, default in payment of principal or interest, occurs. At the point of initial recognition, one-year expected credit loss is measured. One-year expected credit loss is the estimated impairment loss that will arise from credit loss events that are expected to occur within one year. If, after a year, the credit risk of the loan increases from the originally estimated credit risk, lifetime expected credit loss is estimated. Lifetime expected credit loss is the estimated impairment loss, which will arise from credit loss events that are expected to occur over the expected life of the loan.

EXAMPLE 8.12 (Measurement of loan)

Fact pattern: On April 1, 2020, an entity (L) disbursed loan of ₹10,00,000 to an employee (E) at an interest rate of 4% per annum. As per the terms of the loan, E will repay the total amount on April 1, 2023. No interest is payable for one day for which the loan will remain outstanding after March 31, 2022. Interest is payable annually on 31 March. On April 1, 2020, E could borrow from the market the same amount at similar terms and conditions at an interest rate of 10% per annum compounded annually. The financial year of L commences on April 1 and closes on March 31, next year.

Discussion: For the purpose of calculating the fair value, we assume that E will repay the loan on March 31, 2022. Therefore, the cash inflow to E will be as follows:

₹40,000 (interest) on March 31, 2021, ₹40,000 (interest) on March 31, 2022, and ₹10,40,000 (interest plus principal) on March 31, 2023. The effective interest rate is 10%.

Thus,

PV of the cash flows = $[40{,}000/(1.10)] + [40{,}000/(1.10)^2] + [10{,}40{,}000/(1.10)^3]$ = ₹8,50,790

We have assumed that there will be no pre-payment of principal. The loan will be initially measured at ₹850,790.

The opening and closing balances of loan and the calculation of effective interest of B are as follows:

Year/Date	Opening balance (₹)	Interest received (₹)	Effective interest (₹) (2 x 10%)	Closing balance (₹) (2 + 4 – 3)
(1)	(2)	(3)	(4)	(5)
2020–2021	8,50,790	40,000	85,079	8,95,869
2021–2022	8,95,869	40,000	89,587	9,45,456
2022–2023	9,45,456	40,000	94,544	10,00,000

8.4 OTHER CURRENT ASSETS

8.4.1 Advances and Prepaid Expenses

In normal circumstances, the vendor has no obligation to repay the amount paid in advance. The amount is adjusted against the amount that will be payable to vendors on supply of the goods or services as per the contractual arrangement. Therefore, prepaid expenses and advances are non-financial assets.

Prepaid expenses and advances are carried in the balance sheet at the amount paid *less* the amount adjusted till the balance sheet date. An advance or a prepaid expense is classified as current asset if it is expected to be adjusted within 12 months after the balance sheet date.

8.4.2 Marketable Securities

Marketable securities are short-term (12 months or less) securities which are traded in the capital market and convertible into cash easily. They are classified as current asset and viewed as financial instruments held for trading. Therefore, initially and at each balance sheet date, they are measured at fair value. Change in fair value is recognised as profit or loss in the statement of profit and loss.

Marketable securities are short-term (12 months or less) securities which are traded in the capital market and convertible into cash easily.

8.4.3 Cash and Cash Equivalents

Cash and cash equivalents are recognised as current assets, unless there are restrictions on their short-term use. Cash equivalents do not include investment in equity securities. Therefore, cash equivalents, such as commercial papers and short-term government bonds, are measured at amortised cost.

Cash and cash equivalents are recognised as current assets, unless there are restrictions on their short-term use.

REVIEW PROBLEMS

R8.1 Indicate whether the following statements are True or False:

(i) Inventories of stock-in-trade, finished goods and work-in-process are measured at the lower of cost and net realisable value (NRV).

(ii) The cost of units included in inventories should include all the costs incurred to bring those items to the location and condition of sale.

(iii) Warehousing costs incurred to store the finished goods and stock-in-trade closer to the point of sale should be included in the cost of units stored in the warehouse.

(iv) Companies have the choice to value inventories using one of the four cost formulas–specific identification, LIFO, FIFO, and weighted average.

(v) Demurrage charges paid for delay in taking out the material from the port should be included in the material cost.

(vi) Fixed production overheads should be assigned to units in inventories based on the normal capacity irrespective of the capacity utilisation in a particular year.

(vii) Usually, the transaction price is considered to be the fair value of trade receivables for initial measurement.

(viii) Impairment loss of trade receivables should be measured using the life time expected credit loss.

(ix) A single rate should be applied to the total amount due from customers for estimating the provision required for doubtful debts.

(x) Effective interest rate method should be applied in measuring the carrying amount of loan granted to employees at a concessional rate.

R8.2 Fill in the blanks:

(i) The fixed production overhead in a particular financial year is ₹50,00,000. The normal capacity is estimated at 5,00,000 units. The number of quantities produced is 6,25,000. The overhead absorption rate should be ₹................ per unit for assigning overheads to units sold and units in the inventories.

(ii) The fixed production overhead in a particular financial year is ₹50,00,000. The normal capacity is estimated at 5,00,000 units. The number of quantities produced is 4,00,000 units. The overhead absorption rate should be ₹................ per unit for assigning overheads to units sold and units in the inventories.

(iii) An firm that is in the merchandising business sells the goods from 12 large retail stores located in the Delhi NCR. The orders on suppliers are placed centrally and the suppliers deliver goods directly to the central warehouse located in Noida (a city in Delhi NCR). The central warehouse delivers the goods to retail stores based on requisitions received from each store. It provides the following information: (a) the average price of the goods: ₹1,500 per unit; (b) Average warehousing charge: ₹5 per unit; (c) Average cost of transporting goods to stores: ₹3 per unit. The average cost on units included in the inventories at the retail stores is ₹................

(iv) The inventory system under which the entity changes and makes the stock record up to date with each physical addition to or withdrawal from the stock of goods is called .... inventory system.

(v) On the balance sheet date, 50,000 units of a particular product is included in inventories. The entity sells the product at an average price of ₹90 per unit, which is 10 per cent lower than the list price and pays 10 per cent commissions to the salespeople. The net realisable value is ₹................ per unit.

(vi) A vaccine manufacturer holds 100,000 units of a particular vaccine in inventories on the balance sheet date. Out of the stock that the company holds, 50,000 units are to be supplied to the government at a price of ₹500 per unit. The list price of the vaccine is ₹1,200 for private parties. On the face of criticism, before the financial statements are approved by the board of directors after the balance sheet date, the government directed the company to sell the vaccine to private parties at ₹900 per unit. There is no incremental cost for selling the vaccine. The net realisable value of inventories of 100,000 units is ₹................

(vii) A firm granted loan of ₹1,00,000 to an employee at an interest of 4 per cent per annum repayable in equal monthly instalments over a period of 20 years. The employees could borrow from bank the same amount with the same terms and conditions at an interest rate of 8 per cent per annum. The effective interest rate is .... per cent per annum.

(viii) An individual has borrowed ₹1,00,000 from a bank at an interest of 10 per cent per annum. It paid loan processing charge of ₹5,000 to the bank. Interest on the outstanding amount is payable at the end of each year and the loan is repayable is payable repayable in five yearly instalments. First instalment is payable at the end of the first year. The effective interest rate is .... per cent per annum.

ASSIGNMENTS

1. Prema Departmental Stores (PDS) started operations on January 1, 2007. It was engaged in the following transactions during January. Identify the amount that the company should include in the valuation of the merchandise inventory.

(i) Purchases of merchandise on account during January: ₹50,00,000

(ii) Freight cost to transport merchandise to the warehouse of PDS: ₹20,000

(iii) Salary of the purchase manager: ₹50,000

(iv) Depreciation, taxes, insurance and utilities for the warehouse: ₹30,000

(v) Salary of the warehouse manager: ₹20,000

(vi) Cost of merchandise that PDS purchased in part (i) and that was returned to the supplier: ₹10,000

(vii) Cash discount taken by PDS from purchases on account in part (i): ₹5,000

2. Tick the correct answer:

(i) On December 20, 2006, Sanjukta Limited (SL) purchased goods costing ₹5,00,000. The terms were 'Free on Board' (FOB) destination. The following costs were incurred in connection with the delivery of goods:

Packaging and shipment	₹6,000
Shipping	₹4,000
Special handling charges	₹2,000

These goods are included in inventory. What cost should be considered for the purpose of inventory valuation?

(a) ₹5,12,000 (b) ₹5,10,000

(c) ₹5,06,000 (d) ₹5,00,000

(ii) On September 1, 2006, Mrinalini Limited (ML) purchased material from Ketan Limited (KL). The list price of the material was ₹1,00,000. KL allowed trade discount and quantity discount of 30% and 20%, respectively. Credit terms were 2/15, *n*/40 and the sale was made FOB shipping point. The shipping cost was ₹5,000. ML paid the amount due to KL on September 12, 2006. The cost at which the material was recorded in the books of ML is:

(a) ₹68,880 (b) ₹54,880

(c) ₹61,000 (d) ₹59,880

(iii) What is considered to be the normal capacity?

(a) Average production over the previous five year period.

(b) Budgeted production for the period.

(c) Actual production for the period plus the loss of capacity for planned maintenance.

(d) Estimated average production during next three to five years determined after taking into account planned maintenance, and business and industry factors.

3. Indicate against each statement whether it is True or False:

(i) Inventories are necessarily classified as current assets.

(ii) Goods, which are held for sale, are classified as current assets even if they are expected to be sold after 12 months after the balance sheet date.

(iii) Investments in treasury bills are included in cash equivalents.

(iv) Amount of cheques received but not deposited in bank till the balance sheet date (called cheques in hand) is included in cash equivalents.

(v) A firm should determine a single 'normal operating cycle' for a particular business.

(vi) If a firm cannot estimate the normal operating cycle, it is assumed that the normal operating cycle is 12 months.

(vii) Core inventory of crude oil in an oil refinery should be classified as PP&E.

(viii) The balance in escrow account with a bank, which can be used only to purchase the land included in an 'agreement to sale' with the land owner, is a non-current asset.

(ix) Demurrage charge should be included in the cost of the items in the inventory.

(x) By-products are often measured at net realisable value.

(xi) Cash discount should be deducted in calculating the purchase price.

(xii) Interest and other borrowing costs are usually not included in the inventory cost.

(xiii) In estimating the cost of items in inventory, an entity may use any one of the three cost formulas—FIFO, LIFO, and weighted average.

(xiv) In estimating the NRV, transactions between the balance sheet date and the date of approval of the same by the Board of Directors should be taken into account.

(xv) A firm, which is engaged in merchandising business and follows the practice of home delivery, should deduct the estimated home

4. Fill in the blanks:

(i) The installed capacity of the production facility of a firm manufacturing a luxury fountain pen is 100,000 units. The attainable capacity, which is calculated as installed capacity less loss of capacity due to shut down on account of normal maintenance, is 90,000 units. The practical capacity, which is the capacity that the firm intended to use at the time of acquisition of the facility, is 85,000 units. At the beginning of the year 2010–2011, the firm, after taking into account estimated market demand for its product for the next five years, estimates the average use of the capacity over the next five years at 70,000 units. The normal capacity is .... units.

(ii) The normal capacity of a production facility owned by Sunayana Limited (SL) is 80,000 units of table fans. During 2010–2011, it incurred ₹10,00,000 towards fixed factory overheads and produced 70,000 units of table fans. The amount of fixed factory overheads to be included in the conversion cost of table fans in the year-end inventory is ₹................ per unit.

(iii) The normal capacity of a production facility owned by Sunayana Limited (SL) is 80,000 units of table fans. During 2010–2011, it incurred ₹10,00,000 towards fixed factory overheads and produced 90,000 units of table fans. The amount of fixed factory overheads to be included in the conversion cost of table fans in the year-end inventory is ₹................ per unit.

(iv) Kaveri Limited (KL) produces machine tools against confirmed orders from customers. The work-in-progress (WIP) inventory as at the end of the year includes a job order on which cost accumulated till the end of the year was ₹10,00,000. The management estimates that it has to incur ₹5,00,000 to complete the job. The selling price of the job as per the contract is ₹18,00,000. Thus, the estimated gross profit on the job is 20% of the total cost of production. The net realisable value at the balance sheet date was ₹................

(v) Natasha Limited (NL) uses raw material X to produce an electronic safety device that is used by the Railways. One unit of the material is used to produce one unit of the finished product. With increase in the budget allocation for safety items, a large player in the electronic industry has included in its product portfolio a product similar to that is being produced by NL. In order to penetrate the market, it has quoted a price lower than the price at which NL secured orders from Railways in the past. NL has secured a fresh order after matching its price with that of the new player which quoted the lowest price. NL estimates that it will incur a loss of ₹5,000 per unit. The cost of production is estimated at ₹1,60,000. The book value of the material A is ₹25,000 per unit and its replacement cost is ₹28,000 per unit. The year-end inventory of the material X should be valued at ₹................ per unit.

(vi) Manshi Limited (ML) uses raw material Y to produce an electronic choke that is used by Railways. One unit of the material is used to produce one unit of the finished product. With increase in the budget allocation for coach maintenance, a large player in the electronic industry has included in its product portfolio a product similar to that is being produced by ML. In order to penetrate the market, it has quoted a price lower than the price at which ML secured orders from the Railways in past. ML has secured a fresh order after matching its price with that of the new player which quoted the lowest price. ML estimates that it will incur a loss of ₹5,000 per unit. The cost of production is estimated at ₹1,50,000. The book value of the material A is ₹24,000 per unit and its replacement cost is ₹20,000 per unit. The year-end inventory of the material X should be valued at ₹................per unit.

(vii) Sugandha Limited (SL) is in the business of manufacturing potato flakes. The manufacturing facility is located in Dhanekhali in Nadia district of West Bengal. It purchases potato directly from farmers in West Bengal. The quality and the cost of potato flakes depend on the ability of the company to deliver fresh potatoes to the manufacturing facility. The key is speed of delivery to factory after collection from the farmers and maintenance of appropriate temperature inside the container during transportation. SL manages the inward logistics internally. The fixed overhead of the logistic department was ₹500 million. The fixed overhead of the logistic department .... form part of the cost of inventories of potatoes. (Select the right word from the two words 'should' and 'should not'.)

(viii) Aparajita Limited (AL) sold goods to Bidisha Limited (BL) for ₹10,00,000. As per the agreement, BL will pay the amount due to AL after 12 months from the transaction date. AL could borrow the amount for one year at an interest rate of 12% per annum and BL could borrow the amount for one year at an interest rate of 15% per annum. AL should recognise the revenue and receivable at ₹................

CHAPTER 9

INVESTMENTS

CHAPTER OBJECTIVES

The objectives of this chapter is to introduce to readers the nature and accounting for assets that are classified as investments in the balance sheet. In particular, the objective is developing and understanding of:

- Nature and purpose of investments;
- Investments in financial assets—classification and valuation;
- Investment property.

9.1 NATURE AND PURPOSE OF INVESTMENTS

Capital that a firm invests outside the business to earn a regular return and/or to gain from capital appreciation is classified as investment for presentation in the balance sheet. Investments that are included in cash equivalents are not included in investments.

The purposes for which firms invests in financial assets and properties (land, and building) can be summarised in Table 9.1 below.

TABLE 9.1 Investment Purposes

	Purpose	*Description*
1.	Retain excess capital for future use	Companies aim that the excess capital retained in the company earns some return before a new business opportunity is identified.
2.	Earn trade benefits	Companies invest in firms that supply inputs and those who purchase outputs to earn trade benefits. Investee firms are classified as Associate when the company (investor) significantly influences the operating and financing decisions of the investee.
3.	Control other companies (subsidiaries)	Companies operate through subsidiaries to achieve many goals, such as, unfettered attention to a different businesses, controlling the supply chain partners, and horizontal and vertical expansion with financial support from public shareholders.
4.	Share risks and pool skills and capabilities (joint ventures)	Two or more companies form joint ventures for sharing risks and pooling skills and capabilities required for executing a project or operating in a new geographical location.

Investment classifications

Investments can be classified into investments in financial assets, such as investments in equity shares and bonds issued by other companies and investment in property (land, and building). Investment in property is classified as investment property in the balance sheet.

9.2 INVESTMENTS IN FINANCIAL ASSETS

9.2.1 Recognition

Investments in financial assets are recognised when the investor becomes a party to the contract. For example, investment in equity shares and bonds are recognised when the investee allots those to the investors.

9.2.2 Measurement of Investment in Debt Instruments

Investments in a debt instrument is initially measured at fair value, which is usually, the transaction price.

Initial measurement

Investments in a debt instrument is initially measured at fair value, which is usually, the transaction price.

Subsequent measurement

Investments in debt instruments that meet the SPPI criteria and which the entity holds in the *'Held-to-collect'* business model are measured at amortised cost.

1. Investments in debt instruments that meet the SPPI criteria and which the entity holds in the *'Held-to-collect'* business model are measured at amortised cost. In the *'Held-to-collect'* business model, the sale is incidental. SPPI stands for 'solely payments of principal and interest on principal amount outstanding'. Contractual cash flows that meet the SPPI criterion are consistent with a *basic lending arrangement*. In such arrangements, consideration for the time value of money and credit risks are typically the most significant elements of interest.

2. Investments in debt instruments that meet the SPPI criteria and which the entity holds in the *'Held-to-collect and sale'* business model are measured are classified as "Fair value through other comprehensive income' (FVOCI) and are measured at fair value (FV). The change in the FV is recognised in OCI and accumulated in equity. When the investment is sold, the change in FV accumulated in equity is transferred (in accounting jargon, reclassified) to profit or loss. In *'Held-to-collect and sale'* business model the entity sells the investments when needed and the sale is not incidental.
3. Investments in debt instruments that neither meet the SPPI criteria nor held for trading are measured are classified as "Fair value through profit and loss' (FVTPL) and are measured at fair value (FV). The change in the FV is recognised in profit or loss.

Investments in debt instruments that meet the SPPI criteria and which the entity holds in the 'Held-to-collect and sale' business model are classified as FVOCI.

The change in the FV is accumulated in equity, which is transferred to profit or loss when the investment is sold.

Impairment

Investments which are measured either at amortised cost and investments that are classified as FVOCI are tested for impairment loss using the *Expected Credit Loss* method.

9.2.3 Measurement of Investment in Equity Instruments

Initial measurement

Investments in an equity instrument is initially measured at fair value, which is usually, the transaction price.

Subsequent measurement

1. Investments in equity instruments are classified as FVTPL and are measured at fair value (FV). As an exemption, entities can be classified, at the inception, an investment in equity as FVOCI. However, this exemption is not available for investments held for trading. Change in FV of investments classified as FVOCI is recognised in OCI and accumulated in equity. When the investment is sold, the change in FV accumulated in equity is transferred to general reserve directly and not reclassified to profit or loss.
2. Investment in the equity shares of subsidiaries, associates and joint ventures are usually measured at cost. Entities have the option to measure those at FV.

Impairment

Investments are not tested for impairment.

9.2.4 Investment in Mutual Funds

Investments in debt instruments that either does not meet the SPPI criteria or are held for trading are classified as FVTPL. The change in the FV is recognised in profit or loss.

1. Entities should classify investments in units of open-ended mutual funds, including debt mutual funds, as 'Financial assets measured at FVTPL', as they do not meet the SPPI criterion.
2. Investment in a close-ended mutual fund meets the SPPI criterion, if the fund holds only debt instruments that themselves would qualify for amortised cost classification had those instruments been directly held by the unit holder.

Impairment

Investments in closed ended mutual fund that are measured at amortised cost are tested for impairment.

9.2.5 Bid-Ask Spread

Dealers in financial markets (and perhaps in all markets) follow the principle of 'buying low and selling high'. The price they quote to buy is called the *bid price,* and the price they quote to sell is called *ask price.* The difference between the bid price and ask price, which is called the *bid-ask spread,* is their margin. For example, a market maker quotes ₹98 – ₹100 for shares of a listed company. The bid-ask spread is ₹2. The bid-ask spread is considered as transaction cost.

In stock market, which operates under the quote-driven mechanism, market makers give two-way quotes. They quote the bid and ask prices at the same time. In Indian stock exchanges, what exists here is rather the concept of market maker is almost absent, and consequently, the concept of bid-ask spread has no relevance-order-driven trading mechanism where any market participant can enter an order which is visible over the market screen. Other participants view the same and enter a counter order at the same price or a price suitable for them. Trade takes place when orders match.

9.2.6 Effective Interest Rate Method

Effective interest rate is the rate that exactly discounts estimated future cash receipts through the expected life of the financial instrument to the net carrying amount of the financial asset. It is estimated at the time of acquisition of the financial asset. It is also called *yield to maturity* and *internal rate of return (IRR)*. The IRR function in the Microsoft Excel can be used to calculate the effective interest rate. Otherwise, it is calculated by trial-and-error method.

Effective interest rate is the rate that exactly discounts estimated future cash receipts through the expected life of the financial instrument to its net carrying amount. It is estimated at the time of acquisition of the financial asset.

The *initial cash outflow*, which is discounted to measure the effective interest rate, is the cost of the investment plus the transaction costs.

EXAMPLE 9.1 (Effective interest rate)

On January 1, 2018, Satyiki Limited (SL) acquired a bond with face value of ₹1,00,000 and coupon rate of 7% at ₹1,10,000. The remaining period to maturity is four years. Interest is payable by the issuer of the bond at the end of each year (31 December) and the principal will be refunded at the end of the fourth year. The transaction cost was 0.4% of the purchase price.

Effective interest rate: The acquisition cost is ₹1,10,440 (1,10,000 × 1.004). Cash inflow at the end of each of the first three years is ₹7,000. At the end of the fourth year, cash inflow, including repayment of principal, will be ₹1,07,000. Therefore, IRR should be calculated taking cash flow of – (minus) ₹110,440 at the beginning of the first year (January 1, 2018), which is referred to as year 0. Cash flow at the end of each year was as follows:

Year 1, ₹7,000; year 2, ₹7,000; year 3, ₹7,000; and year 4, ₹1,07,000.

IRR is the discount rate at which the present value (PV) of the cash flow stream is zero. Using the IRR function in the Microsoft Excel, we get the IRR of 4.1160%. Therefore, 4.1160% is the effective interest rate. For accounting purpose, we may use the rate of 4.12%, which is correct up to two decimal places.

EXAMPLE 9.2 (Amortised cost)

Consider the facts presented in Example 9.1 above, and assume that SL closes its financial year on 31 December each year.

Discussion: We shall use the following table to explain the accounting for the investment and related interest income.

Year	*Opening balance of investment* (₹)	*Cash Flow* (₹)	*Effective interest* (₹) (2 × 0.412)	*Closing balance of investment* (₹) (2 + 4 – 3)
(1)	(2)	(3)	(4)	(5)
2018	1,10,440.00	7,000.00	4,550.13	1,07,990.13
2019	1,07,990.13	7,000.00	4,449.19	1,05,439.32
2020	1,05,439.32	7,000.00	4,344.10	1,02,783.42
2021	1,02,783.42	1,07,000.00	4,234.68	18.10

SL should recognise the investment initially at ₹1,10,440.

In 2018, SL should recognise interest income at ₹4,550.13. In the balance sheet as at December 31, 2018, it should recognise the investment at amortised cost, which is, ₹1,07,990.13.

In 2019, SL should recognise interest income at ₹4,449.19. In the balance sheet as at December 31, 2019, it should recognise the investment at ₹1,05,439.32.

In 2020, SL should recognise interest income at ₹4,344.10. In the balance sheet as at December 31, 2020, it should recognise the investment at ₹1,02,783.42.

In 2021, SL should recognise interest income at (4,234.68 – 18.10) or ₹4,216.58. The investment will not appear in the balance sheet as at December 31, 2020. It will be derecognised on the realisation of the principal. Note that the approximation error of ₹18.10 will be adjusted against the interest income.

Investment in property (land or a building—or part of a building—or both) is classified as investment property.

9.2.7 Investment Property

Investment in property (land or a building—or part of a building—or both) is classified as investment property.

An investment property is measured initially at its cost. Transaction costs are included in the initial measurement.

9.2.8 Initial Measurement

An investment property is measured initially at its cost. Transaction costs are included in the initial measurement. Principles and methods for accumulating cost of investment property are the same as those for accumulating costs of owner-occupied property.

An entity should subsequently measure an investment property at cost.

9.2.9 Subsequent Measurement

An entity has to measure an investment property at cost. A proposal to provide an option to measure investment property at fair value is an active consideration of the standard-setters in India.

Cost model

The principles and methods used to account for investment property using the cost model are the same as those used to measure items of PP&E.

Fair value model

After initial recognition, an entity that chooses the fair value model measures all of its investment property at fair value. The fair value of investment property should reflect market conditions at the end of the reporting period.

A gain or loss arising from a change in the fair value of investment property is recognised in profit or loss.

REVIEW PROBLEMS

R9.1 Indicate whether the following statements are True or False:

(i) The only purpose for which firms invest a part of capital outside the business is to earn a regular return and gain from capital appreciation.

(ii) Investments in equity instruments should be measured at fair value.

(iii) The method of measuring investments in debt securities depends on the contractual terms and the business model in which they are held.

(iv) A loan with foreclosure option does not meet the SPSS criteria.

(v) Investments in open-ended debt mutual funds should be measured at fair value.

ASSIGNMENTS

1. **Indicate against each statement whether it is True or False:**
   (i) In the balance sheet, investments other than those that augment or maintain the capacity of producing goods and services are classified as investment.
   (ii) Investment in a debt instrument (e.g., debenture), which is issued by another firm, is always classified as measured at FVOCI in the balance sheet of the investor if it intends to hold the same till maturity.
   (iii) The concept of bid-ask spread has no relevance in India.
   (iv) Effective interest rate of a debt instrument held as investment is its yield to maturity at the acquisition date.
   (v) A loan granted by a bank to its constituent usually meets the SPPI criterion.
   (vi) Investments in debt instruments issued by another entity cannot be classified as measured at FVTL in the balance sheet of the investor.
   (vii) A company has a choice to measure its investment in a subsidiary either at cost or at fair value.
   (viii) Apartments owned by an entity and let out to its employees should usually be classified as PP&E in the balance sheet of the entity.
   (ix) Change in the fair value of held for trading investments during a period are included in profit or loss for the period.
   (x) Effective interest rate of an investment in fixed-interest debt instrument, estimated at the time of acquisition of the investment, does not change even if the market interest rate for a similar instrument changes over the life of the instrument.
   (xi) Held for trading investment is not tested for impairment.
   (xii) Investment in equity instrument is not tested for impairment.

2. **Fill in the blanks:**
   (i) On April 1, 2010, Shreyas Limited (SL) purchased 8% debentures (face value ₹1,00,000) from the market for ₹85,000. Interest on the debenture is payable on 31 March every year. The debenture will be redeemed on March 31, 2014. The effective interest rate is ....%.
   (ii) The carrying amount (fair value) of investment in debt securities, which is designated as measured at FVOCI, as at the beginning of the year was ₹750. The fair value of the same at the end of the year was ₹850. The effective interest for the period was ₹75. ₹......... should be recognised as other comprehensive income.
   (iii) Loans are initially measured at ....
   (iv) On April 1, 2010, Anusua Limited (AL) had paid one of its suppliers of goods ₹1,00,00,000 as loan to enable it to upgrade its technology to match the quality requirement of AL. No interest is payable and the loan will be adjusted against the cost of goods to be supplied against future orders. ₹10,00,000 will be adjusted at the end of each quarter beginning from June 30, 2010. The supplier, being categorised as small and medium enterprise (SME), could borrow the amount from a scheduled bank at a concessional interest rate of 9% per annum. AL should recognise vendor development expense in the statement of profit and loss for the quarter ended on June 30, 2010 at ₹..........
   (v) On April 1, 2010, Mitali Limited (ML) paid an advance of ₹1,00,00,000 to Layla Limited (LL) towards advance payment against an order for the supply of equipment. It is expected that LL will supply the equipment after 18 months. LL could borrow the amount from market at an interest rate of 15% per annum. ML should recognise the advance at ₹..........
   (vi) At each balance sheet date, investments held for trading should be carried at ....
   (vii) At each balance sheet date, investments in debt instruments, which are not meeting the SPPI criterion should be carried at ....

CHAPTER 10

LIABILITIES

CHAPTER OBJECTIVES

The objectives of this chapter is to introduce to readers the nature and accounting for liabilities. In particular, the objective is developing and understanding of:

- Measurement of liabilities;
- Measurement of post-retirement employee benefits.

10.1 MEASUREMENT OF LIABILITIES

10.1.1 Measurement of Financial Liabilities

Financial liabilities are contractual obligations to transfer cash or other financial instruments. Examples are borrowings and trade creditors.

Initial measurement

A financial liability is initially measured at fair value (FV), adjusted for transaction costs, which are directly attributable to the assumption of the liability.

A financial liability is initially measured at fair value (FV), adjusted for transaction costs.

Fair value of a financial liability

Fair value is the exit price. In other words, fair value is the price at which the entity can transfer the liability to a third party. In the absence of active markets for financial liabilities, usually, FV is the present value (PV) calculated using the market perception about the interest rate at which the creditor could borrow the amount from the market for the same terms and with similar conditions.

In the absence of active markets, FV is the PV calculated using the market perception about the interest rate at which the creditor could borrow from the market for the same terms and with similar conditions.

Borrowings at an interest rate lower than the market interest rate

If the terms and conditions at which the amount borrowed or liabilities assumed are different from market terms and conditions, the FV will be different from the transaction price. For example, if an entity has borrowed at an interest rate lower than the market rate or receives refundable security deposits from contractors, who execute long-term projects and under terms and conditions that do not require the entity to pay any interest on the same, the FV should be lower than the transaction price (amount borrowed and security deposit received). If the FV is lower than the transaction price, the difference between the two is recognised as income and is presented in the statement of profit and loss under the appropriate line item. The nature of the income should be disclosed.

EXAMPLE 10.1 (Borrowing at market terms and conditions)

Fact pattern: On December 31, 2019, Naina Limited (NL) borrowed ₹100 million from the State Bank of India at the market rate of interest, which is 12% per annum. The loan is repayable in five equal yearly instalments. Each instalment is payable at the end of each year, starting from December 31, 2020. Interest is payable at the end of each year starting from December 31, 2020. Other terms and conditions of the loan are similar to those which are normally imposed by financial institutions. NL had paid 0.2% of the loan amount to the bank towards processing charges. No other transaction cost was incurred by NL which closes its financial year on 31 December.

Discussion: NL should measure the loan initially at (100 – 100 × 0.2%) or ₹99.8 million, which is the fair value *less* transaction costs.

EXAMPLE 10.2 (Security deposit received)

Fact pattern: Contractors who are awarded long-term contract by Lahar Limited (LL) are required to deposit with the company 10% of the project value as refundable security deposit. The company does not pay interest on the refundable security deposit. On January 1, 2019, it has obtained refundable security deposit of ₹10 million from Julia Limited (JL). It is expected to refund the security deposit on January 1, 2021. LL closes its financial year on 31 December.

As per the market perception, the incremental borrowing rate of LL is 12%.

Discussion: Fair value is the present value of the amount revived as refundable security deposit. PV is calculated using the incremental borrowing rate as the discount rate. The fair value is[$10/(1.12)^2$] or ₹7.97 million.

The difference between the transaction price and the fair value of ₹2.03 million should be recognised as other income.

The following will be the journal entries: At the point of receipt of the security deposit

Date	Particulars		*Dr. ₹ million*	*Cr. ₹ million*
Jan 1, 2019	Bank A/c To Security Deposit A/c To other income Cr.	Dr. Cr.	10	7.97 2.03

At the end of the first accounting year

Date	Particulars		*Dr. ₹ million*	*Cr. ₹ million*
Dec 31, 2019	Interest Expense A/c To Security Deposit A/c (Interest is calculated at 12 % on ₹7.97 million)	Dr. Cr.	0.96	0.96

At the end of the second accounting year

Date	Particulars		*Dr. ₹ million*	*Cr. ₹ million*
Dec 31, 2020	Interest Expense A/c To Security Deposit A/c (Interest is calculated at 12 % on (₹7.97 + 0.96) or ₹8.93 million))	Dr. Cr.	1.07	1.07

On repayment

Date	Particulars		*Dr. ₹ million*	*Cr. ₹ million*
Jan 1, 2021	Security A/c To Bank A/c	Dr. Cr.	10	10

EXAMPLE 10.3 (Borrowings at lower than the market interest rate)

Fact pattern: On January 1, 2019, a public sector enterprise received a loan of ₹1,000 million from the government at an interest rate of 6% per annum. Interest is payable at the end of each year beginning from December 31, 2019. The loan is to be repaid in five equal annual instalments. Each instalment is to be paid at the end of each year beginning from December 31, 2019. The entity could borrow the amount from the market at an interest of 12% per annum with similar terms and conditions.

Discussion: The public enterprise should initially measure the borrowing at fair value which is the present value of the cash outflow from the enterprise. PV should be calculated using the discount rate of 12% per annum.

Trade payables and other short-term liabilities are measured at the transaction price.

If the time value of money is material, it is measured at PV calculated by discounting the cash flows associated with the liability by the rate of interest at which the entity could borrow the amount from the market.

$$PV = \frac{260}{1.10} + \frac{248}{1.10^2} + \frac{236}{1.10^3} + \frac{224}{1.10^4} + \frac{212}{1.10^5} = ₹860.478 \text{ million}$$

₹139.522 million, which is the difference between the amount borrowed and the fair value of the borrowing, should be accounted for as government grant.

Short-term liabilities

Trade payables and other short-term liabilities are measured at the transaction price. However, if the time value of money is material, it is measured at PV calculated by discounting to cash flows associated with the liability by the rate of interest at which the entity could borrow the amount from the market. The PV is considered to be the fair value of the liability. As a matter of practical expedient, if the liability is expected to be settled after 12 months from the date of the transaction, it is measured at its present value.

Subsequent measurement

Liabilities, other than those held for trading and derivative instruments, are measured at amortised cost using the effective interest rate method.

Liabilities held for trading (e.g., borrowing of shares by a short seller) and derivative instruments are measured at fair value. The gain or loss arising from the change in the fair value is recognised as profit or loss for the period.

Effective interest method is discussed in Chapter 9.

In example 10.2, the effective interest was 12 per cent per annum.

Liabilities, other than those held for trading and derivative instruments, are measured at amortised cost using the effective interest rate method.

EXAMPLE 10.4 (Effective interest rate and amortised cost)

In case of example 10.3 above, the effective interest rate was 12. The effective interest rate and amortised cost is presented below:

Year	*Opening Amortised cost (₹ million)*	*Cash interest (6% on outstanding loan) (₹million)*	*Effective interest (12% on Opening amortised cost – ₹200 m*) (₹million)*	*Closing balance (amortised cost) (₹million) (2 – ₹200 m* + 4 – 3)*
(1)	(2)	(3)	(4)	(5)
1	860.48	60	103.26	703.74
2	703.74	48	84.45	540.19
3	540.19	36	64.82	369.01
4	369.01	24	44.28	189.29
5	189.29	12	22.71	200.00

*Instalment paid during the year.

Liabilities held for trading and derivative instruments are measured at FV. The change in the fair value is recognised as profit or loss.

10.1.2 Measurement of Provisions

Nature of provision

A provision is a liability of uncertain timing and amount. Examples are provision for product warranty, provision for income tax, and provision for post-retirement benefits like pension.

Measurement

A provision is measured at the *best estimate* of the expenditure required to settle the obligation as on the balance sheet date. The best estimate is the amount that the entity would rationally pay to settle the obligation at the balance sheet date or to transfer to a third party at that time. The entity estimates the financial effects of the liability based on experience and by evaluating available evidence and expert opinion.

A provision is measured at the best estimate of the expenditure required to settle the obligation.

The risk and uncertainties that surround many events and circumstances should be considered in estimating the expenditure. Similarly, future events that may affect the amount required to settle an obligation should be considered in estimating the expenditure that will be required to settle the obligation, provided that there is sufficient objective evidence that those events will occur. For example, the liability to clean up the site when the operation will cease should be measured at an amount that reflects the expected technological changes having a bearing on cleaning costs. In the absence of objective evidence, the enterprise should not anticipate a future event. For example, the enterprise should not anticipate technological developments (which find a place in scientific literature only) that would reduce environment remediation costs.

Gains on expected disposal of assets are not considered in measuring a provision even if the expected disposal is closely linked to the event giving rise to the provision.

The method of estimating the amount of provision depends on the circumstances. For example, where the provision being measured involves a large population, the liability is measured at the expected value, calculated using subjective probabilities.

Where a single obligation is being measured, the most likely individual outcome may be the best estimate of the liability.

EXAMPLE 10.5 (Measuring provision)

Fact pattern: Sarika Limited (SL) sells television sets with a warranty for one year. In 2019, it sold 1,00,000 units. Under the warranty, SL repairs defects that surface during the warranty period. It estimates that 80% of the units sold will have no defects, 15% will have minor defects, and 5% will have major defects. It further estimates that repair of a major defect will cost ₹5,000 per unit, while repair of a minor defect will cost ₹1,000 per unit.

Discussion: The expected value of the cost of repair is:

(0.80 × nil) + (0.05 × 1,00,000 × ₹5,000) + (0.15 × 1,00,000 × ₹1,000) = ₹2,50,00,000 + ₹1,50,00,000 = ₹4,00,00,000

A provision of ₹4,00,00,000 should be recognised in the balance sheet dated December 31, 2019 towards product warranty.

EXAMPLE 10.6 (Measuring provision)

Fact pattern: A customer complaint about a major defect in the plant installed by Sudeshna Transformers Limited (STL) is yet to be attended on the date when financial statements for 2019 are approved by the Board of Directors. STL expects to repair the defect at the first attempt, and in that case, it will cost ₹5,000. However, if the defect cannot be removed at the first attempt, the cost will be much higher. The management of the STL proposes to recognise a provision towards the obligation in the balance sheet as at December 31, 2019 at ₹20,000 because it is quite probable that more than one attempt will be necessary.

Discussion: Where a single obligation is being measured, the most likely individual outcome may be the best estimate of the liability. We may assume that the management's proposal is based on its best estimate, which is formulated on the basis of experience and available evidence. Therefore, it is appropriate to recognise the provision at ₹20,000 towards the cost for rectification of the defect.

10.1.3 Restructuring

Restructuring is a programme that is planned and controlled by the management, and materially changes either the scope of a business undertaken by an entity or changes the manner in which the business is conducted.

Restructuring may involve:

1. Sale or closures of a line of business.
2. Closure of a location or relocation of business activities.
3. Changes in management structure.
4. Changes in the nature or focus of an existing business.

A constructive obligation for restructuring arises when the entity (a) has drawn a detailed formal plan for the restructuring; and (b) has aroused a valid expectation among the people or entity affected by the plan that the plan will be carried out.

An enterprise generates a valid expectation either by initiating the implementation of the plan or by announcing its main features, with sufficient detail, to those who will be affected by the plan.

A restructuring provision includes only the direct expenditure arising from restructuring. That expenditure should not be associated with the ongoing activities of the entity.

A restructuring plan does not generate a valid expectation and does not result in a constructive obligation if a long delay is expected in the commencement of its implementation, or it is expected that the restructuring will take an unreasonably long time. A long timeframe allows the entity to change its plan.

An entity may start implementing a restructuring plan or it may announce its main features after the balance sheet date. In that situation, a disclosure in the financial report is required if the restructuring is of such importance that its non-disclosure will adversely affect proper evaluations and decisions.

A restructuring provision includes only the direct expenditure arising from restructuring. That expenditure should arise necessarily from restructuring and should not be associated with the ongoing activities of the entity. A restructuring provision does not include costs such as retraining or redeployment of continuing employees, marketing, and investment in new systems or distribution networks.

10.1.4 Reimbursement

An entity may expect reimbursement of some or all of the expenditure that it will incur to settle the provision. It should recognise the same as a separate asset if and only if it is virtually certain that the reimbursement will be received. The amount recognised for the reimbursement should not exceed the amount of the provision. In the statement of profit and loss, expense relating to a provision may be presented net of the amount recognised for a reimbursement.

10.1.5 Effect of Time Value of Money

Where the effect of time value of money is material, the amount of a provision should be the PV of the estimated expenditure that will be required to settle the obligation. The same principle should be applied for measuring liabilities other than financial liabilities.

The discount rate should be a *pre-tax rate* that reflects the current market assessments of the time value of money and the risk specific to the liability. The discount rate should not reflect the risks for which future cash flow estimates have been adjusted. For example, provision for asset retirement obligation (ARO) is recognised at the present value of the amount that is expected to be incurred to settle the liability. (ARO has been discussed in Chapter 7.)

10.2 PROVISION OF POST-RETIREMENT EMPLOYEE BENEFITS

Nature and classification

Post-employment benefits include:

1. Retirement benefits, such as, gratuity and pension
2. Other benefits, such as, post-employment life insurance and post-employment medical care

Post-employment benefit plans are deferred payment plans. An employee earns those benefits as he/she renders service. Such entitlement increases with increasing number of years in service. However, after a certain length of service, additional service does not result in increase in the amount of post-retirement benefits. For example, under a pension scheme, an employee earns full pension on completion of 20 years of service. Therefore, if an employee serves for more than 20 years, he/she does not get pension more than what an employee who has completed just 20 years would get, provided other things are equal.

Post-employment benefit plans are classified into:

1. Defined contribution plans.
2. Defined benefit plans.

Defined contribution plan

A defined contribution plan is one in which the employer pays a fixed contribution (e.g., 10% of basic salary) into a separate entity or fund and its obligation is limited to that contribution. The amount of benefit depends on the performance of plan assets. An example of the defined contribution plan is the provident fund. Another example is the contributory pension plan introduced by the Government of India for its employees in 2004.

A defined contribution plan is one in which the employer pays a fixed contribution into a separate entity or fund and its obligation is limited to that contribution.

Defined benefits plan

A defined benefit plan is a post-employment benefit plan other than defined contribution plans. As the name implies, under a defined benefit plan, the benefit to employees is defined. Therefore, under such a plan, the employer has the obligation to provide the agreed benefits to the current and former employees. An example of defined benefit plans is the gratuity scheme under which the amount of gratuity payable to an employee is determined based on the period of service and last pay drawn. It is not linked to the contributions by the employer over the period of employment or on the performance of the plan asset. Plan asset is the asset (such as, a separate fund) that is created to fulfil the obligation. The creditors of the entity have no claim on that asset.

10.2.1 Measurement

Defined contribution plan

An entity recognises contributions payable as an expense in the statement of profit and loss for the period in which the employee has rendered the service. If the amount of contribution paid is less than the amount payable, the difference is recognised as a liability (accrued expense) in the balance sheet as at the end of the period. Similarly, any amount paid in excess of the amount due is recognised as an asset (prepaid expense) in the balance sheet as at the end of the period.

Defined benefit plan

Defined benefit plans may be (a) unfunded or (b) wholly or partly funded by contributions by an enterprise, and sometimes, by its employees.

When a defined benefit plan is funded, the enterprise contributes to an entity or fund that is legally separate from the reporting enterprise. Employee benefits are paid by that entity or from that fund. However, the amount payable does not depend on the financial position and the performance of the entity or fund. Employee benefits are defined in the plan. The enterprise, in reality, underwrites the actuarial and investment risks associated with the plan. Thus, the expense recognised in a defined benefit plan is not necessarily the amount of the contribution due for the period.

Entities use actuarial valuation to determine the present value of defined benefit obligations at the balance sheet date. They use the 'projected unit credit method' to determine the present value of the defined benefit obligations of an enterprise.

Entities use actuarial valuation to determine the present value of defined benefit obligations at the balance sheet date. They use the 'projected unit credit method' to determine the present value of the defined benefit obligations of an enterprise.

Projected unit credit method

The projected unit credit method considers each period of service as giving rise to an additional unit of benefit entitlement and measures each unit separately to build up the final obligation. In short, the projected unit cost method estimates obligations for services already rendered by employees up to the valuation date. However, in estimating the obligations, it makes many assumptions, including the assumption about the rate at which benefits will be payable to the employee. Let us take an example. An employee who has completed 10 years of service at the balance sheet date and is expected to work for another 10 years before retirement, is entitled to gratuity on retirement. The entitlement is determined by a formula that takes into consideration the period of service and the last pay drawn. The projected unit credit method will estimate the obligation on the balance sheet date taking into consideration, among other things, the period of service completed by the employee at the balance sheet date and the estimated salary that he will draw immediately before retirement.

It is assumed that employees earn the benefits as they render service. Therefore, the estimated amount of the benefit is allocated over the estimated period of service that will enhance the benefit. For example, after twenty years of service, the pension might not increase because employees are entitled to full pension after completing twenty years of service. Therefore, estimated benefit is allocated over twenty years.

Set off

An entity measures the liability at the present value of the defined benefit obligation at the balance sheet date minus the fair value of plan assets (if any) on balance sheet date.

REVIEW PROBLEMS

R10.1 Indicate whether the following statements are True or False:

(i) A financial liability is initially measured at fair value (FV), adjusted for transaction costs, which are directly attributable to the assumption of the liability.
(ii) With a few exceptions financial liabilities are measured at the amortised costs.
(iii) Effective interest rate method allocates the transaction cost over the repayment period as a part of interest expense.
(iv) Provisions are measured at the management's best estimate.
(v) Pension liability under the defined contribution scheme is measured based on actuarial valuation.

ASSIGNMENTS

1. Indicate against each statement whether it is True or False:

(i) The concept of constructive obligation leads to early recognition of liabilities.
(ii) Advance received from a customer with an order for supply of goods is a financial liability.
(iii) Security deposit received from a contractor is a financial liability.
(iv) Provision for doubtful debts is a liability.
(v) A firm commitment to purchase materials (to be delivered in future) is an obligation present at the balance sheet date and is recognised as a liability in the balance sheet. (A firm commitment is a binding agreement for the exchange of a specified quantity of resources at a specified price on a specified future date or dates.)
(vi) Incremental borrowing rate should always be higher than the average borrowing rate for an entity.
(vii) Fair value of liability is the amount at which players in the financial market are willing to assume the liability, and the firm may transfer the obligation to a third party.
(viii) In the absence of active markets for financial liabilities, a financial liability is initially measured at the present value of the liability determined using the incremental borrowing rate of the entity.
(ix) Provisions are measured at the best estimate of the management.
(x) Provisions are classified as current liabilities.
(xi) Provision for an onerous contract should be measured at the estimated loss that will arise on execution of the contract.
(xii) Decision of the Board of Directors to restructure the firm does not necessarily lead to recognition of a provision for restructuring expenses.
(xiii) Contributory pension plan is a defined benefit scheme.
(xiv) Pension liability (under a defined benefit scheme) on the balance sheet date, is calculated based on the salary drawn by employees immediately before the balance sheet date.
(xv) Capital commitment is a contingent liability.

2. Fill in the blanks:

(i) On March 31, 2010, Mandakini Limited (ML) borrowed from a bank ₹200 million at the market rate of interest of 12% per annum. It paid 0.2% of the loan as procession charge to the bank. The loan should be carried in the balance sheet as at March 31, 2010 at ₹.........

(ii) On April 1, 2010, Kadambini Limited (KL) borrowed ₹100 million at 12% interest (market rate). The interest is payable on 31 March every year starting from March 31, 2011. The principal amount is repayable in equal yearly instalments over a period of five years. The effective interest rate is ....%. (Correct up to three decimal places).

(iii) On April 1, 2010, Garima Limited (GL) received security deposit of ₹10 million from a contractor against a project awarded to it. GL expects that the security deposit be repaid on March 31, 2013. No interest is payable on the security deposit. The market perception is that GL could borrow the amount from market for a period of three years at an interest rate of 12% per annum. The security deposit should be measured initially at ₹......... million, and ₹......... million should be recognised as other income in the profit and loss account for 2010–2011.

(iv) Suman Limited (SL) sells television sets with a warranty for one year. In 2010, it sold 100,000 units. Under the warranty, SL repairs defects that surface during the warranty period. It estimates that 85% of the units sold will have no defects, 13% shall have minor defects, and 2% shall have major defects. It further estimates that repair of a major defect will cost ₹5,000 per unit, while repair of a minor defect will cost ₹1,000 per unit. SL should recognise provision for the product warranty at ₹......... in the balance sheet as of December 31, 2010.

(v) A customer's complaint about a major defect in the plant installed by Sanchari Transformers Limited (STL) is yet to be attended on the date when financial statements for 2010 are approved by the Board of Directors. STL expects to repair the defect at the first attempt, and in that case, it will cost ₹10,000. However, if the defect cannot be removed at the first attempt, the cost will be much higher and it may go up to ₹50,000. In past 80% cases, defects could be rectified in the first attempt, and only in 20% cases, more than one attempt was required. The management of the STL proposes to recognise a provision towards the obligation in the balance sheet as at December 31, 2010 at ₹30,000 because there is a significant chance that more than one attempt will be necessary. SL should recognise a provision for the cost that it will incur in the next financial year to rectify the defect at ₹..........

(vi) Charu Limited (CL) estimates that execution of a fixed-price contract (to manufacture equipment) awarded by Bakul Limited (BL) will result in a loss of ₹1 million due to sudden spurt of input costs. There is a penalty clause in the contract under which if the company fails to execute the contract, BL will forfeit the security deposit of ₹0.5 million. CL is yet to decide whether to execute the contract. However, it is most likely that it will execute the contract on ethical grounds. The company is finalising the financial statements for 2010–2011. CL should carry a provision for the onerous contract at ₹..........

(vii) Suman Limited (SL) sells television sets with a warranty for one year. In 2010, it sold 1,00,000 units. Under the warranty, SL repairs defects that surface during the warranty period. It estimates that 85% of the units sold will have no defects, 13% shall have minor defects, and 2% shall have major defects. It further estimates that repair of a major defect will cost ₹5,000 per unit, while repair of a minor defect will cost ₹1,000 per unit. Provision should be recognised at ₹.........

CHAPTER

11

INCOME

CHAPTER OBJECTIVES

The objectives of this chapter is to introduce to readers the accounting for income. In particular, the objective is developing and understanding of

- ❖ Classification of income;
- ❖ Recognition and measurement of revenue—income from contracts with customers;
- ❖ Recognition and measurement of interest, and dividend income;
- ❖ Recognition and measurement of government grant.

11.1 INCOME CLASSIFICATIONS

Table 11.1 presents the classification of income.

TABLE 11.1 Classification of Income

	Classification	*Characteristics*
1.	Revenue	Revenue is income from entity's ordinary activities. In case of non-finance companies, income from sale of goods and services is classified as revenue.
2.	Other operating income	Income arising from operating activities, other than from sale of goods and services is classified as other operating income. For example, income from sale of scrap generated during manufacturing activities is classified as 'other operating income'.
3.	Other income	Income, other than those arising from ordinary activities, are classified as other income. For a non-finance entity, interest, and dividend income from investments, and change in fair value of investments classified as FVTPL are classified as other income. Similarly, gain from sale of fixed assets is classified as other income.
4.	Government grant	Government grant is the assistance by government in the form of transfers of resources to an entity in return for past or future compliance with certain conditions relating to the operating activities of the entity. Financial assistance to companies which invest in pollution control equipment is an example of government grant. Similarly, export incentive is a government grant.

11.2 REVENUE

11.2.1 Contract with Customers

Customers are those who buy the output of the entity's operation.

Entities enter into contract with customers. The contract can be in writing or verbal, or contractual terms may be inferred from the customs of the trade.

The contract specifies the rights and obligations of both the parties. The supplier's obligation is to deliver the goods and services specified in the contract and its right is to receive the transaction price in exchange of goods and services delivered. The customer's right is to receive the goods and services promised by the supplier and its obligation is to pay the transaction price to the supplier.

Customers are those who buy the output of the entity's operation.

Entities enter into contract with customers. The contract can be in writing or verbal, or contractual terms may be inferred from the customs of the trade.

The contract specifies the rights and obligations of both the parties.

A contract comes into existence only when *all* of the following criteria are met:

- The parties to the contract have approved the contract and are committed to perform their respective obligations;
- The entity can identify each party's rights regarding the goods or services to be transferred;
- The entity can identify the payment terms for the goods or services to be transferred;
- The contract has commercial substance, in the sense that the risk or timing or amount of the entity's future cash flows is expected to change as a result of the contract; and
- The customer has the *ability* and *intention* to pay the consideration, and thus, it is probable that the entity will collect the same.

A contract has a commercial substance when execution of the contract results in change in the future cash flows. Therefore, usually, revenue is not recognised from barter transactions.

The entity (supplier) should assess the ability and intention of the customer to pay the consideration and its ability to collect the consideration. It implies that until it is reasonably certain that it will collect the amount, it will not recognise the revenue.

Amount received before the contract comes into existence

Amount received before the contract comes into existence should be recognised as a liability. However, it recognises the consideration received as revenue if, the amount received is non-refundable.

Combining the contracts

Two or more contracts should be combined to identify performance obligation if:

(a) they are entered with the same customer or related parties;
(b) they were entered at the same time;
(c) they were negotiated as a bundle or package with a single business objective;
(d) consideration in one contract is tied to the price or performance of the other contract(s); and
(e) promised goods or services in the contracts represent a single performance obligation.

Two or more contracts entered at the same time with the same customer or related parties and negotiated as a package should be combined if certain conditions are fulfilled.

EXAMPLE 11.1 (Combining two contracts)

Fact pattern: A customer enters into a contract with an entity, which deals with used cars, to deliver a fleet of 25 cars. Within two days after the contract for the delivery of 25 car is finalised, the customer enters into another contract with the entity to maintain the fleet for five years.

Discussion: These two contracts should be combined, as the transaction price for maintenance of the fleet might have been tied up with the transaction price for the supply of 25 cars. The combined contract has two distinct performance obligations—delivery of 25 cars and providing maintenance service. However, combining the two contract is important for allocating the combined transaction price to the two distinct performance obligations.

11.2.2 Recognition

General principle

Revenue should be recognised only when:

- the *performance obligation* is fulfilled; and
- the entity expects to collect the *transaction price* to which it is entitled.

Revenue should be recognised only when the performance obligation is fulfilled and the entity expects to collect the transaction price.

Fulfilment of performance obligation: An entity fulfils its performance obligation when it *transfer the control* of the goods to the customer, and in case of service, *delivers the service* to the satisfaction of the customer.

BOX 11.1 SERVICE LEVEL AGREEMENT (SLA)

An entity, which provides services, promises delivery of services at a level expected by the customer or client. Usually, it enters into a service level agreement (SLA) with the customer, which defines the service level. For example, when a customer takes a broadband connection, the telecom company promises to deliver the broadband service and the SLA defines the speed, mean time failure, mean time for recovery and mean time for repair.

Identification of performance obligation

A performance obligation is separate from other performance obligations in the contract, if:

(a) the good or service is distinct from other goods and services in the contract, and
(b) the customer can enjoy the economic benefits embedded in that good or service without depending on the other goods and services to be delivered under the contract.

Separate performance obligations in a single contract

A single contract may have more than one performance obligations against a single transaction price. It is necessary to identify the performance obligations and allocate the transaction price to those performance obligations, as they are fulfilled at different points of time and revenue from each performance obligation is recognised separately.

A single contract may have more than one performance obligations.

EXAMPLE 11.2 (More than one performance obligation)

Fact pattern: The obligation of an automobile dealer in exchange for the transaction price is to deliver the car specified in the car and to provide maintenance service for one year without additional cost.

Discussion: There are two distinct performance obligations–delivering the car and maintaining the care for one year. They are distinct because the customer can enjoy the benefits embedded in the car even if the dealer fails in its promise to deliver the maintenance service, as the customer can obtain maintenance service from other players operating in the market.

The transaction price should be allocated between the car and the maintenance service.

Integrating separate performance obligations in the same contract

Separate performance obligations should be identified as elements of a single performance obligation under certain conditions.

A contract might mention separate performance obligations, but those should be identified as elements of a single performance obligation if:

(a) the supplier uses the inputs to produce a combined output, and
(b) undertakes integration, which is a complex and substantial activity.

In case where integration (e.g., installation) is routine and the customer can engage some other agency for the integration activity, the delivery of goods and integration should be considered as two separate performance obligations.

EXAMPLE 11.3 (Integration of different performance obligations)

Fact pattern: A construction company enters into a contract with a customer to construct the hotel. The contract specifies separate performance obligations, which are: (a) procurement of materials as per specifications mentioned in the contract on or before a specified date, and (b) construction of the hotel.

Discussion: The construction of the hotel, which we can call the combined output, requires use of the inputs delivered and integration of those inputs, which is substantial and complex. Therefore, the construction company should consider the promise to construct the hotel as a single performance obligation, although the contract specifies two separate performance obligations.

EXAMPLE 11.4 (Integration of different performance obligations)

Fact pattern: An firm of architects has entered into a contract for renovating the office of the CEO of a multinational company. The contract has three performance obligations – designing the office, procuring specified furniture, and modifying and arranging those in the office.

Discussion: Although, the contract has three different performance obligations, they should be considered as a single performance obligation, which is the renovation service, as designing the office, and modifying and arranging the furniture involve a complex integration process.

11.2.3 Revenue Measurement

Revenue is measured at the transaction price.

Accounting principle

Revenue is measured at the transaction price.

Transaction price

Transaction price is the amount of consideration to which an entity expects to be entitled in exchange for transferring promised goods or services to a customer, *excluding amounts collected on behalf of third parties.*

Entities estimate the transaction price at contract inception. This is important for allocating the transaction price to different performance obligations in a single contract.

Table 11.2 below presents the elements to be included in the transaction price.

TABLE 11.2 The Elements to be included in the Transaction Price

	Element	*Accounting principle*
1.	**Fixed** Pre-specified transaction price, such as price of a piece of equipment	(a) Amount collected for third parties should not be included in the transaction price. For example, transaction price should not include indirect taxes collected on behalf of the government. Similarly agents should include only the commission to which they are entitled in the transaction price. (b) Time value of money should be considered. Transaction price should be measured at the present value (PV) of the amount if the credit period exceeds 12 months from the delivery of goods or service. The discount rate for calculating the PV should be the market interest rate for financing with similar terms and credit risks.
2	**Variable** *Examples* Discounts (including cash discount), performance bonus, penalty, and customer's right to return	(a) It should be deducted or added to the transaction price only to the extent that it is *highly probable* that a significant reversal in the amount of cumulative revenue recognised will not occur when the uncertainty associated with the variable consideration is subsequently resolved. (b) Time value of money should be considered.
3.	**Non-cash consideration** *Examples* Exchange transaction, and consideration in the form of shares or bonds issued by the customer	The non-cash consideration should be measured at fair value (FV). If an entity cannot reasonably estimate the FV, the entity should measure the consideration indirectly with reference to the stand-alone selling price of the goods or services promised to the customer in exchange for the consideration.
4.	**Consideration payable to customers** *Examples* Vouchers and reward points under the customer loyalty programme	Transaction price should be reduced by the consideration paid or payable to a customer or customer's customer. The management estimates the amount to be returned in the form of future discounts or amount payable to partners and deduct the amount from the transaction price.

Note: Vouchers issued under the customer loyalty programme can be used in subsequent purchases. Similarly reward points (for example, on use of credit cards) can be used for purchases of goods or services from partner entities under a customer loyalty programme.

Variable consideration should be included in the transaction price only to the extent that it is highly probable that a significant reversal in the amount of cumulative revenue recognised will not occur.

BOX 11.2 CONSTRAINED VARIABLE CONSIDERATION

Variable consideration should be included in the transaction price only to the extent that it is *highly probable* that a significant reversal in the amount of cumulative revenue recognised will not occur when the uncertainty associated with the variable consideration is subsequently resolved. For example, contract between a construction company and one of its clients includes a clause that entitles the company for bonus for early completion of the construction. The estimated amount of bonus should be included in the transaction price only if the construction company estimates that it is highly probable that the bonus included in the transaction price *would not be reversed* on completion of the construction due to its inability to complete the construction early.

When the entity is unable to estimate the variable consideration reliably, the variable consideration is a 'constrained variable consideration'. At each reporting date, an entity reassesses the estimated transaction price, including the assessment of whether its estimate of variable consideration is constrained.

When the entity is unable to estimate the variable consideration reliably, the variable consideration is a 'constrained variable consideration'.

EXAMPLE 11.5 (Transaction price)

Fact pattern: An entity allows quantity discount to a customer if the total quantity (or value) of purchase during the accounting year exceeds a predetermined target.

Discussion: At the inception of the contract, the entity should estimate the amount of quantity discount it will allow to the customer. If the entity is unable to estimate the quantity discount to be allowed to the customer, it does not consider the quantity discount in estimating the transaction price.

Estimating the variable consideration

Entities use the expected value method (probability-weighted amount) for estimating variable consideration when they have a large number of contracts with similar characteristics. They use the 'most likely amount' method when they do not have a large number of similar contracts and the contract has only two possible outcomes.

EXAMPLE 11.6 (Estimating the variable consideration)

Fact pattern: An entity enters into a contract for the construction of commercial space. As per the contract, the entity is entitled to a bonus of ₹500,000 if the work can be completed 60 days before the scheduled completions date. The contractual terms are typical in contracts that the entity enters with its customers. In past, in 80 per cent of cases, the entity earned the bonus.

At each reporting date, an entity reassesses the estimated transaction price, including the assessment of whether its estimate of variable consideration is constrained.

Discussion: The entity should estimate the bonus at (0.80 × 5,00,000) or ₹4,00,000.

EXAMPLE 11.7 (Consideration payable to customers)

Fact pattern: AB Limited (ABL), which has a number of stores selling readymade garments, operates a customer loyalty programme. A customer earns 1 point (equivalent to ₹1) for purchase of every ₹10. Points earned during a financial year are redeemable on future purchases during the following three financial years. ABL does not offer any other discount or rebate to customers. During the financial year 2015–2016, customers purchased goods for ₹1,00,000, and thus, earned 10,000 points. The management, on the basis of the past experience, which it assesses as predictive, expects that 90% of the points would be redeemed. The stand-alone selling price of the goods sold to customers without points is ₹1,00,000. During the year 2016–2017, 4,500 points are redeemed; in 2017–2018, 4,000 points are redeemed, and the management has revised estimates of the percentage of points to be redeemed to 95%.

Discussion: *Year 2015–2016*

(i) Stand-alone selling prices: Goods: ₹1,00,000; Points: (₹1,00,000 × 0.90) or ₹9,000

(ii) Total stand-alone selling prices: (₹1,00,000 + 9,000) or ₹1,09,000

(iii) Selling price ratio: Goods: (1,00,000/1,09,000) or 91.74%; Points: 8.26%

Price allocation: Goods: (₹1,00,000 × 0.9174) or ₹91,740; Points: ₹8,260

Thus, in the statement of profit and loss for the year 2015–2016, 'revenue' should be recognised at ₹91,740 and in the balance sheet as at March 31, 2016, 'deferred revenue' (contract liability) should be recognised at ₹8,260.

Year 2016–2017

(i) Management expects total 9,000 points would be redeemed.

(ii) During the year 4,500 points are redeemed.

(iii) Revenue, out of the deferred revenue, should be recognised at: (4,500/9,000) × ₹8,260 or ₹4,130.

(iv) The deferred revenue in the balance sheet dated March 31, 2017 should include deferred revenue of (₹8,260 – 4,130) or ₹4,130 pertaining to the year 2015–2016.

Year 2017–2018

(i) 4,000 points are redeemed resulting in cumulative redemption of 8,500 points.
(ii) Management revised the estimate from total 9,000 points be redeemed to 9,500 points.
(iii) Cumulative revenue, out of deferred revenue, in the first two years should be recognised at should (8,500/9,500) × ₹8,260 or ₹7,391.
(iv) Revenue for the current year should be recognised at (₹7,391 – 4,130) or ₹3,261.
(v) The deferred revenue in the balance sheet dated March 31, 2018 should include deferred revenue of (₹8,260 – 7,391) or ₹869 pertaining to the year 2015–2016.

2018–2019

The opening balance of ₹869 in the deferred revenue account should be recognised as revenue.

Allocation of the transaction price

Often a contract for delivering a bundle of products mentions a single transfer price.

At contract inception, an entity should allocate the transaction price for a bundle of products to each performance obligation.

The transaction price should be allocated to proacts and services in proportion to their respective stand-alone selling prices.

If stand-alone price of one or more products is not available, the entity uses the following values as a proxy for the stand-alone price:

- *Adjusted market assessment approach:* The prices for similar goods or services from competitors in the market in which it sells goods or services, adjusted for entity's costs and margins.
- Expected cost, plus margin.
- *Residual approach:* The sum of the observable stand-alone selling prices of other goods or services promised in the contract from the total transaction price.

Residual approach should be used as a matter of last resort.

The discount identifiable to a particular product should be allocated to that product.

At contract inception, an entity should allocate the transaction price for a bundle of products to each performance obligation.

The transaction price should be allocated to proacts and services in proportion to their respective stand-alone selling prices.

EXAMPLE 11.8 (Allocation of transaction price)

Fact pattern: The stand-alone prices of four products in the bundle are E: ₹3,500, F: ₹2,500, G: 3,000, and H: ₹. 1,000. The ₹10,000. The transaction price is ₹9,500. The entity regularly sells the product E, at 10 per cent discount.

Discussion: The discount offered to the customer is (₹10,000 – 9,500) or ₹500. The entity sells product E, at 10 per cent discount. Therefore, discount of (₹0.10 × ₹3,500) or ₹350, should be allocated to E. The balance of ₹150 should be allocated to F, G, and H in proportion to their stand-alone prices.

11.2.4 Performance Obligations Satisfied Over Time

Usually, performance obligation is satisfied at a particular point in time when the control of the goods is transferred to the customer, or the service is delivered to the customer. However, in the following situations, performance obligation is satisfied over time:

- The customer simultaneously receives and consumes the benefits provided by the entity's performance as the entity performs.
- The entity's performance creates or enhances an asset that the customer controls as the asset is created or enhanced.

Usually, performance obligation is satisfied at a particular point in time.

- The entity's performance does not create an asset with an alternative use to the entity and the entity has an enforceable right to payment for performance completed to date (e.g., the contract stipulates progress payments as the work on producing the asset progresses).

Performance obligation is satisfied over time if (a) the customer simultaneously receives and consumes the benefits; or (b) performance creates or enhances an asset that the customer controls; or (c) the entity's performance does not create an asset with an alternative use to the entity and the entity has an enforceable right to payment for performance completed to date.

EXAMPLE 11.9 (Customer simultaneously receives and consumes the benefits)

Fact pattern: The entity (supplier) provides cleaning service in airport lounges, and office premises of large companies. The contracts between the entity and its customers mentions transaction price in terms of rate per square feet. They require the entity to submit invoice at the close of every month.

Discussion: The customers receive and consume the benefits simultaneously. Therefore, it is appropriate for the company to recognise revenue as and when the invoice is submitted to the customer, provided that the service meets the customer's satisfaction.

EXAMPLE 11.10 (The customer controls the asset as and when created)

Fact pattern: The entity is a construction company. It constructs buildings, bridges etc. at the customers' site.

Discussion: When the supplier creates or enhances an asset at the customer's site, it transfers the control of the work-in-progress to the customer. A typical construction contract requires the construction company to submit invoices for the work certified by the architect. The construction company should recognise revenue as and when it submits invoice.

Usually, entities do not recognise the revenue until at least 20–25% of the work is complete, as in early stages it is difficult to reliably measure the outcome of fulfilling the performance obligation. They measure the revenue at the amount of the cost incurred to the extent they expect to recover the same. In other words, they do not recognise profit in early stages of contracts. The standard of not recognising profit until 20–25 per cent completion of the project is an industry norm. GAAP does not provide any bright line.

EXAMPLE 11.11 (The asset has no alternative use, and the supplier has enforceable right to receive payment)

Fact pattern: The legal opinion based on specific fact pattern has no alternative use. Missiles and other defence equipment produced as per the specifications of the defence establishment have no alternative use. Ship constructed as per the customer's specification has no alternative use. There are many other assets, which have no alternative use.

Discussion: A supplier which creates an asset which have no alternative use cannot sell the assets to any other customer. Therefore, it recognises revenue as the asset is enhanced, provided the contract stipulates that the customer has the obligation to reimburse the cost with a stipulated margin if the project is aborted on the customer's direction without any fault of the supplier.

Progress measurement

In order to recognise revenue over time the progress is measured using either the input method or the output method. Usually, entities use the input method because of its simplicity and cost effectiveness. Measuring output based on survey, etc. involves significant cost.

Under the input method, the progress is measured as the percentage of cost incurred till the measurement date to the estimated total project cost. For example, if the cost incurred till the measurement date is ₹5 lakhs, and the total estimated cost is ₹10 lakhs, it is said that the 50 per cent of the work is completed. Only those costs that are actually incurred is included in measuring the costs incurred till date. For example, the cost of material purchased and not issued is not included in the costs incurred till the measurement date.

11.2.5 Application Issues

Sale with right to return

Entities operating in some industries (such as books, and kitchen appliances) or selling products on platforms (such as, Amazon, and Flipkart) transfer control of a product to a customer, and also grant the customer the right to return the product for various reasons. Accounting for 'sale with a right to return' requires an entity to estimate the expected level of return considering the historical experience of similar contracts. The entity recognises:

1. Revenue, initially measured at the transaction price to which the entity expects to be entitled, based on the expected level of return;
2. A refund liability, initially measured at the amount of consideration received or receivable to which the entity does not expect to be entitled; and
3. An asset (and a corresponding adjustment to the cost of sales) for the right to recover the products from the customer, initially measured with reference to the carrying amount of the products transferred, less expected recovery cost.

Accounting for 'sale with a right to return' requires an entity to estimate the expected level of return considering the historical experience of similar contracts.

An entity updates the measurement of the refund liability at each reporting date. It recognises:

1. Adjustments to the refund liability as revenue; and
2. Adjustments to the refund assets as expense.

EXAMPLE 11.12 (Sale with a right to return)

Fact pattern: BN Publishers Limited (BNPL) sold 100 copies of a particular book in the month of March 2018. It received ₹10,000 towards sales consideration. Under the contract, customers are allowed to return any undamaged book within 30 days and to receive the full refund in cash. The cost of each book is ₹50. The date by which the customers can return the book will expire on April 10, 2018. BNPL estimates that 5% of the books are returned by the customers and the returned books can be sold at a profit. The cost of recovering the books is insignificant.

Discussion: BNPL should pass the following journal entries:

Entry 1

Date	Particulars		Debit (₹)	Credit (₹)
	Cash A/c	Dr.	10,000	
	To Refund Liability A/c	Cr.		500
	To Revenue A/c	Cr.		9,500

Entry 2

Date	Particulars		Debit (₹)	Credit (₹)
	Asset (Right to recover) A/c (₹5 × 50)	Dr.	250	
	Cost of Sales A/c	Dr.	4,750	
	To Inventory A/c	Cr.		5,000

Warranties

There are two types of warranty:

(a) Assurance Warranty, and
(b) Service warranty (also called, extended warranty).

Assurance warranty, which provides an assurance that the product complies with the agreed specifications. It is not a separate performance obligation.

Assurance warranty which provides an assurance that the product complies with the agreed specifications. It is not a separate performance obligation. Customers purchase service warranty separately. It provides the customer with services in addition to an assurance that the product complies with the agreed specifications It is a separate performance obligation.

Non-refundable up front fee

In some contracts, an entity charges a customer a non-refundable upfront fee at or near contract inception. Examples include joining fees in health club membership contracts, activation fees in telecommunication contracts, setup fees in some services contracts and initial fees in some supply contracts.

Usually, the upfront fee is an advance payment for future goods or services, and therefore, it is recognized as revenue when those future goods or services are provided.

In most cases, an entity does not recognise the non-refundable upfront fee as revenue when it is received or receivable. An entity should assess whether the fee relates to the transfer of a promised good or service. Usually, the upfront fee is an advance payment for future goods or services, and therefore, it is recognized as revenue when those future goods or services are provided.

The revenue recognition period extends beyond the initial contractual period if the entity grants the customer the option to renew the contract and that option provides the customer with a material right to acquire future goods or services. If the non-refundable upfront fee relates to a good or service, the entity should evaluate whether to account for the good or service as a separate performance obligation.

EXAMPLE 11.13 (Club admission fee)

Fact pattern: A golf club and charges a non-refundable admission fee of ₹1,00,000. Membership fee is ₹50,000 per year. Club G estimates the average period of membership is 10 years.

Discussion: Entities should recognise revenue only when a distinct good or service is provided. In this case the customer (i.e., the member) receives no benefit from just paying the admission fee on its own. It has to pay separately the annual membership fee to receive the benefit of playing golf. Therefore, the 'admission' is not a 'distinct' good or service. The club should not recognise the admission fee as revenue up front. The admission fee of ₹1,00,000 should be allocated over the average period of membership, which is estimated at 10 years.

Bill and hold sales

The term 'Bill and hold sales' refers to a situation when an entity holds goods on behalf of a customer.

The term 'Bill and hold sales' refers to a situation when an entity holds goods on behalf of a customer. The accounting principle is that the entity should recognise the revenue when the buyer takes the title provided without waiting for the physical delivery of the goods, provided that:

- It is probable that the delivery will be made;
- The item is on hand, identified, and ready for delivery;
- The buyer specifically acknowledges the deferred delivery instructions; and
- The usual payment terms apply.

EXAMPLE 11.14 (Bill and hold sale)

Fact pattern: An entity manufactures tailor-made equipment against firm orders from customers. On the request of a customer the entity holds a piece of equipment ready for dispatch on behalf of a customer until the site for installation is ready.

Discussion: The entity should recognise the revenue immediately when the piece of the equipment is ready for dispatch only if it is holding the good based on the written instruction of the customer, who has taken control of that asset.

In 'lay away sales' the goods are on hand, identified and ready for delivery to the buyer, but delivery is deferred until the final payment is received.

Lay away sales

In 'lay away sales' the goods are on hand, identified and ready for delivery to the buyer, but delivery is deferred until the final payment is received. Usually, sufficient payment is received to support commitment of the buyer take delivery of the goods and the collectability of the sale value. An entity recognises lay away sales as revenue for the period in which the sale occurs.

Repurchase arrangement

Sometimes, entities promise to repurchase goods sold. Repurchase arrangement generally comes in the following three forms:

1. A forward contract—an entity's obligation to repurchase the asset;
2. A call option—an entity's right to repurchase the asset; and
3. A put option—an entity's obligation to repurchase the asset at the customer's request.

Repurchase arrangement generally comes in the following three forms:
(a) a forward contract—an entity's obligation to repurchase the asset;
(b) A call option—an entity's right to repurchase the asset; and
(c) A put option—an entity's obligation to repurchase the asset at the customer's request.

A forward or a call option: If an entity has an obligation or a right to repurchase the asset (a forward or a call option), it does not transfer control of the asset to the customer because the customer is limited in his ability to direct the use of the asset and obtain substantially all of the remaining benefits from it. Consequently, the transaction is not a sale transaction. Such a transaction is either a lease transaction or a financing transaction.

The entity accounts for the contract as a lease contract if the entity can (or must) repurchase the asset for an amount that is less than the original selling price of the asset. For example, if the original selling price is ₹1,000 and the repurchase price is ₹800, the contract is a lease contract; the entity has granted to the customer the right to use the asset over a specified period at the consideration (lease rent) of ₹200.

The entity accounts for the contract as a financing transaction if the entity can (or must) repurchase the asset for an amount that is equal to or higher than the original selling price of the asset. For example, if the original selling price is ₹1,000 and the repurchase price is ₹1200, the contract is a financing arrangement; the entity has lent to the customer ₹1,000 for a specified period to earn an interest of ₹200.

A put option: If an entity has an obligation to repurchase the asset at the customer's request (put option), the entity accounts for the contract as a lease if the customer has a significant economic incentive to exercise that right and it is likely to exercise the right.

If the customer does not have a significant economic incentive to exercise his right at a price that is lower than the original selling price of the asset, the entity should account for the agreement as if it were the sale of a product with a right of return. If the repurchase price of the asset is equal to or greater than the original selling price and is more than the expected market value of the asset, the contract is in effect a financing arrangement. If the repurchase price of the asset is equal to or greater than the original selling price and is less than or equal to the expected market value of the asset, and the customer does not have a significant economic incentive to exercise his right, then the entity accounts for the agreement as if it were the sale of a product with a right of return.

Licensing

A licence establishes a customer's rights to the intellectual property (IP) of an entity. Examples are software and technology; motion pictures, music and other forms of media and entertainment; franchises; and patents, trademarks and copyrights.

A licence may not be a distinct performance obligation.

A licence may not be a distinct performance obligation. For example, a licence that is integral to the functionality of a tangible asset (e.g., equipment) is not a distinct performance obligation. Similarly, a licence that the customer can benefit from only in conjunction with a related service (e.g., licence to access an online service) is not a distinct performance obligation.

If the licence is a distinct performance obligation, the entity recognises the revenue either over a period of time or at a point in time depending on the nature of the licence.

If the licence grants to the customer a right to access the entity's intellectual property as it exists throughout the licence period, the entity recognises the revenue over a period of time because the customer simultaneously receives and consumes the benefit from the entity's performance of providing access to its intellectual property as the performance occurs. This is the case when the activities of the entity significantly change the form or functionality of the intellectual property.

EXAMPLE 11.15 (Licensing use of brand)

Fact pattern: Revenue from granting licence to use a product brand (such as, Raleigh bicycle, a U.K. brand, which is being produced in Ludhiana in India by Naren International, Suncross Bikes) should be recognised over a period of time, as the entity (licensor) continues to manage and augment the value of the product brand through their activities.

Discussion: If the licence grants to the customer a right to use the entity's intellectual property as it exists (in form and functionality) at the point in time at which the licence is granted, the entity recognises the revenue at a point in time.

EXAMPLE 11.16 (License to use a media content)

For example, revenue from granting licence to use a completed media content (such as, films produced by Walt Disney Company) should be recognised at a point of time.

Sale-or usage-based royalty

General revenue recognition principles are not applicable if the sales-or usage-based royalty relates solely to or predominantly to the intellectual property (IP) licence.

Sales-or usage-based royalty is a variable consideration. However, general revenue recognition principles are not applicable if the sales-or usage-based royalty relates solely to or predominantly to the intellectual property (IP) licence.

An entity should recognise revenue for a sale-or usage-based royalty promised in exchange for a licence of intellectual property only when the following events occurs:

1. The subsequent sale or usage occurs; and
2. The performance obligation to which some or all of the sales-or usage-based royalties have been allocated has been satisfied (or partially satisfied).

The second test is required, as the agreement might require the entity to undertake activities which might significantly impact the form and functionality of IP, or the agreement may include other goods or services. For example, entities may sell franchisee licence with consultancy and training services or with supply of equipment and the fees payable by the franchisee is in the form of sales-based or usage-based royalties.

A contract to licence IP may include a fixed element (e.g., minimum royalty guarantee) and a sales-based royalty payment plan. The minimum royalty guarantee element in the transaction price is not a variable consideration, and therefore, normal revenue recognition principles are to be applied in accounting for that part of the consideration. Any additional sales-based or usage-based royalties, in excess of the guaranteed amount, should be recognised using the royalty exception.

11.3 INTEREST AND DIVIDEND

Interest income is recognised using the effective interest method.

Revenue from interests and dividends should be recognised on the following bases:

Interest income

Interest income is recognised using the effective interest method. The effective interest method has been discussed in Chapters 9 and 10. When unpaid interest has accrued before the acquisition of an interest-bearing security, the subsequent receipt of interest is allocated between *pre-acquisition* and *post-acquisition* periods. Only post-acquisition period interest is recognised as revenue, and pre-acquisition period interest is reduced from the cost of investment as a part recovery of the cost.

Dividend from investment in shares should be recognised when the investor's right to receive dividend is established.

Dividends income

Dividend from investment in shares should be recognised when the investor's right to receive dividend is established. In case of investment in the equity shares of a company, right to dividend is established when the shareholder body of the investee approves the dividend payment.

Dividend declared from pre-acquisition net income is reduced from the cost of investment as part-recovery of the cost.

11.4 GOVERNMENT GRANTS

Government grants or other types of government assistance are usually provided to enterprises to encourage certain types of activities. Perhaps, in the absence of government grants, enterprises would not have undertaken those activities. Examples of government grants are export subsidy, subsidy of acquisition of pollution-control equipment, and allotment of land at free of cost for at subsidised rate for establishment of factory, etc. in an under-developed region.

No government grant should be recognised until there is a reasonable assurance that:
(a) the enterprise will comply with the conditions attached to them; and
(b) the grant will be received.

11.4.1 Recognition Principle

No government grant should be recognised until there is a reasonable assurance that:

(a) the enterprise will comply with the conditions attached to them; and
(b) the grant will be received.

Government grants should be recognised in profit or loss on a systematic basis over the periods in which the entity recognises the related costs for which the grants are intended to compensate as expenses.

Government grants should be recognised in profit or loss on a systematic basis over the periods in which the entity recognises the related costs for which the grants are intended to compensate as expenses.

Table 11.3 below presents the application of the general accounting principles discussed above.

TABLE 11.3 Recognition of Government Grant—Application of the General Accounting Principles

	Nature of the grant	*Accounting principle*
1.	Grant related to a specific expense	It should be recognised in profit or loss in the same period as the relevant expense is recognised.
2.	Grant relating to depreciable assets	Entities have a choice to recognise the grant either as a deferred revenue or deduct the grant from the acquisition cost of the asset. Grants recognised as deferred revenue are usually recognised in profit or loss over the periods and in the proportions in which depreciation expense on those assets is recognised.
3.	Grants related to non-depreciable assets	Grants related to non-depreciable assets may also require the fulfilment of certain obligations. If that is the case, then the grant should be recognised in profit or loss over the periods that bear the cost of meeting the obligations.
4.	Non-monetary grants	Entities have an option to measure the grant either at fair value or at a nominal amount. For example, a piece of equipment received as government grant is measured either at fair value or at a nominal amount (say, ₹1)
5.	Grants for financial assistance	In some circumstances, a government grant may be awarded for the purpose of giving immediate financial support to an entity rather than as an incentive to undertake specific expenditures. Such grants may be confined to a particular entity and may not be available to a whole class of beneficiaries. These circumstances may warrant recognising a grant in profit or loss of the period in which the entity qualifies to receive it, with disclosure to ensure that its effect is clearly understood.

EXAMPLE 11.17 (Grant of land for erecting a building)
A grant of land may be conditional on the erection of a building on the site. The entity should recognise the grant in profit or loss over the life of the building.

EXAMPLE 11.18 (Financial assistance to reopen production facilities damaged by cyclone)

Fact pattern: The government declared to provide financial assistance to companies whose production facilities located in the coastal area is damaged by a cyclone hit in the last month of the financial year 2020–2021 immediately after the cyclone. The scheme was finalised in 2021–2022 and the amount was released to companies in the first quarter of 2021–2022 after scrutinizing applications and assessing the extent of damage suffered by each applicant.

Discussion: The government subsidy should be recognised in the financial year 2021–2022.

Repayment of grant

A government grant that becomes repayable should be accounted for as a revision to an accounting estimate.

A government grant becomes repayable due to non-compliance of stipulated conditions or due to disbursement of excess grant by mistake. A government grant that becomes repayable should be accounted for as a revision to an accounting estimate.

REVIEW PROBLEMS

R11.1 Indicate whether the following statements are True or False:

(i) A non-finance company classifies income from the sale of goods and services as revenue.

(ii) A contract with a customer does not come into existence until the entity is reasonably certain that it will collect the transaction price.

(iii) All contracts which are entered at the same time with the same customer or related parties should be combined.

(iv) Cash discount should be deducted from the amount of revenue to be recognised in the statement of profit and loss.

(v) Transaction price should be estimated after fulfilling the promise to deliver the specified of goods.

(vi) A contract with a customer should include one performance obligation.

(vii) Performance obligation is fulfilled only when the control of the goods is transferred to the customer.

(viii) An entity that purchases from a firm scraps generated during the manufacturing process is a customer of that firm.

(ix) Extended warranty is a separate performance obligation while assurance warranty is not a separate performance obligation.

(x) Annual membership fee received by a health club should be recognised as revenue in the financial year in which it is received.

R11.2 Fill in the blanks:

(i) An electrical equipment manufacturing company has entered into a contract with a power producing company to construct a power generating station on a turnkey basis. The contract specifies the specifications of pieces of equipment to be used, individual price of each piece of equipment, and the deadline for delivering those at the construction site. It also indicates the deadline for completing the construction and the value of the total contract. The company .... recognise the revenue after fulfilling the promise to deliver the pieces of equipment. [Chose between, 'should' and 'should not'.]

(ii) A construction company, which has just started its business, has entered into its first construction contract with a multinational corporation. The contract includes a bonus clause for payment of bonus for early completion. The construction company is unable to estimate the probability that it will earn the bonus. At the inception of the contract the bonus .... included in the transaction price. [Chose between, 'should' and 'should not'.]

(iii) Revenue from a contract with a customer for selling goods should be recognised [......] time.[Chose between 'at a point in' and 'over'.]

(iv) Revenue from a contract with a customer to construct a building on the customer's site should be recognised .... time. [Chose between 'at a point in' and 'over'.]

(v) Revenue from a contract with a customer to submit a legal opinion on a particular legal issue faced by the customer should be recognised .... time if the firm has enforceable right to receive from the customer cost incurred plus a specified percentage of profit if the customer cancels the contract without any fault by the firm. [Chose between 'at a point in' and 'over'.]

(vi) Revenue from a contract with a customer to supply an ocean-going ship without any modification of the standard design should be recognised .... time. [Chose between 'at a point in' and 'over'.]

(vii) A construction company estimates that it will incur ₹60 lakhs to construct a building for a customer with whom it has entered into a construction contract during the year 2021–2022. The contract value is ₹100 lakhs. It incurred cost of ₹12 lakhs up to the balance sheet date. It should recognise revenue for the year 2021–2022 at ₹................. lakhs.

(viii) A construction company estimates that it will incur ₹120 lakhs to construct a building for a customer with whom it has entered into a construction contract during the year 2021–2022. The contract value is ₹160 lakhs. It incurred cost of ₹80 lakhs, including ₹20 lakhs towards the cost of material yet to be issued to the site, up to the balance sheet date. It should recognise revenue for the year 2021–2022 at ₹................. lakhs.

(ix) A firm has entered into a contract with a customer to sell a bundle of products-CD, MN, and YZ. The consolidated transaction price is ₹3,20,000. The stand-alone list prices of those products are CD: ₹2,20,000, MN: ₹1,00,000 and YZ: ₹80,000. The firm usually sells CD at 20 percent discount. The transaction price of ₹5,00,000 should be allocated to CD: ₹................., MN: ₹................., YZ: ₹.................

(x) Facilities of a number of companies located in Odisha coastal area was damaged in the last quarter of 2021–2022 by a cyclone that had hit the area. The government immediately announced that each company would be given by the government ₹50 lakhs or the carrying amount of all the assets in the facilities damaged towards financial support to reconstruct the facility. AB & Co. received the government order sanctioning the grant on August 10, 2022, much before the financial statements for the financial year 2021–2022 were placed before the board of directors for approval. The government grant should be recognised in the financial statements for the year.................

ASSIGNMENTS

1. Indicate against each statement whether it is True or False:

(i) There is no significant difference between revenue and other operating income.

(ii) Any entity that purchases an asset or a service from the entity is entity's customer.

(iii) In order to be enforceable in the court law, a contract must be in writing.

(iv) An entity recognises revenue and trade receivables (or cash) simultaneously.

(v) An entity recognises revenue from sale of goods when it transfers the possession of promised goods and services to the customer and expects receiving the promised consideration.

(vi) An entity measures revenue at the amount that is specified as consideration (price) in the contract with the customer.

(vii) An entity recognises revenue when all the distinct performance obligations in the contract are satisfied.

(viii) A contract to install a system with free maintenance for two years might have three distinct performance obligations.

(ix) An entity that promises delivery and installation of television should not recognise until the installation is complete; although installation is a routine and simple activity.

(x) If an entity promises to deliver a combined output (e.g., hospital), it cannot separate other promises (e.g., supply of inputs specified in the contract) from that promise.

(xi) If the entity, which regularly sells building materials in a competitive market, promises to deliver a commercial space as designed by the customer, it allocates the transaction price to the performance obligation to supply building materials and the performance obligation to integrate inputs to deliver the combined output, which is the commercial space.

(xii) If an entity expects that the customer will avail cash discount, the transaction price that is used to measure revenue should be net of cash discount.

(xiii) An entity should not include variable consideration (e.g., performance bonus) in the transaction price.

(xiv) As a practical expedient, an entity is not required to adjust the promised amount of consideration for the effects of a significant financing component if the entity expects, at contract inception, that it will collect money within one year from the date when it transfers a promised good or service to a customer.

(xv) Accounting for customer's loyalty programme is an application of the accounting principle that requires an entity to reduce the transaction price by the consideration paid or payable to a customer or customer's customer.

(xvi) An entity allocates the purchase consideration of a bundle of products to each individual product in the bundle in proportion to their fair values.

(xvii) An entity recognises revenue over time if the customer simultaneously receives and consumes the benefits provided by the entity's performance as the entity performs.

(xviii) In measuring revenue over time, most entities use the input method to measure the progress of the performance obligation satisfied.

(xix) An entity should not recognise revenue from a 'sale with a right to return' until the time allowed to return the goods expires.

(xx) Extended warranty is a separate performance obligation.

2. Fill in the blanks:

(i) A real estate developer, who creates residential complexes, constructs apartments, sells them as it receives clearances from regulators and transfers them to customers by getting them registered on completion of the construction, should recognise revenue.................(Choose between 'over a period of time' and 'at a point in time'.)

(ii) A construction contractor who constructs apartments for a real estate developer should recognise revenue...................... (Choose between 'over a period of time' and 'at a point in time'.)

(iii) Cash discount should be.................... from transaction price. (Choose between 'be deducted' and 'not be deducted'.)

(iv) In measuring the progress of construction work for the purpose of recognising revenue, an entity should .... cost of materials procured specifically for the project but not issued to the site. (Choose between 'include' and 'not include'.)

(v) An entity has sold 100 pieces of a product at a price of ₹1,000 per piece with a right to return within 30 days. The cost per piece is ₹600 and the entity expects that 10% of the goods sold will return. The entity should recognise: (a) revenue at ₹................; (b) refund liability at ₹................; and (c) right to return at ₹................

(vi) A warranty that is required by law is likely to be a...............warranty. (Choose between 'assurance' and 'service'.)

(vii) An entity that produces industrial boilers (of standard specifications) .... recognise revenue when the product is ready for dispatch, if the customer defers the delivery after paying full price and provides a right to the entity to divert the boiler to another customer and deliver him a boiler to be produced later. (Choose between 'should' and 'should not'.)

(viii) An entity that provides health club services, usually, ... the non-refundable joining fee as revenue immediately when it is received or receivable. (Choose between 'recognises' and 'does not recognise'.)

(ix) A contract with a customer under which the entity has an obligation to repurchase the product at a price lower than the selling price should be recognised as ....

(x) Contract asset is a .... asset. (Choose between 'financial' and 'non-financial'.)

CHAPTER

12

DEPRECIATION AND IMPAIRMENT

CHAPTER OBJECTIVES

The objectives of this chapter is to introduce to readers the accounting for income. In particular, the objective is developing and understanding of:

- Classification of income;
- Recognition and measurement of revenue—income from contracts with customers;
- Recognition and measurement of interest and dividend income;
- Recognition and measurement of government grant.

12.1 NATURE OF DEPRECIATION, AMORTISATION, AND DEPLETION

12.1.1 Depreciation

Depreciation is systematic allocation of the depreciable amount of a depreciable asset over its useful life.

- Depreciable amount is the cost of a depreciable asset *less* the amount that the management expects to realise on disposal (called, residual value). In case an asset is revalued, it is the difference between the revalued amount and the estimated residual value.
- Useful life is the period over which the management expects to use the asset.

Depreciation is systematic allocation of the depreciable amount of a depreciable asset over its useful life.

With certain exceptions such as quarries and sites used for landfill, usually land has an unlimited useful life. Therefore, it is not considered as a depreciable asset. All other items of property, plant, and equipment (PP&E) are depreciable assets.

Depreciation is a measure of:

- the wearing out, and
- consumption or other loss of value of a depreciable asset arising from use, efflux of time, or obsolescence through technology and market changes.

12.1.2 Amortisation

Depreciation of intangible assets is called amortisation.

Depreciation of intangible assets is called amortisation.

12.1.3 Depletion

Depletion of natural resources is similar to the depreciation of PP&E. Examples of natural resources are oil and gas reserves, mineral deposits, thermal energy sources, and standing timber.

Depletion of natural resources is similar to the depreciation of PP&E.

12.1.4 Objectives of Charging Depreciation, Amortisation and Depletion

The principle of charging depreciation, etc. is consistent with the principle of accrual accounting. The objective is to match costs and revenue by allocating the cost of the asset to accounting years which will benefit from the use of the asset. Depreciation etc. does not necessarily result in the availability of funds to replace the asset after its useful life. Only if the amount of depreciation is invested outside the business, funds would be available for replacing the asset after its useful life.

12.2 ACCOUNTING PRINCIPLES AND MEASUREMENT OF DEPRECIATION, AMORTISATION AND DEPLETION

12.2.1 Residual Value of Items of PP&E

Residual value is defined as: "The residual value of an asset is the estimated amount that an entity would currently obtain from disposal of the asset, after deducting the estimated costs of disposal, if the asset were already of the age and in the condition expected at the end of its useful life."

Management estimates residual value at zero, if it is immaterial.

Companies Act 2013

The Companies Act stipulates that the residual value cannot exceed five per cent of the original cost.

EXAMPLE 12.1 (Estimating residual value)

Fact pattern: An entity owns a vehicle that it uses in the city periphery for transporting garments. It expects to use it for ten years. As of March 31, 2022, it has to estimate the residual value.

Discussion: Residual value as on March 31, 2022 is the value that a ten-year-old vehicle that is used in the city periphery for transporting material would fetch in the market on March 31, 2022.

The residual value of an asset is the estimated amount that an entity would currently obtain from disposal of the asset, if the asset were already of the age and in the condition expected at the end of its useful life.

12.2.2 Useful Life of PP&E

The useful life of an item of PP&E is either:

- the period over which an asset is expected to be available for use by an entity, usually expressed in years, or
- the number of production or similar units (such as, number of hours) expected to be obtained by that entity.

Usually, the useful life is estimated in years. However, for certain assets, like heavy earth moving equipment, useful life is estimated in production hours.

Factors that determine the useful life

Legal or contractual limits:

Example: The useful life of a commercial vehicle cannot exceed the maximum period for which car can be used as per law. The useful life of a 'right-of-use' asset cannot exceed the lease period.

The useful life of an item of PP&E is either the period over which an asset is expected to be available for use by an entity, usually expressed in years, or the number of production or similar units expected to be obtained by that entity.

Extraction or consumption or use of the fixed asset:

Example: The period over which the ore in a mine will be extracted.

Physical wear and tear: It depends on operational factors, repair maintenance programme of the entity, and similar other factors

Technical or commercial obsolescence: Once the product or the process becomes obsolete the asset cannot be used economically beneficially for producing the product or service.

Entities estimate the useful life of a fixed asset based on the various factors, including experience and corporate strategy.

EXAMPLE 12.2 (Estimating useful life)

Fact pattern: Entities AA and BB produce the same product using the same process and technology. They acquired the piece of equipment on the same day. Both the entities expect that a new technology would be available for use after five years from the acquisition date of the equipment and will stabilise in another three years. AA's policy is to adopt the new technology immediately it is available for use. BB is little risk averse, and its policy is to adopt the new technology once it is stabilised.

Discussion: AA estimates the useful life of the piece of equipment at five years and BB estimates the useful life of the piece of equipment at eight years.

Indicative useful life under the Companies Act, 2013

Schedule II of the Companies Act, 2013 provides the indicative useful life of various assets. A company may use different useful life based on technical assessment. If it uses a different useful life, it must disclose the same.

Technical life, economic life, and useful life

Table 12.1 below explains the difference in technical life, economic life, and useful life.

Technical life is the period over which the asset is expected to produce the intended result.

TABLE 12.1 Technical Life, Economic Life, and Useful Life

	Term	Description
1.	Technical (physical) life	The period over which the asset is expected to produce the intended result. The manufacturer estimates the technical life. It is asset specific.
2.	Economic life	The period over which the use of the asset makes economic sense. In a way, this is specific to the asset. Economic life may be shorter than the technical life of the asset.
3.	Useful life	The period over which the entity that holds the assets intends to use it. It is entity–specific and not asset specific. It cannot exceed the economic life.

Economic life is the period over which the use of the asset makes economic sense.

12.2.3 Depreciation Accounting Principles

Accounting principles for recognising and measuring depreciation is presented in Table 12.2 below.

TABLE 12.2 Accounting Principles for Recognising and Measuring Depreciation

	Topic	Principle
1.	Depreciation method	(a) Entities should choose a method that matches the pattern for allocating depreciable amount with the expected pattern of consumption of the future economic benefits embodied in the asset. (b) Depreciation should not be charged based on revenue, for example, in proportion of the revenue earned in a particular accounting year to the total revenue expected to be earned using the asset over its useful life. This is so because revenue is affected by market forces, and not solely on the physical productivity of the asset. (c) The method should be reviewed at least at the end of each financial year and should be changed if it is assessed that the pattern of the consumption of benefit has changed.
2.	Component accounting	Each component of an item of property, plant, and equipment (PP&E) with a cost that is significant in relation to the total cost of the item of the PP&E should be depreciated separately.
3.	Assets measured using the revaluation model	When an entity uses the revaluation model, it revalues the asset periodically. In that case, depreciation is provided based on (i) the revalued amount, and (ii) the estimate of the remaining useful life of the fixed asset.
4.	Commencement and cessation of charging depreciation	Depreciation on an item of PP&E should be charged from the date when the asset is ready for intended use and should cease at the earlier of the date that the asset is classified as held for sale and the date that the asset is derecognised. Accordingly, depreciation should be charged on assets which were not in use during the financial year.
5.	Depreciation on addition or extension of asset	Any addition or extension to an existing item of PP&E should be depreciated over the remaining useful life of that asset, unless that addition or extension is recognised as a separate asset.
6.	Change in the carrying amount due to cost adjustments	The depreciation on the revised unamortised depreciable amount should be provided prospectively over the remaining useful life of the asset.
7.	Recognition	Depreciation should be recognised in the statement of profit and loss. However, if the asset is used to produce another item of PP&E, the depreciation should be added to the cost of that item.

Entities should choose a method of deprecation that matches the pattern for allocating depreciable amount with the expected pattern of consumption of the future economic benefits embodied in the asset.

12.2.4 Depreciation under the Income Tax Law

The tax law provides depreciation rates and the method to be used in computing depreciation that is allowable as an expense in computing the taxable income. All asses sees (including companies) are required to use the same rates and the same method in computing depreciation irrespective of their own technical estimate of the useful life and the residual value of assets. Tax law is often used as a fiscal instrument to encourage investment in a particular type of asset, and therefore, allows a very high rate of depreciation.

The tax law provides depreciation rates and the method to be used in computing depreciation that is allowable as an expense in computing the taxable income.

In India, the tax law requires use of the reducing balance method of depreciation.

12.2.5 Accounting for Changes in Estimates

Entities revise the estimates for the useful life and residual value based on new information available to them. Change in the depreciation method is also considered a change in estimate, as entities change the methods based on its revised estimate of the pattern of flow of benefits from the item of PP&E.

Entities revise the estimates for the useful life and residual value based on new information available to them. Change in the depreciation method is also considered a change in estimate.

Accounting principle

The general accounting principle is that a change in accounting estimate is applied prospectively. The same account principle is applicable in accounting for changes in useful life, residual value, and depreciation method.

EXAMPLE 12.3 (Revision of estimated useful life and residual value)

Fact pattern: The following are the details of a machine acquired by AA Ltd. in 2016

Acquisition cost	₹110,000
Estimated useful life at initial recognition	10 years
Estimated residual value at initial recognition	₹10,000

AA Ltd. uses the straight-line method of depreciation. In 2019, it reviewed and revised the estimated useful life to five years, and also, revised the estimated residual value to ₹40,000.

Discussion: The amount of depreciation that AA Ltd. should charge per annum over the remaining useful life.

1. The revised useful life of the three-year-old machine is 5 years. Therefore, the remaining useful life is (5 – 3) or 2 years.
2. The depreciable amount estimated at initial recognition was (₹1,10,000 – 10,000) or ₹1,00,000.
3. Cumulative depreciation at the commencement of the year 2019: [(₹1,00,000/10) × 3] or ₹30,000.
4. Carrying amount at the commencement of the year 2019: (₹1,10,000 – 30,000) or ₹80,000.
5. Revised depreciable amount estimated at the close of 2019: (₹80,000 – 40,000) or ₹40,000.
6. Depreciation to be charged in 2019 and 2020: (40,000/2) or ₹20,000 each year.

12.2.6 Depreciation Methods

Table 12.3 presents the commonly used deprecation methods for different types of assets.

TABLE 12.3 The Commonly used Deprecation Methods for Different Types of Assets

	Type of asset	*Depreciation method*
1.	Freehold land	Freehold land is not a depreciable asset.
2.	Leasehold properties	Commonly, the straight-line method of depreciation is used. Those are depreciated over the unexpired period of the lease, or the useful life of the assets, if shorter. Provision should be made for the estimated cost of contractual obligation to make good any obsolescence over the period of the lease, using the latest estimate of the cost of repairs at current prices.
3.	Freehold building	Commonly, the straight-line method of depreciation is used.
4.	Plant and machinery	Commonly, the straight-line method of depreciation is used.
5.	Loose tools	Commonly loose tools, jigs and patterns are depreciated using the revaluation method.
6.	Ships, vehicles, etc.	Commonly, the straight-line method of depreciation is used.
7.	Assets of wasting nature line natural resources	Commonly depreciated on the basis of estimated exhaustion of the asset concerned. The term depletion is used.

Straight-line time method

A uniform amount is allocated over the useful life of the asset by applying a predetermined rate on the depreciable amount.

Under the straight-line method of deprecation, a uniform amount is allocated over the useful life of the asset.

Straight-line use method

The depreciation rate is determined by dividing the depreciable by the total number of units expected to be produced (estimated total number of hours to be operated) over the useful life of the asset. The rate is applied on the actual units produced (or actual hours operated) in the subject financial year.

Reducing balance method

Under this method, a fixed rate is applied on the reducing balance, popularly known as written-down value (WDV). The amount of depreciation reduces every succeeding year.

Under the educing balance method of depreciation, a fixed rate is applied on the WDV. The amount of depreciation reduces every succeeding year.

The formula for calculating that fixed rate can be derived as follows:

Let r be the rate of depreciation. If C represents the cost of acquisition, R is the residual value, and n is the useful life, then,

$$C \times (1-r)^n = R$$

$$(1-r)^n = \frac{R}{C}$$

$$(1-r) = \sqrt[n]{\frac{R}{C}}$$

$$r = 1 - \sqrt[n]{\frac{R}{C}}$$

Sum-of-the-years'-digits method

Under sum-of-the-years'-digits method, the amount of depreciation is calculated by multiplying the depreciable amount by the factor (k/s). If n be the estimated useful life of the asset, then k for year 1 is n, $(n - 1)$ for the year 2, $(n - 2)$ for the year 3, and so on.

Thus, for the *n*th year, *k* is 1. *S* is the sum of the numbers 1 to *n*. Thus, if the useful life is estimated at 10 years, *S* = 55. Thus, (*k/s*) for the year 1 is (10/55). If the depreciable amount is ₹1,00,000, depreciation for the first year is ₹1,00,000 × (10/55) or ₹18,182. Depreciation for the 10th year is ₹1,00,000 × (1/55) or ₹1,818.

EXAMPLE 12.4 (Depreciation methods)

Fact pattern: The following are the details of a machine acquired in 2009:

Acquisition cost	₹110,000
Estimated residual value	₹10,000
Depreciable amount [₹1,10,000 – 10,000]	₹1,00,000
Estimated useful life in years	10 years
Estimated useful life in years in production units	100,000 units
Number of units produced in the year 2009	9,000 units

Discussion:

Straight-line time method of depreciation

Depreciation rate = (1/10) × 100 = 10 per cent

Deprecation per year = (₹1,00,000 × 0.10) = ₹10,000

Straight-line use method of depreciation

Depreciation rate = (₹1,00,000/1,00,000) = ₹1 per unit

Deprecation for 2009 = (₹1 × 9,000) = ₹9,000

Reducing balance method of depreciation

$$\textit{Depreciation rate} = 1 - \sqrt[10]{\frac{₹10,000}{₹1,10,000}} = 21.32\%$$

Year	Opening Written Down Value (₹)	Depreciation (₹) (Column 1 × 0.02132)	Closing Written Down Value (₹) (Column 2–3)
(1)	(2)	(3)	(4)
2009	1,10,000	23,452	86,548
2010	86,548	18,452	68,096
2011	68,096	14,518	53,578
2012	53,578	11,423	42,155
2013	42,155	8,987	33,168
2014	33,168	7,071	26,096
2015	26,096	5,564	20,533
2016	20,533	4,378	16,155
2017	16,155	3,444	12,711
2018	12,711	2,710	10,001

Under sum-of-the-years'-digits method of depreciation, the amount of depreciation is calculated by multiplying the depreciable amount by the factor (*k/s*). If *n* be the estimated useful life of the asset, then *k* for year 1 is *n*, (*n* – 1) for the year 2, (*n* – 2) for the year 3, and so on.

Sum-of-the-Years'-Digits Method

Year	K	S	Depreciation ₹1,00,000 × (K/S)	Written Down Value (₹) (₹1,10,000 – Depreciation)
(1)	(2)	(3)	(4)	(5)
2009	10	55	18,182	91,818
2010	9	55	16,364	75,454
2011	8	55	14,545	60,909
2012	7	55	12,727	48,182
2013	6	55	10,909	37,273
2014	5	55	9,091	28,182
2015	4	55	7,273	20,909
2016	3	55	5,455	15,454
2017	2	55	3,636	11,818
2018	1	55	1,818	10,000

12.2.7 Amortisation: Accounting Principles and Measurement

Accounting principles

Intangible assets with definite (finite) useful life are amortised over its estimated useful life. Intangible assets with indefinite useful life are not amortised. Those are tested for impairment annually.

Intangible assets with indefinite useful life

Intangible assets with definite (finite) useful life are amortised over its estimated useful life. Intangible assets with indefinite useful life are not amortised. Those are tested for impairment annually.

An intangible asset has indefinite useful life if there is no foreseeable limit to the period over which the asset is expected to generate net cash inflows for the entity. In other words, an intangible asset has indefinite useful life if no legal, regulatory, contractual, competitive, economic, or other factors limit its useful life to the reporting entity. Examples are product brand, trade mark renewable at a nominal fee and the entity has the intention and capacity to continue the use the trade mark, and licenses (such as, broadcasting license) renewable at a nominal fee and the entity has the intention and capacity to continue the use of the license.

Goodwill

Goodwill is not amortised. It is tested for impairment annually.

Goodwill is not amortised. It is tested for impairment annually.

Measurement

The principles are similar to those applicable to depreciation. However, many of the principles are not applicable to intangible assets because of the very nature of those assets. Usually, the residual value is considered at zero and straight-line-time method is used.

12.2.8 Depletion

The objective is the same as depreciation of PP&E. Straight-line-use method (cost per unit of extraction) is used to amortise the cost of acquisition, including the capitalised cost of exploration and evaluation, of the natural resource (such as, minerals, oil and gas).

12.3 IMPAIRMENT OF ASSETS

12.3.1 Nature of Impairment

There is an implicit assumption that the enterprise will recover at least the carrying amount of assets either by use or through sale. If at any point in time an entity estimates that it will not be able to recover the carrying amount of the asset, it recognises an impairment loss and reduces the carrying amount to the recoverable amount.

An entity might not be able to recover the carrying amount due to many reasons, including physical damage to the assets, and change in the internal and external contexts (such as, change in the entity's strategy, new government policy, emergence of a competitor, and change in customers' buying behaviour).

12.3.2 Accounting Principles

Table 12.4 below presents the accounting principles for the measurement and recognition of impairment loss.

Impairment loss of an asset is the difference between the carrying amount and the recoverable amount, which higher of the value-in-use and fair value less costs to sell.

Items of PP&E should be tested for impairment only if there are indicators that the asset is impaired.

Intangible assets with indefinite useful life and those that are not put to use should be tested for impairment at least annually.

TABLE 12.4 Accounting Principles for the Measurement and Recognition of Impairment Loss

	Topic	*Principle*
1	Impairment loss measurement	Impairment loss of an asset is the difference between the carrying amount and the recoverable amount.
2.	Recoverable amount	Recoverable amount is the higher of *value-in-use* and the *fair value less costs to sell.*
3.	Value-in-use	Value-in-use is the present value (PV) of *pre-tax* cash flows that the asset will generate from use and on disposal at the end of its useful life. *Discount rate* Market-determined pre-tax discount rate should be used to calculate the PV. Risk-free rate should be used if the projected cash flow is the 'expected cash flow' (in statistical sense), which represents 'risk-free equivalent cash flow'. If the cash flow is not the expected cash flow, the discounting rate should incorporate both the time value of money, and the risks surrounding the cash flow. *Foreign currency cash flow* If the asset is expected to generate cash flows in foreign currency, the entity should discount the forecasted cash flows using a discount rate appropriate for that currency and then translate the PV using the exchange rate at the balance sheet date.
4.	Testing requirement	(a) Items of PP&E should be tested for impairment only if there are indicators that the asset is impaired. Indicators are discussed below. (b) Intangible assets with indefinite useful life should be tested for impairment at least annually. (c) Goodwill should be tested at least annually. (d) An intangible asset that is not put to use (such as, a patent not put in use) should be tested for impairment annually.
5.	Reversal of impairment loss	(a) Entities should estimate the recoverable amount of an impaired asset, if, there is any indication that an impairment loss may no longer exist or may have decreased. An entity should reverse the impairment loss recognised earlier if the recoverable amount is higher than the carrying amount of the asset. The carrying amount of an asset should not be increased above the lower of (a) its recoverable amount, if determinable, and (b) the carrying amount that would have been determined had no impairment loss been recognised for the asset in prior accounting periods. (b) Impairment loss of goodwill should not be reversed.
4.	Cash Generating Unit (CGU) [Discussed below]	If the impairment loss is estimated for a CGU, the loss should be allocated first to the goodwill and the balance, if any, should be allocated to other assets of the CGU in proportion to their carrying amount. However, carrying amount of an asset should not be reduced below the highest of (a) its net selling price (if determinable), (b) its value in use (if determinable), and (c) zero.

12.3.3 Indicators of Impairment Loss

At the minimum an entity should consider the following indicators of impairment:

External sources of information

1. During the period, there is significant decline in an asset's market value as compared to what would be expected as a result of the passage of time or normal use.
2. Significant changes in the technological, market, economic or legal environment having an adverse effect on the entity have taken place during the period or *will take place in the near future.*

3. During the period, there is an increase in market interest rates or other market rates of return on investment that will *materially* affect the discount rate used in calculating an asset's value in use and substantially decrease the asset's recoverable amount.
4. The carrying amount of the net assets is more than its market capitalisation.

Internal sources of information

1. Evidence is available of obsolescence or physical damage of an asset.
2. Significant changes in the extent to which or manner in which an asset is used or expected to be used, having an adverse effect on the entity have taken place during the period or are expected to take place in the near future.
3. Evidence is available from internal reporting that the economic performance of an asset is, or will be, worse than expected.

Evidence available from internal reporting

1. Cash flow required to acquire the asset, or cash needs for operating or maintaining the same are significantly higher than those originally budgeted.
2. Actual net cash flows or operating profit or loss arising from the asset are significantly worse than those budgeted.
3. A significant decline in budgeted net cash flows or operating profit, or a significant increase in budgeted loss arising from the asset.
4. Operating losses or net cash outflows for the asset when current period figures are aggregated with budgeted figures for the future.

12.3.4 Cash Generating Unit (CGU)

A CGU is the *smallest identifiable group of assets.*

A CGU is the smallest identifiable group of assets.

In most situations, it is almost impossible to determine the recoverable amount of an individual asset, as individual assets do not generate cash flows independently from other assets. Therefore, it is important to estimate the cash flows of a group of assets that generates cash flows from continuing use, which are *largely independent* of the cash flows from other assets or group of assets. That group of assets is called the cash generating unit (CGU). Identification of CGU is a matter of judgement. Determination of CGU at a higher level might camouflage the impairment loss of certain assets. On the other hand, any attempt to identify CGU at a very low level of the organisation may result in recognition of impairment loss which does not exist.

Examples of CGU:

1. CGU is the individual store of a retailer that operates number of stores across the country.
2. A factory that produces goods to execute the customers' orders allocated to it by the corporate office based on the capacity available in different facilities of the entity and the location of the customers is not a CGU, as the factory does not generate cash flows independently of other production facilities.

Vertically integrated organisation

If an active market exists for the output produced by an asset or group of assets, that asset or group of assets is identified as a CGU even if some or all of the outputs are used internally.

If an active market exists for the output produced by an asset or group of assets, that asset or group of assets is identified as a CGU even if some or all of the outputs are used internally.

The management's best estimate of future price that could be achieved at arm's length transactions should be used in estimating the value in use of the CGU when measuring (a) the future cash inflows that relate to the internal use of the output for selling CGU, and (b) the future cash outflows that relate to the internal use of the output for buying CGO.

12.3.5 Measuring Impairment Loss of Goodwill

Goodwill is recognised only from a business combination transaction. Therefore, goodwill recognised in financial statements must relate to one or more businesses acquired prior to the balance sheet date, which is the date at which the CGU is being tested for impairment.

An entity should allocate goodwill acquired in a business combination to each of the CGUs (or group of CGUs) that is expected to benefit from the synergies of the combination. An existing CGU, which is not acquired in the business combination transaction, may also benefit from the acquisition. For example, when an entity acquires a business in the value chain, existing businesses benefit from the acquisition.

In certain situations, an entity may not be able to allocate goodwill to CGUs except arbitrarily. In those situations, the entity does not allocate the goodwill to each CGU. The goodwill is tested at the entity level.

The impairment loss, estimated by comparing the carrying amount (with goodwill) with the recoverable amount is first allocated to goodwill and then, to other assets.

Method for testing impairment

An entity compares the carrying amount, including any goodwill, with recoverable amount to test the CGU for impairment. The impairment loss, if any, is first allocated to goodwill to reduce its carrying amount, and then, to other assets.

When goodwill is allocated to a larger CGU, which includes one or more CGUs, testing goodwill involve the steps:

Step 1: Test smaller CGUs, which constitute the larger CGU, for impairment, if there are indications that the CGU might have been impaired.
Step 2: Adjust the carrying amount of the smaller CGUs for impairment loss, if any.
Step 3: Calculate the revised carrying amount, including goodwill, of the larger CGU.
Step 4: Test the larger CGU for impairment.
Step 5: Allocate the impairment loss to goodwill.

When goodwill is allocated to a larger CGU, which includes one or more CGUs, smaller CGUs are tested for impairment and the carrying amount of the larger CGU is adjusted for the impairment losses, if any, before being tested for impairment. the impairment loss is allocated to goodwill.

EXAMPLE 12.5 (Testing goodwill impairment)

Goodwill recognised in a business transaction: ₹20 crores. The goodwill could not be allocated to individual CGUs (smaller CGUs).

The goodwill should be tested as follows with hypothetical carrying amounts and recoverable amounts of smaller CGUs (A, B and C):

Sl. No	Particulars	*CGU A (Amount in Crores)*	*CGU B (Amount in Crores)*	*CGU C (Amount in Crores)*	*Total (Larger CGU) (Amount in Crores)*
1.	Carrying amount without goodwill	40	25	35	100
2.	Recoverable amount	45	24	48	117
3.	Impairment loss	Nil	1	Nil	.
4.	Carrying amount, adjusted for impairment loss	40	24	35	99
5.	Goodwill				20
6.	Carrying amount, adjusted for impairment loss, including goodwill				119
7.	Impairment Loss to be allocated to goodwill (6–2)				2

12.3.6 Impairment of Corporate Office

The key characteristic of corporate assets is that they do not generate cash inflows independently from other assets or groups of assets. Examples of corporate assets are building of the corporate headquarters, EDP equipment, and research centre. The carrying amount of those assets cannot be attributed to a particular CGU under review except on an arbitrary basis. The recoverable amount of an individual corporate asset cannot be determined unless the management decides to dispose of the asset. Therefore, if there is any indication that a corporate asset is impaired, the recoverable amount is determined for the CGU to which the corporate asset belongs. It is compared with the carrying amount of the CGU to determine the impairment loss. Usually, the CGU for corporate assets is the entity as a whole.

REVIEW PROBLEMS

R 12.1 Indicate whether the following statements are True or False:

(i) Depreciation is the amount set aside by the firm to ensure that funds will be available to replace the item of PP&E after its useful life.
(ii) Useful life of items of PP&E are always expressed in terms of number of years.
(iii) Depreciation in a particular accounting year is charged only on those assets that are used during that year.
(iv) Companies are not permitted to us a depreciation method that allocate depreciable amount in proportion to the revenue earned total expected revenue.
(v) Estimated useful life of an item of PP&E cannot be longer than the technical life but can be longer than the economic life.
(vi) A firm that uses the straight-line use method of depreciation does not charge depreciation on temporary idle items of PP&E.
(vii) Accounting principle for recognising impairment loss is an example of the application of the principle of prudence.
(viii) Items of PP&E should be tested for impairment at least once in every financial year.
(ix) An item of intangible asset has indefinite useful life if there is no foreseeable limit to the period over which the asset is expected to generate net cash inflows for the entity.
(x) Goodwill is not amortised but tested for impairment annually.
(xi) Usually, impairment test is applied to cash generating unit (CGU) and impairment loss, if any is allocated to assets that constitute the CGU.
(xii) Impairment loss of items of PP&E, other than goodwill can be reversed.

R 12.2 Fill in the blanks:

(i) The acquisition cost of an item of PP&E is ₹5,00,000 and estimated residual value is ₹50,000, the depreciable amount is ₹......................
(ii) The term .... is used in the context of natural resources in the same sense in which the term depreciation is used in the context of PP&E.
(iii) Land is a .... assets. [Chose between 'depreciable' and 'non-depreciable'.]
(iv) The acquisition cost of an item of ₹5,00,000, estimated useful life is 10 years, and estimated residual value is ₹5,000. The depreciation rate for reducing value method of depreciation is [Blank] per cent.
(v) The carrying amount, value in use, and fair value *less* cost of sell of an item of PP&E is ₹5,00,000, ₹6,00,000, and ₹5,50,000 respectively. The estimated impairment loss is ₹......................

ASSIGNMENTS

1. Indicate against each statement whether it is True or False:

(i) Depreciation measures wear and tear of fixed assets.
(ii) Residual value of intangible assets is usually taken as zero.
(iii) Useful life of an asset is the period over which the asset is expected to produce the intended output/result.
(iv) The economic life of an asset is specific to the asset and useful life of an asset is specific to the entity.
(v) Impairment of an asset necessarily leads to reduction in its useful life.
(vi) Usually, no depreciation is charged on land because there is a general assumption that land has indefinite useful life.

2. In which of the following situations is the unit of production method of depreciation most appropriate?

(i) Service potential of an asset declines with use.
(ii) Service potential of an asset declines with the passage of time.
(iii) An asset is subject to rapid obsolescence.
(iv) An asset, is subject to increasing repairs and maintenance with increasing use.

3. Multiple choice questions:

(i) On January 1, 2003, Naina Limited (NL) purchased a machine for ₹3,00,000 and depreciated it by the straight-line method using an estimated useful life of 10 years with no salvage value. On January 1, 2006, NL determined that the machine had a useful life of six years from the date of acquisition and would have a salvage value of ₹30,000. An accounting change was made in 2006 to reflect the additional data. The accumulated depreciation for this machine should have a balance at December 31, 2006, of:

(a) ₹1,50,000 (b) ₹1,80,000
(b) ₹1,44,000 (d) None of the above

(ii) Rumki Limited (RL) acquired an asset on January 1, 2003. It estimated the useful life of the asset at five years and residual value at 5% of the cost of the asset. On December 31, 2006, accumulated depreciation, using the sum-of-the years' digits method would be:

(a) Original cost *less* salvage value multiplied by 14/15
(b) Original cost *less* salvage value multiplied by 1/15
(c) Original cost multiplied by 14/15
(d) Original cost multiplied by 1/15

5. Problems:

(i) Jose Limited (JL) has three divisions, one of which produces chemicals. The factory producing chemicals emits chemical waste to the nearby canal. The company has recognised a liability of ₹10,00,000 towards the estimated cost of cleaning the canal, as required by a newly enacted environmental law. The assets of JL, which are subject to impairment test, are carried at ₹10,00,00,000. The chemical factory is a CGU. The company can sell the chemical factory as a whole, and the buyer will have to take over the liability for restoration of the environment. The net selling price (fair value less costs to sell) of the factory is estimated at ₹89,00,000. The value in use, considering the present value of expenditure to be incurred for restoration of the environment, is estimated at ₹85,00,000.

Required: Calculate the impairment loss, if any.

(ii) On January 1, 2005, Mallika Limited (ML) acquired Shabnam Limited (SL). ML is in the business of retailing. It has a highly reputed retail stores in the upmarkets in three stores in Dubai. SL is in the textile business. It has two divisions—cloth division and readymade garments division. ML pays ₹1,200 million to the shareholders of SL towards purchase consideration. The estimated fair value of identifiable tangible and intangible assets is ₹900 million. ML recognises goodwill in its balance sheet at ₹300 million. After acquisition, ML has three CGUs—retail division, cloth division, and readymade garments division. ML expects that its retail business will also benefit from this acquisition. Assume the following two situations separately:

(a) ML allocates the goodwill of ₹300 million as follows:

(i) Retail division (Division A): ₹30 million
(ii) Cloth division (Division B): ₹120 million
(iii) Readymade garment division (Division C): ₹150 million

(b) ML is unable to allocate goodwill to individual CGUs.

The carrying amounts of assets (excluding goodwill) of the three divisions are as follows:

Division A: ₹400 million; Division B: ₹350 million; Division C: ₹500 million.

Assume the recoverable amounts of the three divisions are as follows: Division A: ₹450 million; Division B: ₹440 million; Division C: ₹700 million

Required: Estimate the impairment loss of goodwill, taking each situation separately.

CHAPTER

13

TOPICAL ISSUES

CHAPTER OBJECTIVES

The objectives of this chapter is to introduce to readers the following accounting topics briefly:

- Accounting for changes in foreign exchange rates;
- Lease accounting;
- Accounting for business combination;
- Consolidated financial statements;
- Accounting for borrowing costs;
- Employee share based payments.

13.1 ACCOUNTING FOR CHANGES IN FOREIGN EXCHANGE RATES

13.1.1 Important Definitions

Important definitions are provided in Table 13.1 below:

	Term	*Definition*
1.	Exchange rate	Exchange rate is the ratio of exchange for two currencies. Example: 1 USD = 74.50 INR.
2.	Presentation currency	Presentation currency is the currency in which the financial statements are presented. Indian companies have no choice but to present their financial statements in INR. Some countries allow companies to choose the currency for presentation of financial statements.
3.	Functional currency (Discussed in detail below.)	Functional currency is the currency of the primary economic environment in which the entity primarily generates and expends cash. A company maintains its accounting records in its functional currency.
4.	Foreign currency	Foreign currency is a currency other than the functional currency of the entity.
5.	Foreign operation	A foreign operation is a company that is a subsidiary, associate, joint venture or branch of a reporting entity, the activities of which are based or conducted *in a country or currency other than those of the reporting company.* The functional currency of a foreign operation might differ from the same of the reporting entity.
6.	Net investment in foreign operation	Net investment in a foreign operation is the amount of the reporting company's interest in the net assets of that operation. Investment in the equity issued by a foreign operation and a monetary item (such as, long term loan) for which settlement is neither planned nor is likely to occur in the foreseeable future is are parts of the company's net investment in that foreign operation.

Presentation currency is the currency in which the financial statements are presented.

Functional currency is the currency of the primary economic environment in which the entity primarily generates and expends cash.

A foreign operation is a company that is a subsidiary, associate, joint venture or branch of a reporting entity, the activities of which are based or conducted in a country or currency other than those of the reporting company.

Functional currency

A company's functional currency reflects the underlying transactions, events and conditions that are relevant to it. Accordingly, once determined, the functional currency is not changed unless there is a change in those underlying transactions, events and conditions.

A truly global company having activities across different countries and transactions denominated in different currencies might find it difficult to determine the functional currency. When the functional currency is not obvious, management uses its judgement to determine the functional currency that most faithfully represents the economic effects of the underlying transactions, events and conditions.

The following factors are considered in determining its functional currency:

1. The currency in which the sales prices for its goods and services are denominated and settled.
2. The currency of the country whose competitive forces and regulations mainly determine the sales prices of its goods and services
3. The currency in which the costs of inputs (e.g., material and labour) are denominated and settled

The following factors may also provide evidence of a company's functional currency:

(a) The currency in which funds from financing activities (i.e., issuing debt and equity instruments) are generated.
(b) The currency in which receipts from operating activities are usually retained.

13.1.2 Reporting Foreign Currency Transactions in the Functional Currency

Initial Recognition

Entities should record foreign currency transactions in the functional currency using the exchange rate at the transaction date.

Entities should record foreign currency transactions in the functional currency using the exchange rate at the transaction date. For practical reasons, an entity may use a rate that approximates the actual rate at the date of the transaction. For example, in the absence of significant fluctuations in exchange rates, the average rate for a month or for a week might be used for all transactions entered into during that period.

Measuring at subsequent balance sheet dates

General principles

General principles are presented in Table 13.2 below:

Monetary items should be translated using the closing exchange rate on the balance sheet date.

Non-monetary items should be translated using the exchange rate at the transaction date.

TABLE 13.2 Translation of Foreign Currency Items—General Principles

	Asset type	*Accounting principle*
1.	Monetary items	Those should be translated using the closing exchange rate on the balance sheet date.
2.	Non-monetary items measured at historical cost	Those items should be translated using the exchange rate at the transaction date.
3.	Non-monetary items measured at historical cost	Those items should be translated using the exchange rate that existed at the valuation date.
4.	Exchange difference	Exchange difference arises from the following: (a) Settling and/or translating a foreign currency monetary item at an exchange rate different from that used in recording the item initially. (b) Settling and/or translating a foreign currency monetary item at an exchange rate different from that used to translate it for reporting in previous financial statements.
5.	Exchange difference recognition	(a) Exchange differences should be recognised as profit or loss in the period in which they arise. (b) The rule at (a) above is not applicable in recognising exchange differences arising out of a monetary item that forms part of a reporting entity's net investment in a foreign operation. (c) When a gain or loss on a non-monetary item is recognised in other comprehensive income, any exchange component of that gain or loss should be recognised in other comprehensive income. Conversely, when a gain or loss on a non-monetary item is recognised in profit or loss, any exchange component of that gain or loss should be recognised in profit or loss.

EXAMPLE 13.1 (Exchange gain)

Fact pattern: Bravo Limited (BL) exported goods to the USA on April 10, 2021. The consignment was priced at US $ 100,000. The exchange rate (bid rate) on the date of the transaction was 1 US $ = ₹74.45. BL received payment from its customer on June 10, 2021. The exchange rate on that date was ₹74.3716. The functional currency of BL is INR. BL closes its financial year on December 31.

Discussion:

(a) BL should initially (on April 10, 2021) record sales and trade receivables at (74.45 × USD 1,00,000) or ₹74,45,000.

(b) The bank credited the current account of BL by (74.3716 × USD 1,00,000) or ₹74,34,160. This resulted in an exchange difference (gain) of (74,45,000 – 74,34,160) or ₹10,860. BL should recognise the exchange difference as an income in the statement of profit and loss for the year 2021.

EXAMPLE 13.2 (Exchange difference)

Fact pattern: Merry Limited (ML) imported some raw materials from the USA for US $ 1,00,000. It recorded the transaction on February 10, 2010. The company paid the supplier on May 10, 2010. ML closes its financial year on March 31.

Exchange rates: February 10, 2010: US $ 1 = INR 46.4949; March 31, 2010: US $ 1 = INR 44.895; May 10, 2010: US $ 1 = INR 44.85.

Discussion:

(a) ML should record the transaction initially on February 10, 2021, recognising purchase and trade creditors at (46.4949 × USD 1,00,000) = ₹46,49,490

(b) Trade creditors (monetary item) should be presented in the balance sheet as at March 31, 2010 at (44.895 × USD 1,00,000) = ₹44,89,500. Thus, in the balance sheet as at 31 March 2010, trade creditors would be carried at an amount lower than the amount at which it was recorded initially. Consequently, there will be an exchange difference (gain) of(46,49,490 – 44,89,500) = ₹1,59,990. The exchange difference arising from the translation of trade creditors should be recognised as an income in the statement of profit and loss account for the year 2009–2010.

(c) On May 10, 2010 the amount due to the trade creditor was settled by purchasing USD 1,00,000 at (44.85 × USD1,00,000) = ₹44,85,000 This resulted in exchange difference (gain) of (44,89,500 – 44,85,000) = ₹4,500. The exchange difference arising from the settlement of amount due to the trade creditor should be recognised as gain in the statement of profit and loss account for the year 2010–2011.

In practice, exchange difference is presented as an expense in the statement of profit and loss. Gain is presented as negative expense.

13.1.3 Use of Presentation Currency other than Functional Currency

The balance sheet, statement of profit and loss, and cash flow statement of foreign operation with a functional currency different from the reporting entity, are translated in the presentation currency. This is required for incorporating the financial statements of the foreign operation in the consolidated financial statements. For example, if an Indian company with INR as presentation currency has a subsidiary (located in the USA), with USD as functional currency, it prepares the financial statements in USD. Those financial statements are translated in INR for incorporating them in the consolidated financial statements of the Indian company.

The balance sheet, statement of profit and loss, and cash flow statement of foreign operation with a functional currency different from the reporting entity, are translated in the presentation currency.

Accounting principles

General principles are presented in Table 13.2 below:

TABLE 13.2 Translation of Foreign Currency Items of a Foreign Operation in Presentation Currency

	Asset type	*Accounting principle*
1.	Monetary and non-monetary assets and liabilities	Those should be translated using the closing exchange rate on the balance sheet date.
2.	Income and expense items	Those items should be translated using exchange rates at the transaction dates.
3.	Exchange difference	Exchange difference arises from the following: (a) Both the income and expenses at the exchange rates at the date of the transactions and assets and liabilities at the closing date, and (b) The opening net assets at a closing rate that differs from the previous closing rate.

Monetary and non-monetary items should be translated using the closing exchange rate on the balance sheet date.

(Contd...)

	Asset type	Accounting principle
4.	Exchange difference recognition	The resulting exchange differences should be recognised in other comprehensive income (OCI) and is presented as a separate component of equity (e.g., in foreign currency translation reserve). The accumulated exchange difference is recognised in the statement of profit and loss on disposal of the foreign operation. In the case of a partial disposal, only the proportionate share of the accumulated exchange differences is included in the gain or loss.

Reason for different accounting procedure

A foreign operation of an Indian company is integral to the Indian operation if the functional currency of that foreign operation of is INR. It ultimately converts receivables in Indian rupees, must be for remittance to the India operation. Most probably, it makes most of its payments in Indian rupees. Therefore, change in exchange rate has a direct impact on the immediate cash flow of Indian company. Therefore, it is appropriate to recognise exchange differences as gain or loss in the income statement.

A foreign operation (such as, a subsidiary) of an Indian company, whose functional currency is USD is not integral to the Indian operation. It generates and expends cash in USD. The Indian company has interest in the net assets of the company, but it has no commitment to convert its investment in the foreign operation into INR. Therefore, its cash is not be affected by changes in the exchange rate. However, the gain or loss that will arise on disposal of the investment in the subsidiary will include gain or loss arising from changes in the exchange rate between the date when investment was made and the date of disposal. Therefore, it is appropriate to accumulate exchange differences in equity, and to transfer it to the income statement on disposal of the investment in subsidiary.

Financial statements of the foreign operation which is not integral to the Indian operation are incorporated only in the consolidated financial statements.

13.2 LEASE ACCOUNTING

13.2.1 Nature of Leasing Arrangement

In a leasing arrangement, the owner (called lessor) gives the lessee the right to use an identified asset for a period of time (called lease period) in exchange for consideration (called, lease payment).

Leasing is quite common in business. For example, retailers take on lease retail space in shopping malls, companies take office space and cars for use by employees on lease, hospitals take medical equipment on lease and airlines take aircrafts on lease.

In a leasing arrangement, the owner (lessor) gives the lessee the right to use an identified asset for a period of time in exchange for consideration.

The asset specified in the contract is not an identified asset if the supplier has the substantive right to substitute the asset throughout the period of use.

Identified assets

The asset specified in the contract is not an identified asset if the supplier has the substantive right to substitute the asset throughout the period of use.

The supplier's right is substantive if:

(a) it has practical ability to substitute the asset; and
(b) the economic benefit to the supplier exceeds the cost of substituting the asset.

EXAMPLE 13.3 (Identified asset)

Fact pattern: A company enters into a contract with a car dealer for supplying five cars to be used by its executives for five years. The cars are identified by its engine and registration numbers. The contract restrains the dealer to substitute the cars during the contract period.

Discussion: The cars are identified assets and the contract is a lease contract, as the dealer has no practical ability to substitute the cars.

EXAMPLE 13.4 (Identified asset)

Fact pattern: The owner of a shopping mall enters into contracts with retailers giving them the right to use a specified space in the mall. A typical contract requires the mall owner to furnish the space as per the requirement of the customer. The shop owner retains the right to substitute the space.

Discussion: The right is not substantive, as the cost of substitution far exceeds the economic benefits of substituting the asset. The arrangement is a leasing arrangement.

Right to use an asset

The customer has the right to use the asset if it enjoys the right to:

(a) obtain substantially all the economic benefits from using the asset throughout the period of use; and

(b) direct the use of the asset throughout the period.

The customer has the right to direct the use of the asset if it has the right to decide where, for what purpose and how it can use the asset within the constrained placed by the contract.

Right to operate the asset is not the right to use the asset unless the use is predetermined.

The customer has the right to use the asset if it enjoys the right to obtain substantially all the economic benefits from using the asset throughout the period of use and direct the use of the asset throughout the period.

EXAMPLE 13.5 (Right to use asset)

Fact pattern: The customer, who has taken on rent a space in a shopping mall, has the right to use the space if it has the right to decide when to open the shop, what merchandises to sell from the shop and what type of customers to be served, even if the contract stipulates that the shop can remain open within the period for which the shopping mall remains open, and explosives cannot be stored or sold from the shop.

Discussion: The contract is a lease contract, as the customer has the right to direct the use asset within the restrictions imposed by the supplier.

Service contract

A contract is as service contract if the underlying asset is not identified, and the supplier has substantive right to substitute the asset.

A contract is as service contract if the underlying asset is not identified, or the supplier has substantive right to substitute the asset.

EXAMPLE 13.6 (Service contract)

Fact pattern: A company enters into a contract with a travel agency for providing car to its CEO as and when advised by the company. The contract specifies the car model, the age of the car, but does not specify the model and registration numbers.

Discussion: The contract is a service contract, as the underlying asset is not an identified asset.

13.2.2 Accounting by Lessee

Lease term

The lease term is the non-cancellable period of a lease.

The lease term is the non-cancellable period of a lease.

If the lessee has sufficient incentive to exercise the option to extend the lease or not to exercise the option to terminate the lease, and it is reasonably certain the lessee will not exercise those options, the lease period includes those periods. For example, it is more likely that a lessee will exercise an extension option if it has made significant investments to improve the leased asset or to tailor it for its special needs or by extending the lease, it will avoid the cost of signing a replacement lease (e.g., negotiation costs, relocation costs, costs of integrating a new asset and costs of returning the original asset in a contractually specified condition or to a contractually specified location).

The lease term is reassessed only in limited circumstances.

Initial recognition and measurement

A lessee is required to recognise a 'right-of-use asset' and a corresponding lease liability for all lease contracts at the commencement date.

Lessees have option not to apply this accounting principle in case of short-term leases (lease term of 12 months or less) and leases for which the underlying asset is of low value (e.g., office furniture and IT equipment). A lessee, who decides to exercise that option recognises lease payments as expenses on a straight-line basis or another systematic basis that is more representative of the pattern of the lessee's benefit. For certain low value assets (such as assets that are dependent on, or highly interrelated with, other underlying assets), the exemption is not available.

A lessee is required to recognise a 'right-of-use asset' and a corresponding lease liability for all lease contracts at the commencement date.

Initial measurement of the lease liability

The lease liability is initially measured at an amount equal to the present value (PV) of the lease payments during the lease term that are not yet paid. The PV is calculated using the 'interest rate implicit in the lease' as the discount rate. If that rate cannot be readily determined, the lessee should use the lessee's 'incremental borrowing rate'.

The lease liability is initially measured at the present value of the outstanding lease payments, calculated using the 'interest rate implicit in the lease' (or 'incremental borrowing rate' if the implicit interest rate cannot be readily determined) as the discount rate.

Interest rate implicit in the lease

Interest rate implicit in the lease is the rate of interest that causes the PV of (a) the lease payments, and (b) the 'unguaranteed residual value' to equal the sum of (i) the fair value of the underlying asset, and (ii) any initial direct costs of the lessor.

Unguaranteed residual value is that portion of the residual value of the underlying asset, the realisation of which by a lessor is not assured or is guaranteed solely by a party related to the lessor.

Lease payment is the total of fixed payment (net of incentives receivable), variable lease payments that depend on an index or a rate (e.g., variable payments linked to inflation index), residual value guaranteed by the lessee, the exercise price of the purchase option (if the lessee is reasonably certain to exercise that option); and penalties for terminating the lease (if the lease term reflects the lessee exercising the option to terminate the lease).

Initial measurement of the right-of-use asset

The right-to-use asset is initially measured at cost.

The right-to-use asset is initially measured at cost.

The cost consists of:

(a) the amount of the initial measurement of the lease liability, plus
(b) any lease payments made to the lessor at or before the commencement date less any lease incentives received, and
(c) the PV of the initial estimate of restoration costs and any initial direct costs incurred by the lessee. The provision for the restoration costs is recognised as a separate liability.

Subsequent measurement of lease liability and right-of-use asset

The lessee measures the lease liability using the effective interest rate method. It depreciates the right-to-use asset as per its depreciation policy for assets that are similar to the asset covered under the lease. It also tests the same for impairment in accordance with the accounting standard that deals with impairment.

The lessee measures the lease liability using the effective interest rate method. It depreciates the right-to-use asset as per its depreciation policy and tests the same for impairment.

Alternative measurement model: A right-of-use asset can be subsequently measured using the revaluation model if it relates to a class of property, plant, and equipment that the lessee measures using the revaluation model.

13.2.3 Accounting by Lessor

Finance lease and operating lease

At the inception of the lease, that is when the lease contract is signed between the lessor and lessee, the lessor classifies leases as either:

- Finance or
- Operating lease.

It reassesses the same only if there is a lease modification.

Whether a lease is a finance lease, or an operating lease depends on the substance of the transaction rather than the form of the contract.

Finance lease

A lease is classified as a finance lease if it transfers substantially all the risks and rewards incidental to ownership of the underlying asset.

The lessor classifies a lease is classified as a finance lease if it transfers substantially all the risks and rewards incidental to ownership of the underlying asset.

Examples of indicators that signal transfer of risks and rewards incidental to the ownership of the underlying asset substantially to the lessee are: ownership will be transferred to the lessee at the end of the lease; there is bargain purchase option, which gives the right to the lessee to purchase the underlying asset at a price that is expected to be sufficiently lower than the fair value at the date the option becomes exercisable; the present value of the lease payments amounts to at least substantially all of the fair values of the underlying asset; lease term is for the major part of the economic life of the underlying asset even if title is not transferred; the underlying asset is of such a specialised nature that only the lessee can use it without major modifications; and the lease is practically non-cancellable.

Operating lease

A lease is classified as an operating lease if it does not transfer substantially all the risks and rewards incidental to ownership of an underlying asset.

Accounting for finance lease

The lessor accounts for the finance lease as a financing transaction. At the lease commencement, when the right of using asset is given to the lessee, the lessor recognises a receivable at an amount equal to the net investment in the lease. The underlying asset does not appear in the balance sheet of the lessor.

The lessor accounts for the finance lease as a financing transaction.

Net investment is the present value of the aggregate of lease payments receivable by the lessor and any unguaranteed residual value. The lessor uses the interest rate implicit in the lease to measure the net investment in the lease.

Subsequently, the lessor recognises finance income over the lease term, based on a pattern reflecting a constant periodic rate of return on the lessor's net investment in the lease. It applies the lease payments received from the lessee during the period against the 'gross investment in lease' to reduce the principal (receivable) and unearned interest.

Gross investment in lease is the sum of (a) the lease payments receivable by a lessor under a finance lease; and (b) any unguaranteed residual value accruing to the lessor.

Accounting for operating lease

The lessor continues to recognise the underlying asset. It recognises lease payments from operating leases as income on either a straight-line basis or another systematic basis, which it is more representative of the pattern in which benefit from the use of the underlying asset is diminished. The lessor recognises costs, including depreciation, incurred in earning the lease income as an expense.

Manufacturer/dealer vendor

Manufacturers or dealers often offer to customers the choice of either buying or leasing an asset. A finance lease of an asset by a manufacturer or dealer lessor gives rise to profit or loss equivalent to the profit or loss resulting from an outright sale of the underlying asset, at normal selling prices, reflecting any applicable volume or trade discounts.

At the commencement date, a manufacturer or dealer lessor recognises the following for each of its finance leases:

Revenue at the lower of the fair value of the asset and the present value of lease payments discounted at the market interest rate; cost of sale; and selling profit or loss.

In case of operating lease, the lessor continues to recognise the underlying asset. It recognises lease payments from operating leases as income on either a straight-line basis or another systematic basis.

Sale and lease back transaction

Transfer of the asset qualifies as a sale transaction: If the transfer of the asset is sale, seller-lessee measures a right-of-use asset arising from the leaseback as the proportion of the previous carrying amount of the asset that relates to the right to use retained. It recognises the gain (or loss) that is limited to the proportion of the total gain (or loss) that relates to the rights transferred to the buyer–lessor. The proportion of right to use that is retained is the ratio of the present value (PV) of lease payments to the fair value (FV) of the underlying asset.

If the consideration for the sale is not equal to the fair value of the asset, any resulting difference represents either a prepayment of lease payments (if the purchase price is below market terms) or an additional financing (if the purchase price is above market terms). The same logic applies if the lease payments are not at market rates.

The buyer-lessor accounts for the purchase in accordance with the applicable accounting principles and for the leaseback in accordance with accounting principles applicable for accounting for lease contracts.

Transfer is not a sale: The seller-lessee does not derecognise the transferred asset and accounts for the cash received as a financial liability. The buyer-lessor does not recognise the transferred asset, and instead, accounts for the cash paid as a financial asset (receivable).

EXAMPLE 13.7 (Sale and lease back transaction)

Fact pattern: K Ltd. (KL), the seller-lessee, sells a building to M Ltd. (ML), the buyer-lessor for cash at ₹20,00,000. The fair value of the building at the time of sale is ₹18,00,000. The carrying amount of the asset in the books of KL is ₹10,00,000. At the same time, KL enters into a lease contract with ML to lease back the building for 18 years with annual lease rent of ₹1,20,000, payable at the end of each year. KL's incremental borrowing rate is 4.5% per annum.

Discussion:

(a) The fair value of the building is ₹18,00,000, while the consideration for selling the asset to ML (ML's purchase price) is ₹20,00,000. Therefore, there is additional financing of (₹20,00,000 – 18,00,000) or ₹2,00,000 by ML to KL.

(b) The present value of the annual lease payment of ₹1,20,000 discounted at the incremental borrowing rate of 4.5% per annum is ₹14,59,200.

(c) A portion of the lease payments is towards the repayment of the additional financing. The PV of lease payments includes PV of payments towards repayment of additional financing of ₹2,00,000. Therefore, the PV of lease payments that relate to lease is (₹14,59,200 – 2,00,000) or ₹12,59,200.

(d) The proportion of the asset retained is (₹12,59,200/18,00,00). KL should recognise the right-of-use asset at the retained proportion of the carrying amount, which is [(₹12,59,200/18,00,00) × ₹10,00,000] or ₹6,99,556.

(e) The cash received by KL on the sale of the asset, excluding additional financing of ₹2,00,000 is ₹18,00,000, which is the fair value of the asset. Thus, the total gain on the sale of the asset is (₹18,00,000 – 10,00,000) or ₹8,00,000. Out of the total gain, the gain that relates to the proportion of the right on the asset transferred to ML is [(₹18,00,000 – ₹12,59,200)/18,00,000] or ₹8,00,000 or ₹2,40,356. Therefore, KL should recognise the gain on sale of the asset at ₹2,40,356.

Journal entries at the commencement in the books of KL:

Cash	Dr. 20,00,000	
Right-to-use asset	Dr. 6,99,556	
To Building		Cr. 10,00,000
To Financing liability		Cr. 14,59,200
To Gain on sale-and-leaseback		Cr. 2,40,356

13.3 ACCOUNTING FOR BUSINESS COMBINATION

13.3.1 General Principles

Nature of business combination: It is not uncommon that two firms unite to achieve competitive advantages. Similarly, it is quite common that a firm takes over another firm or acquires control over another firm as part of its growth strategy. A business combination is expected to improve the productivity of resources, and thus, benefit shareholders of both the companies. However, in many business combinations, that expectation is not realised.

Business combination occurs when an entity acquires the business of another entity. Business is an integrated set of inputs (assets) and processes. Process is any system, standard, protocol, convention or rule that contributes to the ability of inputs (e.g., assets) to create outputs. Therefore, acquisition of assets is not business combination.

Business combination occurs when an entity acquires the business of another entity. Business is an integrated set of inputs (assets) and processes.

Slump sale

If a company acquires assets of another company for a lump sum consideration (usually called slump sale), the transaction does not result in business combination. Business combination occurs in a transaction involving acquisition of a 'business'. In slump sale, the purchase consideration is allocated to assets acquired.

In slump sale, the company acquires assets of another company for a lump sum consideration.

Types of business combinations

Business combinations may take one of the following firm legal forms:

1. One entity (acquirer) acquires assets and liabilities of a business of another entity (acquirer) through direct negotiation with management. The acquiree continues with other businesses in its portfolio.
2. One entity (acquirer) acquires another entity's (acquiree's) assets and liabilities through direct negotiation with management. The acquiree distributes to its shareholders the assets or securities received from the acquirer and liquidates the firm. The acquirer survives and carries on the combined business.
3. The owners (shareholders in the case of a company) of the acquiree transfer their equity interest to the owners of the acquirer or to the acquirer. This method is known as hostile bid. For example, Company C offers to the shareholders of Company B to sell their shares to Company C. Company C may also buy shares directly from shareholders in capital markets. The management of Company C may liquidate Company B after transferring its assets to Company C.
4. Both the combining entities are dissolved and assets and liabilities of both the entities are transferred to a newly created entity. The new entity carries on the combined business. For example, Companies B and C may agree to create a new Company D and to transfer assets and liabilities to Company D.
5. One company acquires controlling interest in another company either through acquisition of majority of voting shares or otherwise. Both the companies continue to operate as separate but related legal entities. The relationship is referred to as parent-subsidiary relationship. The Parent (investor) controls the subsidiary (investee).

Accounting principle

If the acquiree is wound up, its assets and liabilities find place in the balance sheet of the acquirer. If the acquiree continues to exist as a separate entity, the financial statements of the acquirer (parent) and the acquiree (subsidiary) are combined and presented as consolidated financial statements.

If the acquiree is wound up, its assets and liabilities find place in the acquirer's balance sheet. If the acquiree continues to exist as a separate entity, the financial statements of the acquirer (parent) and the acquiree (subsidiary) are consolidated.

Demerger

In a demerger, an existing entity forms a new entity to hive off one of its businesses (undertaking). All the assets and liabilities of the undertaking of the demerged business are transferred to the new entity. The new entity, which has an economic and legal identity separate from the existing entity, issues shares to shareholders of the demerged undertaking. As a result, a substantial number of shareholders of the existing entity become the shareholders of the new entity.

Accounting method

Business combinations are accounted for using the purchase method. Purchase method assumes that there is always an acquirer in a business combination, who acquires the business of one or more entities. An entity that sales the business is called acquiree. Purchase method is not applicable in case of a business combination involving entities under common control. (In the subsequent section, we shall discuss purchase method of accounting.)

In a demerger, an existing entity forms a new entity to hive off one of its businesses (undertaking).

Pooling of interest method

Pooling of interest method is applied to account for business combination involving entities within the same group. Under pooling of interest method, the equity, assets and liabilities and the balance sheet of combined entity are carried at the total of respective book values of those assets and liabilities in the books of entities before they were combined.

13.3.2 Purchase Method of Accounting

Identification of the acquirer

The first step in applying the purchase method is to identify the acquirer. The acquirer is the combining entity that obtains control of the other combining entities and businesses. If a new firm is formed to take over businesses of more than one existing firms, one of the combining firms that existed before the combination should be identified as the acquirer on the basis of the evidence available. Usually, it is not difficult to identify the acquirer. For example,

1. The company that has significantly greater fair value than that of other combining company is likely to be the acquirer.
2. If the business combination is effected through an exchange of equity interests, the company that issues the equity interests is normally the acquirer.
3. If one of the combining companies dominates the selection of the management team of the combined company, the company which so dominates is likely to be the acquirer.

EXAMPLE 13.8 (Identification of acquirer)

Fact pattern: Assume A, B and C, all existing companies, have decided to form a new Company D to take the control over all the three companies. Company D will issue equity shares to shareholders of Companies A, B and C.

Discussion: One of the three existing companies should be identified as acquirer. For example, if Company A is identified as the acquirer, the measurement of Company A's assets and liabilities is not affected by the transaction. Moreover, the transaction shall not result in recognition of any additional assets or liabilities of Company A (the acquirer) because they are not the subjects of the transaction.

Control

An investor controls an investee if it has the ability to affect variable returns (such as, dividend from investment in equity) to which it is entitled through its power over the investee.

The definition of control is very wide to bring into net all kinds of relationships of the investor with the investee, which give the investor substantive right to control the relevant activities of the investee. Therefore, an investor can control an investee even if it is holding less than 50% of the voting rights of the investee if it has the current ability to direct relevant activities of the investee. Relevant activities are those activities, which significantly affect the investee's return. Usually, operating and financing activities are relevant activities.

An investor controls an investee if it has the ability to affect variable returns to which it is entitled through its power over the investee.

Investor acquires power to direct relevant activities by acquiring voting rights or the right to appoint or approve the appointment of key management personnel of the investee, may be by virtue of shareholder agreement or the right to direct the investee to enter into significant transactions for the benefit of the investor, may be by virtue of special relationship with the investee. It is not necessary that the investor should hold more than 50% of the voting rights to use the voting right for directing relevant activities.

EXAMPLE 13.9 (Control)

The dominant shareholder of a company holding less than 50% of voting right (say, 20%) has the ability to direct relevant activities if other shareholders are dispersed and it is impractical for them to coordinate between themselves. Similarly, if past trend shows that only a very small percentage of non-dominant shareholders vote in AGMs (Annual General Meetings), then it can be assumed that the dominant shareholder has the ability to direct relevant activities even if he/she holds less than 50% of the voting rights of the investee.

Fundamental accounting principle

The acquirer incorporates assets and liabilities in its books at their fair value. Only on rare occasions does it incorporate assets and liabilities at the book values recorded in the books of the acquiree, as the fair value cannot be determined reliably.

Purchase consideration: Purchase consideration is the cost incurred by the acquirer to acquire the assets and liabilities of the acquiree. It may consist of securities, cash and assets. In determining the amount of consideration, non-cash elements should be measured at fair value. In the case of other assets, the fair value should be determined by reference to the market value of the assets given up. When the market value of the assets given up cannot be reliably assessed, such assets may be valued at their respective net book values.

Goodwill and gain from bargain purchase

The acquirer should make special efforts to identify assets and liabilities that can be identified, including assets and liabilities not recorded in the financial statements of the acquiree. For example, a brand not appearing in financial statements of the acquiree may be recognised as a separately identifiable asset in the balance sheet of the acquirer. Similarly, the acquirer recognises in-process research and development even if it was not recognised by the acquiree.

Excess of the net fair value of separately identifiable assets, liabilities and contingent liabilities acquired over the purchase consideration is termed as gain from bargain purchase.

Goodwill is the excess of purchase consideration over the net fair value of separately identifiable assets and liabilities and contingent liabilities acquired by the acquirer.

The acquirer should recognise a contingent liability of the acquiree at the date of acquisition if the fair value of the same can be measured reliably.

Goodwill is the excess of purchase consideration over the net fair value of separately identifiable assets and liabilities and contingent liabilities acquired by the acquirer.

Excess of the net fair value of separately identifiable assets, liabilities and contingent liabilities acquired over the purchase consideration is termed as gain from bargain purchase. The gain from bargain purchase as capital reserve in the balance sheet of the acquirer. IFRS requires that the bargain purchase should be recognised as gain the statement of profit and loss.

EXAMPLE 13.10 (Goodwill and bargain purchase)

(a) KK acquires YY. The purchase consideration is ₹10 lakhs and the fair value of identifiable assets (net of liabilities assumed by KK) is ₹8 lakhs. The goodwill should be recognised at (₹10 – 8) or ₹2 lakhs.

(b) MM acquires PP. The purchase consideration is ₹10 lakhs and the fair value of identifiable assets (net of liabilities assumed by KK) is ₹14 lakhs. The bargain purchase should be recognised at (₹14 – 10) or ₹4 lakhs.

13.4 CONSOLIDATED FINANCIAL STATEMENTS

General principles

The parent is not a passive investor in the subsidiary. The parent benefits if the subsidiary performs well. It provides all kinds of support to the subsidiary. Therefore, investors, lenders and creditors are keen to evaluate the performance and financial position of the group, which is constituted of the parent and its subsidiaries. When a company prepares the consolidated financial statements, it has to incorporate in the consolidated financial statement, the financial statements of its associates and joint ventures.

Associate: An investee is an associate of investor if the investor has the capability of significantly influencing the operating and financial decisions of the investee by participating in those decisions. There is a rebuttable assumption that if the investor holds between 20% and 50% of the total voting rights of the investee, it can significantly influence the operating and financial decisions of the investee. Significant influence may be gained by share ownership, statute, or agreement.

Joint venture: In a joint venture two or more parties jointly undertake an economic activity and they agree sharing of control over that activity. The distinguishing feature of a joint venture is that it is a contractual arrangement, usually in writing, in which two or more companies agree to work together and accept joint control over some economic activities irrespective of their shareholding. Activities that have no contractual arrangement to establish joint control are not joint ventures.

Preparation of consolidated financial statements

If the holding company holds less than 100% of the voting share capital of the subsidiary, balance shares are held by outsiders. Their interest in the subsidiary is called non-controlling interest.

In preparing the consolidated financial statements, the financial statements of the parent and its subsidiaries are consolidated on a line-by-line basis.

Non-controlling interest: If the holding company holds less than 100% of the voting share capital of the subsidiary, balance shares are held by outsiders. Their interest in the subsidiary is called non-controlling interest. In the consolidated balance sheet it is presented as a separate component of equity. The consolidated statements profit or loss presents the share of non-controlling interest in the profit or loss of the subsidiary in the consolidated profit or loss separately.

Consolidation of subsidiary's financial statements: In preparing the consolidated financial statements, the financial statements of the parent and its subsidiaries are consolidated on a line-by-line basis by adding together like items of assets, liabilities, equity, income and expenses. The following steps are involved in the consolidation process:

1. The carrying amount of parent's investment in the subsidiary is eliminated.
2. The parent's portion of the equity in subsidiary is eliminated.
3. The non-controlling interest in the net income of the subsidiary is identified and adjusted against the income of the group in order to determine the net income attributable to the shareholders of the parent.
4 Non-controlling interests in the net assets of the subsidiary are identified and presented in the consolidated balance sheet separately from the parent shareholders' equity.

Accounting principles and methods for incorporating individual assets and liabilities of the subsidiary, and for arriving at the amount of goodwill or gain from bargain purchase (capital reserve) in a business combination should be applied in the preparation and presentation of consolidated financial statements.

Intra-group balances and intra-group transactions: Intra-group balances and intra-group transactions and resulting unrealised profits should be eliminated in full. Unrealised losses resulting from intra-group transactions should also be eliminated unless cost cannot be recovered. The rationale for this requirement is that the transactions within the group do not represent economic events with outside parties. Hence, those transactions should not change the carrying amount of assets, liabilities, and equity of the group.

Consolidation of investments in associates and joint ventures: Investment in associates, and joint ventures should be accounted for in consolidated financial statements using the equity method. However, when the investment is acquired and held exclusively with a view to its disposal in the near future, it should be accounted for using the cost method.

The equity method is a method of accounting whereby the investment is initially recorded at cost and adjusted thereafter for the post-acquisition change in the investor's share of net assets of the investee. Investment in the associate in the consolidated balance sheet is reduced by the dividend received by the investor from the investee. The consolidated statements of profit and loss reflects the investor's share of the results of operations of the investee. Equity method of consolidation is often referred to as on-line consolidation.

13.5 ACCOUNTING FOR BORROWING COSTS

Borrowing cost is the total of interest and other costs that an entity incurs in connection with the borrowing of funds.

Accounting principles are summarised in Table 13.3 below.

TABLE 13.3 Accounting for Borrowing Costs

	Nature of borrowing cost	*Accounting principles*
1.	Borrowing costs directly attributable to the acquisition of a qualified asset	(a) Borrowing cost for the period when the production or construction is in progress should be capitalised. (b) Capitalisation is suspended during extended periods in which active development is interrupted or suspended unless that interruption or suspension is inherent in the production process.
2.	Borrowing costs not capitalised	Borrowing costs not capitalised should be recognised as expense for the period in which the costs are incurred.
3.	Qualified asset	An asset must require a substantial period of time (usually 12 months or more) to get ready for its intended use or sale.
4.	Directly attributable borrowing costs	Borrowing cost is directly attributable if the borrowing could be avoided had the entity did not acquire the asset. It is not necessary that the amount is borrowed specifically to acquire the asset.
5.	Capitalisation method	The weighted average rate is applied on the average carrying amount of the asset during a period, including borrowing costs previously capitalised.

Borrowing costs directly attributable to the acquisition of a qualified asset for the period when the production or construction is in progress should be capitalised.

An asset is a qualified asset if it requires a substantial period of time (usually 12 months or more) to get ready for its intended use or sale.

13.6 ACCOUNTING FOR EMPLOYEE SHARE-BASED PAYMENTS

13.6.1 General Principles

In many companies, share-based payment under the Employee Stock Ownership Plan (ESOP) is one of the components of the total compensation to an employee. Companies usually grant stock options to employees. ESOP is a type of call option. It gives the employees the right to buy from the company its shares at a specified price at a specified date. For example, on April 1, 2010 (grant date), a company may grant option to its employees to buy from the company shares at ₹80 per share after March 31, 2015 (vesting date), but before March 31, 2018 (exercise date) if they continue their services with the company till March 31, 2015. An employee will exercise the option only if the share price moves beyond ₹80. For example, if the share price moves to ₹200 on a date after March 31, 2015, but before March 31, 2018, the payoff to the employee will be (200 – 80) or ₹120 in case she exercises the option on that date. Companies grant stock option to motivate employees to perform at the highest level of productivity so that the share price moves upward, which will benefit both the employees and the shareholders.

Accounting principle

A business recognises the goods or services received or acquired in a share-based payment transaction when it obtains the goods or as the services are received. It recognises a corresponding increase in equity.

A business recognises the goods or services received or acquired in a share-based payment transaction when it obtains the goods or as the services are received. It recognises a corresponding increase in equity. When the goods or services received or acquired in a share-based payment transaction do not qualify for recognition as assets, they are recognised as expenses.

For equity-settled share-based payment transactions, the enterprise directly measures the goods or services received, and the corresponding increase in equity at the fair value of the goods or services received unless that fair value cannot be estimated reliably. If the entity cannot estimate reliably the fair value of the goods or services received, the company measures their value, and the corresponding increase in equity, indirectly, by reference to the fair value of the equity instruments granted.

If the entity cannot estimate reliably the fair value of the goods or services received, the company measures their value, and the corresponding increase in equity, indirectly, by reference to the fair value of the equity instruments granted.

Invariably, an enterprise cannot determine directly the fair value of services rendered by employees. Accordingly, it records the transaction at the fair value of shares or options to acquire shares granted to employees. The fair value of an option has two components—intrinsic value and the time value. Fair value of an option is usually estimated by using an economic model such as the Black-Scholes model. The intrinsic value is the difference between the exercise price and the price of the underlying stock on the date of valuation. For example, if the exercise price is ₹80 and the value of the underlying stock is ₹120, the intrinsic value is ₹40 (₹120 – 80). The time value of an option cannot be estimated directly. It is the difference between the fair value and the intrinsic value. For example, if the fair value is ₹100 and the intrinsic value is ₹40, the time value is ₹60 (₹100 – 40).

The fair value of the share or option is determined at the measurement date, which is the grant date in the case of employee stock option, based on the market price, if available, taking into consideration those terms and conditions upon which those equity instruments were granted.

Grant date

For transactions with employees, the measurement date is the grant date, which is the date at which the company and the employee agree to a share-based payment arrangement.

Vesting date and vesting conditions

The term 'vest' means to become an entitlement. On the vesting date, the equity instrument or the option to acquire equity instrument vests on an employee upon satisfaction of any specified vesting conditions. The period within which all the vesting conditions are to be satisfied is called the vesting period.

Vesting conditions are the conditions that are to be satisfied to become entitled to the share-based payment. Vesting conditions include service conditions which require the employee to complete a specified period of service and performance conditions, which require specified performance targets to be met.

Accounting method

If the share-based payment vests immediately, it is assumed that the payment is made for services already rendered. If the shared-based payment vests on satisfaction of vesting conditions during the vesting period, it is assumed that the payment is made for services to be rendered during the vesting period. In that case, the total fair value at the grant date of the number of stock options estimated to be vested to the employees at the end of the vesting period is amortised over the vesting period.

Each year an expense is recognised in the profit and loss account by credit to stock options outstanding account. The credit balance in that account is presented as a separate component of equity. If at the end of the exercise period, the option is not exercised, the accumulated balance in the stock options outstanding account is transferred to the general reserve. If the option is exercised, the total of the accumulated balance in the stock options outstanding account and the amount (exercise price) received from the employee is allocated to the share capital and share premium account.

Illustration 13.11 (Employee stock option)

Fact pattern: On January 1, 2003 (Grant date) Rishika Ltd. (RL) grants 300 equity options to each of its 100 employees. The face value of each equity share is ₹10. RL estimates the fair value of options at the grant date, based on an option pricing model, at ₹20 per option. The contractual life (comprising the vesting period and the exercise period) of option granted is 6 years. The other relevant terms of the grant are:

Vesting period	3 years
Exercise period	3 years
Expected life	5 years
Exercise price	₹50
Market price	₹50

On December 31, 2003, RL estimates that only 95 employees will satisfy the vesting conditions at the vesting date. On December 31, 2004, RL estimates that only 98 employees will satisfy the vesting conditions at the vesting date. On December 31, 2005, only 90 employees met vesting conditions at the vesting date. In 2006, 40 employees exercised the option, and in 2007, 40 employees exercised the option; 10 employees allowed the option to expire in 2008.

Discussion: At December 31, 2003, RL estimates that only 95 employees will satisfy the vesting conditions at the vesting date. Therefore, expense for services to be received over the vesting period of three years is ₹5,70,000 (₹20 × 300 × 95). RL should allocate ₹5,70,000 over the vesting period of three years. Therefore, in the profit and loss account for 2003, it recognises the expense at ₹1,90,000 (5,70,000/3) with a corresponding credit to stock options outstanding account. The balance in the stock options outstanding account is presented in the balance sheet as at December 31, 2003 as a component of equity.

Accounting in 2004

On December 31, 2004, RL estimates that only 98 employees will satisfy the vesting conditions at the vesting date. Therefore, expense for services to be received over the vesting period of three years is ₹5,88,000 (₹20 × 300 × 98). RL should allocate ₹5,88,000 over the vesting period of three years. Therefore, cumulative expense to be recognised in the first two years is ₹392,000 (5,88,000/3) × 2. Thus, in 2004, RL should recognise the expense at ₹2,02,000 (₹3,92,000 – 1,90,000) with a corresponding credit to stock options outstanding account. The balance (₹3,92,000) in the stock options outstanding account is presented in the balance sheet as at December 31, 2004 as a component of equity.

Accounting in 2005

On December 31, 2005, only 90 employees met the vesting conditions. Therefore, the expense for services to be received over the vesting period of three years is ₹5,40,000 (₹20 × 300 × 90). Thus, cumulative expense to be recognised at the end of the third year is ₹540,000. Consequently, in 2005, RL should recognise the expense at ₹1,48,000 (₹5,40,000 – 3,92,000) with a corresponding credit to stock options outstanding account. The balance (₹5,40,000) in the stock options outstanding account is presented in the balance sheet as at December 31, 2005 as a component of equity.

Accounting in 2006

In this year, 40 employees exercised the option. Therefore, ₹2,40,000 (₹20 × 300 × 40) should be transferred from stock options outstanding account to other equity accounts. In addition, RL receives ₹6,00,000 (₹50 × 300 × 40) against issue of 12,000 shares. Thus, ₹8,40,000 (₹6,00,000 + 2,40,000) is credited to share capital account: ₹1,20,000 (10 × 12,000 shares); and share premium account: ₹7,20,000 [(₹50 + 20 – 10) × 12,000].

Accounting in 2007

In this year, 40 employees exercised the option. Therefore, ₹2,40,000 (₹20 × 300 × 40) should be transferred from stock options outstanding account to other equity accounts. In addition, RL receives ₹6,00,000 (₹50 × 300 × 40) against issue of 12,000 shares. Thus, ₹8,40,000 (₹6,00,000 + 2,40,000) is credited to share capital account: ₹1,20,000 (₹10 × 12,000 shares), and share premium account: ₹7,20,000 [(₹50 + 20 – 10) × 12,000].

Accounting in 2008

In this year, 10 employees allowed their options to expire. Therefore, RL transfers the balance of ₹60,000 (₹5,40,000 – 2,40,000 – 2,40,000) from stock options outstanding account to general reserve.

REVIEW PROBLEMS

R 13.1 Indicate whether the following statements are True or False:

(i) The presentation currency of a firm must be the same as its functional currency.

(ii) ESOP is a type of call option.

(iii) With a few exceptions, the lessor has no option but to recognised the a leased asset as 'right-of-use' asset.

(iv) Lease accounting by the lessee requires classification of a lease as finance lease or operating lease.

(v) In the context of accounting for borrowing costs, qualified asset is one the production of which takes 12 months or more.

(vi) In the context of accounting for ESOP, the grant date and vesting date must be the same.

R 13.2 Fill in the blanks:

(i) A firm has recorded a sale transaction at ₹79,00,000 using the exchange rate of ₹1 = USD 79. On the balance sheet date the exchange rate of ₹1 = USD 78. The exchange difference of ₹.................. should be recognised in the statement of profit and loss as .... [Chose between 'gain' and 'loss']

(ii) If the supplier has practical ability to substitute the underlying asset in a contract with the customer, the contract is a .... contract. [Chose between, 'lease contract', and 'service contract'.]

(iii) Bargain purchase in a business combination transaction should be recognised as .... in the balance sheet.

(iv) The acquirer of a business should account for the transaction using the .... method unless the acquiree is a group company.

(v) In consolidating the financial statements an associate .... method should be used.

ASSIGNMENTS

1. Indicate against each statement whether it is True or False:

(i) A change in foreign exchange rates directly affects cash flows to or from the entity that has entered into a foreign currency transaction.

(ii) Ind AS allows a company domiciled in India to present its financial statements in a currency other than INR.

(iii) In no situation does the choice of the functional currency involve judgement because the primary economic environment in which it operates is obvious.

(iv) If the activities of the foreign operation are carried out as an extension of the reporting firm, rather than being carried out with a significant degree of autonomy, it is quite likely that the functional currency of the foreign operation is the same as that of the reporting firm.

(v) The amount owed by a subsidiary to its holding company against fixed assets supplied on deferred credit basis should be included in calculating net investment of the holding company in the subsidiary.

(vi) The carrying amount of an item of PP&E should be adjusted for gain or loss arising from the translation or settlement of a foreign exchange denominated liability assumed on the acquisition of the asset.

(vii) The effects of gains and losses on foreign currency transactions may result in recognition of a deferred tax asset or a deferred tax liability.

(viii) Exchange differences arising from the translation of assets, liabilities, incomes and expenses of a foreign operation, whose functional currency is different from that of the reporting firm, into the presentation currency of the reporting entity, should be recognised in other comprehensive income and should be presented as a separate component of equity.

(ix) Lease is an off-balance sheet item.

(x) Executory costs should be included in minimum lease payments.

(xi) Interest rate implicit in the lease is the lessor's desired rate of return on investment.

(xii) The lessee should initially recognise the asset at higher of the fair market value and the PV of the minimum lease payment.

(xiii) Finance lease is in substance a financing transaction.

(xiv) A cancellable lease can never be classified as a finance lease.

(xv) A lease of land is classified as an operating lease unless the ownership of the land transfers to the lessee at the end of the lease period.

(xvi) The minimum lease payment (MLP) from the point of view of the lessor and that from the point of view of the lessee is the same.

(xvii) In certain situations, contingent rent is included in the minimum lease payment.

(xviii) For all types of leases, the income tax law allows depreciation on the leased asset to the lessor.

(xix) In the case of finance lease, the lessor presents the leased asset as receivables.

(xx) The lessee includes in the cost of the leased asset all the direct and indirect costs incurred by it in connection with the leasing activity.

(xxi) A lessee recognises the lease rent related to lease of low-cost items and lease for short-term in the income statement for the period in which the lease rent is payable.

(xxii) A manufacturing or dealer lessor uses the commercial rate of interest to determine the PV of minimum lease payment, at which it recognises the sales revenue if the PV is lower than the fair value.

(xxiii) A seller lessee, who takes back the sold asset under a lease classified as finance lease, defers the recognition of profit arising from the sale of asset.

(xxiv) Pooling of interest method is used only for business combination of entities under common control.

(xxv) Purchase consideration, if discharged by issue of securities including equity shares or other assets, is the fair value of those securities or assets on the date of exchange.

(xxvi) If the fair value of an identifiable intangible asset cannot be measured with reference to an active market, the acquirer should measure it at the book value recorded in the books of the acquiree.

(xxvii) The GAAP does not allow the acquirer to recognise a provision that was not a liability of the acquiree.

(xxviii) The amount of 'gain from bargain purchase' should be recognised as income immediately.

(xxix) Demerger does not result in a purchase or sale transaction.

(xxx) In a demerger, if the undertaking which is transferred has a negative net book value, the demerged company should issue shares to the shareholders without receiving cash.

(xxxi) 'Slump sale' means the transfer of one or more undertakings as a result of the sale for a lump sum consideration without value being assigned to individual assets and liabilities.

(xxxii) The terms 'demerger' and 'slump sale' have the same meaning.

(xxxiii) The question of goodwill or gain from bargain purchase does not arise for a slump sale.

2. Tick the correct answer:

(i) A firm is known as an associate of an investor if the investor holds:
   (a) at least 20% of the total voting rights.
   (b) between 20% and 50% of the total voting rights.
   (c) more than 50% of the total voting rights.
   (d) less than 20% of the total voting rights.

(ii) The equity method of accounting stipulates:
   (a) Line-by-line consolidation of financial statements.
   (b) Restatement of the carrying amount of investment based on the net profit reported by the associate.
   (c) Incorporation of the net profit reported by the associate in the statement of profit and loss, and restatement of the carrying amount of investment based on the net profit reported by the associate.
   (d) Incorporation of the net profit reported by the associate in the statement of profit and loss.

(iii) In the equity method of accounting, the difference between investor's share in the fair value of associate's net assets and investor's share in the book value of associate's net assets at the date of investment is:
   (a) Not considered.
   (b) Kept outside the books, but amortised over the useful life of depreciable assets.
   (c) Kept outside the books, but the difference allocated to depreciable assets is amortised over the useful life of those assets through adjustment of income from the associate, and the portion allocated to non-depreciable assets is adjusted against the income from the associate, on disposal of those assets.
   (d) Recognised in the balance sheet.

(iv) In the process of consolidating financial statements of a holding company and those of a subsidiary, unrealised profits or losses in upstream and downstream transactions between an investor and his associate:
   (a) Should not be eliminated.
   (b) Should be eliminated only to the extent of investor's share in those profits or losses.
   (c) Should be eliminated in full.
   (d) May or may not be eliminated.

(v) Joint control in a joint venture is usually established by:
   (a) Equal holding of voting rights by all joint venture partners.
   (b) An informal contractual arrangement.
   (c) A contractual arrangement in writing.
   (d) A statutory requirement.

(vi) Investment in a jointly controlled company is accounted for in the financial statements of joint venture partners:

(a) On cost basis.
(b) By using the proportionate consolidation method.
(c) By using either the proportionate consolidation method or the equity method.
(d) By using the equity method.

(vii) When a venturer contributes or sells an asset to a joint venture and the asset is retained by the jointly controlled entity, the venturer should:

(a) Recognise the total profit or loss attributable to the transaction.
(b) Not recognise any profit or loss attributable to the transaction.
(c) Recognise only that portion of profit or loss which is attributable to the interest of other venturers.
(d) Eliminate that portion of profit or loss which is attributable to the interest of other venturers.

(viii) In the pooling of interest method of accounting, the retained earnings in the balance sheet of the combined entity immediately after amalgamation should be:

(a) Equal to or less than the aggregate of retained earnings of the combining firms.
(b) More than the aggregate of retained earnings of the combining firms.
(c) Less than the aggregate of retained earnings of the combining firms.
(d) Equal to the aggregate of retained earnings of the combining firms.

(ix) In the purchase method of accounting for accounting of business combinations, goodwill or negative goodwill is the difference between:

(a) The purchase consideration and the fair value of identifiable assets and liabilities on the date of the acquisition.
(b) The purchase consideration and the fair value of identifiable assets and liabilities on the dates of exchange.
(c) The purchase consideration and the fair value of identifiable tangible assets and liabilities on the dates of exchange.
(d) The purchase consideration and the fair value of identifiable tangible assets and liabilities on the date of the acquisition.

(x) In preparing and presenting consolidated financial statements, intra-group balances and intra-group transactions and resulting unrealised profits should:

(a) Not be eliminated.
(b) Be eliminated in full.
(c) Be eliminated only to the extent of the holding company's interest in the subsidiary company.
(d) Be eliminated only to the extent of minority interest in the subsidiary company.

CHAPTER 14

FUND FLOW AND CASH FLOW STATEMENTS

CHAPTER OBJECTIVES

The objectives of this chapter is to introduce to readers the fund flow statement and cash flow statement. In particular, the objective is developing and understanding of:

- Method for preparing and presenting the fund flow statement;
- Method for preparing and presenting the cash flow statement—direct and indirect methods;
- Financial ratios to measure cash generating efficiency.

14.1 FUND FLOW STATEMENT

14.1.1 The Concept

A fund flow statement provides information on how, during the reporting period, decisions relating to capital structure, dividend and investment in non-current assets have changed the amount invested in working capital. However, it should be clear that there is no cause-and-effect relationship between investment in non-current assets and financing decisions and the investment in working capital. Management of working capital is a task that can be examined independently of investment in non-current assets and financing decisions. Working capital is measured at the difference between the amount of current assets and the amount of current liabilities at a particular point in time.

A fund flow statement provides information on how, during the reporting period, decisions relating to capital structure, dividend and investment in non-current assets have changed the amount invested in working capital.

In a fund flow statement, the term 'fund' connotes working capital. Movements in non-current assets and liabilities change investment in working capital. For example, purchase of a piece of equipment results in decrease in working capital, as ether the current asset (cash) reduces, or the current liability (sundry creditors) increases. Long-term borrowing increases working capital, as cash increases.

A fund flow statement presents sources and application of funds. Sources imply those movements in non-current assets, non-current liabilities and equity that increase the working capital. Applications imply those movements in non-current assets, non-current liabilities and equity that reduce the working capital.

Usually, the fund flow statement is supported by a 'statement of changes in working capital'.

14.1.2 Sources and Application of Funds

1. **Sources:**
   (i) Funds from business operations
   (ii) Sale of non-current assets
   (iii) Issue of share capital
   (iv) Long-term borrowings
   Total (1)
2. **Applications (or uses):**
   (i) Purchase of non-current assets
   (ii) Redemption of debentures
   (iii) Repayment of other long-term liabilities
   (iv) Buy-back of shares
   (v) Redemption of preference shares
   (vi) Payment of income tax
   (vii) Distribution of cash dividend
   Total (2)
3. **Change in working capital (1 – 2)**
   Equity during the reporting period changes on account of:
   (i) Net profit/(loss) for the period
   (ii) Fresh contribution from shareholders
   (iii) Buy-back of own shares
   (iv) Distribution of cash dividend

Distribution of stock dividend by issue of bonus shares does not change equity. It results in movement between different components of equity, namely, share capital, share premium and retained profit.

A fund flow statement shows changes in different elements of equity, rather than an aggregate figure for change in equity.

Preparation of the fund flow statement does not require analyses of individual transactions. It analyses balance sheet figures of assets and liabilities at the commencement and at the close of the year.

14.1.3 Funds from Operations

Profit from operations is considered to be a long-term source of funds because net profit, unless distributed to owners, enhances the equity. Similarly, net loss incurred by the enterprise reduces the equity. Net profit/(loss) increases/(decreases) the investment in working capital. However, in an accrual accounting system, increase/(decrease) in working capital does not match the reported net profit/(loss). The difference arises because the statement of profit and loss is debited by certain expenses, which represent non-current amortisations. The most common examples of such amortisations are depreciation and amortisation. If the expenditure was incurred in previous years, it does not result in outflow of assets or assumption of liabilities in the current reporting period. Therefore, it does not cause any decrease in working capital. If the expenditure is incurred in the current reporting period, it is exhibited as a separate item under 'application of fund' in the fund flow statement. For example, if equipment is purchased for ₹1,00,000 on cash basis, the fund flow statement exhibits the total amount of such expenditure as a separate item, namely 'purchase of non-current asset, under 'application of funds'. Therefore, even if the expenditure is incurred during the current period, net profit/(loss) should be adjusted for the part of expenditure allocated to the current period and charged to the statement of profit and loss as depreciation.

Profit from operations is considered to be a long-term source of funds because net profit, unless distributed to owners, enhances the equity.

Net profit/(loss) should also be adjusted for incomes or expenses that do not directly relate to the operation of the business. Those items of income and expenses are exhibited as separate items in the fund flow statement.

The following are the most common items for which net profit/(loss) is adjusted to determine the amount of funds from operations:

1. Depreciation on depreciable assets.
2. Amortisation of intangible assets (e.g., goodwill, trademarks and patents) and deferred charges (e.g., discount on issue of securities and preliminary expenses).
3. Profit/(loss) on transactions related to non-current assets.
4. Non-operating expenses.
5. Provision for income tax.
6. Non-operating income.
7. Subsidy credited to the profit and loss account.
8. Credit from reserves (e.g., revaluation reserve).

Illustration 14.1 (Fund from operation)

The statement of profit and loss of Delhi Ltd. for the year 2019 is presented as follows:

(Amount ₹)

Sales			5,000
Less:	Materials consumed	1,000	
	Manufacturing expenses	2,000	
	Administration and selling expenses	750	
	Depreciation	250	
	Amortisation of: Patent	150	
	Preliminary expenses	100	
	Loss on sale of equipment	50	4,300
	Operating profit		700
Add:	Dividend received		100
			800
Less:	Income tax		200
	Net profit		600

Required: Calculate the fund from operation for the year 2019.

Solution:

Funds from operation

		Amount (₹'000)
Net profit as per profit and loss account		600
Add: Loss on sale of equipment (cash flow from sale will be shown as a separate item)	50	
Depreciation (non-current amortisation)	250	
Amortisation of intangible assets (non-current amortisation)	250	550
		1,150
Less: Dividend received (will be shown as a separate item)		100
Fund from operation		1,050

Fund from operation represents increase in working capital due to operating activities of the firm.

14.1.4 Fund Flow Related to Non-current Assets

Transactions relating to non-current assets require special consideration. The carrying amount of a non-current asset reduces due to depreciation/amortisation even without any fresh transaction relating to that asset. Therefore, adjustment for depreciation/amortisation is required to determine the amount of fund flow on account of transactions relating to non-current assets.

Sale of a non-current asset results in increase in working capital by the amount of cash or another current asset received or receivable. Therefore, funds from the sale of the depreciable asset are the aggregate of the asset's WDV and the profit/(loss) on sale of the asset. In order to determine the funds from sale of a depreciable asset, we should collect information on its WDV. Similarly, outflow of funds on account of acquisition of a depreciable asset is presented in the fund flow statement on gross basis. Therefore, in order to determine the cost of a depreciable asset purchased during the year, the difference in the net book value of the depreciable asset at the end and at the commencement of the reporting period should be adjusted for depreciation for the year.

Sale of a non-current asset (such as, items of PP&E) results in increase in working capital by the amount of cash or another current asset received or receivable.

Outflow of funds on account of acquisition of a depreciable asset is presented in the fund flow statement on gross basis.

Illustration 14.2 (Cash from sale of items of PP&E)

A Ltd. has provided the following information relating to its plant and machinery account.

(*Amount* in ₹'000)

	Year 2018	*Year 2019*
Gross book value at the end of the year	100	140
Accumulated depreciation at the end of the year	20	34
Additional information:		
1. Loss on sale of plant and machinery		1
2. Depreciation charged during the year		16
3. Purchase of new machinery during the year		45

Required: Calculate the fund generated in 2019 from the sale of the old item of plant and machinery and the fund flow from the sale of old items of plant and machinery.

Solution:

(*Amount* ₹)

(a) Gross book value of asset sold:		
Balance as on December 31, 2018	1,00,000	—
Purchases during 2019	45,000	—
	1,45,000	—
Sold during 2019 (balance figure)	5,000	—
Balance as on December 31, 2019 (Given)	1,40,000	—
(b) Accumulated depreciation on the asset sold:		—

Balance as on December 31, 2018	20,000
Add: Depreciation for the year 2019 (Given) (Reported in the profit and loss account)	16,000
	36,000
Less: Accumulated depreciation on the item sold (balancing figure)	2,000
Accumulated depreciation as on December 31, 2019 (Given)	34,000
(c) Fund flow from sale of plant and machinery:	
Gross book value of plant sold	5,000
Less: Accumulated depreciation	2,000
Written-down value of the item sold	3,000
Less: Loss on sale of plant and machinery	1,000
Fund flow from sale of machinery	2,000

Illustration 14.3 (Find flow statement)

Sushmita Limited (SL) provides the following information:

(*Amount* (₹'000)

Non-current assets, non-current liabilities, and equity	*Amount at the end of the year*	*Amount at the beginning of the year*
Property, plant and equipment, net of depreciation	290	130
Investment in Rani Limited (RL)	580	270
Debentures	150	500
Contributed capital	800	800
Reserves and surplus	820	475

The following additional information is provided by SL:

(i) Dividends paid during the year ₹80,000.

(ii) A gain on sale of equipment of ₹30,000 has been included in net income. The cost of the equipment and the written down value at the date of sale were ₹1,20,000 and ₹50,000, respectively.

(iii) Depreciation on property, plant and equipment charged in the income statement for the year was ₹90,000.

Required: Prepare the fund flow statement for the year covered by the income statement.

Solution:

Working notes:

(*Amount* in ₹'000)

(a)	**Funds from business operation**	
	Increase in reserves and surplus	345
	Add: Dividends paid	80
	Add: Depreciation on property, plant, and equipment	90
		515
	Less: Gain on sale of equipment	30
		485
(b)	**Sale of equipment**	
	Written down value of the equipment	50
	Gain on sale of equipment	30
	Sale of equipment	80
(c)	**Purchase of equipment**	
	Increase in the net book value of property, plant, and equipment	160
	Add: Depreciation on property, plant, and equipment for the year	90
	Add: Written down value of the equipment sold	50
	Increase in the gross block (purchase)	300

Fund Flow Statement of SL for the year ended ...

Particulars	Amount (₹'000)
Sources of funds	
Funds from business operations	485
Sale of equipment	80
Total (A)	565
Application of funds	
Purchase of equipment	300
Purchase of investment	310
Redemption of debentures	350
Dividends paid	80
Total (B)	1,040
Decrease in working capital (B – A)	475

14.1.5 Analysing the Fund Flow Statement

A fund flow statement may be used to address a variety of questions that help in understanding the dynamics of working capital management:

A fund flow statement may be used to address a variety of questions that help in understanding the dynamics of working capital management.

1. How strong is the enterprise's internal fund generation? Is the fund flow from operations positive? If it is negative, what are the reasons?
2. Have long-term sources been adequate to support long-term applications? If not, what are the reasons? Is it a deliberate policy to reduce investment in working capital?
3. Is the investment in working capital adequate?
4. Has the liquidity position of the firm improved?

Answers to these questions provide an insight into the enterprise's financing strategy and its ability to manage the working capital.

Illustration 14.4 (Interpretation of fund flow statement)
The balance sheets of A Ltd. for a period of three years as on 31 March each year are as follows:

(Amount ₹'Lakh)

	Year 2017	*Year 2018*	*Year 2019*
Liabilities:			
Share capital, in equity shares of ₹10 each	30	35	35
General reserve	10	15	18
Surplus	5	8	9
13% debentures	10	5	10
Bank credit	5	10	15
Trade creditors	10	12	15
Income tax provision for the current year	8	11	14
Proposed dividend	6	10.5	14
	84	106.5	130
Assets:			
Plant and machinery	45	55	70
Investments	10	15	20
Stock	12	15	15
Debtors	14	15	12
Cash and bank	3	6.5	13
	84	106.5	130

Other details:

(i) Depreciation provided in the books:

Year 2017	₹6 lakh
Year 2018	₹8 lakh
Year 2019	₹10 lakh

(ii) A part of the debentures was converted into equity at par in June 2017.

(iii) There was no sale of depreciable asset during the period.

The management seeks your advice on the liquidity position of the company. Use the fund flow statement for the purpose.

Solution:

(Amount ₹Lakh)

	Year 2017	*Year 2018*	*Year 2019*
1. Statement of changes in working capital			
(a) *Current assets*			
Stock	12.00	15.00	15.00
Debtors	14.00	15.00	12.00
Cash and bank	3.00	6.50	13.00
	29.00	36.50	40.00
(b) *Current liabilities*			
Bank credit	5.00	10.00	15.00
Trade creditors	10.00	12.00	15.00
	15.00	22.00	30.00
(c) *Working capital* (a – b)	14.00	14.50	10.00
(d) *Changes in working capital*		0.50	(4.50)
2. Statement of funds from operations			
Increase in retained profit			
Surplus		3.00	1.00
General reserve		5.00	3.00
		8.00	4.00
Proposed dividend		10.50	14.00
Profit for the year		18.50	18.00
Depreciation (non-current amortisation)		8.00	10.00
Tax provisions (To be shown as a separate line item)		11.00	14.00
Funds from operation		37.50	42.00

Working notes:

1. To determine the amount of fund from operations, we have added proposed dividend to the amount of increase in the retained profit. This is because the increase in retained profit represents profit earned during the period reduced by the proposed dividend.
2. The number for purchase of plant and machinery is the total of depreciation for the year and the difference between opening and closing balances of plant and machinery.
3. The balance sheet shows income tax provisions for the current year. It is assumed that the actual tax liability was equal to the provision, and that provision created in one accounting year would be paid in the next accounting period.
4. Proposed dividend becomes the liability on approval by shareholders in the annual general meeting. Unpaid dividend is a current liability. In this case, balance sheets do not show unpaid dividend. Therefore, it is assumed that dividend proposed in one accounting year was paid in the next accounting year.

FUND FLOW STATEMENT

	Year 2018	*Year 2019*
(a) *Sources*		
Funds from operations	37.50	42.00
Issue of 13% debentures	—	5.00
	37.50	47.00

	Year 2018	Year 2019
(b) *Applications*		
Purchase of plant and machinery	18.00	25.00
Purchase of investments	5.00	5.00
Income tax paid	8.00	11.00
Dividend paid	6.00	10.50
	37.00	51.50
(c) *Change in working capital* (a – b)	0.50	(4.50)

Interpretation:

(a) A large part of funds generated from operations were used to pay tax and dividend. It was 37.33% and 51.19% for 2018 and 2019, respectively.

(b) The funds generated from operations in 2019 were more than 2018 by 12%.

(c) In 2018, 62.67% of the funds generated from operations were used in investment activities. Funds generated from operations were adequate to pay tax and dividend, and also to finance acquisition of fixed assets and investment. However, in 2019, the balance (48.81%) left after payment of tax and dividend was not adequate to finance investment activities. Investment activities in that year were financed by funds from operations (68.33%), proceeds from the issue of 13% debentures (16.67%), and reduction in working capital (15.00%).

(d) Reduction in working capital in 2019 might be the result of the conscious policy of the company to maintain a low current ratio. The current ratio of the company declined from 1.93 in 2017 to 1.33 in 2019. The ratio of 1.33 is usually considered acceptable and should not adversely affect the performance of the company. However, further investigation is required to understand whether decline in the current ratio is good or bad for the company. A comparison with industry norms and the company's inventory management policy should be examined.

(e) The firm's debt-equity ratio as on December 31, 2019 is 0.31 : 1. Therefore, the firm has sufficient capacity to borrow, if necessary. It should not worry for liquidity

14.2 CASH FLOW STATEMENT

14.2.1 Purpose of Preparing Cash Flow Statement

Users of financial statements evaluate the ability of an entity to generate cash and cash equivalents and the timing and certainty of their generation.

Information about the cash flows of an entity is useful in providing users with a basis to assess the ability of the entity to generate cash and cash equivalents and the needs of the entity to utilise those cash flows. A statement of cash flows, when used in conjunction with the rest of the financial statements, provides information that enables users to evaluate:

- the changes in net assets of an entity,
- its financial structure (including its liquidity and solvency), and
- its ability to affect the amounts and timing of cash flows in order to adapt to the changing circumstances and opportunities.

Information about the cash flows of an entity is useful in providing users with a basis to assess the ability of the entity to generate cash and cash equivalents and the needs of the entity to utilise those cash flows.

The statement of cash flows enhances the comparability of performance of different entities. This is so because it eliminates the effects of using different accounting policies for the like transactions and events. It also helps one examine the relationship between profitability and net cash flow and the impact of changing prices.

14.2.2 Cash and Cash Equivalents

Cash flows exclude movements between items that constitute cash or cash equivalents because these components are part of the cash management of an entity rather than part of its operating, investing, and financing activities. Cash management includes the investment of excess cash in cash equivalents.

Table 14.1 presents the components of cash and cash equivalents.

TABLE 14.1 Components of Cash and Cash Equivalents

	Component	Description
1.	Cash	Cash comprises cash on hand and demand deposits with banks, which can be withdrawn without prior notice and without payment of any penalty.
2.	Cash equivalents	Cash equivalents are short-term, highly liquid investments, which are readily convertible to known amounts of cash and are subject to an insignificant risk of changes in value. (a) An investment in debt securities having a short maturity, say, three months or less from the date of acquisition. (b) Term deposits with banks with maturity of three months or less. Equity investments are excluded from cash equivalents.
3.	Overdraft	Overdrafts are included in cash and cash equivalents. Usually, overdraft is used for short-term cash management.

Overdrafts are included in cash and cash equivalents. Usually, overdraft is used for short-term cash management.

14.2.3 Classification of Activities

Cash flow statement is presented in three segments—cash flow from operating activities, cash flow from investing activities, and cash flow from financing activities.

Operating activities are principal revenue producing activities of an entity.

Investing activities are activities related to capital expenditure, inter-corporate investments and acquisitions.

Financing activities relate to transactions and activities that change the capital structure.

Operating activities

Principal revenue producing activities of an entity. They generally include the transactions and other events that enter into determination of net income.

Investing activities

Activities related to capital expenditure, inter-corporate investments and acquisitions. Receipt of interest and dividend are investment activities. Disposal of non-current assets is included in investment activities.

Financing activities

Financing activities relate to transactions and activities that change the capital structure. In other words, they are transactions with financiers.

14.2.4 Direct and Indirect Methods

There are two alternative formats for presenting cash flows—direct method and indirect method.

The key difference in these two methods lies in their presentation of cash flows from operating activities. In the *direct method,* operating cash receipts and payments are reported directly. In the *indirect method,* cash flows from operating activities are reported by way of adjustments to the net profit of the reporting period shown in the statement of profit and loss. SEBI requires listed companies to use the indirect method for presenting the statement of cash flows.

14.2.5 Cash Flow from Operating Activities

Nature of operating cash flows

Cash flows from operating activities are primarily derived from the principal revenue producing activities of the firm.

They generally result from the transactions and other events that enter into the determination of net profit or loss. In other words, cash flow measures the amount of cash generated or used by the firm in producing and selling goods and services.

Examples of cash flows from operating activities are as follows:

(a) Cash receipts from the sale of goods and the rendering of services.
(b) Cash receipts from royalties, fees, commissions, and other revenues.
(c) Cash payments to suppliers for goods and services.
(d) Cash payments to and on behalf of employees.
(e) Cash receipts and cash payments of an insurance enterprise for premiums and claims, annuities, and other policy benefits.
(f) Cash payments or refunds of income taxes, unless they can be specifically identified with financing and investing activities.
(g) Cash receipts and payments relating to futures contracts, forward contracts, option contracts and swap contracts when the contracts are held for dealing or trading purposes.

Purchase and sale of dealing or trading securities by dealers

An enterprise dealing in securities hold securities and loans for dealing or trading purposes, in which case they are similar to inventory acquired specifically for resale. Therefore, cash flows arising from the purchase and sale of dealing or trading securities are classified as *operating activities*. Similarly, cash advances and loans made by financial enterprises are usually classified as operating activities since they relate to the main revenue-producing activity of that enterprise.

14.2.6 Methods for Calculating Operating Cash Flows

Table 14.2 below compares the direct and indirect methods for presenting cash flows from operating activities in the statement of cash flows.

TABLE 14.2 Cash Flows from Operating Activities—Direct and Indirect Methods

Direct method	*Indirect method*
CASH FROM OPERATING ACTIVITIES:	**CASH FROM OPERATING ACTIVITIES:**
Cash receipts from customers	Profit before taxation
Cash payments to suppliers	Adjustments for non-cash items
Cash paid to employees	Adjustments for non-operating items
Cash from operations	Changes in working capital
Income tax paid	**Cash from operations**
Net cash flow from operating activities	Income tax paid
	Net cash flow from operating activities

Notes:

1. Examples of non-cash items are depreciation, impairment loss, gain/loss from changes in the fair value of investment in equity, and bad debt.
2. Examples of non-operating items are interest income, dividend income, interest expense, and gain/loss from sale of items of PP&E.
3. In case of financial institutions, interest income, and dividend income are considered cash flows from operating activities.
4. Increase in working capital reduces cash flows and decrease in working capital increases cash flows. Working capital is measured as the difference between the amount of current assets and that of current liabilities. Current liabilities for the purpose of operating cash flows does not included current tax liability, short-term borrowings and current portion of long-term borrowings.

Examples of non-cash items are depreciation, impairment loss, gain/loss from changes in the fair value of investment in equity, and bad debt.

In the indirect method, cash flows from operating activities are reported by way of adjustments to the net profit of the reporting period shown in the statement of profit and loss.

Illustration 14.5 (Cash flow from operating activities)

KK Limited (KKL), which is in the merchandising business, commenced its operation on April 1, 2019. The following is the statement of profit and loss for the year ended March 31, 2020:

Statement of Profit and Loss of KKL for the Year Ended March 31, 2020

	Amount (₹'000)	*Amount* (₹'000)
A. INCOME		
Sales		10,000
B. EXPENSES		
Purchase of goods in trade	8,000	
Increase in inventories of stock-in-trade	(2,000)	
Operating expenses	2,000	
Depreciation	500	
Income tax expense	600	9,100
Net profit (A–B)		900

Examples of non-operating items are interest income, dividend income, interest expense, and gain/loss from sale of items of PP&E.

The following additional information is provided:

(a) As on March 31, 2020, ₹20,00,000 were due from customers.

(b) As on March 31, 2020, ₹10,00,000 were due to creditors for goods and ₹5,00,000 were due to creditors for services.

(c) Income tax expense includes ₹2,00,000 deferred tax expense, and the total amount of current tax liability has already been paid as advance tax.

Required: Calculate the amount of cash flows from operating activities for the year 2019–2020.

Solution:

Direct method

Cash Flow from Operating Activities

	Amount (₹'000)	*Amount* (₹'000)
A. CASH INFLOWS		
Cash receipts from customers (10,000 – 2,000)		8,000
B. CASH OUTFLOWS		
Purchase of goods (8,000 – 1,000)	7,000	
Operating expenses (2,000 – 500)	1,500	8,500
Cash generated from operations (A–B)		(500)
Income tax paid (600 – 200)		(400)
Net Cash Flow from Operating Activities (A–B)		(900)

Indirect method

Cash flow from Operating Activities

	Remarks	*Amount* (₹'000)
Profit before taxation (900 + 600)		1,500
Adjustment for depreciation	Non-cash expense	500
		2,000
Increase in trade receivables (2,000 – 0)		(2,000)
Increase in trade creditors (1,500 – 0)		1,500
Increase in inventories (2,000 – 0)		(2,000)
Cash generated from operations		(500)
Income tax paid		(400)
Net cash flows from operating activities		(900)

Note: Opening balances are zero, as the firm started business in the current year.

Illustration 14.6 (Cash flow from operating activities)

NT Limited (NTL) is in the merchandising business. The following are the balance sheets of NTL as at March 31, 2019 and March 31, 2020:

Particulars	2020/03/31 Amount(₹'000)	2019/03/31 Amount(₹'000)
ASSETS		
PP&E (Net block)	8,000	10,000
Inventory of finished goods	12,000	10,000
Trade receivables	18,000	20,000
Cash and cash equivalents	21,720	2,000
Total	59,720	42,000
EQUITY AND LIABILITIES		
Equity		
Share capital	5,000	5,000
Reserves and surplus	40,100	23,300
Total	45,100	28,300
Liabilities		
Deferred tax liability	500	600
Loan	5,000	5,000
Trade creditors for goods	8,600	7,500
Trade creditors for services	400	500
Income tax liability (net of advance tax paid)	120	100
Total	14,620	13,700
Total of equity and liabilities	59,720	42,000

The following is the statement of profit and loss of NTL for the year ended March 31, 2020:

	Amount(₹'000)	Amount(₹'000)
A. INCOME		
Sales		120,000
B. EXPENSES		
Purchase of good-in-trade	80,000	
(Increase) in inventories of stock-in-trade	(2,000)	
Operating expenses	12,000	
Depreciation	2,000	
Income tax expense	11,200	103,200
C. Net profit (A–B)		16,800

Required: Calculate the cash flows from operating activities of NTL.

Solution:

Direct method

	Amount(₹'000)	Amount(₹'000)
A. CASH INFLOW		
Receipt from customers [120,000 – (18,000 – 20,000)]		122,000
B. CASH OUTFLOW		
Payment for purchase of goods [80,000 – (8,600 – 7,500)]	78,900	
Payment towards operating expenses [12,000 – (400 – 500)]	12,100	
Income tax paid (11,300 + 100 – 120)*	11,280	102,280
C. CASH FLOW FROM OPERATING ACTIVITIES (A–B)		19,720

*Current income tax expense = Income tax expense + Decrease in deferred tax liabilities.

Indirect method

		Amount(₹'000)
Profit before income tax expense (16,800 + 11,200)		28,000
Add: Depreciation	Non-cash expense	2,000
Changes in working capital		

(*Contd...*)

	Amount(₹'000)
Decrease in trade receivables (20,000 – 18,000)	2,000
Increase in trade creditors (9,000 – 8,000)	1,000
Increase in inventories of stock-in-trade	(2,000)
Cash generated from operations	31,000
Income tax paid	(11,280)
Net cash flows from operating activities	19,720

14.2.7 Cash Flows from Investing and Financing Activities

Nature of investing cash flows

Cash flows from investing activities represent the extent to which expenditures have been made for resources intended to generate future income and cash flows.

Investing activities are the acquisition and disposal of long-term assets and other investments not included in cash equivalents.

Cash flows from investing activities represent the extent to which expenditures have been made for resources intended to generate future income and cash flows. Only expenditures that result in a recognised asset in the balance sheet are eligible for classification as investing activities. Examples of cash flows arising from investing activities are as follows:

(a) Cash payments to acquire fixed assets and other long-term assets.
(b) Cash receipts from sales of fixed assets and other long-term assets.
(c) Cash payments to acquire equity or debt instruments of other entities and interests in joint ventures.
(d) Cash receipts from sales of equity or debt instruments of other entities and interests in joint ventures.
(e) Cash advances and loans made to other parties (other than advances and loans made by a financial institution).
(f) Cash receipts from the repayment of advances and loans made to other parties (other than advances and loans of a financial institution).
(g) Cash payments for futures contracts, forward contracts, option contracts and swap contracts except when the contracts are held for dealing or trading purposes or payments.
(h) Cash receipts from futures contracts, forward contracts, option contracts and swap contracts except when the contracts are held for dealing or trading purposes or receipts.
  (i) When a contract is accounted for as a hedge of an identifiable position, the cash flows of the contract are classified in the same manner as the cash flows of the position being hedged. (Discussion on items (h) and (i) above is beyond the scope of this book.)

Nature of financing cash flows

Financing activities are the activities that result in changes in the size and composition of the contributed equity and borrowings of the firm.

The separate disclosure of cash flows arising from financing activities is useful in predicting claims on future cash flows by providers of capital to the firm.

The separate disclosure of cash flows arising from financing activities is useful in predicting claims on future cash flows by providers of capital to the firm. Examples of cash flows arising from financing activities are as follows:

(a) Cash proceeds from issuing shares or other equity instruments.
(b) Cash payments to owners to acquire or redeem the company's shares.
(c) Cash proceeds from issuing debentures, loans, notes, bonds, mortgages and other short-term or long-term borrowings.
(d) Cash repayments of amounts borrowed.
(e) Cash payments by a lessee for the reduction of the outstanding lease liability.

Illustration 14.7 (Cash flow statement)

The following is the statement of profit and loss of Nakusha Ltd. (NL) for 2019 and its balance sheets as on December 31, 2019 and December 31, 2018:

Statement of profit and loss of NL for the year 2019

	Amount (₹'000)	Amount (₹'000)
Sales		700
Cost of goods sold		(520)
Gross margin		180
Operating expenses (including depreciation ₹38)		(150)
Operating profit		30
Other income/(expenses)		
Interest expense	(22)	
Interest income	6	
Gain from sale of investment	10	
Loss on sale of equipment	(2)	(8)
Net profit before tax		22
Income tax expense		(6)
Net profit		16

Balance Sheet as at December 31, 2019 and as on December 31, 2018 (₹'000)

	2019/03/31 Amount (₹'000)	2018/03/31 Amount (₹'000)
ASSETS		
Non-current Assets		
Property, plant, and equipment: Gross Block	720	510
Accumulated depreciation	(105)	(70)
Net Block	615	440
Long-term investments	115	125
Current Assets		
Inventory	145	115
Accounts receivables	45	55
Cash	45	15
Prepaid expenses	1	5
Total assets	966	755
EQUITY AND LIABILITIES		
Equity		
Share capital	460	320
Reserves and surplus	140	132
Total	600	452
Liabilities		
Non-current liabilities		
Bond	300	250
Current liabilities		
Accounts payable	47	38
Accrued liabilities	15	10
Income tax payable	4	5
Total liabilities	366	53
Total equity plus liabilities	966	755

The following additional information on transactions for 2019 is provided by Delhi Ltd:

1. Purchased investments for ₹80,000.
2. Sold equipment that cost ₹10,000 with accumulated depreciation of ₹3,000 on the date of sale.
3. Issued ₹1,00,000 of bonds at face value in exchange for an equipment on December 31, 2019.
4. Issued 1,400 shares of ₹100 each at face value.
5. Paid cash dividends of ₹8,000.

Required: Prepare a cash flow statement using the indirect method.

Solution:

Working notes

1. Purchase piece of equipment
   [Closing gross block – (Opening gross block-Cost of equipment sold) = [₹7,20,000 – (5,10,000 – 10,000)] = ₹2,20,000. Equipment costing ₹1,00,000 was acquired by issuing bond. This had no cash effect. Therefore, cash outflow from purchase of equipment was (₹2,20,000 – 1,00,000) or ₹1,20,000. The non-cash transaction should be disclosed.
2. Proceeds from sale of a piece of equipment
   [(gross block of the item sold – Accumulated depreciation on the same) – Loss on the sale] = (₹10,000 – 3,000) – 2,000 = ₹5,000
3. Proceeds from sale of investment
   [(Opening balance + Purchase during the current period – Closing balance) – Gain on sale] = [(1,25,000 + 80,000 – 1,15,000) + 10,000] = ₹100,000
4. Repayment of bond
   [(Opening balance + Issue of bond during the year) – Closing balance] = [(₹2,50,000 + 1,00,000) – 3,00,000] = ₹50,000
5. Income tax paid = (Opening balance + Income tax expense – Closing balance) = (₹5,000 + 6,000 – 4,000) = ₹7,000
   Cash Flow Statement of NL for the year 2019

	Amount (₹'000)	*Amount (₹'000)*
A. CASH FLOW FROM OPERATING ACTIVITIES		
Net profit before taxation	22	
Adjustment for non-cash items		
Depreciation	38	
Adjustments of non-operating items		
Gains on sale of investments	(10)	
Loss on sale of equipment	2	
Interest expense	22	
Interest income	(6)	
Operating cash flow before working capital changes		68
Changes in working capital		
Decrease in accounts receivable	10	
Increase in inventory	(30)	
Decrease in prepaid expenses	4	
Increase in accounts payable	9	
Increase in accrued liabilities	5	(2)
Cash generated from operations		66
Income tax paid		(7)
Net cash from operating activities		59
B. CASH FLOW FROM INVESTING ACTIVITIES		
Purchase of equipment	(120)	
Sale of equipment	5	
Purchase of investments	(80)	
Sale of investments	100	
Interest received	6	
Net cash from investing activities		(89)
C. CASH FLOW FROM FINANCING ACTIVITIES		
Proceeds from issue of share capital	140	
Issue/(Repayment) of bonds	(50)	
Interest paid	(22)	
Dividends paid	(8)	
Net cash from financing activities		60
Net increase in cash (and cash equivalents) (A + B + C)		30
Cash (and cash equivalents) at beginning of period		15
Cash (and cash equivalents) at end period		45

Disclosure: Issued ₹1,00,000 of bonds at face value in exchange for an equipment on December 31, 2019.

Illustration 14.8 (Cash flow statement)
From the following balance sheet and information, prepare the cash flow statement of Ryan Ltd. for the year ended March 31, 2003:

Ryan Ltd. Balance Sheet for the Year Ended March 31, 2019

	2019/03/31 (*Amount ₹*)	2019/03/31 (*Amount ₹*)
ASSETS		
Non-current assets		
Land and building	1,50,000	2,00,000
Plant and machinery	7,65,000	5,00,000
Investments	50,000	80,000
Current Assets		
Inventory	95,000	90,000
Bills receivable	65,000	70,000
Sundry debtors	1,75,000	1,30,000
Cash and bank	65,000	90,000
Preliminary expenses to the extent not written off	10,000	25,000
Voluntary separation payment	1,25,000	65,000
Total Assets	15,00,000	12,50,000
EQUITY AND LIABILITIES		
EQUITY		
Equity share capital	6,00,000	5,00,000
10% redeemable preference capital	–	2,00,000
Capital redemption reserve	1,00,000	–
Capital reserve	1,00,000	–
General reserve	1,00,000	2,50,000
Profit and loss account	70,000	50,000
Total equity	9,70,000	10,00,000
LIABILITIES		
Non-current liabilities		
9% debentures	2,00,000	–
Current liabilities		
Sundry creditors	95,000	80,000
Bills payable	20,000	30,000
Liabilities for expenses	30,000	20,000
Provision for taxation	95,000	60,000
Proposed dividend	90,000	60,000
Total equity plus liabilities	5,30,000	2,50,000
Total equity plus liabilities	15,00,000	12,50,000

Additional information

(a) A piece of land has been sold out for ₹1,50,000 (cost, ₹1,20,000) and the balance land was revalued. The capital reserve consisted of profit on sale and profit on revaluation.
(b) On April 1, 2018, a plant was sold for ₹90,000 (original cost: ₹70,000 and WDV: ₹50,000) and debentures worth ₹1 lakh were issued at par as part consideration for plant of ₹4.5 lakh acquired.
(c) Part of investments (cost ₹50,000) was sold for ₹70,000.
(d) Pre-acquisitions dividend received (₹5,000) was adjusted against cost of investment.
(e) Directors have proposed 15% dividend for the current year.
(f) A voluntary separation cost of ₹50,000 was adjusted against general reserve.
(g) Income tax liability for the current year was estimated at ₹1,35,000.
(h) Depreciation @ 15% has been written off from the plant account, but no depreciation has been charged on land and building.

Solution:

Assumption:

(a) Income tax expenses for the year ended March 31, 2019 was equal to the income tax liability for the current year. There was no deferred tax expense.
(b) Preacquisition dividend relates to investments in the previous years.
(c) Full year interest was paid on debentures.

Working notes:

1. Revaluation gain on revaluation of land:
Capital Reserve – Gain on sale of land = [1,00,000 – (1,50,000 – 1,20,000)] = ₹70,000
2. Purchase/sale of land:
[Closing balance of land – (Opening balance – cost of the piece sold + Revaluation gain)] = ₹1,00, 000 – (1,50,000 – 1,20,000 + 70,000) = Nil
3. Depreciation for the year:
[Opening WDV + (Purchase – WDV of plant sold) – Closing WDV) = [₹5,00,000 +(4,50,000 – 50,000) – ₹7,65,000 = ₹1,35,000
4. Cash paid to purchase investment:
[Closing balance – (opening balance – cost of investment sold) – preacquisition dividend = [₹50,000 – (80,000 – 50,000 – 5,000) = ₹25,000
5. Net profit reported in the profit and loss account
[Closing General Reserve – (Opening General Reserve – Proposed dividend – Transfer to capital redemption reserve – Transfer from voluntary separation fund – Voluntary separation cost adjusted)] + (Closing balance of profit and loss account – Opening balance of profit and loss account) = ₹1,00,000 – (2,50,000 – 90,000 – 1,00,000 – 50,000) + (70,000 – 50,000) = ₹1,10,000

CASH FLOW STATEMENT

	Amount ₹	Amount ₹
A. CASH FLOW FROM OPERATING ACTIVITIES		
Profit before income tax (`1,10,000 + 1,35,000)		2,45,000
Adjustment of non-cash expenses		
Depreciation		1,35,000
Adjustments for non-operating items		
Interest on debenture (0.09 × ₹200,000)	18,000	
Preliminary expenses written off (₹25,000 – 10,000)	15,000	
Profit on sale of plant (₹90,000 – 50,000)	(40,000)	
Profit on sale of investment (₹70,000 – 50,000)	(20,000)	(27,000)
Cash flow before adjustments for working capital change		3,53,000
(Increase)/Decrease in inventory (95,000 – 90,000)	(5,000)	
(Increase)/Decrease in bills receivable (65,000 – 70,000)	5,000	
(Increase)/Decrease in sundry debtors (1,75,000 – 1,30,000)	(45,000)	
Increase/ (Decrease) in sundry creditors (95,000 – 80,000)	15,000	
Increase/(Decrease) in bills payable (20,000 – 30,000)	(10,000)	
Increase/(Decrease) in liabilities for expenses (30,000 – 20,000)	10,000	(30,000)
Cash flow after adjustments for working capital changes		3,23,000
Voluntary compensation paid during the year		(1,10,000)
Income tax paid		(1,00,000)
Net cash flow from operating activities		1,13,000
B. CASH FLOW FROM INVESTMENT ACTIVITIES		
Sale of plant	90,000	
Sale of investment	70,000	
Sale of land	1,50,000	
Purchase of investment	(25,000)	
Purchase of plant	(3,50,000)	
Net use of cash flow for investing activities		(65,000)

(Contd...)

	Amount ₹	Amount ₹
C. CASH FLOW FROM FINANCING ACTIVITIES		
Dividend paid	(60,000)	
Dividend received	5,000	
Interest paid	(18,000)	
Issue of equity shares	1,00,000	
Issue of debentures	1,00,000	
Redemption of debentures	(2,00,000)	
Net cash flow from financing activities		(73,000)
Net increase in cash and cash equivalents (A + B + C)		(25,000)
Opening balance of cash and cash equivalent		90,000
Closing balance of cash and cash equivalent		65,000

Disclosures

(a) Pre-acquisition dividend of ₹5,000 received during the year relates to investments acquired in one or more prior periods and was adjusted against the 'carrying amount' of investments.

(b) 9% debentures include debentures for ₹1,00,000 towards part payment of plant purchased for ₹4,50,000.

14.2.8 Exchange Difference

General principle

Cash flows arising from transactions in a foreign currency are recorded in a firm's functional currency by translating the foreign currency amount into the functional currency using the exchange rate *at the date of the cash flow*. Cash flows of a foreign subsidiary should be translated using the exchange rates prevailing *at the date of the cash flows*.

For practical reasons, a company may apply a rate (e.g., weighted average rate for the period) that approximates the actual rate.

Cash flows arising from transactions in a foreign currency are recorded in a firm's functional currency by translating the foreign currency amount into the functional currency using the exchange rate at the date of the cash flow.

Cash flows of a foreign subsidiary should be translated using the exchange rates prevailing at the date of the cash flows.

Direct method

When a company enters into a transaction denominated in foreign currency, there are no cash flow consequences until payments are received or paid. The receipts and payments are recorded in the accounting records of the company at the exchange rate prevailing at the date of payment and these amounts are reflected in the statement of cash flows.

For preparing the consolidated statement of cash flows using the direct method, cash flows of the subsidiary are measured at its functional currency and then translated at the presentation currency of the company (parent).

Indirect method

Where the exchange differences relate to operating items such as sales or purchases of inventory by the firm, no adjustment is to be made while calculating cash flows from operating activities using the indirect method. For example, if cash settlement of a sale transaction takes place during the period when the transaction occurred, the net profit includes both the amount recorded at the date of sale and the exchange difference on settlement. Therefore, the net profit is based on the cash flow arising from the sale transaction. If the settlement takes place in a period subsequent to the period in which the transaction occurred, net profit includes exchange difference arising from the translation of the receivables at the closing rate. However, no adjustment is required because the increase or decrease in the amount of receivables during the period is adjusted to determine the cash flows from operating activities for the period. The increase or decrease in receivables includes the exchange difference. [Remember the journal entry for exchange difference (gain): Debit receivables and credit exchange difference.]

Determining the value of non-operating cash flows

Adjustment to net profit is required for exchange difference arising from settlement or translation (at the closing rate) of a transaction relating to non-operating cash flows. An example of non-operating cash flow is the cash flow relating to purchase of an item of property, plant, and equipment. The adjustment is required because the net profit includes the exchange difference while the amount of investment recorded initially is not adjusted. Therefore, the exchange difference should be taken out of the net profit and should be adjusted to the cash flow relating to the purchase of the item of the PP&E. This cash flow should be included in cash flows from investing activities.

Exchange difference relating to cash and cash equivalents

The effect of exchange rate movements on foreign currency cash and cash equivalents is not a cash flow. However, it is necessary to include those exchange differences in the statement of cash flows in order to reconcile the movement in cash and cash equivalents to the corresponding amounts presented in the balance sheet at the beginning and at the close of the period. The exchange difference is presented as a footnote to the statement of cash flows.

14.2.9 Analyst's Perspective

The starting point of an analysis of cash flows is to enquire whether the company has generated positive cash flow from operating activities.

The starting point of an analysis is to enquire whether the company has generated positive cash flow from operating activities. Several factors affect a company's ability to generate positive cash flow from operating activities. Usually, a healthy enterprise in a steady state and operating in a mature industry generates positive cash flow. On the other hand, a growing enterprise that invests significantly in research and development, advertising, training, and working capital to support its future growth may not be able to generate positive cash flow from operations. Cash flow from operating activities should be analysed from this perspective.

The next question that an analyst asks about a company that generates positive cash flow from operating activities is whether it is self-sufficient.

The next question that an analyst asks about a company that generates positive cash flow from operating activities is whether it is self-sufficient. The surplus cash that is available after working capital investment is available for distribution to debtholders (interest and instalment), long-term investment and distribution to shareholders. If the internally generated surplus cash is not sufficient to meet the needs of the company, it resorts to external financing. Analysts analyse the financing policy of the company by examining the different sources that it has used to mobilise additional resources.

Cash flow is analysed from investing activities to understand the company's strategy for long-term growth. A company may achieve growth either through mergers and acquisitions, or through investment in new assets (projects). Analysis of cash flow from investing activities also provides an insight into the company's strategy for spinning-off and disinvestment and its ability to manage surplus cash.

Reconciliation of net profit and cash flow from operating activities helps one understand the quality of net profit reported in the profit and loss account. An examination of the gap between the two provides an understanding of the accounting policy of the company regarding non-current amortisations. It also helps one understand whether increase/decrease in current assets and current liabilities are normal, and whether adequate explanation is available for those changes.

A cash flow statement alone may not provide answers to all questions. An analyst should gather information from the Board of Director's report and the Management Discussion and Analysis presented in the annual report along with annual financial statements. Those two reports provide management's analysis of past performance, management perspective of the business environment, and its projection of future performance. Those reports, to an extent, describe the corporate strategy. A cash flow statement should be analysed in the context of corporate strategy and likely changes in the business environment.

14.3 CASH GENERATING EFFICIENCY

The focus of cash flow analysis is to analyse the efficiency of generating cash flows from operating activities. Analysists calculate the following ratios for evaluating cash generating efficiency: (a) Cash flow yield; (b) Cash flows to sales; and (c) Cash flows to assets.

14.3.1 Cash Flow Yield

$$\text{Cash flow yield} = \frac{\text{Net cash flows from operating activities}}{\text{Net profit}}$$

Net cash flow yield = (Net cash flow from operating activities) ÷ (Net profit)
The cash flow yield ratio helps in evaluating the quality of earnings.

The cash flow yield ratio helps in evaluating the quality of earnings. The ratio is expected to be more than 1. Lower ratio indicates that during the accounting period, either the other income was high or investment in working capital has gone up. We should be careful in interpreting the ratio. In industries and firms, in which investments in fixed assets is high the ratio should be high, as in calculating the net cash flows from operating activities, we add back depreciation to profit before tax and use in the denominator of the ratio net profit after tax.

14.3.2 Cash Flow to Sales

$$\text{Cash flow to sales} = \frac{\text{Net cash flows from operating activities}}{\text{Sales}}$$

The cash flow to sales ratio shows how much cash is generated from one rupee of sales. Interpreting this ratio requires benchmarking the ratio with that of competitors.

14.3.3 Cash Flow to Assets

$$\text{Cash flow to assets} = \frac{\text{Net cash flows from operating activities}}{\text{Average total aseets}}$$

This and other cash flow efficiency ratios are related to overall profitability (Return on Invested Capital), which we shall discuss in Chapter 15.

14.3.4 Free Cash Flows

Free cash flow measures the sufficiency of cash flows assets included in current assets. For example, trade receivable is a better-quality current asset than inventories. Quality of current liabilities is assessed in terms of urgency to settle the liability. For example, trade payable is a better-quality current liability than statutory dues because payment to suppliers of goods and services can be deferred through negotiation with them and because of long-term relationship, but settlement of statutory dues (e.g., income tax deducted at source and employees' provident fund contribution) cannot be deferred.

Free cash flow is the cash flow available for distribution to investors and lenders, after meeting internal needs (investment in fixed assets and working capital)

Financial flexibility

Creditors assess the default risk of extending credit to the company by evaluating the financial flexibility of the company. It refers to the ability of the company to quickly respond to the unexpected interruptions in cash inflows. Assessing financial flexibility requires evaluation of qualitative factors such as ability to borrow at a short notice, ability to sell and redeploy assets quickly, and ability to quickly adjust the direction of its operations to respond to the changes in the business environment. A company's financial flexibility also depends on the extent of debt in the capital structure and availability of open-line of credit, current rating of its bonds, restrictions on the sale of assets, the extent to which the expenses are discretionary, and the ability to negotiate favourably with employees and supply chain partners to adjust to the change in the direction of operations.

Acid-test ratio (Quick ratio)

Acid-test ratio, also called quick ratio, is a more stringent test of liquidity. In the numerator, the total amounts of only those current assets, which are readily convertible into cash, are included.

$$\textit{Quick ratio} = \frac{\text{Currrent Assets} - \text{Inventories} - \text{Prepaid Expenses}}{\text{Current Liabilities}}$$

Inventories are excluded because they are the least liquid current assets. Pre-paid expenses are excluded because they do not get converted into cash. The acid-test ratio suffers from the similar limitations as the limitations of the current ratio. Therefore, the ratio should be interpreted carefully.

The following is the analysis for MRF Tyres, Apollo Tyres and Apollo Hospitals:

		MRF Tyres	*Apollo Tyres*	*Apollo Hospital*
1.	Current Assets (₹ Crores)	8,152	5,481	2,647
2.	Current Liabilities (₹ Crores)	5,225	5,713	2,337
3.	Inventories (₹ Crores)	2,905	3,206	738
4.	Quick Assets (₹ Crores) [(1)–(3)]	5,247	2,275	1,909
5.	Current ratio (Number of times)	**1.56**	**0.96**	**1.13**
6.	Acid–test Ratio (Number of times)	**1.00**	**0.40**	**0.82**

We have taken the year-end (March 31, 2021) figures and not average because we are evaluating year end liquidity position. We have taken the figures from balance sheets directly and not from reorganised balance sheets, as we consider total current assets and total current liabilities.

Cash-to-current asset ratio

Cash-to-Current Assets Ratio

$$= \frac{\text{Cash and Cash Equivalents} + \text{Marketable Securities}}{\text{Current Assets}}$$

Larger the ratio, more liquid are the current assets.

Cash-to-current liabilities ratio

Cash-to-Current Liabilities ratio

$$= \frac{\text{Cash plus Cash Equivalents} + \text{Marketable Securities}}{\text{Current Liabilities}}$$

It is more severe test than quick ratio. It emphasises that ultimately cash is required to settle current liabilities. It is often used as a ratio supplementary to the 'cash-to-current asset' ratio.

14.3.5 Efficiency of Financing Decisions–Credit Analysis Solvency

Solvency refers to the long-term viability of the company. Analysis of solvency involves analysing the capital structure of the company and adequacy of earning to honour long-term financial commitments. In liquidity analysis, the time horizon is fairly short. In solvency it is the amount of cash flow that is available for distribution to investors – equity shareholders and lenders.

Free Cash Flow = Net cash flow from operating activities – Purchase of property, plant and equipment and intangible assets + Sale of property, plant and equipment and intangible assets

REVIEW PROBLEMS

R 14.1 State whether the following statements are True or False:

(i) In case of a non-finance company cash inflow from interest income is classified as cash flow from investing activities.
(ii) In case of a non-finance company cash outflow for interest expense is classified as cash flow from financing activities.
(iii) Change in the overdraft balance is presented as cash flows from financing activities.
(iv) In case of finance companies cash outflow for interest expense is classified as cash flow from operating activities.
(v) Increase in the amount of working capital increases cash flows from operating activities.

R 14.2 Fill in the blanks:

(i) An entity has provided the following information about investments in equity shares, measured at fair value:

(a) Opening balance: ₹6,00,000; (b) Closing balance: ₹7,00,000; (c) Gain from change in the fair value is recognised in the statement of profit and loss; (d) Carrying amount of investments in equity shares sold during the year: ₹1,50,000, including sale of treasury bills classified as cash equivalents with carrying amount of ₹20,000; (e) Gain from sale of investment recognised in the statement of profit and loss: ₹50,000; (f) Gain from change in the fair value of ₹30,000 recognised in the statement of profit and loss.

Cash outflow on purchase of investment ....

(ii) An entity provides the following information about trade receivables:

(a) Opening balance: ₹2,00,000; (b) Cash sales during the period: ₹2,00,000; (c) Credit sales during the year: ₹1,00,0000; (d) Bad debt recognised during the year: ₹50,000; (e) Closing balance: ₹3,00,000.

Total cash collected from customers ₹................

(iii) An entity provides the following information:

(a) Net profit: ₹4,00,000; (b) Depreciation for the year ₹60,000; (c) Tax expense for the year: Current tax: ₹1,00,000, Deferred tax 50,000; (d) Increase in current tax liability: ₹50,000; (e) Increase in working capital: ₹20,000

Cash flow from operating activities ₹................

R 14.3 An entity has provided the following information about PP&E:

(i) Opening Carrying amount (WDV): ₹5,00,000; (ii) Closing Carrying amount (WDV): ₹6,00,000; (iii) Sale of an item of PP&E: WDV: ₹1,50,000, sale proceeds: ₹1,20,000; (iv) Depreciation for the year: ₹2,00,000; (v) Issued bond of ₹1,00,000 in exchange of an item of PPE received.

Required: Calculate cash outflow on purchase of items of PP&E.

R 14.4 An entity has provided the following information for the year 2020–2021:

(i) Net profit for the year: ₹5,000
(ii) Depreciation on fixed asset: ₹ 100
(iii) Impairment of goodwill: ₹20
(iv) Profit on sale of land: ₹150
(v) Loss on sale of furniture: ₹20
(vi) Current tax expense: ₹150
(vii) Trade Receivables: Opening balance: ₹2,000; Closing ₹2,500
(viii) Trade payables: Opening balance: ₹800; Closing ₹600
(ix) Inventories: Opening balance: ₹500; Closing ₹400

(x) Accrued (outstanding) expenses: Opening balance: ₹120; Closing ₹140
(xi) Current tax liability: Opening balance: ₹250; Closing ₹300

Required: Prepare cash flow from operating activities.

R 14.5 The following are the summarised balance sheets of Piyali Limited (PL) as at December 31, 2018 and December 31, 2019:

Balance sheet of Piyali Limited as of December 31, 2019 and December 31, 2018

	2019/03/31 (*Amount* ₹'000)	2018/03/31 (*Amount* ₹'000)
ASSETS		
Non-current Assets		
Plant and equipment Gross Block	2,000	1,030
Accumulated depreciation on property, plant and equipment	900	800
Net Block	1,100	230
Land and buildings Gross Block	1,000	1,000
Accumulated depreciation on land and buildings	550	500
Net Block	450	500
Current Assets		
Short-term investments	560	600
Sundry debtors	2,200	2,500
Inventories	1,500	1,300
Interest receivable	100	60
Cash in hand	300	500
Cash at bank	1,290	780
Total assets	7,500	6,470
EQUITY AND LIABILITIES		
EQUITY		
Contributed capital	2,600	2,200
Reserve and surplus	660	100
LIABILITIES		
Non-Current Liabilities		
15% debentures	2,000	1,800
Deferred tax liability	600	500
Current Liabilities		
Sundry creditors	400	600
Wages outstanding	40	20
Income tax payable	400	450
Provision for dividend	800	800
Total equity plus liabilities	7,500	6,470

Statement of Profit and Loss of PL for Year Ending December 31, 2019

	Amount ₹'000
Sales revenue	45,500
Less: Cost of sales	38,920
Gross profit	6,580
Less: Depreciation	570
Less Selling and administration expenses	3,200
Operating profit	2,810
Other Income/Expenses	
Interest income	80
Dividend income	100
Insurance settlement received	10
Profit on sale of equipment	20
Profit before Interest and tax	3,020

(*Contd...*)

	Amount ₹'000
Interest expense	300
Profit before tax	2,720
Less: Income tax expenses	600
Net profit	2,120

The following additional information is provided by PL (amount, ₹'000) for the year 2019:

(a) 15% debentures of ₹200 were issued.
(b) Equipment costing ₹500 having accumulated depreciation of ₹420 was sold for 100.
(c) ₹1,560 (including interim dividend of ₹760) were distributed as dividend. Assume that there is no dividend tax.
(d) All sales and purchases were made on credit basis.

Required: Prepare a statement of cash flows of PL for 2019 using the indirect method.

R 14.6 From the following information, prepare the cash flow statement for the year ended March 31, 2020:

Balance Sheet as at March 31, 2019 and March, 31 2020

	2020/03/31 (*Amount ₹*)	2019/03/31 (*Amount ₹*)
ASSETS		
Non-current Assets		
Land and building	1,90,000	2,00,000
Plant and machinery	1,69,000	1,50,000
Current Assets		
Inventories	74,000	1,00,000
Sundry debtors	64,200	80,000
Cash	600	500
Bank	8,000	0
Goodwill	5,000	0
Total	5,10,800	5,30,500
EQUITY AND LIABILITIES		
EQUITY		
Share capital	2,50,000	2,00,000
General reserve	60,000	50,000
Profit and loss account	30,600	30,500
Total Equity	3,40,000	2,80,500
LIABILITIES		
Non-Current Liabilities		
Bank loan	0	70,000
Current Liabilities		
Sundry creditors	1,35,200	1,50,000
Provision for taxation	35,000	30,000
Total liabilities	1,70,000	2,50,00
Total equity plus liabilities	5,10,800	5,30,500

Additional information

(a) Dividend of ₹23,000 was paid.
(b) The following assets of another company were purchased for a consideration of ₹50,000 paid in shares: Inventories: ₹20,000; and Machinery: ₹25,000
(c) Further machinery was purchased for ₹25,000 during the year.
(d) Depreciation written off: on building: ₹10,000; and machinery: ₹14,000.
(e) Income tax paid during the year ₹28,000.

ASSIGNMENTS

1. Fill in the blanks:

(i) The net profit presented in the income statement of Ankit Limited (AL) for 2005 is ₹2,000. Depreciation charged during the year is ₹400. The amounts of working capital in the balance sheet in the beginning and at the end of the year are the same. The cash flow from the operation is ₹..........

(ii) The net profit presented in the income statement of Kartina Limited (KL) for 2005 is ₹3,000. Depreciation charged during the year is ₹500, and interest expense for the year is ₹100. The net profit includes interest and dividend income of ₹50 and ₹80, respectively. The amount of working capital in the balance sheet in the beginning and at the end of the year is same. The cash flow from the operation is ₹..........

(iii) The net profit presented in the income statement of Malaika Limited (ML) for 2005 is ₹4,000. Depreciation charged during the year is ₹600, and interest expense for the year is ₹200. The net profit includes interest and dividend income of ₹100 and ₹150, respectively. The amounts of working capital in the balance sheet in the beginning and at the end of the year are ₹2,200 and ₹2,500, respectively. The cash flow from the operation is ₹..........

(iv) The net profit presented in the income statement of Parvinder Limited (PL) for 2005 is ₹3,500. Depreciation charged during the year is ₹550. Interest expense for the year is ₹200. The net profit includes interest and dividend income of ₹100 and ₹200, respectively. The amounts of working capital in the balance sheet in the beginning and at the end of the year are ₹3,000 and ₹2,800, respectively. The cash flow from the operation is ₹..........

(v) The net profit presented in the income statement of Ananya Limited (AL) for 2005 is ₹5,500. The amounts of accumulated depreciation in the balance sheet in the beginning and at the end of the period are ₹3,300 and ₹3,100, respectively. During the year 2005, AL sold equipment costing ₹750; the written down value of the equipment at the time of sale was ₹200. The net profit presented in the income statement includes a profit of ₹100 from the sale of the equipment. The net profit also includes interest and dividend income of ₹100 and ₹200, respectively. Interest expense for the year is ₹300. The amounts of working capital in the balance sheet in the beginning and at the end of the year are ₹3,500 and ₹3,800, respectively. The cash flow from operation is ₹......... and the proceeds from the sale of the equipment are ₹..........

(vi) The net profit presented in the income statement of Sunayani Limited (SL) for 2005 is ₹6,000. The amounts of accumulated depreciation in the balance sheet in the beginning and at the end of the period are ₹3,300 and ₹3,500, respectively. During 2005, SL sold equipment costing ₹1,000; the written down value of the equipment at the time of sale was ₹700. The net profit presented in the income statement includes a loss of ₹200 from the sale of the equipment. The net profit also includes interest and dividend income of ₹100 and ₹200, respectively. Interest expense for the year is ₹400. The amounts of working capital in the balance sheet in the beginning and at the end of the year are ₹3,500 and ₹3,200, respectively. The cash flow from operation is ₹.......... and the proceeds from the sale of the equipment are ₹..........

(vii) The net profit presented in the income statement of Tripta Limited (TL) for 2005 is ₹6,500. The amounts of gross block in the balance sheet in the beginning and at the end of the period are ₹4,800 and ₹5,000, respectively. The amounts of accumulated depreciation in the balance sheet in the beginning and at the end of the period are ₹4,000 and ₹4,100, respectively. During 2005, TL sold equipment costing ₹700 at ₹200. The net profit presented in the income statement includes a profit of ₹100 from the sale of the equipment.

The net profit also includes interest and dividend income of ₹150 and ₹250, respectively. Interest expense for the year is ₹400. The amounts of working capital in the balance sheet in the beginning and at the end of the year are ₹3,500 and ₹4,000, respectively. The cash flow from operation is ₹............... and the cost of equipment purchased is ₹.........

2. Analytical questions:

(i) "The cash flow statement does not provide any additional information, yet it provides important insights into investment and financing decisions of the enterprise." Explain the statement.

(ii) "In the fund flow statement, working capital assumes importance because of the presentation format, otherwise it provides almost no information on working capital management." Do you agree with this view? Write a short note explaining the purpose of presenting a fund flow statement.

(iii) "Treasury function in an enterprise is mainly concerned with day-to-day cash management. A cash flow statement does not provide any information to assess the effectiveness of the treasury function, and therefore, it is an unnecessary addition to the set of financial statements." Examine the statement critically.

(iv) "Operating, investment and financing decisions in a business do not centre around cash; there are many other factors that influence such decisions. Undue importance to cash flow statements might drive managers to unduly focus on cash, which might lead to sub-optimal decisions." Write a note explaining the statement.

3. Problems:

3.1 The profit and loss account of Ludhiana Ltd. for the year 2017 is presented as follows:

	Amount ₹	*Amount ₹*
Sales		8,000
Less:		
Materials consumed	1,600	
Manufacturing expenses	3,000	
Administration and selling expenses	1,000	
Depreciation	400	
Amortisation of Patent	100	
Preliminary expenses	200	6,300
Operating profit		1,700
Loss on sale of fixed assets	(50)	
Dividend receives	350	300
Profit before tax		2,000
Less: Income tax expense		600
Net profit		1,400

Required: Calculate the fund from operations for the purpose of preparing the fund flow statement.

3.2 Nagpur Ltd. has provided the following information relating to its plant and machinery account:

	2017 (*Amount* ₹'000)	2016 (*Amount* ₹'000)
Gross book value at the end of the year	1,000	600
Accumulated depreciation at the end of the year	290	200
Additional information		
(a) Profit on sale of plant and machinery	20	
(b) Depreciation charged during the year	100	
(c) Purchase of new machinery during the year	450	

Required: Calculate the fund flow for the year 2017 from the sale of the old item of plant and machinery.

3.3 Dhaka Ltd. has provided the following information relating to its plant and machinery account:

	2022 (*Amount* ₹)	2021 (*Amount* ₹)
Written-down value at the end of the year	1,000	700
Additional information		
(a) Depreciation charged during the year	150	
(b) Loss on the sale of plant and machinery	20	
(c) Written-down value of the item sold	50	

Required: Calculate: (a) the fund flow for the year 2022, from the sale of the old item of plant and machinery; (b) the cost of new machinery purchased during the year 2022.

3.4 From the following information, prepare the cash flow statement for the year ended December 31, 2019 (making necessary assumptions):

Balance Sheet as at December 31, 2018 and December 31, 2019

	2019/03/31 Amount ₹	2018/03/31 Amount ₹
ASSETS		
Non-current Assets		
Land and building	3,00,000	2,20,000
Machinery	2,80,000	4,00,000
Current Assets		
Stock	90,000	1,00,000
Debtors	1,60,000	1,40,000
Cash	50,000	40,000
Total	**8,80,000**	**9,00,000**
EQUITY AND LIABILITIES		
EQUITY		
Capital	3,50,000	3,00,000
LIABILITIES		
Current Liabilities		
Bank overdraft	2,00,000	3,20,000
Bills payable	80,000	1,00,000
Creditors	2,50,000	1,80,000
Total liabilities	**8,80,000**	**9,00,000**

Additional information:

(a) Net profit for 2019 amounted to ₹1,20,000.

(b) During the year, machinery costing ₹50,000 (accumulated depreciation ₹20,000) was sold for ₹26,000.

(c) The provision for depreciation against machinery as on December 31, 2018 was ₹1,00,000 and on December 31, 2019, it was ₹1,70,000.

3.5 The following is the statement of profit and loss of Vasi Ltd. for the year 2017:

Vasi Ltd. Statement of Profit and Loss Account for Year 2017

	Amount ₹'000
A. INCOME	
Revenue	
Sales	1,500
Other Income	
Income from dividend	10
Profit on sale of machinery	20
Total Income	1,530

(Contd...)

	Amount ₹'000
B. EXPENSES	
Purchases	800
Increase in inventories of stock-in-trade	(20)
Freight inward	40
Manufacturing expenses	260
Administrative and selling expenses	140
Depreciation	50
Amortisation of goodwill	10
Interest expense	50
Income tax expense	80
Total expense	1,410
C. Net profit (A–B)	120

Additional information:

The written-down value as on December 31, 2017 of the item of machinery sold was ₹30. No depreciation has been charged on that item for the year 2017.

Required: Prepare the cash flow statement using the indirect method.

3.6 From the following particulars, prepare a cash flow statement of Sundry Ltd. for the year ended December 31, 2019:

Statement of Profit and Loss for the Year Ended December 31, 2019

	Amount ₹	Amount ₹
Sales		2,16,000
Cost of goods sold		
Purchases	80,500	
Increase in inventories of stock-in-trade	(14,500)	
Loss of stock	(5,000)	
Wages	16,000	77,000
Gross profit b/d		1,39,000
Other income		6,000
Expenses	10,000	
Insurance claim	1,000	
Loss on sale of plant	5,000	
Deferred expenses	5,000	
Depreciation	12,000	
Bad debts	1,000	(34,000)
Profit before tax		1,11,000
Income tax expenses		(10,000)
Net profit		1,01,000
Retained earnings brought forward from the previous years		30,000
Total profit available for appropriation		1,31,000
Appropriations:		
Dividend	8,000	
Reserve	23,000	(31,000)
Retained earnings carried forward		1,00,000

Balance sheets

	2019/12/31 Amount ₹	2018/12/31 Amount ₹
ASSETS		
Non-current Assets		
Fixed assets	1,80,000	60,000
Investments	30,000	68,500
Current Assets		
Stock-in-trade	20,000	5,500
Debtors	55,000	50,000

(*Contd...*)

	2019/12/31 Amount ₹	2018/12/31 Amount ₹
Cash and bank	1,500	3,500
Prepaid expenses	4,000	5,000
Miscellaneous Expenditure to the extent not written off		
Deferred expenses	5,500	10,500
Total	2,96,000	2,03,000
EQUITY AND LIABILITIES		
EQUITY		
Share capital	90,000	80,000
Profit and loss account	1,00,000	30,000
Reserve	73,000	50,000
Total equity	2,63,000	1,60,000
LIABILITIES		
Creditors	20,000	30,000
Liabilities for expenses	10,000	8,000
Advance income	3,000	5,000
Total liabilities	33,000	43,000
Total equity plus liabilities	2,96,000	2,03,000

Additional information:

Machine was sold for ₹10,000

3.7 A fire destroyed the books of accounts of Vikas Ltd. on March 31, 2019. The chief accountant also noticed that the entire cash kept in the cash box was destroyed. However, the following information was available with the chief accountant.

Balance Sheets

	2019/03/31 Amount ₹'000	2018/03/31 Amount ₹'000
ASSETS		
Non-current Assets		
Sundry fixed assets		
Gross block	?	1,600
Less depreciation	?	320
Net block	1,280	1,280
Investment	700	600
Current Assets		
Stock	700	500
Sundry debtors	?	320
Cash-in-bank	120	45
Cash-in-hand	?	5
Total assets	?	2,750
EQUITY AND LIABILITIES		
EQUITY		
Share capital		
Equity shares of ₹10 each	?	1,000
General reserve	?	900
Share premium	?	20
Total equity	?	1,920
LIABILITIES		
Non-current Liabilities		
14% debentures	450	400
Current Liabilities		
Cash credit	?	90
Sundry creditors	220	180
Provision for taxation	?	10
Proposed dividend	?	150
Total liabilities	?	830
Total equity plus liabilities	?	2,750

For the year ended March 31, 2019, the following transactions took place:

1. The company issued 20 lakh equity shares of ₹10 each at a premium of 10%.
2. Fixed assets costing ₹403 lakh were purchased during the year. An old asset (original cost ₹3 lakh and accumulated depreciation ₹1 lakh) was sold for ₹1 lakh.
3. It paid advance tax of ₹70 lakh for 2018–2019 and also the balance tax liability of ₹8 lakh for 2017–2018. The excess provision for 2017–2018 was transferred to the general reserve. The provision for taxation for the year 2018–2019 was ₹90 lakh.
4. Dividend for the year 2017–2018 was fully paid. The company proposed a dividend of 20% for the entire share capital standing as on March 31, 2019.
5. The total increase in cash credit and sundry creditors at the year-end was found to be ₹70 lakh, and the increase with respect to stock and debtors was found to be ₹330 lakh.
6. The chief accountant remembered that the cash from operations for the year was ₹540 lakh.
7. It was decided to write off the cash loss by fire, if any.

   You are required to assist the chief accountant in completing the balance sheet as of March 31, 2019, along with a statement of sources and application of funds.

3.8 The following details are taken from the books of B Ltd. as on two dates:

	2017/03/31 *Amount ₹*	2016/03/31 *Amount ₹*
ASSETS		
Cash	4,05,350	5,04,090
Debtors	7,31,500	7,71,800
Short-term investments	8,40,000	11,05,000
Prepaid expenses	11,550	12,100
Stock	10,55,380	9,21,540
Cash surrender value of insurance policies on employees	53,530	46,070
Land	2,50,000	2,50,000
Buildings and machinery	18,27,820	14,77,780
Debenture discount	28,670	43,050
Total assets	52,03,800	51,31,430
EQUITY AND LIABILITIES		
Creditors	9,56,560	10,30,870
Outstanding expenses	2,16,630	1,27,070
4% mortgage debentures	6,85,000	8,20,000
Accumulated depreciation	8,16,330	9,66,180
Allowance for stock loss	85,000	20,000
Reserve for contingencies	13,41,780	10,67,310
Surplus in profit and loss account	1,02,500	1,00,000
Share capital	10,00,000	10,00,000
Total equity plus liabilities	52,03,800	51,31,430

Further, the following information is available:

(a) Premium on life insurance policies was ₹27,730 of which ₹16,270 was charged to the statement of profit and loss of the year.

(b) Net profit for 2016–2017 as per the statement of profit and loss account was ₹4,90,970.

(c) A 10% dividend was paid during the year.

(d) The allowance for inventory loss was credited by a charge to expense in each year to provide for obsolete items.

(e) A debit to reserve for contingencies of ₹1,14,000 was made during the year. This was in respect of settlement of a past tax liability.

(f) New machinery was purchased for ₹3,13,650, and machinery costing ₹3,26,250 was sold during the year. Depreciation on machinery sold had accumulated to ₹2,91,050 on the date of sale. It was sold as scrap for ₹15,000. The remaining increase in fixed assets resulted from construction of a building.

(g) The mortgage debentures mature at the rate of ₹50,000 per year. In addition to this, the company purchased and retired ₹85,000 of the debentures at ₹103.Both the premium on retirement and the applicable discount were charged to the profit and loss account.

You are required to prepare a statement showing the sources and application of funds for the year 1999–2000.

Note: Schedule of detailed changes in working capital is not required.

3.9 Andaz Ltd. furnishes you with the following information:

(a) Balance Sheet As of March 31

	2017/03/31 *Amount ₹' Crores*	2017/03/31 *Amount ₹' Crores*
ASSETS		
Non-current Assets		
Fixed assets:		
Cost	500	350
Less: Depreciation	300	250
Net	200	100
Investments at cost:		
In subsidiary (wholly owned)	—	60
Current Assets		
Inventory	20	15
Customers dues	135	60
Cash/bank	15	35
Advances	30	60
Total assets	400	330
EQUITY AND LIABIIITIES		
EQUITY		
Equity share capital	100	60
Preference share capital	—	20
Share premium	80	—
Other reserves and surplus	160	100
Total equity	340	180
LIABILITIES		
Non-current Liabilities		
Borrowings	10	70
Current Liabilities		
Creditors	40	60
Tax provision in excess of payment	10	20
Total liabilities	60	150
Total equity plus liabilities	400	330

(b) During the year, the subsidiary merged into Andaz Ltd. The subsidiary had only fixed assets on the date of its merger, and their written-down value was ₹90 crore. These were taken over at ₹90 crore.

(c) Fixed assets costing ₹40 crore and written-down value of ₹15 crore were sold for ₹10 crore.

(d) Andaz Ltd. made a right equity issue of ₹40 crore at an issue price of three times the par value. Preference shares were redeemed at par out of this right issue.

(e) Details of tax assessments.

	2017/03/31 *Amount ₹ Crores*	2016/03/31 *Amount ₹ Crores*
Net tax provision:		
Assessment Year 2014–2015 (FY 2013–2014)	—	9
Assessment Year 2015–1016 (FY 2014–20115)	—	6
Assessment Year 2016–2017 (FY 2015–2016)	—	5
Assessment Year 2017–2018 (FY 2016–2017)	10	
Total	10	20

The tax liability for the various assessment years was settled by payment of ₹4 crore for A.Y. 2014–2015, ₹4.5 crore for A.Y. 2015–2016 and ₹9 crore for A.Y. 2016–2017 on receipt of assessment orders. Advance tax and tax deduction at source totalled ₹30 crore.

(f) Preference dividend of ₹3 crore and equity dividend of ₹30 crore were paid. Interest paid on loans amounted to ₹10.5 crore.

Required: Prepare the following for the year ended March 31, 2017:

(i) Statement of changes in working capital.
(ii) Statement of sources and application of funds.
(iii) Statement of cash flow.

CHAPTER 15

FINANCIAL ANALYSIS

CHAPTER OBJECTIVES

The objectives of this chapter is to introduce to readers the tools for analysing financial statements. In particular, the objective is developing and understanding of:

- Concepts of earnings quality and earnings management;
- Vertical and horizontal analyses;
- Reorganising financial statements for calculating financial ratios;
- Financial ratios;
- Working capital management;
- Altman's Z Score.

15.1 INTRODUCTION

Financial analysis is a part of business analysis, which is the evaluation of a firm's prospect for survival and growth. It starts with the analysis of business environment and strategy. An analyst can draw right conclusions from financial analysis only with an understanding of the firm's strategy and its internal and external contexts.

A firm's sustainability and growth depend on its ability to response quickly to the changes in the business environment. It is important to understand how structural changes affect the firm's performance and financial position. Therefore, an analyst should analyse the firm over a reasonably long period—five to ten years depending on the nature of the industry in which the firm operates.

Lender and creditors analyse financial statements to assess the credit risk in extending credit to the firm. Creditors primarily evaluate the downside risk. Banks and other financial institutions use financial analysis before lending money to a firm. They determine the terms and conditions of loan, including the rate of interest and collateral based on financial analysis. While considering a troubled loan, banks and financial institutions analyse finance from a broader perspective.

Investors and potential investors in the equity shares of a company are interested in the valuation of the company, in particular, in the valuation of the equity. Therefore, they assess both the downside risks and upside potential. In mergers and acquisitions, due diligence includes financial analysis. Analysts with mutual funds, hedge funds, wealth management firms and other financial institutions use financial analysis to identify equity shares which are trading at below or above the fundamental value.

Customers analyse the finance statements to assess supplier's financial strength to support its commitment to supply goods on a long-term basis.

The top management of a conglomerate having a large number of businesses uses financial analysis as a tool for managing subsidiaries and strategic business units.

Immediate earnings (e.g., variable pay) and career development of employees depend on the survival and growth of the firm. Therefore, they use financial analysis to assess survival and growth of the firm.

All stakeholders having an interest in the survival and growth of the firm use financial analysis to protect their interests.

15.2 EARNINGS QUALITY AND EARNINGS MANAGEMENT

15.2.1 Earnings Quality

A high-quality earnings number is one that accurately reflects the company's current operating performance, is a good indicator of future operating performance, and is a useful summary measure for assessing the firm value.

Analysts analyse and interpret financial information to evaluate the firm's current performance, predict its future performance, and based on this analysis, to determine whether the current share price (of listed companies) reflects firm's intrinsic value. From this perspective, a high-quality earnings number is one that accurately reflects the company's current operating performance, is a good indicator of future operating performance, and is a useful summary measure for assessing the firm value. Therefore, generally speaking, the quality of earnings is high if the proportion of earnings from core business activities is high, it is repeatable and reflects only the underlying volatility of the business. Quality of earnings is impacted by the management's discretionary actions, such as choice of inappropriate accounting policy and choice of business decisions focusing on improving earnings of the current period.

15.2.2 Earnings Management

Earnings management is managing earning by bending accounting rules and other actions to match reported earnings with analysts' consensus forecast.

Earnings management is managing earning by bending accounting rules and other actions to match reported earnings with analysts' consensus forecast. Analysts' consensus forecast refers to consensus forecast by analysts that follow the company.

Firms manage earnings also to:

(a) improve variable pay to the members of the top management;
(b) reduce tax liability; and
(c) maintain debt-equity ratio, current ratio, net worth and other financial parameters at a particular level as required by long-term debt covenant.

Strategies for earnings management

Table 15.1 presents the common strategies that companies adopt for earnings management.

TABLE 15.1 Common Strategies for Earnings Management.

	Strategy	Description
1.	Increasing income	Management follows a strategy to increase a period's reported earnings to present the entity's performance favourably. It increases income in this manner over several periods. Usually, in a growth scenario, reversal of accruals is smaller than the current accruals, resulting in increase in income. Management may reverse accruals more than what is appropriate and report income higher than the actual (estimated) earnings. In the long-term, the strategy busts.
2.	Big bath	Management takes as many write-offs as possible in a period of markedly poor performance. It often uses the big bath strategy in conjunction with increasing income strategy in other periods. Management clears all past distortions, which gives an opportunity to resort to increasing income strategy afresh.
3.	Income smoothing	Management decreases or increases reported earnings in order to reduce the volatility in reported earnings from period to period. Income smoothing involves not reporting income in a year of good performance. For example, banks were allowed to create 'secret reserves' for income smoothing.

Big bath strategy refers to earnings management by taking as many write-offs as possible in a period of markedly poor performance.

Income smoothing refers to decreasing or increasing reported earnings in order to reduce the volatility in reported earnings from period to period.

Earnings management and accrual system of accounting

Under accrual accounting, assets and liabilities are carried in the balance sheet at estimated values. In many situations, those estimates depend on the management's perception about uncertainties that surround the inflow or outflow of economic benefits. For example, the carrying amount of receivables in the balance sheet depends on management's estimate of doubtful debts. Moreover, the concepts of allocation and accrual are at the heart of accrual accounting. It is difficult to set out the objective criteria for the selection of the accrual policy. For example, it is difficult to set out the objective criteria to decide the period over which an item of PP&E should be depreciated. Users and auditors can seldom question the bases selected by the management for allocations of expenditure over more than one accounting period. Therefore, the accrual accounting system provides enough opportunities for managing earnings. The most common methods for earnings management are as follows:

The accrual accounting system provides enough opportunities for managing earnings.

1. Under- or over-valuation of inventory.
2. Under- or over-provisioning for depreciation.
3. Amortisation of expenses over a shorter or longer period.
4. Under- or over-provisioning for doubtful debts.
5. Under- or over-provisioning for liabilities.
6. Advance recognition of revenue or deferment of revenue recognition.
7. Derecognition of liabilities on the strength of dubious transactions.
8. Recognition of assets on the strength of dubious transactions.

Safeguards against earnings management

External audit: It is mandatory for limited liability companies and some other types of entities in which public money is invested to get their financial statements audited by a qualified auditor or by a firm of qualified auditors. The auditor asserts whether the financial statements presents a true and fair view of financial position, financial performance, and cash flows.

Accounting standards: Accounting standards aim at minimising opportunities for earnings management by narrowing down the choice of accounting principles and methods and by stipulating detailed conditions for adopting a particular accounting principle or method that has the potential for misuse.

To safeguard stakeholders' interest from earning management, the Companies Act requires directors to report deviations from accounting standards and reasons for such deviations.

Audit committee: Audit committee is another device for minimising the scope for earnings management. Audit committee is a subcommittee of the Board of Directors of a limited liability company. The committee consists of independent directors only. Independent directors are non-executive directors not having any pecuniary relationship with the company. The audit committee is expected to take an independent view on accounting policies. Moreover, the committee provides a communication channel to auditors, thus enhancing the independence of auditors, and consequently, the audit quality.

Director's responsibility statement: The Companies Act requires directors to report deviations from accounting standards and reasons for such deviations. In India, the Companies Act, 2013 stipulates that the Board of Director's report should include a director's responsibility statement. The statement should indicate the following:

In India, the Companies Act, 2013 stipulates that the Board of Director's report should include a director's responsibility statement.

(a) In the preparation of the annual accounts, the applicable accounting standards had been followed along with proper explanation relating to material departures.
(b) The directors had selected such accounting policies and applied them consistently and made judgements and estimates that are reasonable and prudent so as to give a true and fair view of the state of affairs of the company at the end of the financial year, and of the profit and loss of the company for that period.
(c) The directors had taken proper and sufficient care for the maintenance of adequate accounting records in accordance with the provisions of this Act for safeguarding the assets of the company and for preventing and detecting fraud and other irregularities.
(d) The directors had prepared the annual accounts on a going concern basis.

Assertions by directors in the responsibility statement provide a kind of safeguard, particularly when the Board of Directors is a balanced board. A board is balanced when the proportion of non-executive directors is such that the balance of strength is not tilted towards executive directors. It is expected that a balanced board will ensure that the assertions are true.

Certification by CEO and CFO: Certification by CEO and CFO to the Board of Directors about compliance of accounting standards, efficiency and effectiveness of the internal control system, and efficiency and effectiveness of the system that generates information for disclosures in financial statements acts as a safeguard against earnings management. SEBI (Listing Obligations and Disclosure Requirements) Regulation requires such certification.

Potential red flags: An analyst should develop the skill of identifying red flags. The following are some of the common red flags:

1. Unexplained change in accounting policy.
2. Unusual increase in accruals, including receivables, inventory, creditors and depreciation.
3. An increasing gap between reported earnings and cash flow from operations.
4. An increasing gap between a firm's reported income and its taxable income.
5. Increase in securitisation and unusual short-term financing.
6. Large fourth-quarter adjustments.
7. Qualified audit opinion.
8. Change in external or internal auditor.
9. Increase in related party transactions.

An analyst should examine in detail the accounting policy and its implementation to form a judgement on the quality of earnings. Red flags only indicate the potential for noise and distortions in reported earnings.

In case of doubt about the quality of reported earnings, an analyst should examine the information provided in the annual report as a part of the financial statements, and also, the information provided outside the financial statements. He should further investigate any inconsistency noticed in the information provided in different parts of the annual report. It may be a good idea to adjust reported earning with reference to notes, audit report, and reconciliation between reported earnings and cash flow from the operations presented in the cash flow statement.

15.3 VERTICAL ANALYSIS (COMMON-SIZE ANALYSIS)

Vertical analysis requires preparation of common-size financial statements, which present each line item as a percentage of some measure of the size of the firm.

Vertical analysis requires preparation of common-size financial statements, which present each line item as a percentage of some measure of the size of the firm. For a balance sheet, each line item is expressed as a percentage of total amounts of assets, which is equal to the total amounts of liabilities plus equity. For the statement of profit and loss, each line item is expressed as a percentage of the total income. Common-size financial statements provide an insight into the changes in the capital structure of an entity, and also, the changes into relative size of the components of assets, income and expenses. They are prepared as a first step in analysing financial statements of a firm. They are used for trend analysis, and also, to compare the financial statements of two or more companies.

15.3.1 Insights from Vertical Analysis

The limitation of the vertical analysis is that it fails to provide an understanding of the impact of differences in the size of the companies, as common-size statements do not reflect the size of the company.

A meaningful analysis of common-size statements requires understanding the business environment in which the entity operates and the strategy of the entity. For example, the capital structure of an entity depends not only on its past performance but also on the financial strategy of the company. Similarly, for an entity, which outsources a significant part of its manufacturing activities, the proportion of PP&E in total assets should be lower than that of another entity which internally manufactures most of its products. Advertising expense (as a proportion of total expenses) of an entity which relies on the strategy of massive sales promotion through advertisements is likely to be higher than that of another entity which relies more on its salesforce to promote its products. Comparing common–size financial statements of a company with peers and examining the reasons for the differences in assets, liabilities, incomes and expenses provide an insight into the strategy of the competitors. However, the limitation of the analysis is that it fails to provide an understanding of the impact of differences in the size of the companies on the composition of assets, liabilities, incomes and expenses, as common-size statements do not reflect the size of the company.

EXAMPLE 15.1 (Vertical analysis)

The following are the stand-alone balance sheets of three companies as of March 31, 2021. We shall prepare the common size balance sheet based on figures in those three balance sheets.

	Apollo Tyres Limited 2021/03/31 (Amount ₹ Crores)	*Ceat Limited 2021/03/31 (Amount ₹ Crores)*	*Apollo Hospitals Enterprises Limited 2021/03/31 (Amount ₹ Crores)*
A. ASSETS			
1. Non-current Assets			
(a) Property, Plant, and Equipment	9,672	4,556	4,307
(b) Capital work-in-progress	1,030	703	197
(c) Right-of-use assets	524	108	589
(d) Goodwill	—	—	84
(e) Other intangible assets	38	99	58

(Contd...)

	Apollo Tyres Limited 2021/03/31 (Amount ₹ Crores)	Ceat Limited 2021/03/31 (Amount ₹ Crores)	Apollo Hospitals Enterprises Limited 2021/03/31 (Amount ₹ Crores)
(f) Intangible assets under development	—	25	22
(g) Financial assets:			
(i) Investments	2410	118	1,135
(ii) Loans	—	8	31
(iii) Other financial assets	369	1	97
(h) Non-current tax assets (net)		57	125
(i) Other non-current assets	223	46	47
Total non-current assets	14,266	5,721	6,692
2. Current Assets			
(a) Inventories	2,077	1,112	210
(b) Financial assets:			
(i) Investments	90	—	956
(ii) Trade Receivables	732	922	1,204
(iii) Cash and cash equivalents	226	20	239
(iv) Bank balances other than (iii) above	1,174	6	169
(v) Loans	—	—	5
(vi) Other financial assets	290	41	57
(c) Contract assets	—	—	75
(d) Other current assets	309	83	122
Total current assets	4,898	2,184	3,037
Total Assets (1+2)	19,164	7,905	9,729
B. EQUITY AND LIABILITIES			
1. Equity			
(a) Share capital	64	41	72
(b) Other equity	9,409	3,124	5,130
Total equity	9,473	3,165	5,202
Liabilities			
2. Non-current liabilities			
(a) Financial liabilities			
(i) Borrowings	3,662	1,340	1,965
(ii) Lease liabilities	465	67	736
(iii) Other financial liabilities	3	13	7
(b) Provisions	49	45	
(c) Deferred tax liability (net)	674	266	298
(d) Other non-current liabilities	510	—	
Total non-current liabilities	5,363	1,731	3006
3. Current Liabilities			
(a) Financial liabilities			
(i) Borrowings	100	1	—
(ii) Lease liabilities	—	48	32
(iii) Trade payables	1,929	1,942	849
(iv) Other financial liabilities	1,817	756	460
(b) Other current liabilities	219	109	82
(c) Provisions	192	108	98
(d) Current tax liabilities (net)	71	45	
Total current liabilities	4,328	3009	1,521
Total equity and Liabilities (1+2+3)	19,164	7,905	9729

(Contd...)

Table 15.2 below presents Common-size balance sheets of Apollo Tyres, Ceat and Apollo Hospitals:

TABLE 15.2 Common-size Balance Sheets of Apollo Tyres, Ceat and Apollo Hospitals

	Apollo Tyres Limited 2021/03/31 (Amount ₹ Crores)	*Ceat Limited 2021/03/31 (Amount ₹ Crores)*	*Apollo Hospitals Enterprises Limited 2021/03/31 (Amount ₹ Crores)*
A. ASSETS			
1. Non-Current Assets			
(a) Property, Plant, and Equipment	0.5047	0.5763	0.4427
(b) Capital work-in-progress	0.0537	0.0889	0.0202
(c) Right-of-use assets	0.0273	0.0137	0.0605
(d) Goodwill			0.0086
(e) Other intangible assets	0.0020	0.0125	0.0060
(f) Intangible assets under development		0.0032	0.0023
(g) Financial assets:			
(i) Investments	0.1258	0.0149	0.1167
(ii) Loans		0.0010	0.0032
(iii) Other financial assets	0.0193	0.0001	0.0100
(h) Non-current tax assets (net)	0.0000	0.0072	0.0128
(i) Other non-current assets	0.0116	0.0058	0.0048
Total non-current assets	0.7444	0.7237	0.6878
2. Current Assets			
(a) Inventories	0.1084	0.1407	0.0216
(b) Financial assets:			
(i) Investments	0.0047		0.0983
(ii) Trade Receivables	0.0382	0.1166	0.1238
(iii) Cash and cash equivalents	0.0118	0.0025	0.0246
(iv) Bank balances other than (iii) above	0.0613	0.0008	0.0174
(v) Loans			0.0005
(vi) Other financial assets	0.0151	0.0052	0.0059
(c) Contract assets			0.0077
(d) Other current assets	0.0161	0.0105	0.0125
Total current assets	0.2556	0.2763	0.3122
Total Assets (1+2)	1.0000	1.0000	1.0000
B. EQUITY AND LIABILITIES			
1. Equity			
(a) Share capital	0.0033	0.0052	0.0074
(b) Other equity	0.4910	0.3952	0.5273
Total equity	0.4943	0.4004	0.5347
Liabilities			
2. Non-current liabilities			
(a) Financial liabilities			
(i) Borrowings	0.1910	0.1695	0.2020
(ii) Lease liabilities	0.0243	0.0085	0.0757
(iii) Other financial liabilities	0.0002	0.0016	0.0007
(b) Provisions	0.0026	0.0057	0.0000
(c) Deferred tax liability (net)	0.0352	0.0336	0.0306
(d) Other non-current liabilities	0.0266		
Total non-current liabilities	0.2798	0.2190	0.3090
3. Current Liabilities			
(a) Financial liabilities			
(i) Borrowings	0.0052	0.0001	
(ii) Lease liabilities		0.0061	0.0033

(Contd...)

	Apollo Tyres Limited 2021/03/31 (Amount ₹ Crores)	Ceat Limited 2021/03/31 (Amount ₹ Crores)	Apollo Hospitals Enterprises Limited 2021/03/31 (Amount ₹ Crores)
(iii) Trade payables	0.1007	0.2457	0.0873
(iv) Other financial liabilities	0.0948	0.0956	0.0473
(b) Other current liabilities	0.0114	0.0138	0.0084
(c) Provisions	0.0100	0.0137	0.0101
(d) Current tax liabilities (net)	0.0037	0.0057	
Total current liabilities	0.2258	0.3806	0.1563
Total equity and Liabilities (1+2+3)	1.0000	1.0000	1.0000

When analysts prepare common size balance sheets of an entity for sufficiently long period (say, five years), he/she can develop an idea about the changing strategy of the company by examining the composition of assets and liabilities. However, that understanding is not sufficient for forecasting the future cash flows. Comparison of common-size balance sheets of comparable companies provides an idea about the difference in their strategies.

Vertical analysis is the first step in analysing financial statements.

Analyses of common-size balance sheets of an entity for sufficiently long period, an understanding of the changing strategy of the company can be developed. However, that is not sufficient for forecasting the future cash flows.

Comparison of common-size balance sheets of comparable companies provides an idea about the difference in their strategies.

Common-size statements of profit and loss

Common-size statement of profit and loss is prepared by considering revenue (or total income) as 100 and expressing other items as a percentage of revenue (or total income).

EXAMPLE 15.2 (Common size statement of profit and loss)

The following are the statements of profit of loss of Apollo Tyres, Ceat and Apollo Hospital:

	Apollo Tyres 2020–2021 (Amount ₹ Crores)	Ceat Tyres Limited 2020–2021 (Amount ₹ Crores)	Apollo Hospitals Enterprise Limited 2020–2021 (Amount ₹ Crores)
1. Revenue from Operations			
Revenue	11,355	7,573	9,153
Other operating income	378	—	—
	11,733	7,573	9,153
2. Other Income	122	32	18
3. Total Income (1+2)	11,855	7,605	9,171
4. Expenses			
(a) Cost of materials consumed	6,239	4,173	1,330
(b) Purchase of stock-in-trade	695	11	4,155
(c) Change in inventories of finished goods, stock-in-trade, and work-in-progress	7	67	(128)
(d) Employee benefits expense	911	667	1,275
(e) Finance costs	379	173	344
(f) Depreciation and amortisation expense	713	340	436
(g) Other expenses	1,848	1,681	1,573
Total expenses	10,792	7,112	8,985
5. Profit Before Exceptional Items and Tax(3–4)	1,063	493	186
6. Exceptional Items	11	34	(9)
7. Profit Before Tax (5–6)	1,052	459	177
8. Tax Expense			
(a) Current tax	190	37	62
(b) Deferred tax	139	9	10
Total	329	46	72
9. Net Profit for the Year (7–8)	723	413	105

Table 15.3 below presents Common-size statements of profit and loss of Apollo Tyres, Ceat and Apollo Hospitals Common-size Statements of Profit and Loss:

TABLE 15.3 Common-size Statements of Profit and Loss of Apollo Tyres, Ceat and Apollo Hospitals Common-size Statements of Profit and Loss

	Apollo Tyres 2020–2021 (Amount ₹ Crores)	*Ceat Tyres Limited 2020–2021 (Amount ₹ Crores)*	*Apollo Hospitals Enterprise Limited 2020–2021 (Amount ₹ Crores)*
1. Revenue from Operations			
Revenue	1.0000	1.0000	1.0000
Other operating income	0.0333	—	
	1.0333	1.0000	1.0000
2. Other Income	0.0107	0.0042	0.0020
3. Total Income (1+2)	1.0440	1.0042	1.0020
4. Expenses			
(a) Cost of materials consumed	0.5494	0.5510	0.1453
(b) Purchase of stock-in-trade	0.0612	0.0015	0.4539
(c) Change in inventories of finished goods, stock-in-trade, and work-in-progress	0.0006	0.0088	−0.0140
(d) Employee benefits expense	0.0802	0.0881	0.1393
(e) Finance costs	0.0334	0.0228	0.0376
(f) Depreciation and amortisation expense	0.0628	0.0449	0.0476
(g) Other expenses	0.1627	0.2220	0.1719
Total expenses	0.9504	0.9391	0.9816
5. Profit Before Exceptional Items and Tax(3−4)	0.0936	0.0651	0.0203
6. Exceptional Items	0.0010	0.0045	−0.0010
7. Profit Before Tax (5−6)	0.0926	0.0606	0.0193
8. Tax Expense			
(a) Current tax	0.0167	0.0049	0.0068
(b) Deferred tax	0.0122	0.0012	0.0011
Total	0.0290	0.0061	0.0079
9. Net Profit for the Year (7−8)	0.0637	0.0545	0.0115

In preparing the common-size statements of profit and loss, we have considered revenue as 100 and expressed every other item as a percentage of revenue. We may observe that the cost structure and profitability (net profit as a percentage of revenue) are significantly different from Apollo Tyres and Ceat Limited, which manufacture tyre.

Horizontal analysis expresses financial statement items as an index relative to the base year. The index for every line item in the financial statements of the base year, which is the earliest year of the years under analysis, is 100.

Indexed financial statement provides an understanding of how financial statement items have changed over time.

15.4 HORIZONTAL ANALYSIS (TREND ANALYSIS)

Horizontal analysis expresses financial statement items as an index relative to the base year. The index for every line item in the financial statements of the base year, which is the earliest year of the years under analysis, is 100. Indexed financial statement provides an understanding of how financial statement items have changed over time. Calculation of index is not possible if the base year amount is zero. Therefore, in order to develop the index, analysts take the amount of ₹1 for the base year. An analyst uses indexed balance sheets and indexed statements of profit and loss to get an insight into the trend in the financial position and performance of the firm, which helps him/her to plan financial analysis.

As an example, we have considered the statement of profit and loss of Apollo Hospitals for past five years (including 202–21) for horizontal analysis.

EXAMPLE 15.3 (Horizontal analysis)

Statements of Profit and Loss of Apollo Hospitals (Amount ₹' Crores)

Particulars	*2020–2021*	*2019–2020*	*2018–2019*	*2017–2018*	*2016–2017*
1. Revenue from Operations					
Revenue	9,153	9,794	8,337	7,183	6,442
Other operating income	—	—	—	—	—
	9153	9,794	8,337	7,183	6,442
2. Other Income	18	11	12	13	26
3. Total Income (1+2)	9,171	9,805	8,349	7,196	6,468
4. Expenses					
(a) Cost of materials consumed	1,330	1,532	1,392	1,268	1,179
(b) Purchase of stock-in-trade	4,155	3,754	3,049	2,615	2,229
(c) Change in inventories of finished goods, stock-in-trade, and work-in-progress	(128)	(104)	(72)	(81)	(47)
(d) Employee benefits expense	1,275	1,519	1,295	1,118	942
(e) Finance costs	344	426	268	240	200
(f) Depreciation and amortisation expense	436	482	300	272	241
(g) Other expenses	1,573	1,678	1,654	1,433	1,365
Total expenses	8,985	9,287	7,886	6,865	6,109
5. Profit Before Exceptional Items and Tax(3−4)	186	518	463	330	359
6. Exceptional Items	(9)	164	—	—	—
7. Profit Before Tax (5−6)	177	682	463	330	359
8. Tax Expense					
(a) Current tax	62	118	111	74	76
(b) Deferred tax	10	94	49	23	(2)
Total	72	212	160	97	74
9. Net Profit for the Year (7−8)	105	470	303	233	285

Table 15.4 below presents indexed statements of profit and loss of Apollo Hospitals

TABLE 15.4 Indexed Statements of Profit and Loss of Apollo Hospitals

Particulars	*2020–2021*	*2019–2020*	*2018–2019*	*2017–2018*	*2016–2017*
1. Revenue from Operations					
Revenue	1.42	1.52	1.29	1.12	1.00
2. Other Income	0.69	0.42	0.46	0.50	1.00
3. Total Income (1+2)	1.42	1.52	1.29	1.11	1.00
4. Expenses					
(a) Cost of materials consumed	1.13	1.30	1.18	1.08	1.00
(b) Purchase of stock-in-trade	1.86	1.68	1.37	1.17	1.00
(c) Change in inventories of finished goods, stock-in-trade, and work-in-progress	2.72	2.21	1.53	1.72	1.00
(d) Employee benefits expense	1.35	1.61	1.37	1.19	1.00
(e) Finance costs	1.72	2.13	1.34	1.20	1.00
(f) Depreciation and amortisation expense	1.81	2.00	1.24	1.13	1.00
(g) Other expenses	1.15	1.23	1.21	1.05	1.00
Total expenses	1.47	1.52	1.29	1.12	1.00
5. Profit Before Exceptional Items and Tax(3−4)	0.52	1.44	1.29	0.92	1.00
6. Exceptional Items	−9.00	164.00	—	—	—
7. Profit Before Tax (5−6)	0.49	1.90	1.29	0.92	1.00
8. Tax Expense					
(a) Current tax	0.82	1.55	1.46	0.97	1.00
(b) Deferred tax	−5.00	−47.00	−24.50	−11.50	1.00
Total	0.97	2.86	2.16	1.31	1.00
9. Net Profit for the Year (7−8)	0.37	1.65	1.06	0.82	1.00

*Assumed 1 for calculating the percentage.

Horizontal analysis does not tell us the full story. We can develop some understanding of the trend. For example, it is obvious that in terms of overall performance the year 2020–2021 was a pretty bad year, might be due to COVID-19 pandemic. Patients' visit to different hospitals came down sharply. As compared to the base year (2016–2017) the revenue grew by 42 per cent, while expenses grew by 47 per cent. In all other years growth in expenses matched with revenue. We have to analyse financial and non-financial ratios to know the full story.

15.5 FINANCIAL RATIO ANALYSIS–FUNDAMENTALS

For a meaningful analysis, financial ratios should be used in conjunction with non-financial ratios or other non-financial measures of performance in different activities of the firm.

While analysing the performance of a company, which has subsidiaries, it is appropriate to analyse consolidated financial statements.

Financial ratios are extensively used by analysts and managers in a number of metrics that measure the effectiveness of operating and financing decisions of the firm and to predict its future performance and financial position. For a meaningful analysis, financial ratios should be used in conjunction with non-financial ratios or other non-financial measures of performance in different activities of the firm.

While analysing the performance of a company, which has subsidiaries, it is appropriate to analyse consolidated financial statements, as the value of equity of the company depends on the performance of the group, and credit risk of lending to the company increases when the subsidiary is in distress.

The following are the important limitations of accounting measures:

1. Accounting has a bias towards conservatism. Hence, assets are often understated.
2. Different measurement bases (such as, historical cost, fair value, and net realisable value) are used to measure different classes of assets. Accounting figures that represent historical cost are not adjusted for inflation. This causes inconsistency among different figures that appear in financial statements.
3. Accounting principles are inadequate to deal with complex transactions structured by companies.
4. The accrual system of accounting relies much on management's perspective and judgement on the economic impact of transactions and other events. In most situations, no straight jacket objective criteria can be established for deciding the carrying amount of assets and liabilities. For example, in most situations, the choice of the depreciation method for allocating costs of fixed assets over their useful life reflects the firm's preference, rather than the pattern of cash flow that those assets will generate.

A meaningful analysis of financial statements requires adjustments of accounting figures to overcome these limitations. However, care should be taken to ensure that such adjustments do not make computations so complex that the interpretation of results becomes difficult. Care should also be taken those adjustments to figures presented in financial statements are not arbitrary. They should be based on clear understanding of the business and the environment (political, economic, social, and technological) in which it operates.

Trend analysis and cross-sectional analysis

Financial ratios are used for both trend analysis and cross-sectional analysis.

Trend analysis refers to the use of financial ratios to understand the trend, if any, in the financial position and performance of a firm. Ratios based on annual financial results of a particular firm covering more than one accounting years are analysed to understand the trend. It is preferable to analyse financial statements of five years to understand the trend, if any.

Cross-sectional analysis refers to the analysis of the financial position and performance of a firm in comparison to the performance of its peers. Cross-sectional analysis may cover a single period or it may cover more than one period.

Guidelines

The following guidelines may be helpful in analysing financial statements:

1. Ratios by themselves do not provide any insight into the performance of a firm. They help to ask right questions but fail to answer those questions.
2. No inference can be drawn in the absence of a *benchmark ratio*. Trend analysis does not require comparison of actual ratios with benchmark ratios. Selection of appropriate benchmark ratios is important for cross-sectional analysis. Benchmark ratios may be the industry average, or ratios of the firm's immediate competitor or standard ratios set by some industry association or other similar institution. Benchmark ratios should be established carefully. For example, the industry average cannot be used as a benchmark ratio in analysing financial position and performance of a firm, which is the industry leader.
3. Meaningful inferences can be drawn only by comparing ratios of the firm with those of comparable firms. However, it is difficult to define comparability. Comparability between two firms can be established by using a number of parameters. Examples of such parameters include the nature of the business, firm-size, the business environment, and the business strategy. Care should be taken to ensure that the criteria established are appropriate in the given situation and for the given purpose.
4. Consistency should be maintained in selecting the numerator and the denominator of each ratio. In the absence of standard formulas for financial ratios, analyst's report should clearly state the formula used in calculating each ratio.
5. The purpose of financial statement analysis is to develop a *historical perspective* of the operation of the firm. This historical perspective is used to forecast the future performance of the firm. In order to develop the correct historical perspective, non-financial ratios and non-financial information should be used to supplement the financial ratios. Moreover, financial, and non-financial ratios should be integrated with the analyses of the firm's strategy and its environment, both internal and external. Correct historical perspective cannot be developed without such integration.
6. Abnormal years should be excluded from the analysis. The selected period should cover at least a complete business cycle for firms that operate in cyclical industries (e.g., cement and steel).
7. Too many ratios should not be used. A new ratio should be added only if it provides additional insight.
8. The aim should be to be roughly correct. Too much focus on precision might obscure understanding.

15.6 REORGANISING FINANCIAL STATEMENTS

It is important to reorganise financial statements, as some figures that are being used for calculating financial ratios are not directly available from published financial statements.

The most important figures that we aim to derive by reorganising the balance sheet are to derive figures for Net Operating Assets (NOA), and Net Borrowings. The most important figures that we aim to derive by reorganising the statement of profit and loss is to derive the figure for Operating Profit.

It is important to reorganise financial statements, as some figures that are being used for calculating financial ratios are not directly available from published financial statements.

The most important figures that are derived by reorganising the balance sheet are Net Operating Assets (NOA), and Net Borrowings.

15.6.1 Consolidated Financial Statements

We shall provide examples by calculating and analysing financial ratios using consolidated balance sheets and statements of profit and loss of two top Indian tyre companies – MRF Tyres and Apollo Tyres, and Apollo Hospitals for the year 2020–2021. In the following paragraphs, we shall provide a brief overview of consolidated financial statements. The discussion is adequate only for developing an understanding that is necessary for financial statement analysis.

Group

A group consists of the parent and its subsidiaries. An investee is a subsidiary of the investor (parent) if it controls the investee. Investor controls an investee by holding more than 50 per cent of its voting rights. However, holding majority voting rights is necessary to control the investee. Investor can secure control by other means, such as, through shareholder agreement.

A group consists of the parent and its subsidiaries. An investee is a subsidiary of the investor (parent) if it controls the investee.

Consolidated financial statements are prepared by considering the group as a single economic entity.

Consolidated financial statements are prepared by considering the group as a single economic entity.

Consolidated financial statements also incorporate the financial statements of associates and joint venture. An investee is an associate of the investor who has the capability to significantly influence the operating and financial decisions of the investee. There is a rebuttable presumption that the investor has the capability to significantly influence the investee's operating and financial decisions if it holds 20 per cent or more of the investee's voting rights.

In a joint venture, the investors (called, joint venturers) agree to take key decisions jointly irrespective of their respective shareholding.

Consolidated financial statements also incorporate the financial statements of associates and joint venture.

Consolidation of financial statements of subsidiaries

In stand-alone balance sheet of the parent, investment in a subsidiary is presented as a separate line item. It is usually measured at cost, although entities have an option to measure that at fair value. In calculating financial ratios using figures from stand-alone financial statements, investment in subsidiary is treated like any other investment in a financial asset. Investment in subsidiaries disappears in consolidated balance sheet, as the figure against each line item is the total of the carrying amount of that item in the balance sheet of the parent and its subsidiaries, adjusted for claims of group companies against each other. In case the parent holds less than 100 per cent shares of the subsidiary, the claim of non-controlling shareholders in the net worth of the subsidiary is presented as a separate line item with the equity in the consolidated balance sheet. No special treatment is required for non-controlling shareholders' interest. The total book value of equity is used for calculating financial rations.

In the consolidated statements of profit and loss, non-controlling shareholders' share in the reported profit is presented separately. No special treatment is required for the same.

Consolidation of financial statements of associates and joint ventures

In stand-alone balance sheet of the parent, investment in an associate (joint venture) is presented as a separate line item. It is usually measured at cost, although entities have an option to measure that at fair value. In calculating financial ratios using figures from stand-alone financial statements, investment in an associate (joint venture) is treated like any other investment in a financial asset.

In the consolidated balance sheet investment in associates are carried at cost, adjusted for the parent's share in the change in the associate's net worth post-acquisition of shares, and reduced by the dividend received. In the consolidated statements of profit and loss, parent's share in the profit/loss of the associate (joint venture) is presented as a separate line item.

In calculating financial ratios, investment in an associate (joint venture) is considered as operating asset. However, in calculating turnover ratios investment in associate (joint venture) is excluded from net operation assets, as revenue does not include associate's revenue. For the same reason, in calculating operating margin, share in profit/loss of associate is excluded from the operating profit. Both operating margin and turnover ratio are discussed later.

We shall use the consolidated financial statements of MRF Tyres Limited, Apollo Tyres Limited, and Apollo Hospitals Enterprises Limited for the year 2020–2021. MRF Tyres and Apollo Tyres are two top tyre manufacturing companies in India. Apollo Hospitals is a top Indian company in the health care sector. MRF Tyres and Apollo Tyres are comparable because they are in the same industry and their sizes (in terms of value of total assets) are comparable. Apollo Hospital is not comparable with those two companies, as it operates in a different industry. We have selected it to get an insight into how its financial ratios differ from companies operating in tyre industry.

Consolidated balance sheet of MRF Tyres Limited

	MRF Tyres 2021/03/31 (Amount ₹' Crores)	MRF Tyres 2020/03/31 (Amount ₹' Crores)
A. ASSETS		
1. Non-current Assets		
(a) Property, Plant, and Equipment	9,416	8,840
(b) Capital work-in-progress	1,002	1,741
(c) Right-of-use assets	—	—
(d) Goodwill	—	—
(e) Other intangible assets	24	28
(f) Intangible assets under development	—	—
(g) Financial assets:		
(i) Investments	1,130	6
(ii) Loans	3	12
(iii) Other financial assets	94	97
(h) Non-current tax assets (net)	252	232
(i) Other non-current assets	293	334
Total non-current assets	12,214	11,290
2. Current Assets		
(a) Inventories	2,939	2,905
(b) Financial assets:		
(i) Investments	4,744	1,514
(ii) Trade Receivables	2,254	2,299
(iii) Cash and cash equivalents	167	1,179
(iv) Bank balances other than (iii) above	3	3
(v) Loans	7	3
(vi) Other financial assets	61	53
(c) Contract assets	—	—
(d) Other current assets	193	196
Total current assets	10,368	8152
Total Assets (1+2)	22,582	19,442
B. EQUITY AND LIABILITIES		
1. Equity		
(a) Share capital	4	4
(b) Other equity	13,410	12,211
(c) Non-controlling interest	—	—
Total equity	13,414	12,215
Liabilities		
2. Non-current liabilities		
(a) Financial liabilities		
(i) Borrowings	812	779
(ii) Lease liabilities	313	327
(iii) Other financial liabilities	—	—
(b) Provisions	212	190
(c) Deferred tax liability (net)	380	429
(d) Other non-current liabilities	184	250
Total non-current liabilities	1,901	1,975
3. Current Liabilities		
(a) Financial liabilities		
(i) Borrowings	915	731
(ii) Lease liabilities	—	—
(iii) Trade payables	3,441	1,905

(Contd...)

	MRF Tyres 2021/03/31 (Amount ₹' Crores)	MRF Tyres 2020/03/31 (Amount ₹' Crores)
(iv) Other financial liabilities	662	732
(b) Other current liabilities	2,045	1,727
(c) Provisions	200	154
(d) Current tax liabilities (net)	4	3
Total current liabilities	7267	5252
Total liabilities	9168	7227
Total equity and Liabilities (1+2+3)	22,582	19,442
DETAILS OTHER NON-FINANCIAL ASSETS		
Operating	486	530
Non-operating	—	—
Total	486	530
DETAILS OF OTHER FINANCIAL ASSETS		
Operating	80	150
Non-operating	75	—
Total	155	150
DETAILS OF OTHER NON-FINANCIAL LIABILITIES		
Operating	2,229	1,977
Non-operating	—	—
Total	2,229	1,977
DETAILS OF OTHER FINANCIAL LIABILITIES		
Current portion of long-term borrowings	267	344
Accrued interest	26	43
Operating	369	345
Total	662	732

Consolidated balance sheets of Apollo Tyres Limited

	Apollo Tyres 2021/03/31 (Amount ₹' Crores)	Apollo Tyres 2020/03/31 (Amount ₹' Crores)
A. ASSETS		
1. Non-current Assets		
(a) Property, Plant, and Equipment	14,524	13,473
(b) Capital work-in-progress	1,107	1,642
(c) Right-of-use assets	911	1022
(d) Goodwill	220	213
(e) Other intangible assets	764	739
(f) Intangible assets under development	—	—
(g) Financial assets:		
(i) Investments in associates and joint ventures	5	5
(ii) Other investments	15	15
(iii) Loans	—	—
(iv) Other financial assets	379	243
(h) Non-current tax assets (net)	—	—
(i) Deferred tax asset (net)	219	45
(ii) Other non-current assets	231	371
Total non-current assets	18,375	17,769
2. Current Assets		
(a) Inventories	3,319	3,206
(b) Financial assets:		
(i) Investments	90	—

(Contd...)

	Apollo Tyres 2021/03/31 (Amount ₹' Crores)	Apollo Tyres 2020/03/31 (Amount ₹' Crores)
(ii) Trade Receivables	1,381	940
(iii) Cash and cash equivalents	971	739
(iv) Bank balances other than (iii) above	1,174	11
(v) Loans	—	—
(vi) Other financial assets	324	108
(c) Contract assets	—	—
(d) Other current assets	429	477
Total current assets	7,688	5,481
Total Assets (1+2)	26,063	23,250
B. EQUITY AND LIABILITIES		
1. Equity		
(a) Share capital	63	57
(b) Other equity	11,380	9,873
Total equity	11,443	9,930
Liabilities		
2. Non-current liabilities		
(a) Financial liabilities		
(i) Borrowings	4,808	5,148
(ii) Lease liabilities	735	822
(iii) Other financial liabilities	3	3
(b) Provisions	156	168
(c) Deferred tax liability (net)	921	748
(d) Other non-current liabilities	1,267	718
Total non-current liabilities	7,890	7,607
3. Current Liabilities		
(a) Financial liabilities		
(i) Borrowings	303	1,432
(ii) Lease liabilities	—	—
(iii) Trade payables	2,807	2,309
(iv) Other financial liabilities	2,735	1,360
(b) Other current liabilities	503	266
(c) Provisions	288	274
(d) Current tax liabilities (net)	94	71
Total current liabilities	6,730	5,713
Total liabilities	14,620	13,320
Total equity and Liabilities (1+2+3)	26,063	23,250
DETAILS OTHER NON-FINANCIAL ASSETS		
Operating	660	848
Non-operating	—	—
Total	660	848
DETAILS OF OTHER FINANCIAL ASSETS		
Operating	703	351
Non-operating	—	—
Total	703	351
DETAILS OF OTHER NON-FINANCIAL LIABILITIES		
Operating	1,770	984
Non-operating	—	—
Total	1,770	984
DETAILS OF OTHER FINANCIAL LIABILITIES		
Current portion of long-term borrowings	1,322	184
Accrued interest	153	75
Operating	1,263	1,104
Total	2,738	1,363

(Contd...)

Consolidated balance sheet of Apollo Hospitals Enterprises Limited

	Apollo Hospitals 2021/03/31 (Amount ₹' Crores)	Apollo Hospitals 2020/03/31 (Amount ₹' Crores)
A. ASSETS		
1. Non-current Assets		
(a) Property, Plant, and Equipment	5,350	5,404
(b) Capital work-in-progress	212	209
(c) Right-of-use assets	983	1,647
(d) Investment property	5	6
(e) Goodwill	375	346
(f) Other intangible assets	64	28
(g) Intangible assets under development	22	27
(h) Financial assets:		
(i) Investments in equity accounted entities (associates and joint ventures)	308	324
(ii) Other investments	37	35
(iii) Loans	18	23
(iv) Other financial assets	144	234
Deferred tax assets (net)	25	50
(i) Non-current tax assets (net)	171	281
(j) Other non-current assets	61	77
Total non-current assets	7,775	8,691
2. Current Assets		
(a) Inventories	250	738
(b) Financial assets:		
(i) Investments	998	75
(ii) Trade Receivables	1,331	1,027
(iii) Cash and cash equivalents	425	381
(iv) Bank balances other than (iii) above	299	86
(v) Loans	5	7
(vi) Other financial assets	60	102
(c) Contract assets	101	66
(d) Other current assets	172	165
Total current assets	3,641	2,647
Total Assets (1+2)	11,417	11,338
B. EQUITY AND LIABILITIES		
1. Equity		
(a) Share capital	72	70
(b) Other equity	4,530	3,270
(c) Non-controlling interest	200	130
Total equity	4,802	3,470
Liabilities		
2. Non-current liabilities		
(a) Financial liabilities		
(i) Borrowings	2,473	2,852
(ii) Lease liabilities	1,230	1,868
(iii) Other financial liabilities	590	507
(b) Provisions	22	10
(c) Deferred tax liability (net)	261	294
(d) Other non-current liabilities	—	—
Total non-current liabilities	4,576	5,531
3. Current Liabilities		
(a) Financial liabilities		
(i) Borrowings	21	498
(ii) Lease liabilities	70	158
(iii) Trade payables	1,161	908

(Contd...)

	Apollo Hospitals 2021/03/31 (Amount ₹' Crores)	Apollo Hospitals 2020/03/31 (Amount ₹' Crores)
(iv) Other financial liabilities	551	461
(b) Other current liabilities	127	189
(c) Provisions	109	123
(d) Current tax liabilities (net)	—	—
Total current liabilities	2039	2337
Total liabilities	6615	7868
Total equity and Liabilities (1+2+3)	11,417	11,338
DETAILS OTHER NON-FINANCIAL ASSETS		
Operating	233	242
Non-operating	—	—
Total	233	242
DETAILS OF OTHER FINANCIAL ASSETS		
Operating	204	336
Non-operating	—	—
Total	204	336
DETAILS OF OTHER NON-FINANCIAL LIABILITIES		
Operating	127	189
Non-operating	—	—
Total	127	189
DETAILS OF OTHER FINANCIAL LIABILITIES		
Current portion of long-term borrowings	364	246
Accrued interest	17	35
Operating	760	687
Total	1,141	968

The following are the consolidated statements of profit and loss of MRF Tyres, Apollo Tyres, and Apollo Hospitals for the year 2021

	MRF Tyres 2020–2021 (Amount ₹' Crores)	Apollo Tyres 2020–2021 (Amount ₹' Crores)	Apollo Hospitals 2020–2021 (Amount ₹' Crores)
1. Revenue From Operations			
Revenue	16,163	16,955	10,560
Other operating income	—	442	—
	16,163	17,397	10,560
2. Other Income	210	129	45
3. Total Income (1+2)	16,373	17,526	10,605
4. Expenses			
(a) Cost of materials consumed	8,952	7,065	1,623
(b) Purchase of stock-in-trade	16	2,009	4,187
(c) Change in inventories of finished goods, stock-in-trade, and work-in-progress	354	320	(125)
(d) Employee benefits expense	1,415	2,513	1,601
(e) Finance costs	275	443	449
(f) Depreciation and amortisation expense	1,141	1,315	573
(g) Other expenses	2,483	2,692	2,137
Total expenses	14,636	16,357	10445
5. Profit Before Exceptional Items and Tax(3–4)	1,737	1169	160
6. Exceptional Items	—	(608)	61
7. Profit Before Tax (5+6)	1,737	561	221

(*Contd...*)

	MRF Tyres 2020–2021 (Amount ₹' Crores)	Apollo Tyres 2020–2021 (Amount ₹' Crores)	Apollo Hospitals 2020–2021 (Amount ₹' Crores)
8. Tax Expense			
(a) Current tax	498	225	76
(b) Deferred tax	(38)	(14)	9
Total tax expense	460	211	85
9. Net Profit For The Year (7–8)	1,277	350	136
10. Share in the profit/(loss) of associates and joint venture	—	—	1
11. Net profit for the year (9+10)	1,277	350	137
DETAILS OF OTHER INCOME			
Income from investments	157	83	30
Foreign exchange difference (net)	—	26	(4)
Other	53	20	19
Total other income	210	129	45

15.6.2 Reorganising Balance Sheet

Revisiting accounting equation

Assets = Equity + Liabilities

Assets can be classified into operating and non-operating assets. Operating assets are used in the operation of the firm. Non-operating assets are investments outside the business.

Liabilities can be classified into borrowings and operating liabilities. Borrowings result from financing decisions, and operating liabilities arise from operating decisions.

We may write:

(Operating Assets + Investments) = Equity + (Borrowings + Operating Liabilities)

Transposing,

(Operating Assets – Operating Liabilities) = Equity + (Borrowings – Investments)

Thus,

Net Operating Assets = Equity + Net Borrowings.

Net operating asset (NOA) measures the capital that is invested in the business. Therefore, the terms NOA, invested capital (IC) and capital employed (CE) are used interchangeably.

Net operating asset (NOA) measures the capital that is invested in the business. Therefore, the terms NOA, invested capital (IC) and capital employed (CE) are used interchangeably.

Net borrowings = Borrowings – Investment in financial assets.

Firms invest in property, classified as investment property. However, unless the investment is large, they do not disclose the rent income separately. Therefore, analysts deduct investment property from equity and deduct only investments in financial assets from borrowings to calculate net borrowings. In analysing financial statements, we shall follow this practice. We may write,

NOA = (Equity – Investment property) + (Borrowings – Investment in financial assets)

or

NOA = (Equity – Investment property) + Net borrowings

NOA = (Equity – Investment property) + Net borrowings.

We should look into the details of 'other non-current assets', 'other non-current financial assets', 'other current assets' and 'other current financial asset' in the notes to accounts to identify operating and non-operating assets.

Lease liability is in the nature of borrowings. Therefore, it is included in borrowings.

Table 15.5 below presents the reorganised consolidates balance sheets of MRF Tyres Limited.

TABLE 15.5 Reorganised Consolidates Balance Sheets of MRF Tyres Limited.

	2021/03/31 (₹ Crores)	2020/03/31 (₹ Crores)	Average (₹ Crores)
A. OPERATING ASSETS			
1. Fixed Assets (PP&E, Right-of-Use assets, goodwill, and intangible assets)	9,440	8,868	9153
2. Capital Work-in-progress	1,002	1,741	1372
3. Intangible assets under development	—	—	—
4. Tax assets (current and non-current)	252	232	242
5. Operating current assets (Inventories, trade receivables, cash and cash equivalents, and contract assets)	5,360	6,383	5,872
6. Other operating financial assets (non-current and current)	80	150	115
7. Other operating non-financial assets (non-current and current)	486	530	508
8. Deferred tax asset	—	—	—
Total	16,620	17,904	17262
B. OPERATING LIABILITIES			
1. Provisions (Non-current plus current)	412	344	378
2. Trade payables	3,441	1,905	2,672
3. Other operating liabilities (Non-current plus current)	2,229	1,977	2,103
4. Other operating financial liabilities (Non-current plus current)	369	345	357
5. Current tax liability	4	3	4
6. Deferred tax liability	380	429	405
Total	6,835	5003	5,919
C. NET OPERATING ASSETS (A–B)	9,785	12,901	11,343
D. INVESTMENTS OTHER THAN INVESTMENT PROPERTY			
1. Invoctmont in financial assets other than bank deposits (Non-current plus current)	5,874	1,520	3,697
2. Bank deposits not included in cash and cash equivalents (Non-current plus current)	3	3	3
3. Loans (Non-current plus current)	10	15	13
4. Other non-operating financial assets (Non-current plus current)	75	—	—
Total	5,962	1,538	3,750
E. BORROWINGS AND LEASE LIABILITY			—
1. Borrowings (Non-current borrowings, current borrowing, current portion of long-term borrowings, and interest accrued on the same)	2,020	1,897	1,959
2. Lease liability	313	327	320
Total	2,333	2,224	2,279
F. NET BORROWINGS (E–D)	(3,629)	686	(1,472)
G. EQUITY			
Share of controlling shareholders	13,414	12,215	12,815
Non-controlling interest	—	—	—
Investment property			
Total	13,414	12,215	12,815
G. NET OPERATING ASSETS (F+G)	9,785	12,901	11,343

Table 15.6 below presents the reorganised consolidates balance sheets of Apollo Tyres Limited.

TABLE 15.6 Reorganised Consolidates Balance Sheets of Apollo Tyres Limited.

	2021/03/31 (₹ Crores)	2020/03/31 (₹ Crores)	Average (₹ Crores)
A. OPERATING ASSETS			
1. Fixed Assets (PP&E, Right-of-Use assets, goodwill, and intangible assets)	16,419	15,448	15,934
2. Capital Work-in-progress	1,107	1,642	1,375
3. Intangible assets under development	—	—	—
4. Tax assets (current and non-current)	—	—	—
5. Operating current assets (Inventories, trade receivables, cash and cash equivalents, and contract assets)	5,671	4,885	5,278
6. Other operating financial assets (non-current and current)	703	351	527
7. Other operating non-financial assets (non-current and current)	660	848	754
8. Deferred tax asset	219	45	132
9. Investments in associates and joint ventures	5	5	5
Total	24,784	23,224	24,005
B. OPERATING LIABILITIES			
1. Provisions (Non-current plus current)	444	442	443
2. Trade payables	2,807	2,309	2,558
3. Other operating liabilities (Non-current plus current)	1,770	984	1,377
4. Other operating financial liabilities (Non-current plus current)	1,263	1,104	1,183
5. Current tax liability	94	71	83
6. Deferred tax liability	921	748	835
Total	7,299	5,658	6,479
C. NET OPERATING ASSETS (A–B)	17,485	17,566	17,526
D. INVESTMENTS OTHER THAN INVESTMENT PROPERTY			
1. Investment in financial assets other than bank deposits (Non-current plus current)	105	15	60
2. Bank deposits not included in cash and cash equivalents (Non-current plus current)	1,174	11	593
3. Loans (Non-current plus current)	—	—	—
4. Other non-operating financial assets (Non-current plus current)	—	—	—
Total	1,279	26	653
E. BORROWINGS AND LEASE LIABILITY			
1.Borrowings (Non-current borrowings, current borrowing, current portion of long-term borrowings, and interest accrued on the same)	6,586	6,840	6,713
2. Lease liability	735	822	779
Total	7,321	7,662	7,492
F. NET BORROWINGS (E–D)	6,042	7,636	6,839
G. EQUITY			
Share of controlling shareholders	11,443	9,930	10,687
Non-controlling interest	—	—	—
Investment property	—	—	—
Total	11,443	9,930	10,687
G. NET OPERATING ASSETS (F+G)	17,485	17,566	17,526

Table 15.7 below presents the reorganised consolidates balance sheets of Apollo Hospitals Enterprises Limited.

TABLE 15.7 Reorganised Consolidates Balance Sheets of Apollo Hospitals Enterprises Limited.

	2021/03/31 (₹ Crores)	*2020/03/31 (₹ Crores)*	*Average (₹ Crores)*
A. OPERATING ASSETS			
1. Fixed Assets (PP&E, Right-of-use assets, goodwill, and intangible assets)	6773	7,425	7099
2. Capital Work-in-progress	212	209	211
3. Intangible assets under development	22	27	24
4. Tax assets (current and non-current)	171	281	226
5. Operating current assets (Inventories, trade receivables, cash and cash equivalents, and contract assets)	2,107	2,212	2,160
6. Other operating financial assets (non-current and current)	204	336	270
7. Other operating non-financial assets (non-current and current)	233	242	238
8. Deferred tax asset	25	50	37
9. Investments in associates and joint ventures	308	324	316
Total	10,055	11,106	10,581
B. OPERATING LIABILITIES			
1. Provisions (Non-current plus current)	131	133	132
2. Trade payables	1,161	908	1,035
3. Other operating liabilities (Non-current plus current)	127	189	158
4. Other operating financial liabilities (Non-current plus current)	760	687	724
5. Current tax liability	—	—	—
6. Deferred tax liability	261	294	277
Total	2,440	2,211	2,326
C. NET OPERATING ASSETS (A–B)	7,615	8,895	8,255
D. INVESTMENTS OTHER THAN INVESTMENT PROPERTY			
1. Investment in financial assets other than bank deposits (Non-current plus current)	1,035	110	572
2. Bank deposits not included in cash and cash equivalents (Non-current plus current)	299	86	193
3. Loans (Non-current plus current)	23	30	27
4. Other non-operating financial assets (Non-current plus current)	—	—	—
Total	1,357	226	792
E. BORROWINGS AND LEASE LIABILITY			
1. Borrowings (Non-current borrowings, current borrowing, current portion of long-term borrowings, and interest accrued on the same)	2,875	3,631	3,253
2. Lease liability	1,300	2,026	1,663
Total	4,175	5,657	4,916
F. NET BORROWINGS (E–D)	2,818	5,431	4,124
G. EQUITY			
Share of controlling shareholders	4,602	3,340	3,971
Non-controlling interest	200	130	165
Investment property	(5)	(6)	(5)
Total	4,797	3,464	4,131
G. NET OPERATING ASSETS (F+G)	7,615	8,895	8,255

Table 15.8 below presents the reorganised statements of profit and loss of MRF Tyres, Apollo Tyres, and Apollo Hospitals Enterprises Limited.

TABLE 15.8 Reorganised consolidates statements of MRF Tyres, Apollo Tyres, and Apollo Hospitals Enterprises Limited for the year 2020–2021

	MRF Tyres 2020–2021 (Amount ₹' Crores)	*Apollo Tyres 2020–2021 (Amount ₹' Crores)*	*Apollo Hospitals 2020–2021 (Amount ₹' Crores)*
1. Income from Operating Activities			
Operating Income (revenue plus other operating income)	16,163	17,397	10,560
2. Operating Expenses			
(a) Cost of materials consumed	8,952	7,065	1,623
(b) Purchase of stock-in-trade	16	2,009	4,187
(c) Change in inventories of finished goods, stock-in-trade, and work-in-progress	354	320	(125)
(d) Employee benefits expense	1,415	2,513	1,601
(e) Depreciation and amortisation expense	1,141	1,315	573
(f) Other expenses	2,483	2,692	2,137
Total expenses	14361	15,916	9,996
3. Operating Profit Before Income Tax (1 – 2)	1,802	1,483	564
4. Income tax expenses on operating profit (See the calculation in note 1)	484	534	206
5. Net Operating Profit Adjusted for Tax (Nopat) (3 – 4)	1,318	949	358
6. Net Borrowing Expense			
(a) Finance cost, net of tax (1 – 0.35)			
*Finance costs	179	288	292
(b) Investment income, net of tax (1 – 0.35)			
*Investment income	102	54	20
Net borrowing expense (a – b)	77	234	272
7. Net Profit Before Exceptional Items and other Income (5 – 6)	1,243	715	86
8. Other Income Net of Tax (0.35 × Other Income)	34	30	11
9. Exceptional Items Net of Tax (0.35 × Exceptional Income/Expense)	—	(395)	40
10. Net Profit 7 – (+) 8	1,277	350	137

Notes:

(a) We have considered income tax rate at 35 per cent, which is approximately the actual tax rate applicable to the Assessment Year 2021–2022 (corresponding to the financial year 2020–2021).

(b) Income tax on operating income = Total tax Expenses + Income tax on finance – Income tax on other income – (+) income tax on exceptional items – Income tax on investment income

(c) MRF Tyres: ₹460 + (0.35 × 275) – (0.35 × 53) – 0 – (0.35 × 157) = ₹460 + 96.25 – 18.55 – 54.95 = ₹482.75

(d) Apollo Tyres: ₹211 + (0.35 × 443) – (0.35 × 46) + (0.35 × 608) – (0.35 × 83) = ₹211 + 155.05 – 16.10 + 212.8 – 29.05 = ₹533.70

(e) Apollo Hospitals: ₹85 + (0.35 × 449) –(0.35 × 15) – (0.35 × 61) – (0.35 × 30) = ₹85 + 157.15 – 5.25 – 21.35 – 9.6 = ₹205.95

15.7 SUMMARY MEASURES OF OVERALL PERFORMANCE

15.7.1 Return on Net Operating Assets (RONOA)

Firms formulate and implement strategies to improve the return on capital invested in the business (Net operating assets), measured by RONA. RONA is also called, return on invested capital (ROIC).

RONOA = (NOPAT ÷ Average NOA) × 100
RONOA = Operating Margin × Asset Velocity

$$\text{RONOA} = \frac{\text{NOPAT}}{\text{Average Net Operating Assets}} \times 100$$

In ratios where we us a figure from statement of profit and loss in the numerator and a figure from the balance sheet in the denominator, we use the average of the balance sheet figures in the denominator. The average is calculated by adding opening and closing balances and dividing the same by two. The logic is that assets and liabilities are built over the year, therefore, neither the opening nor the closing NOA was available throughout the year.

Using figures from the reorganised consolidated balance sheets and reorganised statement of profit and loss we have calculated the RONOA for the year 2020–2021 as follows:

		MRF Tyres	*Apollo Tyres*	*Apollo Hospital*
1.	Average NOA (₹ Crores)	11,343	17,526	8,255
2.	NOPAT (₹ Crores)	1,318	949	358
3.	RONOA (Per cent)	11.62	5.41	4.34

MRF Tyres and Apollo Tyres are in a way comparable because they operate in the same industry. However, the size (measured by NOA) of the Apollo Tyres is 1.55 times of that of MRF Tyres. Therefore, they do not meet the size criterion for establishing comparability.

RONOA of MRF at 11.62 per cent is much higher than that of Apollo Tyres at 5.41 per cent. We may conclude that MRF Tyres better managed their NOA than the Apollo Tyres.

Apollo Hospital operates in the health care industry. Without a benchmark ratio, we cannot comment whether RONOA of $.34 per cent is good or bad. Moreover, the year 2020–2021 was a bad year for the hospital industry, as due the outbreak of the pandemic COVID-19, visits of the patients, other than those suffering from COVId-19, in hospitals dropped significantly. Only by comparing the performance of 2020–2021 with that of earlier years, we may comment of the company's efficiency and effectiveness in managing RONOA.

Decomposition of RONA

The drivers of RONOA are operating margin and asset velocity (also called, asset turnover). Every firm aims to enhance the RONOA, as that the growth rate determines the firm's value. Increase in operating income might result in reduction in the operating margin, while increasing the asset velocity. Therefore, the management's challenge is to formulate the right strategy.

The RONOA may be calculated as follows:

Operating Margin = (NOPAT ÷ Operating Income) ×100
Asset Velocity = (Operating Income ÷ Average NOA)

$$\text{RONOA} = \left(\frac{\text{NOPAT}}{\text{Operating Income}} \times 100\right) \times \left(\frac{\text{Opearing Income}}{\text{Average NOA}}\right)$$

The first factor in the above equation measures operating margin and the second factor measures the asset velocity.

The following is the analysis for MRF Tyres, Apollo Tyres and Apollo Hospitals:

		MRF Tyres	Apollo Tyres	Apollo Hospital
1.	Average NOA (₹ Crores)	11,343	17,526	8,255
2.	NOPAT(₹ Crores)	1,318	949	358
3.	Operating income(₹ Crores)	16,163	17,397	10,560
4.	RONOA (Percent)	11.62	5.41	4.34
5.	Operating margin (percent)	8.154	5.455	3.390
6.	Asset velocity (Number of times)	1.425	0.993	1.279

The equation is used to incorporate a measure for tax management efficiency.

RONOA = [(Operating Profit Before Tax ÷ Average NOA) ×100] × Asset Velocity × (NOPAT ÷ Operating Profit Before Tax)

The following equation is used to incorporate a measure for tax management efficiency:

$$\text{RONOA} = \left(\frac{\text{OPBT}}{\text{Operating income}} \times 100\right) \times \left(\frac{\text{Operating income}}{\text{Average NOA}}\right) \times \left(\frac{\text{NOPAT}}{\text{OPBT}}\right)$$

OPBT stands for Operating Profit Before Tax. In the above equation operating margin is calculate by dividing OPBT by operating incomes, a modification over our previous measure of operating margin. The last factor is called Tax Adjustment.

The following is the analysis for MRF Tyres, Apollo Tyres and Apollo Hospitals:

		MRF Tyres	*Apollo Tyres*	*Apollo Hospital*
1.	Average NOA (₹ Crores)	11,343	17,526	8,255
2.	NOPAT(₹ Crores)	1,318	949	358
3.	Operating profit before income tax	1,802	1,483	564
4.	Operating income(₹ Crores)	16,163	17,397	10,560
5.	Operating margin (percent)	11.149	8.524	5.341
6.	Asset velocity (Number of times)	1.425	0.993	1.279
7.	Income tax adjustment(Number of times)	0.731	0.640	0.635
8.	RONOA (Percent) [(5) × (6) × (7)	11.62	5.41	4.34

15.7.2 Return on Equity (ROE)

ROE measures how the management has used the equity capital provided by investors. The book value of equity might be higher or lower than the NOA. If the firm invests a part of the equity outside the business, NOA should be lower than the book value of equity. If the firm finances a part of NOA through borrowings, NOA should be higher than the book value of equity.

ROE = (Net Profit ÷ Average Equity) ×100

$$\text{ROE} = \frac{\text{Net profit}}{\text{Average equity}} \times 100$$

The following is the analysis for MRF Tyres, Apollo Tyres and Apollo Hospitals:

		MRF Tyres	*Apollo Tyres*	*Apollo Hospital*
1.	Average Equity (₹ Crores)	12,815	10,687	4,131
2.	Net Profit (₹ Crores)	1,277	350	137
3.	ROE (Per cent)	9.964	3.275	3.316

ROE is an important measure from the investor's perspective.

Trading on equity

A firm provides higher return than RONOA if it can borrow at an after-tax interest rate lower than RONOA.

EXAMPLE 15.4 (Trading on equity)

Fact pattern: ROIC of a firm in a particular financial year was 15 per cent. Average NOA was ₹1,00,000. It financed 60 per cent of Average NOA by equity and balance 40 per cent by borrowing money from a bank at an after-tax interest rate of 10 percent.

Discussion: NOPAT = (₹1,00,000 × 0.15) or ₹15,000
Borrowing cost (after tax): ₹15,000 – (0.10 × ₹40,000) = ₹11,000

$$\text{ROE} = (₹11{,}000/60{,}000) \times 100 = 18.33 \text{ per cent}$$

ROE is higher than RONOA, as the firm could borrow at an interest rate (net of tax) lower than RONOA, which was 15 per cent.

Trading on equity refers to the phenomenon that a firm provides higher return than RONOA when it borrows at an after-tax interest rate that is lower than RONOA.

Decomposition of ROE

The driver of ROE is the RONOA, the proportion of equity to borrowings and the borrowing cost.

ROE = RONOA + FLEV × Spread FLEV stands for Net Financial Leverage

$$\text{ROE} = \text{RONOA} + \left(\frac{\text{Average borrowings}}{\text{Average equity}} \times (\text{Spread})\right)$$

Spread is the difference between the RONOA and borrowing cost (after tax). The ratio, (Average Borrowings/Average Equity) is called Net Financial Leverage (NFLEV) or simply, financial leverage (FLEV)

EXAMPLE 15.5 (Decomposition of ROE)

Fact pattern: ROIC of a firm in a particular financial year was 15 per cent. Average NOA was ₹100,000. It financed 60 per cent of Average NOA by equity and balance 40 per cent by borrowing money from a bank at an after-tax interest rate of 10 per cent.

(Fact pattern is the same as in example 15.4 above)

FLEV = (Average Borrowings ÷ Average Equity)
Spread = RONOA – NBC
NBC stands for After Tax Net Borrowing cost

Discussion: ROE = 0.15 + (40,000/60,000) × (0.15 – 0.10) = 0.15 + 0.0333 = 0.183 or 18.33 per cent. This result agrees with the result in example 15.4.

Firms often invest a part of the total capital outside the business, classified as investment in the balance sheet. In that situation, one should consider the net borrowing cost (NBC). In calculating NBC, one has to calculate Net Borrowings (NB) and Net borrowing Expense (NBE). NB is the amount borrowed reduced by amount invested outside the business. NBE is the finance costs reduced by after-tax income from investments outside the business.

NBC = (Net Borrowing Expense ÷ Average Net Borrowings) ×100

$$\text{NBC} = \frac{\text{NBE}}{\text{NB}} \times 100$$

Net profit includes other income and exceptional items. Return on equity from those income and exceptional item (income/expenses) should also be considered in deriving ROE from RONOA.

The following is the analysis for MRF Tyres, Apollo Tyres and Apollo Hospitals:

		MRF Tyres	*Apollo Tyres*	*Apollo Hospital*
1.	Average Equity (₹ Crores)	12,815	10,687	4,131
2.	Net Profit(₹ Crores)	1,277	350	137
3.	RONOA (Per cent) (Calculated above)	11.619	5.415	4.337
4.	Average Net Borrowings (₹ Crores)	−1,472	6,839	4,124
5.	FLEV (number of times) [(2)/(1)]	−0.115	0.640	0.998
6.	Net borrowing expenses (Net of tax) (₹ Crores)	75	234	272
7.	Net borrowing cost(Net of tax) (Per cent)[(6/4) × 100	−5.095	3.422	6.596

(Contd...)

		MRF Tyres	*Apollo Tyres*	*Apollo Hospital*
8.	Spread (Percentage)(3–7)	16.715	1.988	–2.256
9.	Other income (after tax) (₹ Crores)	34	30	11
10.	Other income as a percentage of equity (Per cent)	0.265	0.281	0.266
11.	Exceptional items (after tax) (₹ Crores)	—	(395)	40
12.	Exceptional items as a percentage of equity (Per cent)	—	–3.696	0.968
13.	ROE (Per cent)	9.962	3.273	3.320

ROE

1. MRF Tyres: 11.619 + (–0.115 × 16.715) + 0.265 = 9.962
2. Apollo Tyres: 5.415 + (0.640 × 1.988) + 0.282 + (– 3.696) = 3.273
3. Apollo Hospitals: 4.337 + [0.998 × (– 2.256)] + 0.266 + 0.968 = 3.320

Observations

In all the three companies, the ROE is lower than RONOA. MRF Tyres invested a part of the equity and total money borrowed outside the business, which earned a very low return. Exceptional expenses were very high in case of Apollo Tyres. Exceptional items being non-recurring items, we may exclude that in analysing ROE. Excluding those items, ROE comes to 6.97 per cent, which is higher than RONOA. Apollo Hospitals net borrowing costs was higher than RONOA.

Financial ratios do not answer questions. Therefore, in order to find an answer to such questions like why Apollo Tyres performance was so poor compared to MRF Tyres, we need to go through the management commentary, examine the company's market segment and business model, and also analyse the trend over past few years.

15.8 DuPont Model

DuPont Model (also known as the DuPont analysis), breaks down the return on equity (ROE) into different elements.

DuPont Model (also known as the DuPont analysis), breaks down the return on equity (ROE) into three parts, as presented in exhibit in Figure 15.1.

The name comes from the DuPont Corporation of U.S.A that invented and started using this formula in the 1920s. The model is widely used for its simplicity.

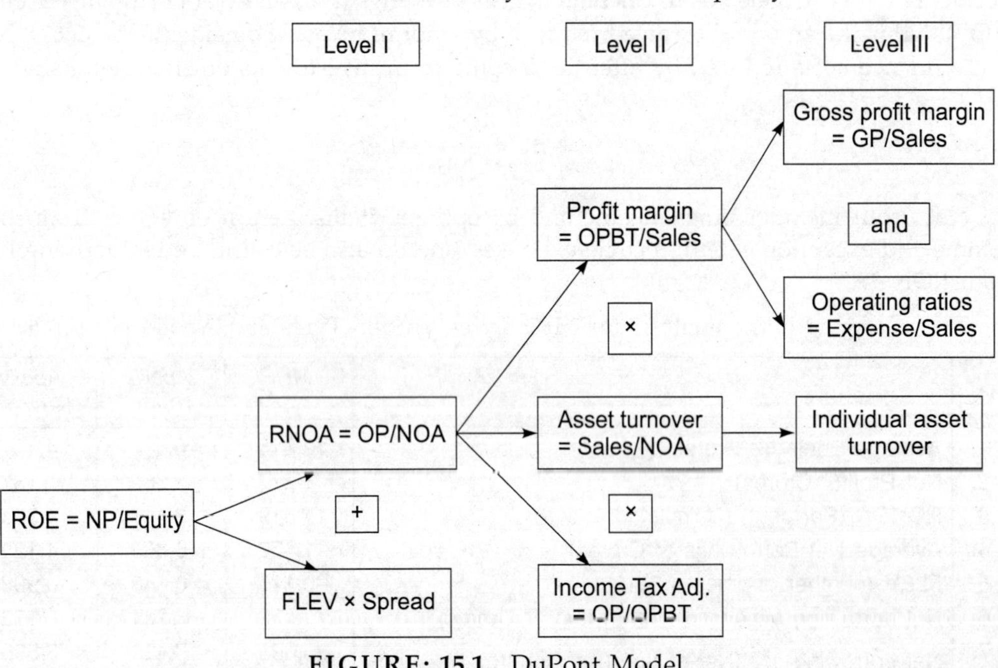

FIGURE: 15.1 DuPont Model

The DuPont Model has not considered the other income and exceptional items in decomposing the ROE. Firms can modify that model. We can exclude the exceptional items, being non-recurring items and calculated ROE before exceptional items. In case of MRF Tyres, Apollo Tyres and Apollo Hospitals, other income was not material. Therefore for the purpose of DuPont analysis, we may start the analyses with ROE before other income and exceptional items.

We have analysed up to Level II. For Level III analysis we have to calculate gross profit ratio, operating ratios and turnover ratios of each class of assets.

We shall discuss those in the following sections–profitability ratios and activity ratios.

15.9 PROFITABILITY AND ACTIVITY RATIOS

15.9.1 Profitability Ratios

Gross profit ratio

Gross Profit Ratio = (Gross Profit ÷ Sales) ×100

Gross profit = Sales – Cost of sales

Cost of sales and cost of goods sold are often used interchangeably.

Indian companies analyse expenses in the statement of profit and loss using the natural classification model. Therefore, cost of sales is not available in the at statement. The information in that statement is inadequate to calculate cost of sales precisely. However, we may roughly calculate gross profit.

The following is the analysis for MRF Tyres, Apollo Tyres and Apollo Hospitals:

		MRF Tyres	*Apollo Tyres*	*Apollo Hospital*
1.	**Operating income (₹ Crores)**	16,163	17,397	10,560
2.	Cost of materials consumed	8,952	7,065	1,623
3.	Purchase of stock-in-trade	16	2,009	4,187
4.	Change in inventories of finished goods, stock-in-trade, and work-in-progress	354	320	(125)
5.	Depreciation and amortisation	1,141	1,315	573
6.	Cost of sales (2+3+4+5) [See note below.]	10,463	10,709	6,258
7.	Gross profit (1−5)	5,700	6,688	4,302
8.	**Gross profit ratio [(6)/(1) × 100] (Per cent)**	35.265	38.443	40.738

Note: A part of the employee cost and a significant part of deprecation should have been included in the cost of goods sold. In order to improve our estimate of gross profit, we have included the total depreciation and amortisation expense in the cost of sales.

Gross profit ratio is used to measure the procurement and operating efficiency.

Apollo Tyres earned marginally higher gross profit than that of MRF Tyres.

Operating ratio

Operating ratio is calculated by dividing total operating expenses by the total operating income. It is expressed as a percentage.

Operating ratio should be calculated for each major expenses.

Operating ratio is calculated by dividing total operating expenses by the total operating income. It is expressed as a percentage. Operating ratio should be calculated for each major expenses.

The following is the analysis for MRF Tyres, Apollo Tyres and Apollo Hospitals:

		MRF Tyres	*Apollo Tyres*	*Apollo Hospital*
1.	**Operating income(₹ Crores)**	**16,163**	**17,397**	**10,560**
2.	Employee benefits expense	1,415	2,513	1,601
3.	Other expenses	2,483	2,692	2,137
4.	Total operating expenses	3,898	5,205	3,738
5.	**Operating ratio (per cent) [(4)/(1) × 100]**	**24.117**	**29.918**	**35.397**
6.	**Employee benefits expenses to operating income ratio (per cent)[(2)/(1) × 100]**	**8.754**	**14.445**	**15.161**

The operating ratio of Apollo Tyres is significantly higher than that of MRF Tyres. This has resulted in reduced RONOA and ROE. Employee benefits expense as per centage of operating income is much lower for MRF Tyres than that of Apollo Tyres. Further enquiry is required to understand the reasons for this difference. For example, if a company subcontracts manufacturing, employee benefits expense should be lower than a company that manufactures the product itself.

EBIT Ratio = (EBIT ÷ Operating Income) ×100

EBIT ratio (EBIT margin)

EBIT stands for Earnings before interest and tax. EBIT ratio is calculated by dividing EBIT by operating income. It is expressed as a percentage. EBIT is often used as a proxy for operating profit. EBIT approximates operating profit of the amount of other income is not material.

EBITDA Ratio = (EBITDA ÷ Operating Income) × 100 EBITDA is often used as a proxy for cash profit.

EBITDA ratio (EBITDA margin)

EBITDA stands for Earnings before interest, tax, and depreciation and amortisation. EBITDA ratio is calculated by dividing EBITDA by operating income. It is expressed as a percentage. EBITDA is often used as a proxy for cash profit, as it excludes depreciation and amortisation, which are non-cash expenses. EBITDA is comparable among comparable companies of different ages, as it is not impacted by the cost of creating production facilities, which increases in an inflationary economy. It is also used as a multiple for valuation of companies operating in capital intensive industries where periodical capital expenditure is not significant (such as, mobile tower). In difficult times, firms focus on EBITDA ratio, as a positive ratio helps it to remain afloat. A positive ratio indicates that the firm is recovering its cash expenses from sales.

Net profit ratio

Net profit ratio is calculated by dividing net profit by operating income. It is expressed as a percentage. It does not provide any significant insights.

15.9.2 Economic Value Added (EVA)

EVA = Net Operating Profit After Tax (NOPAT) – Cost of Capital Employed (COCE)

where,

COCE = Weighted average cost of capital (WACC) × Average invested capital

We may write the formula as follows:

EVA = Average Invested Capital × (ROIC – WACC)

The terms 'invested capital' and net operating assets (NOA) are used interchangeably.

EVA = Average Invested Capital × (ROIC – WACC)

EVA is residual income after charging the company for the cost of capital provided by lenders and shareholders. It represents the value added to the shareholders by generating operating profits in excess of the cost of capital employed in the business. A company creates value when its ROIC is greater than WACC, so the factor (ROIC – WACC) is positive. A company destroys value when its ROIC is lower than WACC, so the factor (ROIC – WACC) is negative. A company neither creates nor destroys value when its ROIC is equal to WACC, so the factor (ROIC – WACC) is equal to zero.

Managers endeavour to increase EVA by:

1. Improving operating efficiency resulting in growth in operating profits without additional capital;
2. Investing in projects that return more than the cost of obtaining new capital additional capitals; or
3. Liquidating unproductive capital by curtailing activities that do not cover the cost of capital.

15.9.3 Earnings Per Share (EPS)

Companies are Required to disclose basic EPS and diluted EPS in the statement of profit and loss.

Basic EPS

$$\text{Basic EPS} = \frac{\text{Profit or loss attributable to equity shareholders}}{\text{Weighted average number of equity shares outstanding}}$$

Basis EPS = (Profit or loss attributable to equity shareholders) ÷ (Weighted average number of equity shares outstanding).

Usually, profit or loss (after tax) from continuing operations is used for computing EPS. However, Indian companies are required to disclose EPS from continuing operations and EPS based on net profit, including profit or loss from discontinuing operation.

Weighted average number of equity shares

The weighted average number of equity shares outstanding during the period is the number of equity shares outstanding in the beginning of the period, adjusted by the number of equity shares bought back or issued during the period, multiplied by a time weighting factor. The time weighting factor is the number of days during which shares are outstanding as a proportion of the total number of days in the period. For additional shares where no consideration received (e.g., bonus issue), time weighted average number of shares from beginning of year/date of issue of shares with consideration should be considered.

EXAMPLE 15.6 (Weighted average number of shares)

Fact pattern: PQ Limited (PQL) provides the following information for calculating the weighted average number of shares for calculating basic EPS for the year 2017–2018:

(i) Number of outstanding shares as at April 1, 2021(beginning of the year): 1,250
(ii) Number of shares bought back on June 30, 2021: 250
(iii) Number of new shares issued on September 30 to settle a liability: 1,000
(iv) Balance as at March 31, 2022: 2,000

Discussion: The weighted average number of shares

$= (3/12 \times 1{,}250 + 3/12 \times 1{,}000 + 6/12 \times 2{,}000) = 1{,}562.50.$

Diluted EPS

Dilution is a reduction in EPS or an increase in loss per share resulting from the assumption that convertible instruments (e.g., convertible debentures) are converted, options or warrants are exercised, or ordinary shares are issued upon the satisfaction of specified conditions. The first step in calculating diluted EPS is to assess whether the issue of potential equity shares will dilute the EPS. If it dilutes the EPS, the potential equity share is called *dilutive potential equity share.*

Earnings for calculating diluted EPS include increase in earnings due to avoidance of the expenses associated with the dilutive instruments.

Earnings for the purpose of calculating diluted EPS is the profit or loss considered for calculating basic EPS, adjusted for increase in earnings, if any, due to avoidance of the expenses associated with the instrument (e.g., convertible bond).

For the purpose of calculating diluted EPS, the number of equity shares should be the weighted average number of equity shares calculated for computing basic EPS, plus the weighted average number of equity shares that would be issued on the conversion of all the dilutive potential equity shares into equity shares. It is assumed that dilutive potential equity shares have been converted into ordinary shares at the beginning of the period. However, if the date of issue is later, the same is considered.

For the purpose of calculating diluted EPS, the number of equity shares includes the weighted average number of equity shares that would be issued on the conversion of all the dilutive equity shares into equity shares.

EXAMPLE 15.7 (Weighted average number of shares)

Fact pattern: At the end of 2017–2018, NM Limited (NML) had 10,00,000 equity shares of face value of ₹1 each. In 2016–2017, NML had issued 1,000, 10% convertible bonds with face value of ₹100 at par. Each bond is convertible into 20 equity shares on demand. Both equity shares and convertible bonds were outstanding for the whole year (2017–2018). NML's equity share price is ₹4.50 per share. Net profit (after tax expense) for the year was ₹5,25,000, of which ₹25,000 (after tax expense) was from discontinuing operations. The tax rate applicable to the company is 40%.

Discussion:

Basic EPS

Net profit (after tax expense) from continuing operations is to be considered for computing EPS.

Basic EPS = (₹5,00,000/10,00,000) or ₹0.50 per share.

Diluted EPS

Conversion of the bond is not rational because face value of each bond is ₹100. While after conversion, the market value of 20 equity shares would be (20 × ₹4.5) or ₹90. Yet, for computing diluted EPS, we have to assume that convertible bonds were converted in the beginning of the year.

The first step is to assess whether the potential equity shares (convertible debentures) are dilutive. On conversion, interest on the bond will be saved, and to that extent, profit will increase. Interest after tax is 1000 × ₹100 × 0.10 × (1 – 0.40) = ₹6,000.

Increase in number of equity shares will be 1,000 × 20 = 20,000. Net profit per incremental equity share = (₹6,000/20,000) = ₹0.30

The bond is dilutive because net profit per incremental equity share of ₹0.30 is lower than the basic EPS of ₹0.50.

The second step is to calculate diluted EPS.

Diluted EPS = (₹5,00,000 + 6,000)/(10,00,000 + 20,000) = ₹0.496 per share

15.9.4 Activity Ratios

Asset turnover ratio = (Total operating income) ÷ (Average asset value).

Asset turnover ratios are called activity ratios. Turnover ratios are also called asset velocity ratios. They are calculated by dividing the total operating income They measure how much operating income is generated using one rupee of the asset. Thus it measure's the asset's productivity and consequently, managerial efficiency in using the asset. The inverse of the asset turnover ratio is called asset intensity ratio. It measures how much asset is required to generate one rupee of revenue.

$$\text{Asset turnover ratio} = \frac{\text{Total Operating Income}}{\text{Average Asset Value}}$$

Asset intensity ratio = (Average asset value) ÷ (Total operating income).

$$\text{Asset intensity ratio} = \frac{\text{Average Asset Value}}{\text{Total Operating Income}}$$

We calculated NOA turnover ratio while decomposing the RONOA above. We can calculate activity ratios of different classes of assets. Analysts also calculate the turnover ratio of working capital. Working capital is measured at the difference between current assets and current liabilities.

The following is the analysis for MRF Tyres, Apollo Tyres and Apollo Hospitals:

		MRF Tyres	*Apollo Tyres*	*Apollo Hospital*
1.	Operating income(₹ Crores)	16,163	17,397	10,560
2.	Fixed asset (₹ Crores)	9,153	15,934	7,099
3.	Operating current assets (₹ Crores)	5,872	5,278	2,160
4.	Fixed asset turnover (number of times)[(2)/(1)	1.766	1.092	1.488
5.	Operating current asset turnover (number of times)[(3)/(1)	2.753	3.296	4.889

The fixed asset turnover ratio of Apollo Tyres is significantly lower than that of MRF Tyres. This indicates that the productivity of fixed assets is higher for MRF Tyers than that of Apollo Tyres. On the other hand, Apollo used lowers current assets to generate one rupee of revenue than that of MRF Tyres. The ratios do not indicate the reasons. Further investigation is required for identifying the reasons for the difference. For Apollo Hospital no benchmark is available. Therefore, it is impossible for us to comment on whether the ratios are good or poor. In absence of a benchmark ratio, a financial ratio communicates nothing.

Managers use the following formulas to calculate turnover of each component of current assets:

$$\text{Inventory turnover ratio} = \frac{\text{Cost of goods sold}}{\text{Avergae inventory}}$$

Inventory turnover ratio = (Cost of goods sold) ÷ (Average inventory).

Some analysts use the term *cost of revenue* to refer to the cost of goods sold.

$$\text{Raw material inventory turnover} = \frac{\text{Cost materials consumed}}{\text{Average RM inventory}}$$

$$\text{Work-in-process inventory turnover} = \frac{\text{Cost of production}}{\text{Avergae WIP inventory}}$$

$$\text{Finished goods inventory turnover} = \frac{\text{Cost of goods sold}}{\text{Average FG inventory}}$$

$$\text{Trade receivables turnover ratio} = \frac{\text{Revenue}}{\text{Average trade receivables}}$$

Trade Receivables turnover ratio = (Revenue) ÷ (Average trade receivables).

$$\text{Trade payables turnover} = \frac{\text{Purchases}}{\text{Average trade payables}}$$

Managers usually express turnover of the assets included in current assets as number of days. The formula for calculating the number of days is:

$$\text{Number of days of holding} = \frac{365}{\text{Turn over}} \text{ days}$$

15.10 FINANCIAL HEALTH LIQUIDITY AND SOLVENCY

15.10.1 Efficiency of Financing Decisions—Credit Analysis—Liquidity

Liquidity refers to the ability of the company to meet short-term financial commitments.

Liquidity of a firm depends on its ability to convert assets into cash or to generate cash through operations in a short period to meet short-term obligations. When a firm finds it difficult to arrange enough cash to meet short-term obligations, it is said that it is facing liquidity problem. A firm that continually faces liquidity problem might face closure, as its supply chain might get choked due to non-payment to supply chain partners and employees, and failure to meet terms and conditions of debt covenant. Therefore, liquidity is vital for the survival of a company. One-year period may be considered as short-term.

Current ratio

Conventionally current ratio is used to evaluate the liquidity of a firm.

$$\text{Current Ratio} = \frac{\text{Current Assets}}{\text{Current Liabilities}}$$

Current ratio = (Current Assets) ÷ (Current Liabilities).

Number of days holding = (365) ÷ (turnover).

Current ratio measures the following:

1. *Current liability coverage:* Higher the current ratio, greater is the assurance that current liabilities will be met.
2. *Safety margin:* Higher the current ratio, larger is the buffer against the risk that carrying amount of a non-cash current asset may not be realised in full.
3. *Reserve of liquid funds:* Higher the current ratio, larger is the reserve of liquid funds, which is required to sail through difficult cash flow situations.

It is difficult to establish what the optimal current ratio is. A thumb rule of 2 is widely used. However, the use of the thumb rule might misguide us. Managers manage working capital to achieve higher working capital turnover. Adequacy of working capital from managerial perspective differs from the same from creditors' perspective. We should be careful in interpreting the current ratio. We should be cautious about the limitations of current ratio.

The following are the limitations of current ratio:

1. Assessing liquidity is about assessing the ability of the firm to generate adequate cash inflows in the short-term. Unfortunately, current ratio does not help us either in predicting future cash flows or in measuring the adequacy of future cash flows.
2. It is less relevant for a going concern. Investments in most current assets do not get unlocked except in liquidation. For example, investments in trade receivables and inventories do not get unlocked, except in liquidation. A going concern does not use or liquidate current assets to settle current liabilities.
3. Current liabilities do not include some prospective cash outlays. For example, a firm commitment to purchase equipment might result in cash outflow within 12 months after the balance sheet date, but the same is not included in current liabilities. Companies disclose commitments in notes to accounts. Analysts may adjust current liabilities for commitments for the purpose of calculating current ratio.
4. Prospective cash inflows are not included in current assets. For example, unused portion of an open-credit arrangement (e.g., pre-approved revolving credit like cash credit limit or credit limit on credit cards) with banks is not included in current assets. Companies can always use open-credit arrangements to draw cash in order to settle current liabilities.

Creditors, other than bankers, do not use current ratio to assess liquidity. Bankers use current ratio to evaluate the ability of the company to settle current liabilities in the worst situation, which is when the company will stop generating future cash inflows. Therefore, they always include current ratio in debt covenant and use the ratio in deciding the limit for short-term credit (e.g., working capital loan and cash credit limit). Bankers look into the quality of current assets and current liabilities. Quality of current assets is assessed in terms of liquidity of the assets included in current assets. For example, trade receivable is a better-quality current asset than inventories. Quality of current liabilities is assessed in terms of urgency to settle the liability. For example, trade payable is a better-quality current liability than statutory dues because payment to suppliers of goods and services can be deferred through negotiation with them and because of long-term relationship, but settlement of statutory dues (e.g., income tax deducted at source and employees' provident fund contribution) cannot be deferred.

Financial flexibility

Financial flexibility refers to the ability of the company to quickly respond to the unexpected interruptions in cash inflows.

Creditors assess the default risk of extending credit to the company by evaluating the financial flexibility of the company. It refers to the ability of the company to quickly respond to the unexpected interruptions in cash inflows. Assessing financial flexibility requires evaluation of qualitative factors such as ability to borrow at a short notice, ability to sell and redeploy assets quickly, and ability to quickly adjust the direction of its operations to respond to the changes in the business environment. A company's financial flexibility also depends on the extent of debt in the capital structure and availability of open-line of credit, current rating of its bonds, restrictions on the sale of assets, the extent to which the expenses are discretionary, and the ability to negotiate favourably with employees and supply chain partners to adjust to the change in the direction of operations.

Acid-test ratio (quick ratio)

Acid-test ratio, also called quick ratio, is a more stringent test of liquidity. In the numerator, the total amounts of only those current assets, which are readily convertible into cash, are included.

$$\text{Quick Ratio} = \frac{\text{Current Assets} - \text{Inventories} - \text{Prepaid Expenses}}{\text{Current Liabiities}}$$

Quick ratio = (Current Assets – Inventories – Prepaid expenses) ÷ (Current Liabilities)

Inventories are excluded because they are the least liquid current assets. Pre-paid expenses are excluded because they do not get converted into cash. The acid-test ratio suffers from the similar limitations as the limitations of the current ratio. Therefore, the ratio should be interpreted carefully.

The following is the analysis for MRF Tyres, Apollo Tyres and Apollo Hospitals:

		MRF Tyres	*Apollo Tyres*	*Apollo Hospital*
1.	Current Assets (₹ Crores)	8,152	5,481	2,647
2.	Current Liabilities (₹ Crores)	5,225	5,713	2,337
3.	Inventories (₹ Crores)	2,905	3,206	738
4.	Quick Assets (₹ Crores) [(1)–(3)]	5,247	2,275	1,909
5.	Current ratio (Number of times)	**1.56**	**0.96**	**1.13**
6.	Acid–Test Ratio (Number of times)	**1.00**	**0.40**	**0.82**

We have taken the year-end (March 31, 2021) figures and not average because we are evaluating year end liquidity position. We have taken the figures from balance sheets directly and not from reorganised balance sheets, as we consider total current assets and total current liabilities.

Cash-to-current asset ratio

Cash-to-Current Assets Ratio = (Cash and Cash Equivalents + Marketable Securities) ÷ (Current Assets)

$$\text{Cash-to-Current Assets Ratio} = \frac{\text{Cash and Cash Equivalents} + \text{Marketable Securities}}{\text{Current Assets}}$$

Larger the ratio, more liquid are the current assets.

Cash-to-current liabilities ratio

Cash-to-Current Liabilities Ratio = (Cash and Cash Equivalents + Marketable Securities) ÷ (Current Liabilities)

$$\text{Cash-to-Current Liabilities Ratio} = \frac{\text{Cash plus Cash Equivalents} + \text{Marketable Securities}}{\text{Current Liabilities}}$$

It is more severe test than quick ratio. It emphasises that ultimately cash is required to settle current liabilities. It is often used as a ratio supplementary to the 'cash-to-current asset' ratio.

15.10.2 Efficiency of Financing Decisions—Credit Analysis—Solvency

Solvency refers to the long-term viability of the company. Analysis of solvency involves analysing the capital structure of the company and adequacy of earning to honour long-term financial commitments. In liquidity analysis, the time horizon is fairly short. In solvency analysis, the time horizon is fairly long. Long-term forecasts are less reliable than short-term forecasts. Therefore, solvency analysis is less precise than the liquidity analysis.

Financial leverage

It is calculated as follows:

$$\text{Financial Leverage} = \frac{\text{Net Financial Obligations}}{\text{Book Value of Equity}}$$

We have already discussed financial leverage while discussing ROE.

Gearing ratios

The gearing ratio measures the proportion of a company's borrowed funds to its equity. Book value of equity is used in calculating the gearing ratio. Gearing is expressed as a percentage. The following are the various formulas used to measure gearing:

Net gearing = (Total Liabilities – Cash and Cash Equivalents) ÷ (Book Value of Equity) × 100

$$\text{Net Gearing} = \frac{\text{Total Debt} - \text{Cash and Cash Equivalents}}{\text{Book Value of Equity}} \times 100$$

Total debt should include all liabilities, including current liabilities. Cash and cash equivalents and marketable securities are deducted from the total debt to calculate net debt, which is used in the numerator.

Gross gearing = (Total Liabilities) ÷ (Book Value of Equity) ×100

$$\text{Gross Gearing} = \frac{\text{Total Debt}}{\text{Book Value of Equity}} \times 100$$

Analysts use the following alternative formulas to calculate gross gearing:

$$\text{Gross Gearing} = \frac{\text{Total Debt}}{\text{Total Assets}} \times 100$$

Debt-Equity = (Total Debt) ÷ (Book Value of Equity) ×100

$$\text{Debt-Equity Ratio} = \frac{\text{Total Debt}}{\text{Book Value of Equity}} \times 100$$

Appropriate gearing ratio

Gearing ratio roughly measures the financial risk to which a business is subjected, as excessive debt can lead to financial difficulties. In a business downturn, a company with high gearing ratio (often called highly leveraged firm) may have trouble in meeting its debt repayment schedules and could risk bankruptcy. Generally, investors and creditors should worry if net gearing is 50% or above. Net gearing of 100% and above is dangerous.

A low gearing ratio may be indicative of conservative financial management. However, firms operating in highly cyclical industries cannot afford to have high debt in its capital structure in the face of an inevitable downturn in operating income and profits. Prosperous firms usually work with very low debt, as they view debt covenants restrictive.

The appropriate gearing ratio depends on the nature of the industry. It depends on the proportion of fixed costs in the total cost of delivering products or services to customers. If the proportion of fixed costs is high, the firm prefers low debt in its capital structure. If the proportion of fixed costs is low, the firm has the flexibility to have high debt in its capital structure. Gearing ratio also depends on the volatility in input prices or supply of inputs, and also, on volatility in demand for the products or services of the firm. Low debt in the capital structure provides the desired flexibility that helps the firm to manage difficult situations.

Operating leverage

The proportion of fixed costs in the cost structure is measured by operating leverage, which is calculated as follows:

$$\text{Operating Leverage} = \frac{\text{Total Contribution}}{\text{EBIT}}$$

Operating leverage is also called operational gearing.

'Contribution' is the difference between sales and variable costs of sales. For example, if the sale value is ₹10 lakh and variable cost of sales is ₹6 lakh, contribution is (₹10 lakh – 6 lakh) or ₹4 lakh. EBIT is the difference between total contribution and fixed costs. For example, if contribution is ₹4 lakh and fixed cost is ₹1 lakh, the EBIT is (₹4 lakh – 1 lakh) or ₹3 lakhs. If other income is substantial, EBIT should be replaced by 'operating income before tax'. In that case, operating leverage is (4/3) or 1.33. On the other hand, if 'sales' is ₹10 lakh, variable cost is ₹4 lakh, and fixed cost is ₹3 lakh, operating leverage is (6/3) or 2. In both the cases, sales and EBIT are ₹10 lakh and ₹3 lakh, respectively, but the operating leverage is higher in the second case, as the fixed cost is higher than that in the first case. Higher operating leverage signifies higher fixed cost in the cost structure. A firm with high operating leverage faces challenges when the going is not good.

Operating Leverage = (Total Contribution) ÷ (EBIT)

Total Contribution = Sales – Total Variable Cost of Sales

Earnings coverage

Analysts use capital structure for screening purpose, i.e., to understand whether debt is high in the capital structure, and thus, require further investigation. Assessing the earning capacity provides greater insights, as a leveraged firm does not face difficulties if it generates enough cash inflow to meet its commitments to pay interest on outstanding borrowings and to repay the principal as per schedule. The following are the coverage ratios:

Interest coverage

$$\text{Interest Coverage} = \frac{\text{EBIT}}{\text{Interest Expense}}$$

Interest Coverage = (EBIT) ÷ (Interest Expense)

Interest expense must include the amount of interest capitalised during the year. Interest coverage of 3 and above is considered good because empirically, it is established that firms having interest coverage ratio of 3 do not file bankruptcy petition.

The following is the analysis for MRF Tyres, Apollo Tyres and Apollo Hospitals:

		MRF Tyres	*Apollo Tyres*	*Apollo Hospital*
1.	Total liabilities (₹ Crores)	9,168	14,620	6,615
2.	Cash and Cash Equivalents (₹ **Crores)**	167	971	425
3.	Borrowings + Lease Liability + Accrued Interest(Percentage)	2,333	7,321	4,175
4.	Book value of equity (₹ Crores)	13,414	11,443	4,802
5.	EBIT (₹ Crores)	2,012	1,612	609
6.	Interest Expense (₹ Crores)	275	443	449
7.	Gross gearing (Percentage) [(1)/(4) × 100]	**68.35**	**127.76**	**137.76**
8.	Net gearing (Percentage) [((1) – (2))/(4) × 100]	**67.10**	**119.27**	**128.90**
9.	Interest coverage (Number of times)	**7.316**	**3.638**	**1.356**
10.	Debt-Equity Ratio (Number of times) [(3)/(1)]	**0.714**	**0.639**	**0.869**

We have taken the year-end (March 31, 2021) figures from the balance sheet and not average because we are evaluating year end solvency position. We have taken the figures from balance sheets directly and not from reorganised balance sheets. For calculating debt-equity ratio, we have considered borrowings only. Lease liability is also of the nature of borrowings. Interest expense (finance cost) is available in the statement of profit and loss.

The financial position of MRF Tyres is sound. The net gearing of Apollo Tyres is more than 100 per cent, and therefore, worrying. However, interest coverage of 3.638 gives comfort. The financial position of Apollo Hospital is bad, as the net gearing is at 128.90 per cent and interest coverage at 1.356 is much below 3.

Fixed charge coverage ratio

$$\text{Fixed Charge Coverage} = \frac{\text{EBIT} + \text{Fixed Charge}}{\text{Interest Expense} + \text{Fixed Charge}}$$

Fixed Charge Coverage Ratio= (EBIT + Fixed Charge) ÷ (Interest Expense + Fixed Charge)

Usually, lease rent is considered as fixed charge.

Debt service coverage ratio (DSCR)

Debt-Service Coverage Ratio (DSCR) = (EBIT – Current Tax) ÷ (Instalment of Principal + Interest Expense + Lease Rent)

$$\text{DSCR} = \frac{\text{EBITDA} - \text{Current Tax}}{\text{Instalment of Principal} + \text{Interest} + \text{Lease Rent}}$$

Usually, financial institutions use DSCR to evaluate loan applications. Each financial institution establishes its own benchmark DSCR. However, usually, less than 1 is not acceptable, as it indicates that the company may not be able to generate enough cash inflows to meet its commitment to pay interest and instalment of principal due during the year.

15.11 MARKET-BASED RATIOS

Two market-based ratios, which are used for equity valuation, are the following:

1. Market value to book-value ratio,
2. Price-to-earnings (PE) ratio,
3. PE Growth (PEG) ratio,

A ratio that is being used by traders in the capital market to identify undervalued and overvalued shares is the PE Growth (PEG) ratio.

15.11.1 Market Value to Book Value Ratio (PB Ratio)

PB Ratio = (Market Value of Equity) ÷ (Book Value of Equity)

PE Ratio = (Market price per share) ÷ (EPS)

The ratio is often called Price-to-Book (PB) ratio. It is calculated as follows:

$$\text{PB Ratio} = \frac{\text{Market Value of Equity}}{\text{Book Value of Equity}}$$

PB ratio shows the market's (investors collectively) perception about the company's ability to generate cash flows in future.

The ratio is often used as a multiple to estimate the market value of equity. For example, if the book value of equity is ₹100 crore and average PB ratio of comparable companies is 1.5, the estimated market value of the company's equity is (₹100 crore × 1.5) or ₹150 crore.

15.11.2 Price-to-Earnings (PE) Ratio

PE ratio is calculated as follows:

$$\text{PE Ratio} = \frac{\text{Market Price Per Share}}{\text{EPS}}$$

EPS stands for earnings per share.

PE ratio is often used as a multiple to estimate the market price per share. For example, if the EPS is 100 and the average PE of comparable companies is 16, the estimated market price per share is (₹100 × 16) or ₹160.

PE ratio is called trailing P/E, when annual EPS used in the ratio is calculated based on the earnings of past four quarters. PE ratio is called forward P/E or leading P/E, when annual EPS used in the ratio is calculated based on the expected earnings for next 12 months. PE ratio cannot be calculated for companies having no earnings or having negative earnings.

15.11.3 PE to Growth Ratio (PEG Ratio)

PEG ratio is calculated as follows:

$$\text{PEG Ratio} = \left(\frac{P}{E}\right) \div (\text{Estimated Short-term Earnings Growth})$$

PEG ratio is widely used as a stock-screening matrix. It is calculated as follows:

For example, if the PE ratio is 20 and the expected short-term growth rate is 20%, PEG is (20/20) or 1. Proponents of this ratio classify a share as overvalued if PEG is more than 1, and undervalued if PEG is less than 1.

The validity of PEG ratio is yet to be demonstrated empirically.

15.12 WORKING CAPITAL MANAGEMENT

15.12.1 Working Capital Cycle

Working capital cycle is measured in number of days. It comprises the inventory holding period, receivable days and payable days.

Working capital cycle is measured in number of days. It comprises the inventory holding period, receivable days and payable days. For example, if the 'receivable days' are 30 days, 'inventory holding period' is 60 days and 'payable period' is 45 days, the working capital cycle is (30 + 60 – 45) days or 45 days.

An analysis of working capital cycle provides significant insights into the company's efficiency in managing working capital. The shorter the working capital cycle, the faster the company is able to free up its cash stuck in working capital.

Receivable days are calculated by dividing average trade receivables by total operating income per day. Inventory holding period is calculated by dividing average inventories by total operating income per day. Payable days are calculated by dividing average trade payables by purchases per day. Usually, the figure for purchase, other than purchase of sock-in-trade, is not available directly from the statement of profit and loss. However, it can be derived from the information available in that statement.

To calculate inventory holding period more precisely, the holding periods of raw materials, work-in-progress and finished goods should be calculated separately. Raw material holding period is calculated with reference to consumption of raw material per day. Work-in-progress holding period is calculated with reference to cost of production per day. Finished goods holding period is calculated with reference to cost of sales per day.

The working capital cycle does not take into account locking of funds in loans and advances, and current assets other than receivables and inventories. Similarly, it does not take into account operating current liabilities (including provisions and advance from customers).

15.12.2 Conversion Cycle (Operating Cycle)

Conversion cycle, also called operating cycle, is the total of receivable days and inventory holding period.

Conversion cycle, also called operating cycle, is the total of receivable days and inventory holding period. For example, if the receivable days are 30 days and inventory holding period is 60 days, the conversion cycle is (30 + 60) or 90 days. Conversion cycle measures how many days the company takes to both sell its inventories and to collect the receivables. It is a useful inventory liquidity measure.

Altman's Z score = Z = 0.717X1 + 0.847X2 + 3.107X3 + 0.420X4 + 0.998X5

X1= Working capital/ Total assets
X2= Retained earnings/ Total assets
X3= EBIT/Total assets (Signifies profitability)
X4= Equity/Total liabilities X5= Sales/Total assets

15.13 ALTMAN'S Z-SCORE

The most well-known model of financial distress is Altman's Z-score. Altman's Z-score uses a statistical technique (multiple discriminant analysis) to produce a predictor that is a linear function of several explanatory variables. This predictor classifies or predicts the likelihood of bankruptcy or non-bankruptcy.

The following five financial ratios are included in the Z-score:

- X_1 = Working capital/Total assets (signifies liquidity)
- X_2 = Retained earnings/Total assets (Signifies age of the firm and cumulative profitability)
- X_3 = EBIT/Total assets (Signifies profitability)
- X_4 = Equity/Total liabilities (Signifies financial structure)
- X_5 = Sales/Total assets (Signifies capital turnover rate)

The Altman Z-score is computed as follows:

$$Z = 0.717\ X_1 + 0.847\ X_2 + 3.107\ X_3 + 0.420\ X_4 + 0.998\ X_5$$

A score of less than 1.20 suggests a high probability of bankruptcy. Z-score above 2.90 implies a low probability of bankruptcy. Scores between 1.20 and 2.90 are in grey area.

Z-score is a useful screening, monitoring and attention-directing tool. However, integrated analysis of ratios discussed in this Chapter also helps in predicting financial distress.

REVIEW PROBLEMS

R 15.1 State whether the following statements are True or False:

(i) In calculating interest coverage ratio, amount of interest capitalised during the period should not be included in interest expense.

(ii) Market value to book value ratio should be relatively higher in case of companies which invest in creating intangible resources than the companies that use mostly tangible assets.

(iii) The terms net operating asset, invested capital and capital employed are used interchangeably.

(iv) Operating profit is the profit from operating activities after interest and tax.

(v) Asset intensity ration is the inverse of the asset turnover ratio.

(vi) In analysing consolidated financial statements, investments in associates and joint ventures should not be including in Net Operating Assets for calculating ROIC.

R 15.2 Fill in the blanks:

(i) An entity provides the following information: Fixed assets (net block): ₹5,00,000; Investment in equity shares: ₹2,00,000; Trade Receivables: ₹50,000; Trade payables ₹20,000; Advance from customers: ₹30,000; Inventories: ₹70,000; Cash and bank balance: ₹5,000.

Capital employed (Net Operating Assets) is ₹................

(ii) The Basic EPS is ₹5.00. There are 100 outstanding 10 per cent convertible debentures with face value ₹1,000. Assuming 40 per cent income tax rate, the conversion rate should be, at the minimum, ... shares for 1 debenture to make the debenture dilutive. Ignore fraction.

(iii) An entity provides the following information: Net profit: ₹4,00,000, interest income: ₹50,000, finance costs: ₹40,000, gain from change in the fair value of investments in equity: ₹20,000, and exceptional items (income): ₹5,000.

Assume marginal tax rate at 35 per cent.

Operating profit is: ₹................

(iv) RONOA is 15 per cent, NOA turnover is 2, Operating margin is .... per cent

(v) RONA is 30 per cent, Net Financial leverage (FLEV): 0.40, Net borrowing cost 20 per cent.
ROE is .... per cent. Ignore fraction.

(vi) Balance sheet shows the following information: Fixed asset (Net block): Opening balance ₹200,000, closing balance 1,80,000; Trade receivables classified as current: Opening ₹20,000, Closing: ₹25,000; Trade receivables classified as non-current: Opening ₹4,000, Closing: ₹4,000; Inventories: Opening: ₹30,000 (including non-moving stock of ₹5,000), Closing: ₹25,000 (including non-moving stock of ₹5,000); Cash and cash equivalents: Opening ₹40,000 (including excess cash of 35,000), Closing ₹42,000 (including excess cash of 37,000), Investments in equity shares: Opening ₹20,000, Closing ₹22,000; Fixed deposits with bank (not included in cash equivalents): Opening ₹8,000; Closing ₹8,500.
Average net operating asset is ₹................

(vii) During the year ended on March 31, 2011, a limited liability company earned a net profit of ₹10,00,000. The number of outstanding shares at the beginning and at the end was 20,000 and 40,000, respectively. It had issued 20,000 shares on October 1, 2010. The basic EPS for 2010–2011 was ₹……..

R 15.3 Choose the most appropriate answer to each of the following questions:

(i) Increase in the amounts of current assets and current liabilities by the same amount:
(a) Increases current ratio
(b) Decreases current ratio
(c) Current ratio remains the same
(d) None of the above

(ii) In calculating the gross gearing ratio, the numerator is:
(a) Average total liabilities
(b) Long-term debt at the end of the
(c) Total liabilities at the year-end
(d) None of the above

(iii) Current ratio below 2 always indicates:
(a) Weak liquidity position
(b) Strong liquidity position
(c) Efficient working capital management
(d) None of the above

(iv) Cash yield ratio is used to evaluate:
(a) Earnings quality
(b) Quality of current assets
(c) Change in working capital
(d) None of the above

(v) Operating profit is:
(a) Sustainable if the business environment in which the firm operates is not full of uncertainties.
(b) Sustainable irrespective of the characteristics of the business environment in which the firm operates.
(c) Not sustainable
(d) None of the above

(vi) For the purpose of financial analysis, year-end balance of Cash and cash equivalents is considered a:
(a) Non-operating assets
(b) Operating assets
(c) Allocated between operating assets and non-operating assets
(d) None of the above

ASSIGNMENTS

1. Tick the correct answer:

(i) SET A

(a) Return on invested capital (ROIC) improves with revenue growth without further investment.

(b) Return on invested capital (ROIC) improves with revenue growth with same margin and without further investment.

(c) Return on invested capital (ROIC) improves with improvement in margin.

(d) None of the above.

(ii) SET B

(a) Return on equity (ROE) can be improved by borrowing at a cost lower than ROIC.

(b) Return on equity (ROE) improves if net borrowing cost is lower than ROIC.

(c) Return on equity (ROE) is greater than ROIC, if return on net investments in financial assets is lower than ROIC.

(d) None of the above.

(iii) SET C

(a) ROIC depends on industry attractiveness and not on capital structure of the company.

(b) ROIC depends on industry attractiveness and on capital structure of the company.

(c) ROIC depends on industry attractiveness and competitive position of the company and not on capital structure of the company.

(d) None of the above.

(iv) SET D

(a) EBITDA is a proxy for cash profit, but not a measure of cash flows from operating activities.

(b) EBITDA measures cash flows from operating activities.

(c) EBITDA is a proxy for cash profit and EBITDA to operating revenue ratio provides more meaningful insights than those provided by operating margin when the industry is facing downturn.

(d) None of the above.

(v) SET E

(a) Gross profit ratio is useful in measuring the procurement and production efficiency.

(b) Gross profit ratio is useful in measuring the procurement and production efficiency, but it may improve without improvement in procurement and production efficiency.

(c) Gross profit ratio is useful in measuring the procurement efficiency of a merchandising company and not useful for a manufacturing company.

(d) None of the above.

(vi) SET F

(a) Pressure on price affects operating margin only and not assets turnover.

(b) Pressure on price affects both operating margin and assets turnover if the company fails to increase quantity (in terms of units) sold.

(c) Pressure on price necessarily affects ROIC and ROE adversely.

(d) None of the above.

(vii) SET G

(a) Managers aim to work with high current assets turnover.

(b) Managers aim to work with high current assets turnover, while creditors are comfortable with low current assets turnover.

(c) Managers aim to work with high current assets turnover, while creditors are comfortable with low current assets turnover, but sudden increase or decrease in current assets turnover should be taken as a red flag.

(d) None of the above.

(viii) SET H

(a) Current ratio is useful in assessing liquidity of a firm.

(b) Current ratio is not at all useful in assessing liquidity of a firm.

(c) Current ratio is not at all useful in assessing liquidity of a going concern.

(d) None of the above.

(ix) SET I

(a) Gearing ratio does not help in assessing solvency of a company.

(b) Gearing ratio does not help in assessing solvency of a company but helps in screening to decide whether further investigation is required.

(c) Gearing ratio and interest coverage ratio should be used together for assessing solvency of a company.

(d) None of the above.

(x) SET J

(a) Economic value added (EVA) measures the value created by the company during the accounting period.

(b) Economic value added (EVA) measures the value created by the company during the accounting period, but improves without managerial efforts if, the bench mark interest rate reduces.

(c) Economic value added (EVA) can be used to measure managerial efficiency because it can be improved only through managerial efforts.

(d) None of the above.

SOLUTIONS TO REVIEW PROBLEMS

R1.1

(i) F; (ii) T; (iii) T; (iv) T; (v) T; (vi) T; (vii) F; (viii) T; (ix) T; (x) F; (xi) T; (xii) F; (xiii) T; (xiv) F; (xv) T

R2.1

(i) T; (ii) F; (iii) F; (iv) T; (v) T; (vi) F; (vii) T; (viii) T; (ix) F; (x) T; (xi) T

R2.2

(i) ₹2,00,000; (ii) one annual accounting; (iii) current; (iv) 2; (v) ₹140; (vi) ₹50,000; (vii) ₹10,00,000

R3.1

(i) T; (ii) T; (iii) F; (iv) F; (v) T; (vi) T; (vii) F; (viii) F; (ix) F; (x) True

R3.2

(i) ₹2; (ii) Descending; (iii) (a) Liability (b) ₹200,000

R4.1

(i) T; (ii) T; (iii) F; (iv) T; (v) T; (vi) T; (vii) T; (viii) T; (ix) T; (x) T

R4.2

(i) Continuing; (ii) ₹4,94,000; (iii) Discretionary

R5.1

(i) T; (ii) T; (iii) T; (iv) F; (v) F; (vi) F; (vii) F; (viii) F; (ix) T; (x) T

R5.2

	Transaction	Account to be debited	Account to be credited
1.	The owner introduced capital in the form of cash	Cash Account	Capital Account
2.	The owner introduced capital in the form of stock-in-trade	Purchases Account	Capital Account
3.	The owner introduced capital by transferring the amount to the firm's bank account	Bank Account	Capital Account
4.	Cash is withdrawn from bank	Cash Account	Bank Account
5.	Purchased stock-in-trade on credit	Purchase Account	Trade Payables Account
6.	Purchased stock-in-trade by cash	Purchases Account	Cash Account
7.	Purchased a piece of equipment on credit	Equipment Account	Sundry Creditors
8.	Sold stock-in-trade to a customer on credit	Trade Receivables Account	Sales Account
9.	Sold stock-in-trade to a customer on cash	Cash Account	Sales Account
10.	Goods sold on credit returned by a customer	Sales Return Account	Trade Receivables
11.	Goods purchased on credit returned to the suppliers	Trade Payables Account	Purchase Return Account
12.	Stock-in-trade issued to the owner for personal use	Drawings Account	Purchase Account
13.	Stock-in-trade distributed as free samples	Sales Promotion Account	Purchase Account
14.	Carriage inwards paid in cash	Carriage Inward Account	Cash Account
15.	Carriage outwards paid in cash	Carriage Outward Account	Cash Account
16.	Insurance premium paid by cheque	Insurance Premium Account	Bank Account
17.	Stock-in-trade lost by fire	Loss of Stock-in-Trade by Fire Account	Purchase Account
18.	Amount received from customers by cheque against the amount due against credit sales	Bank Account	Trade Receivables Account
19.	Discount allowed to a customer	Discount Paid Account	Trade Receivables Account
20.	Discount received from a supplier	Trade Payables Account	Discount Received Account
21.	Cheque received from a customer is dishonoured	Trade Receivables Account	Bank Account
22.	Amount due to a supplier of stock-in-trade paid by cheque	Trade Payables Account	Bank Account
23.	Deposited cash in bank	Bank Account	Cash Account
24.	Amount borrowed form bank and the amount is transferred by the bank to the entity's bank account	Bank Account	Borrowings Account
25.	Amount invested in mutual fund units, pay by transfer to the Fund's bank Account	Investment Account	Bank Account
26.	Interest earned on investments in bond, received by transfer to bank account	Bank Account	Interest Received Account
27.	Dividend received on investment in equity by transfer to bank account	Bank Account	Dividend Received Account

(Contd...)

Transaction	Account to be debited	Account to be credited
28. Interest paid to the lender by transfer from the bank account	Interest Expense Account	Bank Account
29. Loan disbursed to employees by cheques	Loan to Employees Account	Bank Account
30. Maintenance charges for the maintenance of plant and machinery paid in cash	Repairs and Maintenance of Machinery Account	Cash Account

R6.1

(i) T; (ii) F; (iii) T; (iv) T; (v) T; (vi) F; (vii) T; (viii) F; (ix) F; (x) T

R6.2

(i) Sales: ₹15,00,000
Cost of goods sold: (6,00,000 + 50,000 – 60,000 + 60,000 + 10,000 – 30,000) = ₹6,30,000
Gross profit = 15,00,000 – 6,30,000 = 8,70,000
Net profit = ₹8,70,000 – 20,000 – 1,00,000 – 1,00,000 – 10,000 – 10,000 – 80,000 = ₹5,50,000

(ii) Sales less return: ₹10,00,000
Cost of goods sold: (6,00,000 + 20,000 + 50,000 – 40,000 – 60,000) = ₹5,70,000
Gross profit = ₹10,00,000 – ₹5,70,000 = ₹4,30,000

(iii) Corrected figure of plant and machinery: (₹5,00,000 + 60,000 – 1,50,000) = ₹4,10,000
Depreciation on plant and machinery: 10% of ₹4,10,000 = ₹41,000
Gain on the sale of the item of the plant and machinery: [₹60,000 – (1,50,000 – 1,10,000)] = ₹20,000
Net profit after adjustments: (₹2,00,000 – 41,000 + 20,000) = ₹1,79,000

(iv) [₹10,00,000 – (80,000 – 75,000) + (30,000 – 55,000)]= ₹9,70,000

(v) Revenue for the current year = ₹5,00,000 – 15,000 = ₹4,85,000

(vi) 2 per cent of ₹5,00,000 = ₹10,000
Existing provision= ₹8,000
Additional provision required = (10,000 – 8,000) = ₹2,000

(vii) Prepaid insurance = (₹24,000/4) = ₹6,000

(viii) Answer: 0
An investor in equity shares recognises revenue when it becomes entitled for the same after the shareholder body of the investee approves payment of dividend.

(ix) Adjusted Plant and machinery Gross block = (₹20,00,000 – 4,00,000 + 5,00,000 – 2,00,000) = ₹19,00,000
Accumulated depreciation on assets held on the balance sheet date: (₹8,00,000 – 1,80,000 + 1,90,000) = ₹8,10,000
Net block = (₹19,00,000 – 8,10,000)= ₹10,90,000

(x) 2 per cent of (₹8,00,000 +100,000) = ₹18,000

R6.3

Working notes

1. Goodwill

Assets taken over from Chandni	*Amount (₹)*
Stock	2,400
Furniture and fittings	2,540
Buildings	12,000
Trade debtors	2,560
Total	19,500
Less: trade creditors taken over	2,500
Net assets taken over	17,000
Purchase consideration	28,000
Goodwill (Purchase consideration minus value of net assets taken over)	11,000

2. Adjusted Trial balance incorporating assets acquired in business combination

Particulars	Debit (₹)	Credit (₹)
Capital (₹28,000 + ₹2,000)		30,000
Goodwill	11,000	
Opening stock	2,400	
Furniture and fittings	2,540	
Building	12,000	
Debtors	6,580	
Prepaid rates	300	
Creditors		2,160
Outstanding wages and salaries		450
Cash-in-hand and balance at bank	560	
Drawings	10,400	
Sales		86,980
Purchases	55,230	
Carriage inward	1,250	
Wages and salaries (₹8,700 + ₹450)	9,150	
Advertising	4,680	
Rates and insurance (₹1,950 – ₹300)	1,650	
Electricity	870	
Sundry office expenses	420	
Discounts allowed to customers	560	
Total	1,19,590	1,19,590

Trading, profit and loss account of Suraj for the year ended on March 31, 2019

Particulars	Amount (₹)	Amount (₹)
I. Income		
Sales	86,980	
Discount allowed	560	86,420
II. Cost of Goods Sold		
Purchases		55,230
Increase in stock of goods		(2,160)
Carriage inward		1,250
Total II		54,320
III. Gross Profit		32,100
IV. Operating Expenses		
Wages and salaries		9,150
Advertising		4,680
Rates and insurance		1,650
Electricity		870
Sundry office expenses		420
Depreciation Building		600
Depreciation F&F		508
Provision for doubtful debts		329
Total III		18,207
VI. Operating Profit		13,893

Balance sheet of Suraj as on March 31, 2019

Particulars	Amount (₹)	Amount (₹)
ASSETS		
Non-current Assets		
Goodwill		11,000
Property, plant, and equipment		
Building	12,000	

(Contd...)

Particulars	Amount (₹)	Amount (₹)
Less: Depreciation	600	11,400
Furniture and fittings	2,540	
Less: Depreciation	508	2,032
Total non-current assets		24,432
Current Assets		
Stock-in-trade		4,560
Sundry debtors	6,580	
Less: Provision for doubtful debts	329	6,251
Pre-paid rates and insurance		300
Cash and bank balance		560
Total current assets		11,671
Total assets		36,103
EQUITY AND LIABILITIES		
Capital		
As at April 1, 2018	30,000	
Add: Net profit for the year 2018–2019	13,893	
	43,893	
Less: Drawings	10,400	33,493
Liabilities		
Non-current liabilities		Nil
Current Liabilities		
Sundry creditors		2,160
Outstanding wages and salaries		450
Total liabilities		2,610
Total Equity and liabilities		36,103

R 6.4

Trial balance as on March 31,2019

Particulars	Amount (₹)	Amount (₹)
Creditors		10,000
Bills payable		560
Long-term loan from bank		5,000
Capital account		45,400
Sales		63,000
Purchase returns		500
Discount earned		100
Bad debt recovered		350
Interest on investments		300
Fixed assets	30,000	
Opening stock	7,500	
Trade receivables	20,500	
Bills receivables	1,000	
Investments	5,000	
Cash-in-hand	500	
Cash-in-bank	1,000	
Drawings	900	
Purchases	52,500	
Sales returns	1,000	
Carriage inward	140	
Freight outward	200	
Duty paid on purchases	160	
Primary packing expenses	200	
Rent paid	300	
Insurance premium paid	360	
Office and administrative expenses	1,320	

(*Contd...*)

Particulars	Amount (₹)	Amount (₹)
Discount allowed	200	
Bad debts	500	
Interest on loan from bank	250	
Delivery expenses	660	
Selling and distribution expenses	1,000	
Income tax paid	100	
Value added tax (VAT) collected		200
Loose tools	200	
Apprentice premium received		50
Commission received		30
Total	1,25,490	1,25,490

Trading, and profit and loss account for the year ended on March 31, 2019

Particulars	Amount (₹)	Amount (₹)
I. Income		
Sales	63,000	
Sales return	(1,000)	
Discount	(200)	61,800
II. Cost of Goods Sold		
Purchase	52,500	
Purchase returns	(500)	52,000
Decrease (Increase) in inventories of stock-in-trade		3,500
Duty on purchases		160
Carriage inward		140
Packaging expenses		200
Total II		56,000
III. Gross Profit (I–II)		5,800
IV. Operating Expenses		
Freight outward		200
Rent		360
Insurance premium		270
Delivery expenses		660
Selling and distribution expenses		1,000
Office and administrative expenses		1,320
Bad debt		500
Depreciation on fixed assets		3,000
Depreciation on loose tools		120
Total IV		7,430
V. Operating Profit (III–IV)		(1,630)
VI. Other Income		
Commission		20
Interest on investment		450
Apprentice premium received		50
Bad debts recovered		350
Discount received		100
Total IV		970
VII. Interest Expense		375
VIII. Income Tax Expense		100
IX. Net Profit (V+VI–VII–VIII)		(1,135)

Balance sheet on March 31, 2019

	Amount (₹)	Amount (₹)
ASSETS		
Non-current Assets		
Fixed assets	30,000	
Provision for depreciation	(3,000)	27,000

(Contd...)

	Amount (₹)	Amount (₹)
Investments		5,000
Total non-current assets		32,000
Current Assets		
Closing stock		4,000
Trade receivables		20,500
Bills receivables		1,000
Pre-paid insurance		90
Loose tools (₹200–120)		80
Interest accrued on investments		150
Cash-at-bank		1,000
Cash-in-hand		500
Total current assets		27,320
Total assets		59,320
EQUITY AND LIABILITIES		
Capital		
Opening balance		45,400
Net loss for the year		(1,135)
Drawings		(900)
Total equity		43,265
Non-current Liabilities		
Loan from banak		5,000
Current Liabilities		
Outstanding interest on long-term bank loan		125
Creditors		10,000
Bills payable		560
VAT collected		200
Deferred commission		10
Outstanding rent		60
Total current liabilities		10,955
Total liabilities		15,955
Total Equity plus Liabilities		59,320

R7.1

(i) F; (ii) F; (iii) T; (iv) T; (v) T; (vi) T; (vii) F; (viii) T; (ix) F; (x) T; (xi) T; (xii) T; (xiii) F; (xiv) T; (xv) F

R7.2

(i) Right of use asset; (ii) Fair value; (iii) ₹2,00,000; (iv) 2,97,287; (v) Natural resources; (vi) 60,000; (vii) 100; (viii) 43,60,000

R8.1

(i) T; (ii) T; (iii) F; (iv) F; (v) F; (vi) F; (vii) T; (viii) T; (ix) F; (x) T

R8.2

(i) 8; (ii) 10; (iii) 1,508; (iv) perpetual (v) 81; (vi) 7,00,00,000 (vii) 8; (viii) 12.157

R9.1

(i) F; (ii) T; (iii) T; (iv) F; (v) T

R10.1

(i) T; (ii) T; (iii) T; (iv) T; (v) F

R 11.1

(i) T; (ii) T; (iii) F; (iv) T; (v) F; (vi) F; (vii) T; (viii) F; (ix) T; (x) F

R 11.2

(i) Should not; (ii) Should not; (iii) At a point; (iv) Over; (v) Over; (vi) At a point in time; (vii) 12; (viii) 80; (ix) CD:1,58,202, MN: 89,888, YZ:71,910; (x) 2022–2023

R 12.1

(i) F; (ii) F; (iii) F; (iv) T; (v) F; (vi) T; (vii) T; (viii) F; (ix) T; (x) T; (xi) T; (xii) T

R 12.2

(i) 4,50,000; (ii) Depletion; (iii) Non-depreciable (iv) 36.90; (v) 0

R 13.1

(i) F; (ii) T; (iii) T; (iv) T; (v) T; (vi) F

R 13.2

(i) 1,00,000, loss (ii) Service contract; (iii) Capital reserve; (iv) Purchase method; (v) Equity

R 14.1

(i) T; (ii) T; (iii) F; (iv) T; (v) F

R 14.2

(i) 2,00,000; (ii) 10,50,000; (iii) 5,40,000

R 14.3

	Amount (₹)
Opening WDV	5,00,000
Less: WDV of asset sold	1,50,000
	3,50,000
Less: Depreciation for the year	2,00,000
	1,50,000
Addition during the year (Balancing figure)	4,50,000
Closing WDV	6,00,000
Addition during the year	4,50,000
Acquisition through a non-cash transaction	1,00,000
Cash outflow from purchase of items of PP&E	3,50,000

R 14.4

Particulars	*Amount (₹)*	*Amount (₹)*
Profit before income tax (5,000 + 150)		5,150
Add: Non-cash expenses:		
Depreciation	100	
Impairment of goodwill	20	120
		5,270
Adjustments for non-operating items:		
Profit on sale of land	(150)	
Loss on sale of furniture	20	130

(*Contd...*)

Particulars	*Amount (₹)*	*Amount (₹)*
		5,140
Adjustments for change in working capital:		
Increase in trade receivables	(500)	
Decrease in trade payables	(200)	
Decrease in inventories	100	
Increase in accrued expenses	20	(580)
Cash flow from operating activities		4,560
Income tax paid (250 + 150 – 300)		(100)
		4,460

R14.5

Cash Flow Statement of PL for the year 2019

	Amount ₹'000	*Amount ₹'000*
A. CASH FLOW FROM OPERATING ACTIVITIES		
Net profit before taxation		2,720
Adjustments for non-cash expenses		
Depreciation	570	
Adjustments for non-operating items		
Interest income	(80)	
Dividend income	(100)	
Interest expense	300	
Profit on sale of equipment	(20)	670
Operating profit before working capital changes		3,390
Decrease in sundry debtors	300	
Increase in inventory	(200)	
Decrease in sundry creditors	(200)	
Increase in wages outstanding	20	(80)
Cash generated from operations		3,310
Income tax paid		(550)
Net cash from operating activities		2,760
B. CASH FLOW FROM INVESTING ACTIVITIES		
Purchase of equipment	(1,470)	
Proceeds from sale of equipment	100	
Proceeds from sale of investment	40	
Interest received	40	
Dividend received	100	
Net cash used in investing activities		(1,190)
C. CASH FLOW FROM FINANCING ACTIVITIES		
Proceeds from issue of share capital	400	
Proceeds from issue of debentures	200	
Interest paid	(300)	
Dividend paid	(1,560)	
Net cash used in financing activities		(1,260)
Net increase in cash and cash equivalents (A + B + C)		310
Cash and cash equivalents at the beginning		1,280
Cash and cash equivalents at the end		1,590

R 14.6

Cash Flow Statement for 2020

	Amount ₹	Amount ₹
A. CASH FLOW FROM OPERATING ACTIVITIES		
Profit before income tax	66,100	
Adjustment for non-cash items		
Depreciation for the year	24,000	
Cash flow before adjustment for changes in working capital		90,100
Adjustments for changes in working capital		
Decrease in stock	46,000	
Decrease in debtors	15,800	
Decrease in sundry creditors	(14,800)	47,000
Cash generated from operations		1,37,100
Income tax paid		(28,000)
Net cash flow from operating activities		1,09,100
B. CASH FLOW FROM INVESTING ACTIVITIES		
Purchase of machinery	(25,000)	
Sale of machinery	17,000	
Net use of cash for investing activities		(8,000)
C. CASH FLOW FROM FINANCING ACTIVITIES		
Repayment of bank loan	(70,000)	
Dividend paid	(23,000)	
Net use of cash for financing activities		(93,000)
Net increase in cash and cash equivalents		8,100
Opening balance of cash and cash equivalents		500
Closing balance of cash and cash equivalents		8,600

Disclosures

Non-cash transactions: The following assets of another company were purchased for a consideration of ₹50,000 paid in shares: Inventories: ₹20,000, Machinery: ₹25,000, and Goodwill: ₹5,000.

R 15.1

(i) F; (ii) T; (iii) T; (iv) F; (v) T; (vi) F

R 15.2

(i) 5,75,000; (ii) 13; (iii) 3,77,250; (iv) 7.5; (v) 34; (vi) 2,49,000; (vii) 33.33

R 15.3

(i) b; (ii) c; (iii) c; (iv) a; (v) c; (vi) b;

Index